Reading Africa into American Literature

Reading Africa
into
American Literature

Epics, Fables, and Gothic Tales

Keith Cartwright

THE UNIVERSITY PRESS OF KENTUCKY

Publication of this volume was made possible in part by a grant from the National Endowment for the Humanities.

Editorial and Sales Offices: The University Press of Kentucky
663 South Limestone Street, Lexington, Kentucky 40508–4008

02 03 04 05 06   5 4 3 2 1

Library of Congress Cataloging-in-Publication Data

Cartwright, Keith, 1960-
Reading Africa into American literature : ethics, fables, and gothic
tales / Keith Cartwright.
p. cm.
Includes bibliographical references and index.
ISBN 0-8131-2220-1 (acid-free paper)
1. American literature—African influences. 2. American
literature—African American authors—History and criticism.
3. African literature—Appreciation—United States. 4. American
literature—History and criticism. 5. Gothic revival
(Literature)—United States. 6. Fables, American—History and
criticism. 7. African Americans in literature. 8. Africa—In
literature. 9. Slavery in literature. 10. Ethics in literature.
I. Title.
PS159.A35 C37 2002
810.9'896073—dc21   2001002582

For my path-openers—
my parents and grandparents,
and for Eileen Julien, John Locke,
and the family of Moustapha Diaw

Contents

Introduction

Tropical Trees: Towards a *Hippikat* Poetics

Here, root yourselves beside me.
I am that Tree planted by the River,
which will not be moved.

> Maya Angelou, "On the Pulse of Morning," read at the
> inauguration of President William Jefferson Clinton, 1993

If I am child of the foundation tree,
the origin of all things,
I am child of the dead child.

All things awaken, under the tree,
to be finished; even the dead
gnarl up to the tree for breath.

> Jay Wright, *The Double Invention of Komo*

I

A strong body of scholarship from Melville Herskovits (1940) to Gwendolyn Midlo Hall (1992) has shown that enslaved Africans were among the primary shapers of emergent American cultures. But as Eric Sundquist argues in *To Wake the Nations: Race in the Making of American Literature* (1993), "it remains difficult for many readers to overcome their fundamental conception of 'American' literature as solely Anglo-European in inspiration and authorship, to which may then be added an appropriate number of valuable 'ethnic' or 'minority' texts, those that closely correspond to familiar or semantic paradigms" (7).[1] Even contemporary multiculturalism often works to keep the unhyphenated American, understood as white and Anglo, still fixed at the unreconstructed center. What I hope to trace here is something of the historical routes and semiotic systems by which Africa may by recognized as a foundational source of the American mainstream. The African presence runs deep, as does the Anglo-American response to the call (real and imagined) of that presence. When we remind ourselves, for example, that Thomas Jefferson's first memory was of being carried on a pillow by a black servant, we can be certain that the presence of Africans and their American-born children played a significant role in shaping the emergent Virginian/American identity of the man who would give compelling voice to our nation's yearnings for freedom.[2]

By reading Africa into American literature, I hope to render greater visibility to some previously invisible or misread *African* American cultural currents that have long shaped American language and consciousness. Along with Albert Murray, I recognize America's black presence as its "Omni-American" presence. The very first Americans were those who were most fully forced to navigate the chaos of New World changes: the Africans of many nations who responded to situations imposed upon them by European settlers to become a New World people. The collective memory and reinventions of Afro-Creole cultures serve par excellence as channels for navigating the tragedies and transitions of our shared national and hemispheric experience. As Paul Gilroy argues in *The Black Atlantic* (1993), it is no real irony that Afro-Atlantic music "produced out of the racialized slavery that made modern civilisation possible, now dominate[s] its popular cultures" (80). A strong African presence was indeed one of the factors that most clearly differentiated America from Europe, and transatlantic slavery was a major force in shaping a New World central to any understanding of modernism.

My reading of America's Africanity follows critical pathways bushwhacked and charted by Joel Chandler Harris, W.E.B. Du Bois, William Faulkner, Zora Neale Hurston, Ralph Ellison, and Toni Morrison. And while following the signposts and going into the territory of scholarly works like Sundquist's *To Wake the Nations*, Gilroy's *The Black Atlantic*, and Henry Louis Gates's *Figures in Black* (1987), my study departs from these groundbreaking predecessors in looking to one specific region of Africa (Senegambia) for African models—and to the American South's core Creole regions (Louisiana and the Sea Islands) for the clearest crossroads whereby one identifiable group of African nations entered American life. Gates's *The Signifying Monkey* (1988) provides valuable precedent in its modeling of the Yoruba Ifa corpus as a possible source and analogue of the signifying traditions operative within African American vernacular culture. But Gates's powerful comparativist reading is grounded in poststructuralist readings of the African American tradition's self-conscious intertextuality, through which he lays claim to equivalent modes of discourse from the Yoruba Ifa corpus. My aims and methods benefit immeasurably from his Eshu/Derrida-inspired refigurations but operate a bit differently. I am interested in calling readers to reconsider the age-old paradigms through which the roots of American literature and identity are seen to be solidly British, while African sources—when recognized at all—find location in what is perceived to be the "ideological," ever-separate and ghettoized domain of black studies. I would move us to recognize that the study of all American literature demands deep, historically conscious reassembly.

Perhaps because I am a Southerner whose true education began with the eye-opening experience of spending some of the formative years of my young adulthood in Senegal (where having one's inner eyes open makes one—in Wolof—the "*hippikat*" familiar to American musical/countercultural longings), I find texts like the Mandinka Sunjata epic or the Senegalese animal fables of Birago Diop to be a bit less "otherly" than the Beowulf epic or the plays of Samuel Beckett.[3] Having been forced to develop a new set of eyes in Senegal to see through some of the limiting assumptions and moral pathologies of my Southern upbringing and undergraduate education, I began to develop the means to trace routes by which an African presence has been an active and ever-repressed agency at the foundation of American culture. This study is the result of my effort to read traces, re-creations, and shadows of Africa into American texts that have always been fully inhabited by Africans—both real and imagined. So with the Senegambian region as my African reference point and the American South as primary crossroads of study, I will examine three Africa-informed currents in American literature: 1) epic-like narratives of African ancestry by Americans of African descent; 2) folk-infused, fabulous narratives by white Americans revealing Afro-Creole cultural descent; and 3) Africanist, gothic-historicist narratives by Americans responding to the literacy and scriptural religion of Senegambian Muslims, revealing what Toni Morrison has called "the racial disingenuousness and moral frailty" at the heart of the American design (*Playing in the Dark* 6).

Like Toni Morrison, I will be charting a "critical geography" in order to arrive at a more accurate map of American literary and psychic history. Though I will be speaking of "Africa" and "America" rather broadly, I think it best to focus upon specific landscapes in order to achieve sufficient reliability and detail. My familiarity with the Senegambian region of West Africa provides this study's African focal point or benchmark. Several years of teaching at Coastal Georgia Community College reinforced my desire to look closely at the Georgia/Carolina Gullah coast and at Louisiana (areas with creole languages) so that I might examine the Senegambian crossroads into American culture at the strongest ports of entry—New Orleans, Charleston, and Savannah. But if we are to make the most sense of the stories told in Senegambian-Creole contact zones, it would be useful to supplement geographic-historical focus with generic focus.

Having been called by Eileen Julien's *African Novels and the Question of Orality* to consider the way generic tendencies work as "tools of social vision," I see in the patterns of genre, "the underlying assumptions of a work, its struggle to reconcile new historical situations with what we might call—following Fredric Jameson's lead—'ideology of form'" (46). African American narratives of epic impulse tend to treat Africa (particularly the old Islamic empires of Greater Senegambia) in one almost enshrined set of ways, as the epic engenders and reassembles a community's sense of identity and difference. The folktale or fable tends to be more transgressive and ethically ambiguous, and I am particularly interested in the master class's use of "fabulous" black cultural forms and language as emblems of Southern identity and as a masked means of "rebel" freedom from "white" forces of social/psychic constraint.[4] And finally, scripture itself—writing—has been seen in both Muslim Senegambia and in America as the sign of reason; and the very fact that enslaved Senegambians could produce Arabic scripture provoked shocks of recognition that fueled some of the nation's most explosive writing in modes of deferral, repression, and compulsive explication that we have come to recognize as American/Southern gothic.[5] Attention to Africa-impacted genres should provide a means of understanding the enduring power of the stories we tell at the geographic and literary crossroads of Africa and Europe in America. Part of what we will find here is a particular set of American responses to what Toni Morrison calls "a dark, abiding, signing Africanist presence" (*Playing in the Dark* 5). And it is this presence, "this unsettled and unsettling population," that—contemporaneous with the extermination and forced relocations of America's indigenous peoples—provided "the very manner by which American literature distinguishes itself as a coherent entity" (6).

In treating the pervasive "Africanisms" shaping American texts, we must recognize that we are dealing with at least two different but historically blended forces. We are looking at a landscape infused with the cultural presence of Africans and their descendants. Simultaneously, however, we are looking at a landscape shaped by racial ideologies that have worked to deny African humanity and in doing so have denied the full humanity of America and the narratives that represent and divine our paths.

For one understanding of Africanism we may turn to Melville Herskovits's *The Myth of the Negro Past* (1941), in which he traced adaptations and transformations of African cultural practice in America. Herskovits's recognition of African cultural agency in North America inspired important projects such as the Georgia Writers' Project's *Drums and Shadows* (1940) and Lorenzo Dow Turner's *Africanisms in the Gullah Dialect* (1949), as well as the work of Peter Wood (1974), Charles Joyner (1984), Gwendolyn Midlo Hall (1992), and Michael Gomez (1998), to name just a few of the historians, linguists, and folklorists who have been the truest trailblazers of my own path of study. Herskovits had a good understanding of the interlocking self-perpetuation of power and knowledge, as revealed in the opening chapter of *The Myth of the Negro Past*, entitled "The Significance of Africanisms": "The myth of the Negro past is one of the principal supports of race prejudice in this country. Unrecognized in its efficacy, it rationalizes discrimination in everyday contact between Negroes and whites, influences the shaping of policy where Negroes are concerned, and affects the trends of research whose theoretical approach, methods, and systems of thought presented to students are in harmony with it. . . . its acceptance is so little subject to question that contradictions are not likely to be scrutinized too closely" (1). The orthodox myth was that enslaved Africans "presented a cultural *tabula rasa* on which to receive this New World experience" (14). Through comparative study of "Africanisms" (African cultural "survivals," "syncretizations," and "acculturations"), Herskovits sought to demonstrate the falsity of the myth and to lay the framework for our eventual understanding of the fact "that the civilizations of Africa, like those of Europe, have contributed to American culture as we know it today" (30). For Herskovits, awareness of America's African heritage would work to deconstruct the white racial myth of the American past and move us all to an understanding of our nation's foundational multiculturalism.

Another, quite different understanding of Africanism arises from Christopher Miller's *Blank Darkness: Africanist Discourse in French* (1985), a work that owes much to Edward Said's *Orientalism* (1978). In *Blank Darkness*, Miller differentiates Europe's invention of Africanist discourse from its centuries-old construction of an Orientalist discourse producing an Orient that although inferior to Europe possesses identifiable cultures, its own religion (Islam), scriptural texts, and history (15). Africanist discourse, on the other hand, constructs an Africa that is a "nullity," a "blank slate" void of culture, history, and religion; it is "an otherness that appears to have no 'actual identity'" (23). European fixation upon the dark blank slate of Africanist nullity creates a dreamlike (and often nightmarish) discourse of wish fulfillment as Africa becomes whatever the subject desires or fears. As a result, Africa tends to be presented in "dual, polarized evaluations" and "has been made to bear a double burden of monstrousness and nobility" (5).

This European discourse evoked Africanist monstrosity and nobility in one set of ways when addressing a distant, exotic Africa separated from home (France or England) by thousands of miles of sea. But things changed utterly in the New World. As home became some American town or plantation, some colony or nascent nation, Africanist wish fulfillment laden with desires and fears was suddenly addressing a familiar, even intimate "other," even as the context and grounds for this forced familiarity were so utterly perverse. Toni Morrison's *Playing in the Dark* (1992) rings true in asserting that "a real or fabricated Africanist presence," an "American Africanism," provided American writers with "a way of talking about and a way of policing matters of class, sexual license, and repression. . . . a way of contemplating chaos and civilization, desire and fear, and a mechanism for testing the problems and blessings of freedom" (7). But in America the line between "a real or fabricated Africanist presence" may be incredibly elusive since the primitivist/antebellum representations of Africans that enabled plantation slavery became so entrenched in America's racialized configurations of power and knowledge, so hauntingly real, that to speak of discursive inventions of Africans is to speak of a strange double agency: 1) Africans shaping new American identities and culture (variously but also centrally for all Americans) within the context (and against the grain) of a thoroughly racist society; and 2) an ideologically dominant "master" discourse, inventing ideas and economies of Africans and their descendants in such a way as to shape and warp us all. I join Morrison in defining America's "Africanist" discourse as the "denotative and connotative blackness that African peoples have come to signify, as well as the entire range of views, assumptions, readings, and misreadings that accompany Eurocentric learning about these people" (6–7). But we must be wary of easy separation between the ideologies (Althusser's "imaginary relations to the real") of America's Africanist discourse and the reality of what Morrison calls the "varieties and complexities of African people and their descendants who have inhabited this country" (6). Since in some of the most engaging American works Africanist ideology is often intertwined with real Africanisms, and since real Africanisms are forced to navigate America's Africanist ideologies, what we are essentially called to do is to develop a complex set of bifocals. My real goal in establishing Senegambian benchmarks for a rereading of American literature does not lie in proposing an alternative Afrocentrism (which is too often a mirror image of Eurocentrism and thus a reaction almost wholly predicated by the boundaries of Eurocentric racial discourse). Ultimately, my project would work towards opening our eyes and ears to a crossroads from which we may perceive some of the unsettling double agencies and something of the parallax effect of a contrapuntal, often polyrhythmic consciousness that is our true New World heritage.[6]

II

The Senegambian/Old Mali region of the Sahel—an area stretching from the Senegal River in the north to the Casamance River and Futa Jallon mountains in the south, and from the Atlantic coast eastward to the middle Niger Valley—will serve as my study's African focal point. The region's Muslim, often monumental cultures and texts rose from a succession of famed empires, offering an attractive cultural patrimony that has served as one of the easiest, most obvious refutations of the racist notion of African cultural/ historical nullity. But I do not intend to argue that the cultures and texts of the Senegambian region (and the old empires of Ghana, Mali, Songhay) are inherently more valuable than others, nor will I argue that Senegambia has always been the single most important source of African contributions to American culture. Rather, I focus here on Old Mali and the Senegambian region because of the difficulty of generalizing about a continent as vast and diverse as Africa, and because the Senegambian region is the part of Africa I know best.

Boubacar Barry has outlined the historical/cultural contours of what he calls "the Greater Senegambia" (extending well beyond the contemporary borders of Senegal and the Gambia) as he has argued for the region's "profound cultural cohesiveness" (*Senegambia* 3). Barry goes on to note that the Senegambian region's cultural and geographic diversity should not be underestimated, but he emphasizes how much is indeed shared among its dominant Mande, Fulfulde, and Wolof speakers. Thomas Hale has outlined shared narrative patterns among the descendants of the Ghana, Mali, and Songhay empires of the Sahel (*Griot, Scribe, Novelist* 167). And Stephen Belcher argues that "the effects of the succession of states, trade, Islam, and colonialism in the region have made the Sahel from Senegal to the republic of Niger a region of related and interpenetrating traditions" ("Of Birds" 55).

Important to any study of Africa in America is the fact that American planters valued Africans according to ethnicity and region of embarkation, and placed particular value upon the Senegambian region as a desirable source. We must acknowledge that the very term "Senegambia" is an invention of European slave traders who viewed the ports between the Senegal and Gambia Rivers as prime sources of highly marketable Wolof, Fulbe, and Mande captives. And we must also acknowledge the complexities and historical complications in speaking of Senegambian ethnic and linguistic groups. Spread even further than the far-flung boundaries of their Old Mali empire, "Mande peoples may be defined either linguistically, as a group of peoples speaking closely related languages or historically, as a group of peoples defined by belief in a common origin, generally centered on the towering figure of Sunjata" (Johnson et al 8). Mande-speaking peoples include Maninka, Mandinka, Bamana (known by their neighbors and in the historical literature as Bambara), Dyula, and Sierra Leonian groups such as the Kuranko and Mende. Fulbe (singular Puulo) peoples, speaking dialects of Fulfulde/Pulaar, are even more widespread in West Africa and are known throughout the region as Peul, Fula, Fulani, or Tukolor, and were identified in the slave trade as Fula, Pholey, or Poulard. Wolof populations (also referred to as Jolof) have been more centered in Senegal proper. If the language for identifying West African ethnicities and language groups is often elusive, we might keep in mind that the people most interested in "pinning down" such categorizations were usually the slave traders and colonial administrators whose business it was to turn a profit on subdividing the region's population. So, following Boubacar Barry and tracing the murderous routes of the transatlantic slave trade, I will use the term "Senegambian" in its largest sense to speak primarily of Wolof, Fulbe, and Mande peoples from an area once controlled by the Mali empire, peoples who when shipped into slavery most often left from ports in Senegal, Gambia, and Sierra Leone. And I will read "Senegambian" bodies of epic, folk narrative, and scripture to develop lenses through which we may read American texts.

As a Peace Corps fisheries agent assigned to counsel Wolof rice farmers on an ill-advised aquaculture program, I spent countless hours with members of the Guidakhar rice cooperative beneath the village *pench*, the palaver tree that provided a shaded location for public discourse. Throughout the region, such trees have long been perceived as primal, spirit-inhabited locations. Barry notes in *Le Royaume du Waalo* that Louis Chambonneau visited the Wolof Kingdom of Waalo in 1675 and reported that each family was represented by a totemic animal and that several sacred trees received offerings (69–70). And Mande/Bamana creation myths collected by Germaine Dieterlen describe how Pemba, a deity incarnate in a tree, descended to earth and enabled creation (10–29). Even with the spread of Islam, trees such as the ones Maninka bards call "origin of origins" continue to serve as dialogic sites of mediation in the region (Johnson 207–8).

No single performance piece could provide a richer discourse upon origins or a more widespread cultural encyclopedia than the region's best-known epic, the Sunjata. And at the base of the Sunjata, animating its action, lies a powerful psychic concept: the agency of *nyama*. The Sunjata epic finds emplotment and voice through Mande articulations of *nyama*, "energy of action," described by Patrick McNaughton as "the energy that animates the universe . . . prerequisite to all action . . . emitted as a by-product of every act," a "natural and mystical . . . source of moral reciprocity" (15). While *nyama* could be described as being a divine current, it may also be linked to pollution, to catastrophic destruction resulting from disembodied forces unleashed through acts of hubris, even through the killing of plants and animals necessary to daily sustenance. If we think of the enormous charges of *nyama* released by transatlantic slavery and centuries of violent racial oppression, then we might understand the need for a "*nyama*-handling" griot (Mande *jali* or *jeli*, Wolof *gewel*, Fulbe *gawlo* or *mabo*) who—like Faulkner or Morrison—understands that the past is never truly past, that old actions hold a wild power and "rememory" of their own.

Most Senegambian cultures recognize a special class of artists who are born with the means to handle these wild energies of transition.[7] Among Mande speakers, this endogamous caste of professionals, *nyamakala*, is composed of all who craft *nyama* in leather, wood, metal, music, and language. The endogamous caste status of *nyamakalaw* allows them to inherit the biological and social means or *nya* "to perform particular acts and, more importantly, to be protected from the consequences of those acts" (Bird and Kendall 16). Thus, *nyamakalaw* are "holders of the *nyama*" (Keita 113); they are the ones who handle wild forces and fetch them for the community.

The *nyamakalaw* (and notably the griots) provide the socially ambiguous channels by which innovation and conformity to tradition are navigated. So fraught with tension is this mediating artistic role, that Wolof griots have traditionally been buried inside large hollow baobab trees at the margins of the bush rather than in the cemetery (Hale, *Griots* 193–96). The baobab's emblematic linkage to the griot's authoritative witnessing comes across in Waly Mbaye's transmission of "The Baobabs Nderexeen and Werugeen," which speaks of the importance of two particular baobabs as fonts of royal election and authority in the old Wolof kingdom of Baol. Mbaye addresses the "electing" baobab Nderexeen by name, aware that kingdoms have come and gone beneath a baobab that endures: "Nderexeen, the one / The king knows he's chosen by. / That's where he's taken. / Maali Kumba Njaay / Was taken to Nderexeen" (Kesteloot and Mbodj 193). Mbaye tells of how the king was bathed and covered with protective amulets before being buried "up to the shoulders" at the base of Nderexeen, where the nobles and griots would dance a "crowning" ring dance around him. The griot then narrates the procession's movement to another baobab, Werugeen, where all strata of Wolof society gather for the newly chosen king's ritual boasts by the baobab of authoritative power:

> I'm the best of us!
> I'm the best of my mother's offspring!
> I'm the best of my father's offspring!
> I'm the best of my maternal uncle's offspring!
> So only I can hear the title "King"! (195)

Asserting that he is the strongest product of collective roots, the new king engages an almost hubristic energy of action—since it is normally the griot who sings the noble's praises. But his language of individuation and collective identity rises from traditional structures of family life.

Ideas of mothering and fathering developed from polygamous marriage engender much of Mande ideology around a fertile tension between *fadenya* or "father-child-ness" (Fulbe *fandirabe*), rivalry between a father's children from different wives, and *badenya* or "mother-child-ness" (Fulbe *bandirabe*), the affection between full siblings of the same mother. *Fadenya*-oriented behavior tends toward innovation and individualistic social transgression, while *badenya*-oriented behavior tends toward conformity, social cohesion, and group-affiliated action. This engendering of ways to assimilate foreign or wild material for the benefit of the community (by way of *fadenya/badenya* and professional groups like the *nyamakalaw*) leads to an orientation toward tradition that values dialogic openness and improvisation without undue fears of losing identity. When, for example, the Fulbe griot Bani Gisse (between interludes on his *hoddu*, ancestral to the banjo) recounts the orthodox Muslim holy warrior al-hajj Umar Taal's visit to a spirit-inhabited tree to secure a supernatural army for his jihad (Kane and Robinson 125), he mediates between localized ancestral repertoires and the power of universalist scriptural Islam. This West African "polyrhythmic sensibility" navigated the chaos of transatlantic slavery and came to be central to contrapuntal Afro-New World "soul" cultures, religions, and music.[8]

Polyrhythm and complementarity are so fundamental to West African worldview that we may speak of the soul itself as being a polyrhythmic unity. Traditionally, the individual soul in the Mande-speaking world (as in Yoruba spiritual systems and in Cuban santería, Haitian vodou/voodoo, Afro-Creole Christianity, and more recently, Freudian psychology) consists of several constituent parts: the elemental life force (*ni*), its shadow or double (*ja*), and a force of essential character or personality (*tere*, which may be shared with animals and is not reincarnated but dispersed as *nyama* after death). It is this pluralistic, polyrhythmic sensibility noted by Chernoff (155–60) and alluded to by Du Bois as "the singular spiritual heritage of the nation" (178), a psychic "twoness," a veiled gift of "second sight" (3) that offers America our most profound understanding of *e pluribus unum*.

III

Despite pervasive appropriations and commodifications (and most often in the very face of them), African American soul music has transmitted sustaining energies of action uniquely charged for navigating New World/modern/post-modern uprootings and re-routings. We see something of this when Langston Hughes enters the cabaret of "Jazzonia" and finds figuration for the deep embodiment of African American spirituality in the Africa-based trope of the tree:

In a Harlem cabaret
Six long-headed jazzers play.
A dancing girl whose eyes are bold
Lifts high a dress of silken gold.

Oh, singing tree!
Oh, shining rivers of the soul! (226)

Hughes's linkage of the vernacular singing tree with "shining rivers" of soul embodied in dance embraces the erotics of a music that is now moving the world. This expansive (non-Puritan) sense of the erotic has been best described by Audre Lorde in an essay entitled "The Erotic as Power": "The erotic functions for me in several ways, and the first is in providing the power which comes from sharing deeply any pursuit with another person. This sharing of joy, whether physical, emotional, psychic, or intellectual, forms a bridge between the sharers which can be the basis for understanding much of what is not shared between them, and lessens the threat of their difference" (56). Lorde goes on to speak of the erotic as "a resource within each of us that lies in a deeply female and spiritual place, firmly rooted in the power of our unexpressed or unrecognized feeling" (53). Charged with its own powerful *nyama*, the erotic works as a bridge to what Michelle Cliff calls "intimacy informed with identity" (368), a sharing of powerful mother-child-ness bonds that may be used in an abstract sense to call people "to suspend their differences and find solidarity in a common mother," a "Mother Mande" or "Mother Africa" (Diawara 159). In America as well, the deepest sharing of the joys of vernacular traditions often becomes feminized as a kind of "mother wit." An occult(ed) realm of birthing and language acquisition, song and culinary art, finds location in a female/spiritual zone close to what Julia Kristeva calls the semiotic: "the rhythms, intonations, and echolalias of the mother-infant symbiosis—intense, pre-Oedipal, predating the father" (157). I am interested in exploring patterns in Senegambian and African American expressive traditions whereby certain realms of vernacular identity have been feminized and "guarded" against a scriptural patrimony that often aims at destroying them. The literary and legal language of English, working through deft hierarchies like patrimony/matrimony, has worked against articulation of the soul semiotics of Afro-Creole mother-child-ness and has created anxieties of patrimony for writers who would emplot claims to an African heritage.

Responding to similar anxieties, Henry Louis Gates has written in *The Signifying Monkey* that "[b]ecause of the experience of diaspora, the fragments that contain the traces of a coherent system of order must be reassembled" (*xxiv*). Gates goes on to demonstrate, however, that the process of African American cultural reassembly is as old as America and has never lost coherence. From the moment of arrival in the New World, Africans and their descendants faced the daunting task of mediating between various African, European, and emergent American vernacular traditions. Indeed, it requires the kind of comparatist perspective that Gates advocates, mindful of "complex double formal antecedents, the Western and the black" (xxiv), for us to see how enslaved descendants of Africans appropriated Hebrew myths (familiar to Muslims) around an old *pench* of knowledge:

> Of this tree you must not eat,
>   Dese bones gwine rise ergain.
> If you do you'll have to skeet,
>   Dese bones gwine rise ergain.
>
> Sarpent wound aroun' the stump,
>   Dese bones gwine rise ergain,
> At Miss Eve his eye he wunk,
>   Dese bones gwine rise ergain. (Newman White 84)

This tree of knowledge is more fully erotic (in both the conventional sense and Lorde's extended sense, linking freedom of body and soul) than the Anglo-Christian tree that more often marks the guilt of original sin and the fall from grace. The tree of the spirituals is Christian, but its composite soul has grown from West African palaver trees of mediation and cultural reassembly.

Mande epic euphemisms for one's true lover—"sharer of secrets," "sharer of hopes" (Camara 107)—get to the core sustenance of soul identity and community. A secret-sharing sense of mother-child-ness enabled slaves to sing of a tree of life that could as easily mark heavenly shores north of the Ohio as it could heaven's side of the Jordan:

> I have a right to the tree of life,
>   And how I long to be there!
> With them that fought my Jesus' fight,
>   And how I long to be there!
>   . . . . .
> If you get there before I do,
>   O, how I long to be there!
> Look out for me, I'm coming too,
>   O, how I long to be there! (Barton 83)

Whether sharing plans to escape, as in spirituals such as "Steal Away," or whether sharing the open secret of black Christianity's singular adherence to Christ-consciousness, the spirituals are imbued with an energy of action, a mother-child-ness and mother wit aptly described as "soul."[9]

America's most steadily repeated trope of African mother-child-ness finds panegyric expression in Paul Laurence Dunbar's "Ode to Ethiopia," in which Dunbar invokes "MOTHER RACE," and sings of how African seed, though crushed by slavery, managed to "spread its leaves so fresh and young— / Its blossoms now are growing" (15). Dunbar's praise-song concludes in bardic style:

> Go on and up! Our souls and eyes
> Shall follow thy continuous rise;
>   Our ears shall list thy story
> From bards who from thy root shall spring
> And proudly tune their lyres to sing
>   Of Ethiopia's glory. (15)

Though masked in standard English, worn poetic diction, and nineteenth-century racial ideology, West African energies of action branch from a familiar trope. And if Dunbar's "lyres" seem to be producing a sound unfamiliar to Senegambian griots, we might look again and see a mask; elsewhere he is more clear in sharing the secret: "We strum our banjo-strings and call them lyres" (117).

True to form, Alain Locke's anthology *The New Negro* (1925) features the singing tree as Harlem's repeated trope of renaissance. Within its pages, Langston Hughes links the singing tree of "Jazzonia" to Egypt and Eden, while Jean Toomer's "Georgia Dusk" evokes "folk songs from soul sounds," and "Song of the Son" claims inheritance from "A song-lit race of slaves" through "An everlasting song, a singing tree, / Caroling softly souls of slavery" (137). Countee Cullen's "In Memory of Colonel Charles Young" turns its praise-song to an old *pench*: "No lie is strong enough to kill / The roots that work below; / From your rich dust and slaughtered will / A tree with tongues will grow" (133). And finally, Jamaica-born Claude McKay contributes a sonnet that rings with *nyama*-filled boasts:

> Like a strong tree that reaches down deep, deep,
> For sunken water, fluid underground,
> Where the great-ringed unsightly blind worms creep,
> And queer things of the nether world abound.
>
> So I would live in rich imperial growth,
> Touching the surface and the depth of things,
> Instinctively responsive unto both,
> Tasting the seeds of being, fearing no stings,
> Sensing the subtle spell of changing forms,
> Like a strong tree against a thousand storms. (134)

Throughout the Americas, black modernists responded to *The New Negro* with a revalorization of African ancestry. In the poetry of Nicolás Guillén and Aimé Césaire we can see the arboreal tropes and hear the contrapuntal sound of a reenergized "counter-culture of modernity" (Gilroy 1).[10]

From attentiveness to the Sunjata epic, we can trace specific energies of action that informed black vernacular culture in America, patterns that found reassembly in epic-like narratives of ancestry by writers such as W.E.B. Du Bois, Jean Toomer, Zora Neale Hurston, Ralph Ellison, Alex Haley, and Toni Morrison. Vernacular "mother wit" (nourished by a number of Afro-Creole repertoires—a whole "soul semiotics") drew sustenance from many sources, including bonds of mother-child-ness between Senegambia and America, while Islam and accompanying narratives of glorious black empire worked to render the Senegambian patrimony ideologically attractive in the face of forces that would present Africa as a cultural nullity.

Chapter 1 will look to the Sunjata epic as a cultural catalogue and to the griots' multigeneric epic forms (mixing narrative, panegyric, and song modes) in order to chart something of the vast matrix of West African energies of action that informed black folk culture and gave sustenance to Du Bois's articulation of double consciousness, the veil of second sight, and the idea of "soul beauty" in *The Souls of Black Folk*. Through close comparative reading, we can find enough of a Senegambian impact upon African American vernacular culture to insist that the Senegambian region should be regarded as one of several sources of Du Bois's psychic reassemblies in *The Souls of Black Folk*.

Chapter 2 examines patterns by which three novelists—Toomer, Hurston, and Ellison—articulate something of an Africa-informed "soul" heritage from occulted sources of song, folktale, and spirituality. As Toomer, Hurston, and Ellison capture a nodal moment of black cultural transformation from Afro-Southern sources of authority to the freer ground of northern urban migration, their fiction often feminizes the Southern vernacular tradition and reveals a sometimes anxious search for black patrimony. From tireless efforts at antiphonal patterns engaging the *nyama* of Afro-Southern semiotics, Toomer's *Cane* (1923) seeks to "become the face of the South . . . my lips being the lips of its soul" (81). Zora Neale Hurston offered High John de Conquer as the hoodoo root figure of a semiotic system that is "the source and soul of our laughter and song," come from Africa "walking on the waves of sound" (542–43). And although Ellison's *Invisible Man* (1947) works to undermine concepts of rooted identity, his novel remains so immersed in Afro-Southern systems of expression that a much hybridized Senegambian *nyama* emerges in scenes that locate shared soul identity in Brer Rabbit, Carolina yams, and the entire jazz-inflected system of "mother wit."

Chapter 3 will address attractions and problems of epic quests for Senegambian Muslim patrimony. *The Autobiography of Malcolm X*, Alex Haley's *Roots*, and Toni Morrison's *Song of Solomon* respond to the loss of African patronyms and the dislocations of black families with narratives that seek griotlike marriage of soul semiotics and epic-heroic African Muslim patrimony. *The Autobiography of Malcolm X* voices the clearest call for an Afrocentric Islam as a means of black nationalist salvation, but the work's undervaluation of certain aspects of the Afro-Creole soul heritage shares something of the Western Devil's discourse. Alex Haley's *Roots* offered the Mande/Muslim Kinte patronym as a foundational epic replacement for the Nation of Islam's variable "X" in a work of unparalleled popular success, a much attacked text that single-handedly re-introduced America to the griot profession. Finally, I want to pay close attention to how Toni Morrison handles and revises the project of epic renaming and narration of transcendent heroic flight in *Song of Solomon*, which lays claim to yet another Senegambian Muslim forefather.

IV

Although the Deep South's subtropical landscape, substantial black populations, and colonial immigrations of people and institutions from the West Indies (to Carolina from Barbados, to Louisiana from Haiti, and to Florida from Cuba) ensured its position as a Creole matrix, too few Americans have recognized the vigor of the Afro-Creole foundational presence. Joseph Murphy has called our country "a creole country. . . . [t]he denial of our Africanity is the great myth that Herskovits succeeds in exposing" (115). Likewise, W.E.B. DuBois called black music "the singular spiritual heritage of the nation" (178), and J.E. McTeer, who served as sheriff in Beaufort, South Carolina, for thirty-nine years while working for fifty years as a root doctor and white colleague of the famous Dr. Buzzard, observed how "over the years of our country's growth, the white American has become a 'hybrid'" (96).

We must pay more attention to the ways in which the word "creole" may represent us all. By "creole" I refer to a multiplicity of New World forces and identities, a new crossroads of being, and an awareness of (and often a resistance to) becoming something new. "Creole," with its ever-present association with race, tends to refer to an Africa-informed New World presence. The first New World writer of distinction, Inca Garcilaso de la Vega, gave early mention of this most American of words in *La Florida* (1605): "The Negroes designate all persons *criollos* who have been born in the Indies of either pure Spanish or pure Negro parents, thus indicating that they are natives of the Indies. . . . Likewise, the Spaniards have already introduced the word *criollo* into their language, attaching to it the same significance" (106). George W. Cable wrote in *The Creoles of Louisiana* (1884) that *criollo* is "a corrupt word made by the negroes, said to be a contraction of *criadillo*, diminutive of *criado*—one educated, instructed, or bred up, pp. of *criar*, lit. to create, also to nurse, instruct" (41). While "creole," in its earlier sense

came to signify New World peoples, cultures, products, and identities (anyone or anything born/produced in the Americas), and carried traces of the
racial and vernacular "corruption" alleged by Cable, the word has also been
applied by linguists to name the Afro-Atlantic languages born of New World
contact situations, languages spoken primarily (though never exclusively)
by the descendants of enslaved Africans. My understanding of creolization,
informed by linguistic models, is supplemented by the broader vision of the
Caribbean poet/historian Edward (Kamau) Brathwaite, who has defined it
as "a cultural action—material, psychological, and spiritual—based upon
the stimulus/response of individuals within the society of their environment and—as white/black, culturally discrete groups—to each other" (296).
Extending linguistic models into the realm of culture, we may speak of
creolization in folktales, religion, cooking, music, and worldview. In the
United States, core geographic centers of creolization may be located in
areas of long-standing creole language use (the Carolina/Georgia coast as
well as the area popularly synonymous with "Creole" culture—with a capital "C"—South Louisiana). Energies of action that created Afro-Creole languages and cultures in these core areas may also be traced throughout the
plantation economy, and—following routes of urban migration—throughout America's cities, and across the world.

In summary, by "creole" I am referring to New World identities and
cultures deeply impacted by Africans, as well as the languages born of New
World contact situations. I follow the lead of the Martinican writer, Edouard
Glissant, who in writing of Faulkner speaks of creolization as "the unstoppable conjunction despite misery, oppression, and lynching, the conjunction that opens up torrents of unpredictable results. . . . the unpredictability
that terrifies those who refuse the very idea, if not the temptation, to mix,
flow together, and share" (30). Anxieties of creolization are distinctly registered in Anglo-America's foundational colony of Virginia, which was the
native soil of Thomas Jefferson, the site of the varied hauntings of Edgar
Allan Poe and Nat Turner, and the source of the antebellum banjo sound of
Joel Walker Sweeney, "'the Elvis Presley of his time'" (Rosenberg 12).

But when we look farther south, to South Carolina, which according
to an eighteenth-century traveler's comment, looked "more like a negro country than like a country settled by white people" (Wood 132), we find white
anxieties and repression of creolization to be intensified. In an early issue of
the *South Carolina Gazette,* a poet who signed himself "The Cameleon Lover"
(1732) feared for the white minority's moral/racial survival, arguing that
whites who took black lovers would "imbibe the Blackness of their Charmer's
Skin," while a responding poet soon countered with "Cameleon's Defense"
in verse sympathetic to "the dark beauties of the Sable Race" (234–35). The
development of varying degrees of chameleon or gumbo consciousness was

certain in the colony, given its substantial black majority and the fact that Carolina, according to Philip Curtin, offered "the closest mainland approximation to the West Indian plantation pattern" (*Atlantic Slave Trade* 145).

Although the rice belt of South Carolina and Georgia was a strong center of African cultural dissemination, Gwendolyn Midlo Hall writes that "the most significant source of Africanization of the entire culture of the United States" is Franco-Creole Louisiana (157). We find this Creole presence evoked in Dominique Rouquette's "La jeune fille des bois" (1857), which links Louisiana's landscape to "une brune, ami, comme ces jeunes filles / Que dore de ses feux le soleil des Antilles" (a dark girl, friend, like those young girls / that bake in the heat of the Antillean sun), and begs more of "ses longs cheveux d'ébène (her long ebony hair) and more of "ces chants . . . dans la forêt créole" [her songs . . . in the Creole forest (4598–99)]. In a landscape in which the majority language was a creole language, it should come as no surprise that the Creole forest, Afro-Creole song, and a repressed/projected/romanticized/often pornographic eroticism emerges from white Creole texts. This Creole forest was a new landscape inhabited by an African majority that in some way inhabited almost every thought of the French, Spanish, British, and American-born residents who claimed title to it all.

As we have seen with South Carolina's "Cameleon Lover," America's Creole forest often aroused white anxieties. William Gilmore Simms's "The Edge of the Swamp" (1853) laments the Carolina low country's lack of resemblance to the English landscape:

Here are no gardens such as he desires,
No innocent flowers of beauty, no delights
Of sweetness free from taint. The genial growth
He loves, finds here no harbor. Fetid shrubs,
That scent the gloomy atmosphere, offend
His pure patrician fancies. On the trees,
That look like felon spectres, he beholds
No blossoming beauties . . . (491)

Increasingly, however, America's emergent vernacular tradition took shape from grounding in Afro-Creole soil, as can be seen in the banjo playing of early minstrels, the animal tales of Joel Chandler Harris, and the fresh voice of Huck Finn. In the 1920s, in the midst of the jazz-modernist-primitivist vogue, the Charleston Poetry Society nurtured some of white America's most forthrightly creolist writers, including DuBose Heyward, Julia Peterkin, and Beatrice Ravenel. Heyward's *Porgy* (1925) provided the basis for his collaboration with George and Ira Gershwin in the making of "Porgy and Bess." And Peterkin, the first Southern novelist to win a Pulitzer Prize, launched her career with work grounded in Gullah traditions of tree-talking (a tradition shared with Senegambian spiritual seekers): "Me an' dis ol' tree / Sets heah togedder. / I wonder ef e know me / Lak I know him" (242). Beatrice Ravenel, the most powerful poet among the members of the Charleston Poetry Society, is now almost forgotten, but she managed to combine the group's local colorist interest in the Carolina low country with a keen intellect informed by a modernist jazz-era aesthetic. Her *Arrow of Lightning* (1925) affirms Creole difference from European sources in the title poem's address to a mockingbird: "Oh, what have you to do / With English wood-rides, / Trees pampered like horses in a stall?" (31) When Ravenel was in her sixties, she wrote an astonishingly strong body of work in Haiti, arguing (in "Judge Achille Fontain") that "Folk-ways are final, supreme, holding the only authority; / Crystallized they are Law" (89). This "crystallization," furthermore, is revealed to be nothing more than political and social power, as she stresses in having her Haitian judge state that with freedom from American Marines, the old Creole ways "would be ours once more. / O Legba! O Dumballo! O Voodoo Pantheon! / Our folk-ways then would be Law. / They would be right" (89). What many Southern writers began to sense was that old differences of valuation between high canonical culture and black folk culture had been rooted not in any intrinsic correctness or value but in ideology: in the workings of economic and political power.

This study's second section of chapters (4–6) proposes that by reading texts from Gullah and Louisiana Creole repertoires through the lens of Senegambian folktales, we may begin to trace processes of Africa-informed creolization at work elsewhere in the South and in the country as a whole. Calling attention to the fact that African cultural currents were strong enough to cross the color line, I will focus upon white writers' representations of Afro-Creole fables and language in order to address questions about how Afro-Creole cultural forms have answered the peculiar needs of whites.

Chapter 4 will turn to Senegambian folk narratives to show that the Afro-Creole repertoires of South Carolina, Georgia, and Louisiana sometimes preserve Senegambian tales almost wholly intact and regularly transmit Mande/Wolof/Fulbe plot structures, motifs, performance techniques, language features, and names. We will examine how enslaved Senegambians came to be in position to impart so much of their culture through all strata of plantation life. Animal fables, moralistic tales, and shape-shifting hunters' narratives worked upon their listeners as a civilizing force capable of harsh criticism of the hubristic savageries of the plantation system, and worked simultaneously to encourage the kind of openness to wild forces of innovation that has made American vernacular culture truly powerful.

Chapter 5 highlights the means by which Joel Chandler Harris might arguably be called one of our most *African* American authors, as we look at how his immersion in Afro-Creole semiotic systems enabled his fidelity to the plots and performance techniques of Senegambian fables. By examining the different political and psychic needs that Uncle Remus and Brer Rabbit answered for Harris and for America as a whole, we may begin to note Harris's major contribution to the development of a folk vernacular voice, noting too that Harris's Africanist voice and knowledge tended to be used to support white Southern governance of black subjects.

In Chapter 6 we will chart double forces in Harris's work (a realistic Creole-vernacular voice and a perniciously sentimental arcadian mask) that inform routes taken by other white writers—particularly in representations of the enculturating force of the black "mammy" or "maum" in the fiction of Susan Petigru King, Alfred Mercier, Julia Peterkin, and Faulkner. In retraversing the charged space of racialized weaning from what King called her "maumer tongue," these writers often entered a personally liberating, fabulous, masked zone in order to move through repression toward otherwise unaskable questions of soul erotics and pornography, legitimacy and illegitimacy, morality and immorality, freedom and control. While their efforts to find vision in Afro-Creole "spiritual soil" are fraught with all sorts of violence, these texts create more openings than closures, and they prefigure current pop-culture movements toward an African American-inflected voice in a nation still struggling toward the kinds of intimacies informed with identity that would mark full acceptance of our creolization.

V

If, as I will argue, there is an Afro-Creole *nyama* (an "energy of action" with identifiable Senegambian roots) at work in the shaping of American cultures, there has also been a counterforce working to close the pathways of Afro-Creole energy of action; this counterforce is also an agent of creolization. Following the aforementioned lead of Miller and Morrison, we may refer to this counter-Creole (yet still creolizing) agency as Africanist discourse. By regarding African culture as a nullity, Africanist discourse in America churned up the most unsettling and relentless national obsessions, as Ralph Ellison has pointed out, "For out of the counterfeiting of the black American's identity there arises a profound doubt in the white man's mind as to the authenticity of his own image of himself" (*Shadow and Act* 68). While Harlem Renaissance writers were reclaiming African heritage through the singing tree, Nashville's celebrated Fugitive poets were beginning to recognize that a foundation tree rooted in white Anglo-American identity was doomed by its dependence on unmixed purities.[11] Developing a pruned high-formal style, John Crowe Ransom sought enracination in the virgin space of English foundations—"A green bough from Virginia's aged tree" that might stay "the world of outer dark"—but found only doom there: "this was the old tree's late branch wrenched away, / Grieving the sapless limbs, the shorn and shaken" (38). Following the shocks of World War I and the rising resistance of colonized peoples throughout the world, white modernists had good reason to question the roots of the Western image, as we see most famously in Eliot's "The Waste Land": "What are the roots that clutch, what branches grow / Out of this stony rubbish?" and found "only / A heap of broken images, where the sun beats, / And the dead tree gives no shelter, the cricket no relief" (29–30). Forces of creolization led Eliot to mimic and resist jazz voices singing "OOOO that Shakespeherian Rag" amidst "a heap of broken images," a "dead tree" choked by multiplicity.[12] But Eliot was far from alone among American artists in drawing upon this polyphonic rag-time sound even as he felt threatened by "something oddly amorphous and denaturing . . . the distorting shape of the Other" (Glissant, *Faulkner* 31).

In the hands of American writers, Africanist disorientation (and dialogic intervention with it) takes many modes and masks. So again entering the frontier territory charted by Ellison and Morrison, I will examine America's most powerful mode of Africanist writing—the "gothic." It is no accident that the Southern literary tradition and the "gothic" inhabit a shared crossroads. The gothic novel, with its obsessions with history, haunted edifices and bloodlines, shadowy curses, moral and supernatural blackness, and romance gone awry, provides a framework for labyrinthine excavation of the repressed knowledge at the base of our national edifice. As Eric Sundquist writes, "The essence of the gothic is the eruption from below of rebellious or unconscious forces and the consequent violation of boundaries, whether racial, sexual, or abstractly moral" ("Faulkner, Race, and Forms of American Fiction" 18). Even the Fugitive poet Allen Tate, who yearned to connect with the Confederate dead, could not avoid gothic "knowledge / Carried to the heart" (21), a knowledge that is clearer in a later poem, "The Swimmers," which recalls a childhood memory of standing in creekbank shadows and discovering a lynched "nigger" on a "giant sycamore," embodying unspeakable sin: "Alone in the public clearing / This private thing was owned by all the town, / Though never claimed by us within my hearing" (135).

Gothic tends to work most powerfully as a medium not when it is sharing the open secret of white guilt or hypocrisy, but when it gives energy of action to insurrectionist shades. Operating at such a juncture, the New Negro poet Angelina Grimke presented "Tenebris" (1927):

There is a tree, by day,
That, at night
Has a shadow,

A hand huge and black.
　　All through the dark,
Against the white man's house,
　　In the little wind,
The black hand plucks and plucks
　　At the bricks.
The bricks are the color of blood and very small.
　　Is it a black hand,
　　Or is it a shadow? (945)

By showing how America took shape from sources other than European roots, as well as from racial "othering" of peoples deemed enslaveable, I seek to help, as Jay Wright does in his Mande-informed *The Double Invention of Komo*, "a spirit uneasy in its double knowledge" (39) lay claim to its "complex body" (43). This study's concluding section of chapters (7–9) will trace the explosive gothicism and passages through which American writers have repressed, outrageously recapitulated, boomeranged, and remembered the nation's denial of African (and indeed its own) humanity.

By focusing upon the Arabic scriptural tradition of Senegambian Muslims, Chapter 7 argues that literate Senegambian slaves presented a unique challenge to the "providential" ideology of racial slavery. Arabic texts produced by enslaved black "gentlemen" registered shocks of recognition (and elaborate dodges) in white responses to African literacy/humanity. Particularly charged Africanist disorientations take place when "masters" confront literate Muslim slaves and thereafter find it increasingly difficult to defend racial assumptions and even more difficult to minimize dangers of insurrection and damnation. Plantation romances such as William A. Caruthers's *The Kentuckian in New York* (1834) face mounting pressures in repressing the violent "dark side of things."

Chapter 8 calls attention to the fact that Senegambian insurrectionists provided some of nineteenth-century America's most haunting shadows of Africans in texts that violently explode white America's imaginary relations to its real conditions of existence. Melville's "Benito Cereno" (1855), in spite of its obvious "Ravenesque" foreshadowing, anticipates that the reader's complicity with racist ideologies will allow Senegalese Babo (and author) to plot a spectacular revolt in a narrative that reenacts energies of action for which American literature has had no adequate language. George W. Cable's *The Grandissimes* (1880) also uses an exceptional Senegalese rebel around which to build an attack on the foundations of American racial ideologies and thereby reveal "the double damage of all oppression," but the very exceptionalism attached to Senegalese in the narrative entraps Cable's efforts to move most meaningfully through the violence he reemplots.

After establishing that some of America's most haunting shadows of Africans were cast by the glare of whiteness in recognition of Senegambian Muslim humanity, I will move to examine ways in which three twentieth-century novelists sound the racialized depths of the American romance gone awry. In the labyrinthine prose of Faulkner, we may find a truly New World medium of foundational designs and events that continue to channel present actions since "*Maybe nothing ever happens once and is finished*" (*Absalom* 261). Faulkner, Ellison, and Morrison help us to read African and Africanist energies of action into a body of literature already channeled by their thick enmeshment. In engagement with the eye-opening poetics of our strongest crossroads writers, my tracing of the most historically visible African strand of the American heritage (the Senegambian presence) seeks to sharpen the focus of our ever-emergent *hippikat* vision.

I

Epic Impulses/Narratives of Ancestry

The little white gauze veil clung to the oval of a face of full contours. Samba Diallo had been fascinated by this countenance the
first time he had beheld it: it was like a living page from the history
of the Diallobé country. Everything that the country treasured of
epic tradition could be read there. All the features were in long
lines, on the axis of a slightly aquiline nose. The mouth was large
and strong, without exaggeration. An extraordinarily luminous gaze
bestowed a kind of impervious lustre upon this face. All the rest
disappeared under the gauze, which, more than a coiffure would
have done, took on here a distinct significance. Islam restrained
the formidable turbulence of those features, in the same way that
the little veil hemmed them in.

Cheikh Hamidou Kane,
L'aventure ambiguë (1961),
translation, Katherine Woods

1

Imperial Mother Wit, Gumbo Erotics

From Sunjata to *The Souls of Black Folk*

With cotton seed
With fresh okra
And flour of eggplant leaf
They set forth to Mèma
In search of Nare Magan Kònatè

Fa-Digi Sisòkò, *The Epic of Son-Jara*

I

Following Fa-Digi Sisòkò's narration of a royal search party's journey to foreign markets to locate the exiled Sunjata, I will be bringing some of the occulted signs and semiotic systems of Senegambian cultures into the marketplace of American literatures in an effort to discover telling moments of recognition. Deep Senegambian/Mande "soul" signs such as okra (and the thick "gumbo" of griot performance traditions) may help Americans to bear more articulate witness to how a community of shared *badenya* (mother-child-ness) identity has remembered Africa out of diaspora and exile.[1] Whether we are exploring provocative analogies to Senegambian traditions—as in Eric Sundquist's connection of W.E.B. Du Bois "to Africa through the role of the bard, or griot, as a communal singer and historian" (488)—or whether we are looking to the ways in which Du Bois does indeed handle enduring currents of *nyama* in his treatment of the spirituals and second sight, we can sharpen our reception of American narratives of African (and Afro-Creole) ancestry through an understanding of *nyama*, the repertoires of the *nyamakalaw*, and the griots' epic interweavings of heroic *fadenya* and collective *badenya* modes of power. As we proceed, we should bear in mind that wide-ranging contemporary use of the word "griot" testifies to the ideological appeal of Senegambian/Mande cultures and their old Muslim empires, and testifies as well to the enormous global impact of Alex Haley's celebration of griots in *Roots*. The word "griot," descriptive of a hereditary class of professional bards in the Senegambian/Sahelian region, has come to be applied to almost any African performance artist and is used in African American communities and beyond "as a sign of respect for those who know about the past, are artists in various media, or are simply high achievers" and also "to symbolize awareness of and attachment to Africa" (Hale, *Griots* 4, 255). The very word "griot" has come to be read beyond its home region as an Africa-centered sign of African mother-child-ness. The best-known text of the griots, the Sunjata epic, offers an exemplary narrative of national (even transnational) mother-child-ness identity. The Sunjata's use as a kind of cultural charter throughout much of the Mande diaspora, along with its growing popularity as a "world text," makes it a good benchmark from which to read African energies of action in African American quests to reunite the tastes and language of mother wit with an epic-heroic soul patrimony.

Throughout much of West Africa, Sunjata Keita is celebrated as the epic founder of the thirteenth-century Mali empire, which absorbed the remnants of old Ghana and expanded from its core in the Manden (or Manding) along the upper Niger to colonize the Senegambian coast to the west, Timbuktu and Gao to the east, Mauritanian oasis towns to the north, and forest lands of Guinea and Ivory Coast to the south. By the mid-sixteenth century, the Mali empire was in decline, but its imperial heroic age would continue to be celebrated among nationally fragmented Mande-speakers in Africa's best known and most widespread epic of empire. While tellings of the Sunjata epic differ with each set of regional interests and traditions, with each narrator, and with each performance, most performances of the epic begin by tracing Sunjata's patrilineage from famous Mande hunter-ancestors to Mecca and to Muhammad's servant Bilali. At the same time, Sunjata's mother is connected to the rampaging Buffalo-Woman of Du in an extended folkloric narrative that works to endow Sunjata with considerable occult *nyama*. As a child, Sunjata is a cripple who finally overcomes the sorcery of the Queen Mother (his own mother's rival co-wife), rises to his feet, and uproots a baobab tree. Sent into exile because of his growing threat to the rule of his half-brother, Sunjata ends up in distant Mema, after which the invading blacksmith-king Sumamuru Kante conquers the Manden. Summoned from Mema by an okra-wielding group of Manden ambassadors seeking him, Sunjata assembles an army, finds the occult means to destroy Sumamuru, and moves on to conquer surrounding regions and establish the Mali empire.

Mande epic is performed with musical accompaniment (usually a banjo prototype such as the *ngoni*) and supported by an "amen corner" of apprentice respondents or *naamu*-sayers. Similar to African American sermonic styles, Mande epic performance shifts between what Charles Bird has de-scribed as three differing metrical/generic modes: praise-proverb, narrative, and song mode ("Mande Hunters" 283–90). A body of shared plots and motifs, shared aesthetics, ideological concerns, and bardic institutions is discernable in the Senegambian/Mande region's epic traditions, which aside from the Sunjata, include such epics as the Kambili and the Monzon cycle (Bamana), the epics of Silamaka and Samba Gueladio Djegui (Fulbe), and the epic of Njajaan Njaay (Wolof).[2] Valorizing ideas and institutions attrib-uted to the days of founding ancestors, each of these epics voices a call of ancestral challenge, demanding response.

Mikhail Bahktin has argued that "the authorial position immanent in the epic and constitutive for it . . . is the environment of a man speaking about a past that is to him inaccessible, the reverent point of view of a de-scendant" (13). But in turning to the aggrandized past of West African epic, what we see is not as wholly inaccessible as we might expect, nor are the heroes (aside from Muslim saints like al-hajj Umar) valorized in the abso-lute manner of an Aeneas or Charlemagne. West African bards are schooled in the ethical ambiguities of power and in the ways that energy of past ac-tions may remain active in the present.[3] The griots' understanding of *nya* (occult means), *nyama* (energy of action), and their inherited role as *nyamakalaw*—professional handlers or "holders of the *nyama*" (Keita 113)—has shaped the emplotment of epic confrontation and determined who may give it voice.

From his opening lines, "Nare Magan Kònatè! / Sorcerer-Seizing-Sor-cerer! / A man of power is hard to find" (Johnson 100), Fa-Digi Sisòkò's Sunjata performance is explicitly concerned with power and its acquisition, which "is keyed to the notion of *nya*" (Bird and Kendall 16). A gendered ideology of power informs the epic's beginning as the hero's genealogy ac-counts for differing patrilineal and matrilineal inheritance of the means (*nya*) through which he wields the occult powers essential to West African epic-heroic action. Although the worldview of the Sunjata (its narrative "energy of action") has been described as "essentially pagan," the epic's many invo-cations of Islam "lend the sanction of an established world religion to the commemoration of the hero" (Irele 2336), as most griots ground Sunjata's patrilineal means in the authority of scriptural texts: "Almighty God created Adam, the forefather, / And caused him to stand upon the earth, / And said that all creation's beings should submit to him" (Johnson 101).

The epic patrilineage (moving from the Manden to Mecca and all the way back to Eden) traces the scriptural channels by which Sunjata receives *barakha*, the Islamic grace or power inherited by descendants of the early Muslim saints. Having established that imperial authority was Islamic, from the East, and conferred through patrilineal ties to Bilali the Ethiopian

(Muhammad's personal servant and Islam's first muezzin), Fa-Digi Sisòkò cites further scriptural authority in his genealogy of Sunjata's leading general, Tura Magan Traore, referring to Arabic chronicles to doubly authenticate the Islamic patrilineage of the founders:

> In our chronicles,
> It was written this way, my father,
> Amongst the Arabs:
> Among the Quraysh and Hashim,
> 'Abd al-Muttalib was the forefather of the Hashim Clan.
> 'And al-Muttalib begat 'Abdullah.
> 'Abdullah begat Muhammad.
> Muhammad begat Fatimah Bint. (108)

Tracing *barakha* received from the Prophet's daughter (because he had no son) through a male line to Sunjata's general, Sisòkò's second citation of textual authority is intent on persuasive verification, "the written being endowed with truth partly because of the high status of that channel (the language of sacred books)" (Goody 299). The epic thus provides African precedent for African American mediation between scriptural authority and the "veiled" oral voice of ancestral energies of action.

Even when bowing to Islam, griots often seem more interested in tapping bifocal, syncretic powers. For instance, when Sisòkò ends his textual citation of Tura Magan's patrilineage and reverts back to an "oral," more vernacular authority, he does so through explanation of the origins of Tura Magan's clan name, arriving at an ancestor who

> Could see in front
> And see behind.
> The name they gave him was Tarawere,
> "The man of two visions."
> That is the meaning of being Tarawere. (108)

Second sight, whether understood as a culturally constituted parallax effect or an extrasensory ability to divine the workings of spirits and power(s), is a gift the griots exploit in epic performance. After initial submission to Islamic authority, within which griots are at an authoritative disadvantage to scribes and clerics, Fa-Digi Sisòkò explores Sunjata's matrilineage in narrative detail, evoking a traditional authority threatened by Islam. Though they sanction male control, male griots have strategic interests in valorizing occulted, extra-Islamic realms of power accorded to women. Born into their bardic *nyama*-handling position, griots have had much to lose to literate clerics championing Islam and have been among the groups most hostile to Islam (Klein 420). Practitioners of indigenous African religions—and women in particular—found themselves excluded from the new literacy, and as illiterates, found access to authoritative readings of power increasingly limited to realms marginalized by orthodox Islam. As Nancy Hartsock asserts about Christian and Enlightenment thought, since orthodox Islam tends to divide the world into "A and not-A," regularly associating the not-A side "with disorder, irrationality, chance, error, impurity," what is not-Islam may easily become feminized, even demonized as magic or witchcraft (162). Griots' strategies of conserving a core Mande tradition and their own authority as its sanctioned ancestral voices led them to preserve and reforge an aesthetic complementarity of gender, expressed in the epic as an assimilated Muslim patrilineage and an often feminized Mande tradition. Islamic authority is acknowledged but is not the substance or style of the epic; an older semiotics operating from an old set of tensions is maintained and feminized (through folktales, indigenous spirituality, and a wide range of "erotic" joy-sharing cultural patterns) in a manner similar to African American bodies of knowledge known as "mother wit." Sunjata performances seek to get to the soul of Mande mother-child-ness. They do so by exploring realms of occult *nyama*, "conferred upon the hero . . . through his mother's ancestry" (Johnson 5).

Although the patrilineal claims cover more geographic space and historical time, the maternal inheritance is the real story. An extended narrative arises from a rupture of royal familial relations between Du Kamisa Konde (an ancestral mother figure to Sunjata's mother) and a nephew whom Du Kamisa raised to become king. Foolishly disregarding the power of motherly bonds, the king excludes Du Kamisa from a sacrificial feast early in his reign. She then confronts her nephew/son with kinship claims: "I and your father are of the same cause, / And suckled the same breast" (112). When the enraged young king reacts by slashing her breasts and ordering her to remain in the bush, Du Kamisa dips into an old calabash for signs of the transgressed motherly bonds. The items she produces bear a kind of *nyama* that no discerning South Carolinian would want to see in the hands of a root doctor:

"Do you not see your navel cord?
"Did I not bear a child?
"The water breaking at your birth,
"The cloth on which it spilled,
"Behold that cloth before you! (112)

Following this revelation of her knowledge and occult power, Du Kamisa transforms into the murderous, shape-shifting Buffalo of Du.

It takes a hunter of considerable means to kill the rampaging Buffalo-Woman, so two second-sighted Tarawere brothers enter the forest after receiving divination from a spirit who gives them knowledge of "an old woman to the West of Du" to whom they must offer "yesterday's rice" (115). Accepting the rice, Du Kamisa identifies herself as the Buffalo, binds the Taraweres to an oath of goodwill with the Konde clan, and then gives the brothers the means by which she may be vanquished—two eggs, a piece of green wood, a charcoal chunk, and a spindle stick. Du Kamisa reveals that when thrown by the fleeing hunters, these items will transform into forests and rivers to impede her progress. The spindle, when shot from a bow, is the only way to kill her, for she is invulnerable to metal weapons. This widespread West African folktale of the Buffalo-Woman and the hunters, yoked to Sunjata's matrilineal means, migrated to the American South by way of the forced relocations of transatlantic slavery, as Chapter 5 will explore more fully.

Whether in the Senegambian/Mali region or in the Americas, the Buffalo-Woman tale reminds male listeners of the need for discernment in their dealings with women, who are the surest source of their own psychic means—received from the maternal side (Bulman 174). Fundamental respect for women's power keeps the hunters' pathways open, lest all life be rendered an unnavigable wilderness. After killing the Buffalo, the Tarawere brothers win their choice of the kingdom's virgins. However, staying true to their oath of cooperation, they claim ugly Sugulung Konde of the Buffalo's clan, a choice that suggests the continued presence of the Buffalo-Woman. Many griots insist that this hunchbacked virgin, who will give birth to Sunjata, is indeed Du Kamisa's spirit double: her *ja*, capable of taking totemic buffalo form (Niane 8). While griots may not explicate the obscurity of occult matters, it is clear that Sunjata's maternal ancestry offers him extensive means for harnessing *nyama*. Delving into indigenous belief systems and realms of knowledge outside of orthodox Islam, the Buffalo of Du narrative locates what is not-Islam in the *nyama*-charged body of a noble but wild Mother Mande (Diawara 159).

Mande epic uses of genealogy trace the tuggings of *fadenya* rivalry (between a father's children from different wives) against *badenya* cohesion (between full siblings of the same mother). *Fadenya* tendencies toward innovation and aggressively individualistic action find balance in *badenya* tendencies toward conservative social cohesion and group-affiliated enabling action. These sustaining forces of complementarity reflect "tenets of Mande/Bamana cosmology [that] remain in place in spite of Islamic influence" (Johnson 21). Mande creation myths explain these forces of cosmological balance "as traits of the personality of God" (21). It is into this dynamic matrix of cohesion and dislocation that Sunjata is born. Fa-Digi Sisòkò tells us that after Sugulung Konde resisted the hunters' efforts to possess her, she was given to the king of the Manden and eventually gave birth to Sunjata, who was forced into immediate *fadenya* competition since the king's first wife gave birth to her own first son on the day of Sunjata's birth. Since "That which causes co-wife conflict / Is nothing but the co-wife's child" (49), the first wife moved to protect her son's birthright (and her own power) by soliciting both a Muslim "holy man" and a traditional "Omen Master" to render Sunjata lame and unfit to inherit power.

Sunjata's overcoming of lameness marks the beginning of his empowerment, which the griots link to a core trope of enduring power—the tree. When Sugulung is mocked for having mothered a lame son and is refused baobab leaf for use in a sauce, Sunjata blames his mother, his truest source of means. Serving as her son's "Answerer-of-Needs," Sugulung proceeds to a custard apple tree, "glossed in folk etymology as 'origin of origins'" (Johnson 207–08), carves a staff from the tree, and swears on her marital fidelity that Sunjata shall rise. With this staff charged by the *nyama* of his mother's oath, Sunjata rises to a praise-song of familiar tropes: *"Behold his way of standing: danka /O Kapok Tree and Flame Tree!"* (139). Avenging his mother's humiliation (the deepest "fighting" insult to the psyche, as in the American "dozens"), he uproots the baobab around which she was mocked and—in an act of aggressive *fadenya* individuation—transplants it in her courtyard, foreshadowing a transfer of power from the rival half-brother (enthroned during Sunjata's lameness) to himself. In the process, his violent uprooting of the tree earns him the *nyama*-laden praise-songs and praise-names so important to Senegambian/Mande ideas of heroic action.

When his transgressive acts finally force Sunjata and his mother into exile, he must move quickly to amass and control the almost radioactive *nyama* needed for his epic triumph. As in the confrontations of Moses with Pharaoh, the heroic narrative will not focus on battlefield confrontation with Sumamuru Kante—the new invading conqueror of the Manden—but will cloak Sunjata with enough energy of action to defeat an opponent who wears pants of human skin. The epic's cloaking of Sunjata with *nyama* parallels the practice of Senegambian heroes and hunters sporting the *nyama*-laden amulets that they introduced into Louisiana: *gris-gris, zinzin*, and knotted string *tafo* amulets.[4]

Sunjata's power quest in exile leads him to many Muslim city-states destined to become part of the Mali empire, but it also leads him to a secret society consisting of nine "Queens-of-Darkness" equipped with "invisible eyes . . . to see in the night" (Diedhiou 45). With their second-sighted night vision, the Nine Queens-of-Darkness are each capable of taking a person's night-wandering soul and sharing it in a meal with the members of their group (Diedhiou 34). Like the conjurers and witches described in the Works Progress Administration (WPA) coastal Georgia interviews collected in *Drums and Shadows*, these Queens-of-Darkness might "change deah shape at night an come in duh house an ride yuh" (108) since, as one informant put it, "dem folks wuz detuhmined tuh git muh spirit" (61). Upon entering this obscure, predominantly female realm, Sunjata steps furthest outside of scriptural religion as he comes to wield transgressive *nyama* to the point of near-invulnerability. He keeps his own *ja* ("shade" or "dual soul") from being devoured and emerges further empowered by generously offering food to the "Queens," just as the Taraweres vanquished the Buffalo with their gift of rice. In these battles of psychic warfare and protection (familiar to anyone acquainted with hoodoo or root-work of the Deep South), food items appear as fundamental units of exchange; even relatively antisocial witches have strict regard for manners, hospitality, and the reciprocity of meals.

It is through Sunjata's sister's use of a few Mande food items that the epic orchestrates its crucial recognition scene in a reversal of the action from *fadenya* dislocation to location in bonds of imperial mother-child-ness. During Sunjata's exile, his full-sister Sugulun Kulunkan, left behind in the Manden, begins to replace their mother as supporting sorceress and "Answerer-of-Needs." Sugulun Kulunkan's powers enable her to organize a group to search for Sunjata "With fresh okra, / And flour of eggplant leaf" (160). We might ask, why the okra and eggplant leaf? As emblematic signs of an intimate group knowledge, these Mande food items locate the exiles in the *nyama*-laden, joy-sharing, bridging of empathy and identity described by Audre Lorde in "The Erotic as Power." The nostalgic exile could not help but be affected by culinary signs of the Manden in a foreign market where okra, for example, would discretely signify an extended understanding of *badenya*, "commonly used as an abstraction that suppresses the presence of different mothers and unites all children as offspring of the same mother, 'mother Mande'" (Diawara 159). In the Mema market, okra and leaf thickener are veiled signs of *badenya* intended to spark recognition, solidarity, and the reintegration of a Mande diaspora. It is this market scene that probably best points to the function of the epic itself, which despite its celebration of transgressive heroic actions, is ultimately concerned with bringing its audience to recognize a sense of shared Mande mother-child-ness, a "soul" erotic, that is—according to Lorde—"a resource within each of us that lies in a deeply female and spiritual plane, firmly rooted in the power of our unexpressed or unrecognized feeling" (53). Linking extra-Islamic Mande spirituality and heritage to a kind of Mande "mother wit," the Sunjata seeks to make its listeners aware of feelings that might otherwise be unexpressed or unrecognized. The epic brings attention to what its audiences share—linguistic, cultural, and historical identity—and seeks to recapitulate the erotic *nyama* of the market recognition scene throughout its performance, bringing postimperial exiles to dip hands into a shared gumbo.

Griots repeatedly show how Sunjata, through sagacious dealings with women and respect for supportive *badenya* bonds, accrues the means to face the powerful blacksmith Sumamuru Kante. At Sunjata's moment of greatest need, a woman again steps forward as epic "Answerer-of-Needs." Sunjata's sister simply approaches the gates of Kante's fortress, willing to answer the sexual desires of her brother's adversary. By seducing him, she coaxes Kante into revealing the occult source of his strength—his one taboo vulnerability, the spur of a white cock. When Sumamuru's mother reprimands her son for spilling his secret, he responds by slashing his mother's breasts (in a repetition of the Du Kamisa story), further diminishing his resources and cutting into the very fabric of his power as his mother then rips his birth cloth, the sign of his deepest *nya*. Following Sumamuru's seduction and the dissolution of his *nya*, the battle's outcome is assured. In fact, Bird and Kendall write of a bard who sang for three hours of Sunjata's efforts to discover his enemy's means, and then described the final battle in three lines (20). Still, in almost every epic telling, Sumamuru is defeated but not killed, since he has the powers of disappearance and birdlike flight so common in African American tales of flight back to the motherland.[5]

The Sunjata is an epic of imperial mother wit, ideologically feminizing much that is locally or nationally Mande, mediating realms of *fadenya* and *badenya*, Islam and not-Islam, Arabic and Mande language use, collisions and readjustments of worldview. Mande epic tradition celebrates aggressive—even transgressive—*fadenya* action, enabling the hero to serve the community as "Answerer-of-Needs" during times of crisis. The hero is often ruthless and is celebrated with ambivalence, as reflected in the proverb, "The hero is welcome only on troubled days" (Johnson 42). Sunjata is no Charlemagne or Aeneas. Like the "bad" men of contemporary hip-hop or early blues, he is the embodiment of transgressive *fadenya*, as his praisenames attest: "Destroyer of Origins," "Kinsman-Killing-Hunter," "Sorcerer-Seizing-Sorcerer," "Devourer-of-the-Knower." The Mande hero fetches wild forces to be integrated into established cultural patterns (Jackson 20–21). Well equipped for handling the *nyama*-laden task of mediating innovation and tradition, griots weave the Manden's fragmented strips into the birth cloth of empire. Sharing something of the second-sightedness of the Tarawere hunters, griots—with their gendered complementarity in treating bipolar forces, their use of deep "soul" semiotics to spark empathetic recognition of group identity, and their rootedness in the call and response of epic's mix of song/praise-proverb/narrative performance—bequeathed a rich body of navigational means to their ethnic kin enslaved across the Atlantic. As we shall see, griots and griot-nurtured Senegambian cultures contributed significantly to emergent African American musical styles and an accompanying "*hippikat*" culture. With their open-eyed "ability to tell and retell 'the story,'" griots provided a clear precedent for black Baptist preachers' sermonic styles and their "transformation, renewal, and reimagination" of the gospel message (Gomez, *Exchanging* 281). Senegambian cultures nourished a "veiled" vernacular mother wit that offers Americans the means to see in front and behind, the *nya* to read and wield *nyama*-charged signs.

II

Although the Sunjata was almost certainly told throughout the American colonies in the early days of the slave trade, only a trace of its imperial memory and a stronger vein of the folktales, worldview, and Mande/Senegambian semiotics at work in it seem to have survived the transformations of American acculturation. Even in West Africa, the epic went through substantial transformation as it entered the repertoires of the vassals and pioneers of the expanding Mali empire. For instance, griots from the Manden heartland often conclude their Sunjata performances with a short episode covering the conquest of Kambi (Gambia), but Mandinka griots of contemporary Gambia expand this section to take up as much as a third of the entire narrative, often dispensing with the extensive genealogy important to griots from the Manden. A Wolof Sunjata performed on the *halam*, a five-stringed ancestor of the banjo, condenses the epic even more, ignoring the building of empire to focus on Sunjata's dealings with a local jinn who lived in a baobab where powerful "medicine was kept" (Ames 75). This Wolof variant describes the hero as a second-sighted *ya-bopa* ("wide-head") who controlled storehouses of ancestral power lodged in the roots of baobabs. Through the horrible dislocations of North American slavery, what was successfully adapted from Sunjata's cultural storehouse was (along with narrative motifs and modes of performance that will be treated more fully in chapters 4 and 5) a deep matrix of cultural reenactments, a semiotics that shaped patterns of language, music, worship, cookery, and spiritual traditions such as divination and second sight. It was from this griot-informed legacy of soul medicine that W.E.B. Du Bois articulated his notion of double consciousness and sought to bring readers to recognize African American music as "the singular spiritual heritage of the nation" (178).

Second sight, an ability to discern the workings of power, occult or otherwise, to see spirits and look "not merely at things but into them—and through them" (Bass 386), is a gift that seems to have traveled from Senegambian and other West African cultural repertoires to American ones. Ruth Bass's conversations with the Mississippi tree-talker, Old Divinity, reveal that like Sunjata he was a double-sighter possessed of two spirits, "one that wanders and one that stays in the body" (Bass 386). Born "from a tree-tawkin' family" (385), "de gran'son ob a witch. . . . wid a veil ovah ma face. . . . er dubble-sighter," (386) he developed his inherited powers through apprenticeship, much as Mande/Bamana *nyamakalaw* develop *jiridon* or "knowledge of the trees" (McNaughton 42). Divinity had learned to read trees' signs: "If yo heah murmurin' in de trees when de win' ain't blowin,' dem's sperrits . . . effen yo know how tuh lissen yo kin git dey wisdom," and was convinced that man is "Jes' a part uv de livin souls. . . . Man aint all" (385–86). The Carolina rice planter Elizabeth Allston Pringle wrote similarly of an encounter related to her by her maid Chloe, who had seen a spirit known in the low country as a plat eye. The plat eye (like Du Kamisa Konde) "tu'n 'eself unto a bull, en rare up befo' me," and Chloe "say to meself 'Trow down yu fader h'art, en tek up yu murrer h'art . . . 'Kase yu kno..'. yu' murrer h'art is always stronger dan yu fader h'art. . . . 'Oman h'art is stronger dan man h'art w'en yu cum to speret en plat eye" (215). These reports of tree-talking dual souls, shape-shifting bull-spirits, and the special spiritual powers of the "mother heart" suggest rootedness in Mande/Senegambian traditions of knowledge and power.

The dynamic worldview emergent from Divinity and Chloe's double-sighted powers finds an analogue in West African music, which "uses the interplay of two or more metrical frameworks as the primary material out of which the music is built" (Waterman 88). Though the communicative tones and polyrhythms of West Africa's drums were generally (but not completely) suppressed in North America, a profoundly pluralistic African sensibility informed American music as string instruments, body, and voice kept the music's *nyama* alive. Murph Gribble, a black banjo player from Tennessee, claimed to play "the way the old folks played" and called his favorite style "broke-legged" rhythm; his broke-legged rhythms, "not hitting all the up-beats and downbeats," and filled with "sudden startling gaps and hesitations" (Charles Wolfe, *Altamont* 1–2), closely resemble the frailed rhythms of banjo prototypes used in the Mande epic's narration of Sunjata's rise from lameness. The banjo, recognized by Thomas Jefferson as "brought hither from Africa" (257), developed from the Wolof *halam*, the Fulbe *hoddu*, and the Mande/Bamana *ngoni*.[6] The Wolof term equivalent to our own "banjo player"—*halamkat*—made up of *halam* plus the Wolof agentive suffix *kat* familiar to American jive-cats and hip-cats, signals extensive Senegambian impact upon the language and performance styles of an American musical culture intimately bound to Africa (Dalby 138).

Not only did Senegambian musicians make strong contributions to American music, but they have also contributed to the music of their northern, Mauritanian neighbors—Moors (Hassiniya) whose enslavement of phenotypically "blacker" Africans both preceded and outlasted the Atlantic slave trade. Moors generally play the *tidinit* (their *halam* equivalent) in either of two tuning styles: a "black" tuning preferred by the musicians for the range of effects that it allows, and a "white" tuning preferred by their upper-class patrons for its fidelity to Arab/Berber tradition; likewise, many Fulbe *hoddu* players use a "white" tuning when playing for Moorish patrons, and a "black" one when playing for their own communities (Coolen 122–29). These black and white tunings, like the differing modes and origins of action that Fulbe weavers distinguish as "white knowledge" (Islamic/clerical) and "black" (caste-craft/ancestral) knowledge (Dilley 142), provide evidence of bifocal, possibly racialized, repertoires developed within Africa.

Because of their role in articulating and navigating the Senegambian region's tripartite social structures (consisting of free, endogamous professional, and slave groups), Mande, Fulbe, and Wolof griots would have prepared Senegambians with useful means and manner for facing the intense social stratification of plantation slavery. Wolof griots developed a style of speech (*waxu gewel*), which in contrast to the restraint and near silence of a noble style is, according to Judith Irvine, noted for an emotionally charged "fluency of expression" that is inseparable from the "lack of inhibition" that, for example, helps griot women "be the best dancers, since high-caste women are 'too stiff' and 'too ashamed' to perform in the sexually suggestive manner deemed the most skillful" (131–34). Irvine observes that "extreme versions of the 'griotlike' prosody are found in those public situations where the greatest differences in social rank are most pertinent" (137). At meetings or celebrations hosted by prominent noble families, griotlike speech styles assume their greatest difference from other speech modes, and the griot, in a manner similar to that of many contemporary American rappers (or the frenetic pacing that necessitates the "whoops" of country preachers), "stands and shouts as loudly as possible to the assembled crowd; he sways and jabs at the air with dramatic and forceful gestures, pointing at his addressees and holding up the money he has received in largesse. . . . His voice rises into a falsetto pitch, and the rate of his utterance increases to more than 300 syllables a minute" (137). The African component of the repertoires of musicians enslaved in America went beyond West African musical instruments and styles to include Senegambian double-voiced discursive modes expressive of social differences and proud griot identity. Once enslaved in America, a *halamkat* named "Samba" might find himself in demand as a "hip" doubly conscious banjo-cat called "Sambo."

While Americans are only beginning to be able to read the veiled depths and ironies of banjo-cats or the "Sambo Boogie Woogie paper dolls" of Ellison's *Invisible Man*, the dialogic, antiphonal patterns of African American music and speech, particularly prominent in the art of preaching, have long derived their special power from the way in which call and response work to create forms of shared identity, pain, and pleasure. As John Chernoff remarked of West African musical sensibility (intimately linked to speech patterns), rhythm in Africa may be perceived less as something to "get with" than as something to "respond to"; it demands dialogue, the call and response of fully engaged conversation (55). This dialogic aesthetic base is evident in Sunjata performances, from the ideological tuggings of *fadenya* and *badenya* to the antiphonal interplay of the bard and his *naamu*-sayer, who punctuates the epic with "amens":

Our grandparent Eve and our ancestor Adam,	*(Indeed)*
They sought each other out,	*(Indeed)*
For forty days,	*(Indeed)*
They were seeking each other.	*(Indeed)*
The mount whereon they met,	
Its name was Arafan.	*(True)*
Ask the ones who know of this!	*(True.*
	That's true Fa-Digi)
	(Johnson 104)

Substitute the *naamu*-sayer's interjections with those of an animated Christian congregation, and it would be possible to confuse this passage from the Mande-Muslim epic with a transcription from Georgia Sunday radio. Indeed, many of our terms of response may come from peoples of Old Mali. In Wolof conversation, one might respond by saying *degg-na*, "I hear," rendered in America as "dig"; however, a truly responsive addressee might add an emphatic *waw kay*, combining the Wolof "yes," (*waw*) with the emphatic particle *kay* to convey a sense of "yes indeed, all right," corresponding closely, in sound and meaning, to our "OK" (Dalby 139).

Since it is not only the antiphonal form of the Sunjata that seems familiar but also some of its scriptural base, we must remember that Mande, Fulbe, and Wolof peoples enslaved in the Americas would have been able to use their Islamic scriptural knowledge to question American interpretations of Biblical texts. Unintimidated by Christian texts treating well-known stories, Muslims were in authoritative position to interpret holy scripture to other enslaved Africans. Arabic literacy signaled an alternative knowledge, and the Arabic alphabet could even be employed to transcribe the vernacular (as Senegambian Fulbe had done); in fact, a Georgia slave named London wrote several texts that were successfully "translated" only when the translator stopped looking for Arabic vocabulary and transliterated the Arabic letters into Afro-English sounds that revealed the following:

Fas chapta ob jon.
Inde be ginnen wasde wad;

ande Wad waswid Gad,
    ande wad was Gad. (Hodgson, "The Gospels" 10)

As the first West Africans to come into regular contact with Europeans, Senegambians were particularly important in the early days of the transatlantic slave trade and contributed significantly to the formative base of African American culture. During the eighteenth century, Senegambian cultures were the dominant African cultures in Louisiana (Hall 159) and played strong roles in the formation of Creole cultures in low country Carolina and Georgia (Joyner 204–07). Because Senegambians often served as house servants and "had extensive and close contact with European-Americans" (Holloway 4), enslaved Wolof, Fulbe, and Mande men, women, and children were able to Africanize European patterns of speech, narrative, music, dance, worship, cookery, etc., to such an extent that Southern whites were acculturated into Afro-Creole styles (as Chapters 4–6 will examine). The most valued Africans in the slave markets of the Old South, Senegambians were considered the most civilized, attractive, and intelligent of slaves, due to contact with "Semitic" cultures, and were desired as drivers, cooks, nurses, and personal servants (Holloway 13, Gomez 82). Southern planters often proved willing to learn from Africans, profiting from Senegambian knowledge of rice culture and livestock (see Wood 30–62). The men who served as houseboys and cowboys and the women who nursed and mothered the Europeans' children were mediating translators in the reciprocal process of acculturation between Africans and Europeans in America.

For the clearest picture of the tenacity of a reassembled African (and identifiably Senegambian) cultural matrix in North America, we can turn to coastal Georgia in a composite reading of three closely related, intersecting texts: the Georgia Writers' Project's *Drums and Shadows* (1940), Lydia Parrish's *Slave Songs of the Georgia Sea Islands* (1942), and Lorenzo Turner's *Africanisms in the Gullah Dialect* (1949), all of which presented material from the same group of communities and shared many of the same informants. When the Georgia Writers' Project interviewed ex-slaves from the rice coast, many Muslims were remembered, including two Fulbe men who served as plantation overseers—both named Bilali after the Prophet's muezzin (whom the griots claim as Sunjata's ancestor). Katie Brown, whose grandmother was a daughter of Bilali Muhammad, recalled Muslim names of great-aunts Bintu, Medina, and Fatima, as well as the family's manner of prayer: "Belali an he wife Phoebe pray on duh bead. Dey wuz bery puhticluh bout duh time dey pray an dey bery regluh bout duh hour. Wen duh sun come up, wen it straight obuh head an wen it set, das duh time dey pray. Dey bow tuh duh sun an hab lill mat tuh kneel on. Duh beads is on a long string. Belali he pull bead an he say, 'Belambi, Hakabara, Mahamadu.' Phoebe she say, 'Ameen,

Ameen'" (161). Katie Brown spoke of Sapelo Island's Islamic clothing styles
and recalled the process of pounding rice in a mortar to make sweet "saraka"
cakes that were distributed from a Senegalese-style rice fanning basket to
celebrate the end of Ramadan.[7] Another Bilali Muhammad descendant, Shad
Hall, provided a wealth of information concerning his recollections of his
grandmother Hester's talk of Africa, of her father Bilali, and of her sisters
Medina, Yaruba, Fatima, Bintu, and Charlotte. He spoke of how his grandmother "Hestuh an all ub um sho pray on duh bead. . . . At sun-up and face
duh sun on duh knees an bow tuh it tree times, kneelin on a lill mat" (166).
On St. Simons Island the interviewers found descendants of Salih Bilali.
Bilali's grandson, Ben Sullivan, used a West African-style gender-neutral
pronoun to speak of one Muslim woman: "I membuh a ole uhman name
Daphne. . . . He weah loose wite veil on he head" (180). Sullivan also told of
Old Israel, who prayed on a mat with a book he kept hidden and "alluz tie
he head up in a wite clawt" (179). Susan Maxwell recalled a grandmother's
religious difference: "Friday wuz duh day she call huh prayuh day" (145).
The semiotics of imperial Mali clearly lived in patterns of cloth, music, language, worship, and the tastes of folk who would "gadduh wile okra" to
"cook sumpn fuh nyam . . . sumpn fuh tuh eat" (144).

Lydia Parrish's collection of Gullah songs and shouts (which, following Lorenzo Turner, she connects to the Arabic *saut*, signifying a circling
dance around the Kaaba) points to Afro-Creole synthesis of Christian, Islamic, and indigenous African worship patterns, and a more general process that Charles Joyner has called the creolization of culture.[8] In Parrish's
presentation of Bilali Muhammad descendant Katie Brown's song of seeking
religion in the wilderness "on your bending (knees)," we can see—in the
Gullah churches' insistence upon initiatory "seeking" of divine vision in the
woods—a continuation of West African socioreligious institutions requir-
ing initiation bush-retreats, along with probable synthesis of Islamic and
Christian modes of prayer (132).[9] The shout entitled "Knee-bone" offers
the times and actions of Islamic prayer: "Knee-bone in the mornin' / Ha-ah
Lord knee-bone bend. / Knee-bone in the evenin' / H-a-nn knee-bone" (81).
Another shout, "Down to de Mire," called shouters even more deeply into
Islamic styles of prayer as each participant would individually enter the
ring's circle and get on her knees to touch forehead to the floor while the
shouters circled, clapped, stomped, and sang: "You must bow low to de
mire" (72). "Mire," pronounced "myuh" by *Drums and Shadows* informants,
ambiguously signifies depths or bottom, but it also bears traces of the Fulbe/
Pulaar "*maayo*" used by Salih Bilali in an interview with his master concerning rice culture (Austin 400): Bilali said he was born "in the Kingdom of
Massina . . . within half a mile of a great river, nearly a mile wide, which is
called Mayo" (Hodgson, *Notes* 70). The "myuh" sung of by Bilali's descen-

dants may be a creolized convergence of Islamic/West African worship patterns, Christian baptism, and memories of water rites by rivers such as the Niger, Senegal, and Gambia. Certainly the shout itself—the "holy dance"—is a Creole mediation reconciling West African worship styles with Anglo-Protestant prohibition of dance and drums. As Parrish's work and the WPA interviews reveal, the ring shout was so important to early Afro-Creole worship and conversion that Michael Gomez is right in arguing that the ring shout was the primary vehicle by which Christianity was "grafted onto the tree of African tradition" (*Exchanging* 267). Along with her descriptions and collections of shout songs, Parrish also describes "The Buzzard Lope," a dance resonant with the "Douga" or Vulture dance central to Mande representations of heroism. Even today, Senegambian Muslim influence upon Christian practice remains evident along the Georgia coast. In McIntosh County, members of the Mt. Calvary Baptist Church usher in the New Year with black-eyed peas and a watch-night shout (amazingly similar to Senegalese *gamut* celebrations of Muhammad's birth). Across the salt marsh, the Sapelo Island First African Baptist congregation prays to the east, and individuals often direct prayers eastward, since as Bilali Muhammad's descendant Cornelia Bailey says, "the devil is in the other corner" (Gomez, *Exchanging* 87).

Lorenzo Turner's *Africanisms in the Gullah Dialect* (1949) examines not only the residual African roots of Gullah but also the composite, creolized transmutations through which growth is routed. Mande and Fulbe sources show up repeatedly. Two of Turner's informants could count from one to nineteen in the Pulaar spoken by their Fulbe ancestors, suggesting both the strength of the Fulbe cultural contribution and the attractive power of alternative means of knowledge. Turner also found that in a manner parallel to Senegambian peoples' uses of names to indicate birth order and maternal descent (complementing a system in which first names tend to be derived from Islamic hagiography, while family names are patrilineal), his Sea Island informants used two given names: one English name used at school and in dealing with strangers, and another nickname or "basket name," often African in origin, used at home or among close acquaintances. Turner's extensive list of African basket names retained in Gullah is filled with many of Mande, Fulbe, and Wolof origin, and he argues for the vitality of a West African ideological dualism through which the "erotic" familiar element may be veiled and transmitted as mother wit. A number of texts collected by Turner reveal a strong Mande-speaking Sierra Leonian connection to Gullah culture.[10] Of particular interest is Turner's translation of a Mende funeral song performed by Amelia Dawley [also presented by Parrish, "I wock om a mo-na / Cum bul-le al-le / Lilli—quam-be" (48), and—in a slightly different version—by a *Drums and Shadows* interviewee (54)]:

In the evening we suffer; the grave not yet; heart, be cool perfectly.
In the evening we suffer; the grave not yet; heart be cool continually.
Death quickly the tree destroys, steals [it]; the remains disappear slowly;
Death quickly the tree destroys; be at rest, heart, continually. (Turner 256)

Although none of the singers could (or would) recall the song's meaning, they remained true enough to the sounds for the song to be recognized by contemporary Mende speakers. That the surviving song is a funeral song attests to the honor offered to African ancestors. The song proved to be so filled with a venerated ancestral *nyama* that Dawley's daughter Mary Moran continued singing the song, and once located by one of coastal Georgia's ubiquitous Gullah-researchers in the late 1990's, managed to travel to Sierra Leone where she sang the funeral hymn in duet with Baindu Jabati.[11]

Taken as a whole, Turner's, Parrish's, and the Georgia Writers' Project's works allow us to see something of the worldview and culture of an American community deeply informed by African cultural systems, a community that traced genealogies to specific African (particularly Muslim) founders, and in creolized performances evoked an African past from the reverent point of view of descendants. Like Salih Bilali descendant Ben Sullivan, they felt a mixture of feelings about their African ancestors (but mostly pride) in recalling that "all ub em ain tame" (Georgia 179). Wild, unbroken energies of action inform the way in which Moses (or perhaps the Muslim Moussa) is claimed as a Sunjata-like African ancestor revered for his formidable means to do occult battle with a powerful enemy to answer the needs of an oppressed people: "Dat happen in Africa duh Bible say. Ain dat show dat Africa wuz a lan uh magic powuh since duh beginnen uh history? Well den, duh descendants ub Africans hab duh same gif tuh do unnatchul ting" (28). We hear, time and time again, a *nyama* akin to Alejo Carpentier's "marvelous real" claimed with pride by descendants of Africans, for whom snippets of a Mende funeral song might marry the soul erotics of mother wit with a patrimony enabling (as with Sumamuru Kante) disappearing flight:

> "[M]uh gran say ole man Waldburg down on St. Catherine own some slabes wut wuzn climatize an he wuk um hahd an one day dey wuz hoein in duh fiel an duh dribuh come out an two un um wuz unuh a tree in duh shade, an duh hoes wuz wukin by demsef. Duh dribuh say 'Wut dis?' an dey say, 'Kum buba yali kum buba tambe, Kum kunka yali kum kunka tambe,' quick like. Den dey rise off duh groun an fly away. Nobody ebuh see um no mo. Some say dey fly back tuh Africa. Muh gran see dat wid he own eye." (79)

Since scholars such as Daniel Littlefield (1981), Gwendolyn Midlo Hall (1992), and Michael Gomez (1998) have established that Mande, Fulbe, and Wolof captives contributed significantly to the foundations of Creole cultures in North America, I have taken for granted that in various ways the energies of action transmitted by enslaved Senegambians shaped America's emerging African American cultures. Indeed, we may see that the semiotics of Sunjata performances (in essence the "gumbo erotic" shared in performance) successfully migrated to America. The Sunjata epic's musical instruments and musical patterns—even some of the language of performance—lived on in the banjo, in antiphonal patterns of music and speech, and in some of the language and styles of American "hip-cats." On a spiritual plane, we see evidence that Senegambian energies of action contributed to Afro-Southern tree-talking, patterns of worship and initiatory vision-seeking, a tradition of dual or componential souls, belief in second sight, and even a tendency to "feminize" such repertoires of knowledge as "mother wit." Spiritualist possession, ring shouts, and the body of song known as "spirituals" drew from a well of corporal spirituality that provided a joy-sharing/erotic bridge between West Africa and America. A vernacular synonym for this "erotic" that emerged out of plantation-forged Afro-Creole semiotic systems might be "soul." For vernacular ideas of "soul" integrate corporality with "the spiritual," signify an animate force kin to *nyama*, and offer in-group mother-child-ness associations: soul music, soul food, soul brother/sister. Among American texts that attempt epic articulation of African American "soul," there is one unavoidable bible: W.E.B. Du Bois's *The Souls of Black Folk* (1903).

III

When Du Bois developed his trope of the veil as a figure of the peculiar powers of vision arising from the duality of African American experience, he was working from means that would be familiar to *nyama*-handling griots who have navigated gaps between a localized mother wit and a scriptural universalist ideal. He announced that "the Negro is a sort of seventh son, born with a veil, and gifted with second sight in this American world" (3). True to his second-sighted Afro-Creole sources, Du Bois's articulation of double consciousness offers a visionary gift accompanied by shadow-haunted habitation in two worlds: "One ever feels his twoness,—an American, a Negro; two souls, two thoughts, two unreconciled strivings" (*Souls* 3). This veil of second sight is a kind of crossroads figure of Afro-Creole "soul" and of the racially constructed limits of the American dream, allowing peculiar vision of the ways African American dual strivings are "woven . . . into the very warp and woof of this nation" (187). Resonating with the Sunjata epic's summoning of Sunjata—and the Mande diaspora—out of exile, Du Bois's task was nothing less than an epic reassembly of African American patrimony called out of exile via a revalorization of the "soul" semiotics of African American mother-child-ness. Eric Sundquist has noted that it is this "bardic function" of Du Bois's plural *Souls* that allows his performance as "epic singer of the New Negro Nation—and of a nation, the United States, that was Negro in critical ways" (*To Wake the Nations* 489). Each chapter's frame, with a literary quote alongside musical notation of a "sorrow song," reinforced the duality of *Souls* while seeking integration of discursive and musical styles. Like Mande epic's mix of song, narrative, praise-proverb, and genealogy, Du Bois added to sociology "history, fiction, autobiography, ethnography, and poetry . . . [to create] a polyphonic form" (Gilroy 115). Because of similarities of polyphonic genre and aim, it is no surprise that analogies to griot traditions may come easily when we speak of *The Souls of Black Folk*. What has not been sufficiently understood, however, is the degree to which Du Bois actually came to handle something of Senegambian/West African energies of action in his epic articulation of his plural *Souls*. The means by which he did so lie in his studied attentiveness to an Africa-informed vernacular culture that offered him the spiritual veil of second-sighted double consciousness and the powerfully coded sounds of the spirituals.

The birth veil that Du Bois crafted into a racial sign of "double consciousness, this sense of always looking at one's self through the eyes of others" (3), enabled his truly novel text.[12] Similar to Bakhtin's "polyglot consciousness," a consciousness "existing in a field illuminated by another's language" (62–65), the consciousness of *The Souls of Black Folk* is so thoroughly double that it would be difficult to pick out which is its "other" language. One is tempted to say that the vernacular language of the sorrow songs is the text's "other" language since, as Arnold Rampersad writes, Du Bois "did not enjoy exploiting black dialect" and wrote his "epic" text following the classical rhetorical patterns of his Fisk and Harvard education (69). But like its controlling trope of the veil, the vision revealed by the language of *Souls* is nourished by a vernacular mother wit that knows the "official" consciousness of letters and law to be terribly lacking. The opening lines of *The Souls of Black Folk* establish the boundaries between self and other: "Between me and the other world there is ever an unasked question. . . . How does it feel to be a problem?" (1). Du Bois's response to "the other world" came after a studied immersion in Afro-Southern expressive traditions and required a polyphonic form since, according to Bakhtin, such a quarrel of languages and worldviews "could not pass on to a further phase by means of abstract and rational dialogue, nor by a purely dramatic dialogue, but only by means of complexly dialogized hybrids" (82). Du Bois's veil of second sight emerges as the dialogic trope through which the reader may come to see that only a person possessing dual souls can gain a truly inclusive, whole vision of America.

According to the Georgia Writers' Project's *Drums and Shadows* informants, a veil or birth caul allows a person to "be birthed with wisdom" and to "talk wid duh spirits" (15, 77). The Mande tradition of saving the umbilicus and afterbirth—seen in Du Kamisa's moment of occult revelation and in the revenge of Sumamuru's mother—resurfaces in a coastal Georgia resident's means for conversing with a spirit from the "shadduh worl": "I kin tell duh fewchuh jis by lookin at duh pusson . . . cuz I wuz bawn wid a double cawl wut wuz sabe fuh me till I wuz grown" (39). Du Bois's second-sighted trope of vision and prophecy is lodged in traditions kin to Mande ideas of inheritable *nya* for wielding *nyama* but is also lodged in the history of American racial/power relations and nineteenth-century ideas of race that led Du Bois to embrace this "veil of Race" (55) and to argue that "Negro blood has a message for the world" (3). However, when Du Bois reaches toward Africa as origin of racial soul and spirit, his vision is not as clear as when it is focused on American soil. He may ask, "What did slavery mean to the African savage?" and answer such a question by proposing a genealogical study of changes "from the heathenism of the Gold Coast to the institutional Negro church of Chicago" (135). Du Bois's double consciousness, a product of an often antierotic Victorian patrimony and a more fully soulful mother wit, worked at times to distance him from the bodies and souls of the folk, as he acknowledged in his commentary on the black artist's "waste of double aims": "The innate love of harmony and beauty that set the ruder souls of his people a-dancing and a-singing raised but confusion and doubt in the soul of the black artist; for the beauty revealed to him was the soul-beauty of a race which his larger audience despised" (4).

Du Bois comes up against the problem that Kwame Anthony Appiah noted in Alexander Crummell (whom Du Bois invokes in a panegyric chapter of *Souls*); Appiah writes that "even those African-Americans like Crummell, who initiated the nationalist discourse *on* Africa in Africa, inherited a set of conceptual blinders that made them unable to see virtue in Africa, even though they needed Africa, above all else, as a source of validation" (5). Du Bois, who finally chose Ghana over pre–civil rights America, certainly saw virtue in African "soul-beauty." He needed that virtue if he was to cling to the idea of racial soul. But this virtue of the veil of race was a troubled, uneasy virtue for a Hegel-indebted Harvard Ph.D. whose faith lay in "the talented tenth" rather than in the "superstition" of the folk. If in his valorization of African American gifts to America we see dialogic difficulties, even "othering" of Africa, we must remember that although Du Bois was "novel," he was trapped by haunting shadows of oppressive discursive modes even as he forged new modes of seeing.

Although the child born with a veil is gifted with second sight, the veil may also be a source of haunting since it enables vision of (even dialogue with) ghosts or "shadows." As one Georgia midwife remarked of children born with a veil, "Folks hab tuh be mighty keahful wen duh chile is bawn lak dat. Ef dey dohn do sumpn bout it, duh chile will be hanted all its life" (Georgia Writers' Project 128). From the opening "Forethought" in which Du Bois states his aim to raise the veil so that the world without "may view faintly its deeper recesses," he prepares the reader for revelations of "haunting melodies" beyond (xxxi). He writes that "the very soul of the toiling, sweating black man is darkened by the shadow of a vast despair" (7) formed by shadows of the color line and a growing uneasiness over cultural patrimony: "The shadow of a mighty Negro past flits through the tale of Ethiopia the Shadowy and of Egypt the Sphinx" (3). Du Bois saw that "the awful shadow of the Veil" (45) haunts not just the souls of black folk but also a nation that "has not yet found peace from its sins" (5). He would have all Americans find the means to see how it is "a hard thing to live haunted by the ghost of an untrue dream" (54).

The veil's dual functions are most fully operative in a mythologized South where we encounter something "outside of written history" (127): Africa-based traditions/cultures that, according to Hegel, had no history, had contributed nothing to the sweep of history, and were in essence a virginal tabula rasa to be inscribed with the gifts of Western civilization. As Du Bois takes readers into the "Black World Beyond the Veil" (56), into the Georgia "Black Belt,—that strange land of shadows, at which even slaves paled in the past, and whence come now only faint and half-intelligible murmurs to the world beyond" (79), he posits an enduring trace of an original Africanity in "half-intelligible murmurs" occulted by the psychic vertigo of the Georgia (and New World) landscape's cultural/economic realities. Seizing upon the South as locus of an African past and as haunting site of a national sin of biblical proportions, Du Bois announces that this "Cotton Kingdom,—the shadow of a marvellous dream" (82), is "the Egypt of the Confederacy" (87). The Georgia Black Belt becomes, according to Robert Stepto, a ritual site of the narrator's "immersion in a source of culture and of what Du Bois would term 'race-spirit,'" providing a locus for "the first true narrative expression of a distinctly Afro-American cultural immersion ritual" (66). Du Bois's ritual immersion finds West African precedent in Mali Kumba Njaay's coronation burial at the base of the baobab Nderexeen, in Sunjata's journey to the Nine Queens-of-Darkness (and his spirit-enabled *hajj*), in initiation societies like Bamana Komo and Mende Poro/Sande, all of which informed Afro-Creole traditions of retreating to the woods while "seeking" initiatory experience of salvation. Du Bois's own journey of "seeking" is haunted by the Southland of ritual immersion where "trees spring from a prodigal luxuriance of undergrowth; great dark green shadows fade into the black background, until all is one mass of tangled semi-tropical foliage, marvellous in its weird savage splendor" (85). Emerging as a tangled Africanist landscape of "double consciousness," the "weird savage splendor" of this "semi-tropical" Georgia Black Belt grows from Du Bois's ties to European racial discourse, even as a certain clairvoyance rises from Afro-Southern experience to reveal how it is the South's racist, ritualized savagery that has cast the weirdest "shadows" upon the land. Seeking articulation and transmission of "half-intelligible murmurs" from behind the veil, Du Bois—like the griots (and like theorists such as Julia Kristeva)—locates core identity in the semiotics of a world "outside of written history" even as he faces the conflict of crafting his appeal to the values and prejudices of a scriptural world (79).

More successfully than his seeking of ritual immersion in the Georgia Black Belt, and more successfully even than his appropriation of the folk birth veil as trope of double consciousness, Du Bois's treatment of African American song grounded the epic aspirations of *The Souls of Black Folk* in foundational African mother-child-ness. Much of the visionary power of *The Souls of Black Folk* came through Du Bois's belief that America's finest indigenous art was born from deep structures of the African American vernacular: "the siftings of centuries; the music is far more ancient than the words" (180). More often than not, the African rhythms and tones of this soul semiotics are bound to and transmitted by the child's responsive relationship to the mother's body, as with fragments of song passed from Du Bois's great-great-grandmother, who "crooned a heathen melody to the child between her knees," a "voice of exile" repeated for two hundred years: "Do ba-na co-ba, ge-ne me, ge-ne me! / Do ba-na co-ba, ge-ne me, ge-ne me! / Ben d'nu-li, nu-li, nu-li, nu-li" (180). Du Bois's revoicing of his great-great-grandmother's African song marks *Souls'* deepest call to cultural/spiritual reassembly. As with Amelia Dawley's Mende funeral song and the use of its refrain as the magic password in coastal Georgia tales of flight back to Africa, the "voice of exile" that Du Bois notes in "the sorrow songs" yearns for mother-child-ness, motherland, and is filled with "eloquent omissions and silences," singing of "[m]other and child . . . but seldom father," singing of death "familiarly and even fondly as simply a crossing of the waters, perhaps—who knows?—back to . . . ancient forests again" (183–84). Du Bois writes that "[s]uch a message is naturally veiled and half articulate," but "[o]nce in a while we catch a strange word of an unknown tongue, as the 'Mighty Myo,' which figures as a river of death" (182). This "Mighty Myo" of Du Bois's *Souls* is most likely the *maayo* (Pulaar—"river") remembered by Salih Bilali and his Georgia descendants who sang "Down to de Myuh." In a very real sense, the African rivers referred to as *maayo* (the Senegal, the

Gambia, and the Niger) have been sources of our mighty rivers of song, deep sources of the polyphonic music that Du Bois called "the singular spiritual heritage of the nation" (178).

By immersing himself and his readers in an *African* American semiotic, Du Bois sought to articulate the dual strivings in *The Souls of Black Folk*. He wrote of powerful yearnings for home and intense feelings of homelessness. His eventual decision to take up residence in Ghana, where he embarked on his final homecoming and was buried, testifies to the strength of the African component of his African American double consciousness and to his frustration with the tenacity of American racism. Given that West African and Gullah traditions insist upon the importance of burial at home, one can only hope that some deep component of Du Bois's plural souls found rest in Ghana's soil.[13] If the spirits of enslaved Africans flew home to rest in peace, where might home lie for their Georgia-born or Virginia-born descendants, and how would the cycles of reincarnation proceed—once broken by the Atlantic and by American slavery?[14] The WPA coastal Georgia interviews and works of contemporary scholarship reveal what mother wit should tell us anyway—that the connection to Africa was never broken and that the descendants of Africans relied upon Afro-Creole means to make a way out of no way. But Du Bois's vernacular-informed soul text was truly a landmark of psychic reassembly offered at a low water mark of appreciation of Africa-based (or Creole) cultures.[15] Prophetic in its transformative action as well as in its intent, *The Souls of Black Folk* "redefined the terms of a three-hundred-year interaction between black and white people and influenced the cultural and political psychology of peoples of African descent throughout the Western hemisphere, as well as on the continent of Africa. It was one of those events epochally dividing history into a before and an after" (Lewis 277). In this epic of self-definition and collective "soul," Du Bois's studied search for rootedness, his journaling of the routes taken—southward to Fisk, Atlanta, and the Georgia Black Belt, and eastward across the Atlantic—led him down paths the griots helped to divine for him in the Sunjata's doubled consciousness and polyphonic form, and its attempts to reconnect an exiled diaspora through semiotics of mother-child-ness.[16]

2

Of Root Figures and Buggy Jiving

Toomer, Hurston, and Ellison

Way down yon'er in Guinea Gall,
De Niggers eats de fat an' all.
Way down yon'er in de cotton fiel,'
Ev'ry week one peck o' meal.

> Thomas Talley's *Negro Folk Rhymes*
>
> *(Wise or Otherwise)* (1922)

All it takes to get along in this here man's town is a little shit, grit and mother-wit. And man, I was bawn with all three. In fact, I'mas eventhsonofaseventhsonbawnwithacauloverbotheyesandraisedonblack catboneshighjohntheconquerorandgreasygreens . . . You dig me daddy?

> Ralph Ellison's Peter Wheatstraw, *Invisible Man* (1952)

I

Amidst the many banjo and fiddle songs from an American repertoire shared across the color line were others, such as "Guinea Gall," that turned to valorized traces of Guinea—or more likely *Senegal*—to elicit a doubly conscious critique of American realities. In "Guinea Gall" the old imperial memories have been reduced to a metathetic confusion of place; nevertheless, the old place's *nyama* shows its vitality in the song's banjo instrumentation and "soul" semiotics.[1] Songs like "Guinea Gall" and Du Bois's "Mighty Myo," as Ralph Ellison explained in an interview with Hollie West, often contain words or concepts that "have just become a mumble" and that might take their listeners "way back to the South" and even "back to Africa" (39). Having come to active "seeking" of the means bequeathed by an African heritage at the very moment when that heritage was perceived to be little more than an inarticulate "mumble," writers such as Jean Toomer, Zora Neale Hurston, and Ralph Ellison followed Du Bois's path of immersion in the roots of Afro-Southern culture. Filling a bardic role and answering an epic impulse for reassembly/remix of core values at challenging moments of cultural change, these three writers lie at the heart of twentieth-century black fiction's rearticulation of the Afro-Creole soul sounds and semiotics that Du Bois embraced in *The Souls of Black Folk*.

As Chris Bonghie has pointed out in a statement quite relevant to the situation of Toomer, Hurston, and Ellison, "Modernist literature of the Americas—or at least of the 'other America' . . . has as one of its defining features an anxiety about cultural origins and traditions that are in the process of becoming ever more occulted under conditions of modernity" (167). The occult(ed) *nyama* of a griot-informed black vernacular tradition works differently in the texts and psyches of each of these three black modernists. Toomer was most like Du Bois in being an incredibly perceptive but somewhat unlikely and "foreign" soul-seeker in the "veiled" Africa-based cultures of the Deep South, while Hurston—bred and born in Brer Rabbit's briar patch—worked more familiarly to evoke "the meaning of 'Africa' found within the rich folklife of the African-American community" (Wilentz xxx).[2] Although Ellison rarely showed explicit concern with reaching toward a reassembled "original" Africanity, his appreciation of and fidelity to black vernacular traditions was such that he simply assumes Africa as a primary "Omni-American" (modernist-informing) source.[3] Sharing Hurston's confidence in the enduring power of soul repertoires, he could do his "seeking" in the streets of Harlem or in the grooves of a Louis Armstrong record as easily as in backwoods Alabama. What all three writers found in Afro-Creole soul sounds, soul foods, and mother wit was a base of deep identity and cultural power calling for textual articulation. Immersed in the epic/prophetic vision of Du Bois's veil, their narratives of descent into soul consciousness gave answer to the "mumble" of "Guinea Gall's" ancestral call through patchwork reassemblies of *nyama*-traced vernacular traditions.

II

In the spirit of the Sunjata and Du Bois's *Souls*, Jean Toomer's *Cane* (1923) weaves song, narrative, and praise modes in a polyphonic performance of occulted soul traditions. Like Mande griots, Toomer engages a scriptural religion and retains a good ear for the African semiotics alive and kicking in its practice. He is sensitive to the dialogic role of language in this tension; instead of the tuggings of Arabic against Mandinka, *Cane* is woven of literary English and a black vernacular. As for West African griots, a gendered ideology identifies God as paternal and may at times represent elements of his scriptural culture as "white." Maternal tropes identify black elements rooted in the land and in the semiotics of a tradition that produces "folk songs from soul sounds" (13). Seeking through a multigeneric transformation of enduring *nyama* to "become the face of the South. . . . my lips being the lips of its soul" (81), Toomer attempts to bind a northern diaspora with core traditions from its Southern heartland, which serves as a spiritual locus of an African past.

The first section of *Cane* offers the novel's most successful sequence of immersion narratives. Toomer's journey to cultural roots led him south to Georgia, following routes to an African semiotic embodied by figures of women and trees, as in "Carma": "Pungent and composite, the smell of farmyards is the fragrance of the woman. She does not sing; her body is a song. She is the forest, dancing. Torches flare . . . juju men, greegree, witchdoctors . . . torches go out . . . The Dixie Pike has grown from a goatpath in Africa" (10). The narrative explicitly reclaims African heritage as it explores the forest crossroads connecting Dixie to African goatpaths. Carma knows the path. She is both of the African motherland and the Georgia earth. Though juju men are here, it is Carma who is clearly "the forest," whose "body is a song" signaling, like the song of Du Bois's great-great-grandmother, African modes of communication preexisting an African American vernacular but still inside it, a semiotics transmitted in rhythmic relationship to the mother's body.[4] For Toomer, Carma *is* West African energy of action, a kind of karma that can not cease to exist—as long as birth and mothering, language acquisition and bodily movement exist. But the Georgia Black Belt of *Cane* faces so many kinds of trauma that it risks being reduced to near sterility.

"Song of the Son," the poem that follows "Carma," marks Toomer's most successful immersion of griotlike desires in the folk culture of the Deep South. Urgently returning, as if to the deathbed of a family member, *Cane*'s prodigal griot claims inheritance from a "song-lit race of slaves" through mastery of familiar tropes:

> O Negro slaves, dark purple ripened plums,
> Squeezed, and bursting in the pine-wood air,
> Passing, before they stripped the old tree bare
> One plum was saved for me, one seed becomes
>
> An everlasting song, a singing tree,
> Caroling softly souls of slavery,
> What they were, and what they are to me,
> Caroling softly souls of slavery. (12)

The son receives his song from the tree that bears the joy-sharing secrets of slave culture. Upon eating the fruit, he gains knowledge of continuity and transformation as the seed becomes a new song for the page—a textual singing tree singing of precursory trees that are "everlasting." Seed is secreted and germinated in the *jouissance* between song and singer, call and response. Clearly a plum tree is not a baobab, but the textual path that Toomer cleared from the Dixie Pike to Africa was one the folk culture had long navigated. The very earth of the Southern Black Belt had been rendered an Afro-Creole landscape by the slaves who cultivated her and by the planters who raped her, engendering a new people who acquired the paternal European symbolic language but guarded a maternal West African semiotics.[5] "Song of the Son" seeks ritual immersion in the soil of that soul semiotics and emerges with a familiar tropic boast.

Toomer's "Georgia Dusk" continues the act of listening for an originary truth as "some genius of the South" is "[s]urprised in making folk-songs from soul sounds."[6] Here, too, trees are more than trees, are markers of old African culture and spirituality:

> Smoke from the pyramidal sawdust pile
> > Curls up, blue ghosts of trees, tarrying low
> Where only chips and stumps are left to show
> > The solid proof of former domicile.

> Meanwhile, the men, with vestiges of pomp,
> > Race memories of king and caravan,
> High-priests, an ostrich, and a juju-man,
> > Go singing through the footpaths of the swamp. (13)

While the stump traces of virgin woods provide race memories and vestiges of African culture, black song (as with Du Bois) remains the "privileged signifier of black authenticity" (Gilroy 91), and—more importantly—the sustaining medium of the spirit. Emerging from "mumble" and "moan" like the repeated sounds of Amelia Dawley's Georgia/Mende funeral song, Toomer's "Georgia Dusk" offers "folk-songs from soul sounds" as the clearest link to "blue ghosts of trees" rising over the sawdust pyramids of a monumental African past. In eerie repetition of the sense behind Dawley's Mende song ["Death quickly the tree destroys, steals it; the remains disappear slowly" (Turner 256)], the "chips and stumps" of "Georgia Dusk" work—like the repeated soul sounds that Dawley sang but could not translate—"to show / The solid proof of former domicile."

Toomer's immersion in Southern folk culture comes to climax in the tree-talking of "Fern," as the narrator enters the action to share a moment of vision with a hauntingly beautiful woman who reads old trees: "Under a sweet-gum tree . . . we sat down. Dusk, suggesting the almost imperceptible procession of giant trees, settled with a purple haze about the cane. I felt strange, as I always do in Georgia, particularly at dusk. I felt that things unseen to man were tangibly immediate. . . .When one is on the soil of one's ancestors, most anything can come to one"(17). Ancestral soil and giant trees fill Fern's face with vision, and as the artist holds this woman whose name suggests the vegetal, she becomes the singing tree: "Her body was tortured with something it could not let out. Like boiling sap it flooded arms and fingers till she shook them as if they burned her. It found her throat, and splattered inarticulately in plaintive convulsive sounds, mingled with cries to Christ Jesus" (103). Her possessed fervor of song opens oracular (but hardly articulate) contact with the South's pained spirit(s).

Another narrative of the first section that dramatizes oracular vision, the story "Esther," led critic Barbara Bowen to the observation that "If there is a single gesture which characterizes Jean Toomer's *Cane* . . . it is the gesture of listening for a voice" (12). Having established its trope of origin in the singing trees and women of the book's first sketches and poems, *Cane* moves toward its task of epic reassembly of Afro-Southern *nyama* "by trying to recover an unexiled continuity of speaker and listener" (Bowen 15). Bowen writes that in *Cane*, Toomer discovered the formal power of "call-and-response—the drama of finding authority through communal voice" (15). This formal power is readily apparent in "Esther," in which an itinerant preacher known as King Barlo delivers a short sermon that doubles as a foundational text. As Barlo speaks of receiving the call of Jesus, the crowd hums response, and Barlo then revoices the call, to which a woman cries "Ah, Lord" (20–21). Receiving the call is the first step. What follows is the vision the preacher articulates and the audience response that authorizes and further enables vision and voice:

> "I saw a vision. I saw a man arise, an he was big an black an powerful—"
>
> Some one yells, "Preach it, preacher, preach it!"
>
> "—but his head was caught up in th clouds. An while he was agazin at th heavens, heart filled up with th Lord, some little white-ant biddies came an tied his feet to chains. They led him t th coast, they led him t th sea, they led him across th ocean an they didn't set him free. The old coast didn't miss him, an th new coast wasnt free, he left the old-coast brothers, t give birth t you an me. O Lord, great God Almighty, t give birth t you an me."
>
> Barlo pauses. Old gray mothers are in tears. Fragments

of melodies are being hummed. White folks are touched and awed. . . . Barlo rises to his full height. He is immense. To the people he assumes the outlines of his visioned African. (21)

Out of "fragments of melodies" and mumbles risen to "being hummed," Toomer reassembles heroic possibilities through participatory, antiphonal epic assent. Barlo becomes the foundational African of his sermon, but an African hero of such stature is too revolutionary to be sustainable in the Georgia of *Cane*— as the story's end suggests when we are left with a drunken, repulsive Barlo to whom "dictie" Esther offers herself before fleeing in revulsion since "conception with a drunken man must be a mighty sin" (25). Here again the calling proves unable to sustain a response (or "conception").

Cane's second section takes us to northern settings, where according to Friedrike Hajek, the speaker's voice "is left without a response" (187). In "Box Seat," Dan would "[s]tir the root-life of a withered people" (56), but he is stopped by "endless rows of metal houses" that separate "root-life" from the "rumble [that] comes from earth's deep core. . . . the mutter of powerful underground races" (57). As Dan seeks to articulate the "mutter" at the "deep core" of soul "root-life" emanating from his vision of a woman sitting in the Washington theatre, the response he receives differs from Barlo's reception in a rural Georgia dirt street:

A soil-soaked fragrance comes from her. Through the cement floor her strong roots sink down. They spread under asphalt streets. . . . Her strong roots sink down and spread under the river and disappear in blood-lines that waver south. Her roots shoot down. . . . Dan's heart beats violently. He sees all the people in the house rush to the walls to listen to the rumble. A new-world Christ is coming up. Dan comes up. He is startled. The eyes of the woman dont belong to her. They look at him unpleasantly. From either aisle, bolted masses press in. He doesnt fit. The mass grows agitant. For an instant, Dan's and Muriel's eyes meet. His weight there slides the weight on her. She braces an arm against the brass rail, and turns her head away. (62)

What in rural Georgia might be accepted as divinely sanctioned is taken as a sign of mental imbalance in Washington, D.C.

Answering needs born of the displacement of urban migration, *Cane* cast a backward glance to the Dixie Pike fed by its goat path in Africa as Toomer sought to record and channel moments of monumental change. Friederike Hajek writes that *Cane* emerges from "a crisis of cultural authority in the course of which an old authority was replaced by a new one" and that *Cane* distinguishes itself "by the author's effort to make this change the very subject of his discourse, which he structured accordingly" (186). *Cane* traces (and channels) the rerouting of a rural folk authority as it faces and enters an urban modernity. It is the kind of moment out of which epic has often been born. Stephen Belcher notes the tendency of West African epic to construct "heroes whose stories are associated with the period immediately preceding this power-shift" (between pre-Islamic and Islamic authority), and speaks of the epic impulse as arising from needs to affirm "self-identity in the face of a powerful, demanding, and alien world-view" ("Construct-ing" 86). *Cane* indeed seeks epic expression of Southern folk culture and its Afro-Creole roots—and does so nowhere more explicitly than in its final section, one long piece entitled "Kabnis." "Kabnis" dramatizes the ritual of immersion that is often merely a trope in *The Souls of Black Folk*. At the heart of the underground drama of "Kabnis," Father John, an old ex-slave who is "symbol, flesh, and spirit of the past," appears as possible source of a soul epic's rearticulation of *nyama*. But a quarreling crisis of languages, be-liefs, and authorities threatens and possibly dooms young Ralph Kabnis's yearning to "become the face of the South. . . . my lips being the lips of its soul. Soul. Soul hell. There aint no such thing" (81).

Kabnis, northern, "lemon-hued," a troubled embodiment of double consciousness, seeks artistic voice and vision while teaching in Georgia. Throughout the opening pages we see a "divided Kabnis . . . and we are reminded of his doubleness by his constant injunctions to himself to pull himself together" (McKay 155). He scorns the antiphonal church shouting that Du Bois had also found unsettling, but in spite of a teacherly desire for a monologic sermon, Kabnis has the potential to serve as bridge between the soulful but needy rural Georgia community and the modern urban world with its open possibilities and soul dangers. After being fired from his teaching job, he is taken in as apprentice by the blacksmith Halsey and given a posi-tion that offers better access to the *nyama* that he, "[s]uspended a few feet above the soil whose touch would resurrect him," seeks to wield (96). Soul semiotics and the land itself—racialized, feminized—offer sustenance while the scriptural white world of logos and law holds a withering supremacy: "The earth my mother. God is a profligate red-nosed man about town. Bas-tardy: me" (82–83).

Cane's concluding immersion scene occurs during a night's revelry beneath the blacksmith shop and is framed by the landscape's lyrical call: "Night, soft belly of a pregnant Negress. . . . throbs a womb-song to the South" (103). Kabnis, Halsey, a political activist named Lewis, and two party-women descend into the ritual drinking space in the basement ("the Hole"), where they encounter the mute presence of an old man "like a bust in black walnut," seen as a patinaed avatar of the root cellar, a "John the Baptist of a new religion—or a tongue-tied shadow of an old" (104). Like the jinn guarding medicinal roots beneath a baobab in Bani Gisse's Wolof Sunjata, and like the monadic source beneath the roots of the coronation baobab Nderexeen, Father John is a figure of ancestral power and wholeness, imagined as a Geechee visionary "who saw Jesus in the ricefields and began preaching to his people" (105). Although Father John's signs are scriptural, "Moses- and Christ-words used for songs" (105), the African rhythms, tones, and semiotics of the songs are pre-scriptural. He is in fact the male root figure of a residual African heritage previously figured in Barlo's sermon and in the oracular tree-women of *Cane's* first section. True to Senegambian narrative codes, Toomer cloaks Kabnis with a "gaudy ball costume" that serves as a *nyama*-charged ritual garment allowing him the means to "seek" Father John's monadic source. But the enrobed "blueblood" Kabnis tries to renounce genealogical links to Father John—and by implication a heritage from slavery—bringing Lewis to try to force Kabnis to face the racial realities of early-twentieth-century Georgia: "Master; slave. Soil; and the overarching heavens. Dusk; dawn. They fight and bastardize you" (107). Kabnis's transgressive language finally hits verbal attack mode, "shapin words t fit m soul," as the pain of his ritual immersion releases the kind of language that shaped much of today's rap: "Ugh. Th form thats burned int my soul is some twisted awful thing that crept in from a dream, a godam nightmare, an wont stay still unless I feed it. An it lives on words. Not beautiful words. God Almighty no. Misshapen, split-gut, tortured, twisted words. . . . You hear me? . . . you little snot-nosed pups who've been making fun of me, an fakin that I'm weak. Me, Ralph Kabnis weak. Ha" (110). His *fadenya* boasts summon supportive, need-answering responses from one of the women, as she wants "to take Kabnis to some distant pine grove and nurse and mother him" (110). For Lewis, the "pain is too intense," so he leaves the initiatory action he has helped to provoke.

In the aftermath of the revelry, as dawn's eastern sun appears, the "girls, before the mirror, are doing up their hair. It is bushy hair that has gone through some straightening process. Character, however, has not all been ironed out. . . .they are two princesses in Africa going through the early-morning ablutions of their pagan prayers" (112). In similar fashion, the ending of *Cane* seeks synthesized vision in which character has not been ironed out. The group goes upstairs, leaving Kabnis alone to sleep at the feet of Father John in a final immersion through which Kabnis becomes a tree-talker of sorts. Responding to the old man's silence-breaking voice, Kabnis unleashes a torrent of insults upon him in an attack that is essentially a self-inflicted wound: "Your soul. Ha. Nigger soul. A gin soul that gets drunk on a preacher's words. An screams. An shouts. God Almighty, how I hate that shoutin" (113). But even in mocking Father John, Kabnis begins to sense needs that the old man fills: "Th old man is a good listener. He's deaf; but he's a good listener. An I can talk t him. Tell him anything" (114).

When this figure of a "mute" ancestral past begins to nod his head and respond, Kabnis is so haunted by the repeated word "sin" that he misreads the message, shouting back at the old man, "[I]t was only a preacher's sin they knew in those old days, an that wasn't sin at all. . . . th only sin is whats done against th soul" (115). With the impetuosity of youth, Kabnis thinks that his own sense of sin is more concrete, embodied in his yellowish skin: "Th whole world is a conspiracy t sin, especially in America, an against me. I'm th victim of their sin. I'm what sin is" (115). But encouraged by Halsey's young niece Carrie and by Kabnis's misreading, Father John strains to voice an authoritative "black knowledge" (similar to what Georgia Muslims must have argued) as he attempts to get to the deep source of America's haunting sin: "Th sin whats fixed . . . upon th white folks . . . f tellin Jesus—lies. O the sin th white folks 'mitted when they made th Bible lie" (115). Carolyn Mitchell writes that Father John's message underscores the a-spiritual blasphemy of white Christianity, for "[i]n creating chattel slavery in America, the dominant class stripped Christ consciousness of its redemptive spiritual qualities and institutionalized Christianity as a religion that justifies deceit and brutality" (304). Father John's soul message completes the revelation begun earlier in *Cane* by Barlo. After collapsing, "ashamed, exhausted," Kabnis hangs up his robe "with exaggerated ceremony" and emerges hung over but impacted by dialogue with an ancestral figure offering renewed possibilities of patrimony. Meanwhile, Carrie, whispering "Jesus, come," tends to the old man as the morning's "birth-song" arrives "down gray dust streets and sleepy windows of the southern town" (116). The initiatory assembly of Father John, Kabnis, and Carrie achieves a "conception" that is found nowhere else in the prose pieces of *Cane*.

Although Kabnis seeks to become "the face of the South. . . . the lips of its soul," a growing, almost absolute distance seems to separate an occulted epic-soul past from his lived world. The old antiphonal patterns that assented to communal voice give way in *Cane* to fractured voicings that break the certitude of each narrator's call. But if Toomer saw *Cane* as an elegy to a culture destined for extinction, his patchwork reassembly of the "root-life" of a *nyama*-laden semiotics achieves a transmission similar to the way in which jazz was then reassembling and transmitting earlier "soul-sounds." *Cane*'s labored "birth-song" announces possibilities of a modern African American art/spirituality encompassing many forms, voices, and modes of experience. Its antiphonal performance attempts to answer the call of its soul-seeking at the crossroads of African goat paths and the Dixie Pike.

III

Following Toomer's descent into the root cellar of the South's Africa-based culture, Zora Neale Hurston reached even more deeply into her Afro-South-ern native soil. The heroine of Hurston's *Their Eyes Were Watching God*, Janie Woods, undertakes her own "ritualized journey of immersion with Teacake into the 'muck' of the Everglades" (Stepto 164–65). In a manner similar to Toomer's *Cane*, the tree is the figure of Hurston's book and Janie's vitality: "Janie saw her life like a great tree in leaf with the things suffered, things enjoyed, things done and undone. Dawn and doom was in the branches" (8). Janie's blossoming pear tree offers a more fully erotic vision than anything we read in *Cane*: "She saw a dust-bearing bee sink into the sanctum of a bloom; the thousand sister-calyxes arch to meet the love em-brace and the ecstatic shiver of the tree from root to tiniest branch creaming in every blossom and frothing with delight" (10–11).[7] After yearning "to be a pear tree—*any* tree in bloom!" (11) Janie survives two ugly marriages and meets Tea Cake Woods, who "could be a bee to a blossom—a pear tree blossom in the spring" (101), finding soul fulfillment as "Mis' Woods."

Their Eyes Were Watching God may be a bit more rooted in initiation tales and bildungsroman than in epic-heroic panegyric to mother-child-ness, but there is one true epic figure in the novel: Big John de Conquer, who like Sunjata, is seen as that something shared that gives a "soul" flavor to iden-tities and in-group tales.[8] John de Conquer is "uh man wid salt in him. He could give uh flavor to *anything*" (62–63). Located in a Bakhtinian "abso-lute past," John de Conquer is spoken of in Sunjata-like praise-proverb mode: "[H]e was uh man dat wuz more'n man. 'Tain't no mo' lak him. He wouldn't dig potatoes, and he wouldn't rake hay: He wouldn't take a whipping, and he wouldn't run away" (63). At the most dangerous moment in the action—as a hurricane is approaching—the storytellers of the Muck summon epic courage by "handling Big John de Conquer and his works. How he had done everything big on earth, then went up tuh heben without dying atall. Went up there picking a guitar and got all de angels doing the ring-shout round and round de throne" (148–49).

Hurston's figure of epic reassembly of occulted African traditions, Big John de Conquer stands at the center of a coherent system of soul semiotics. But he leaves the earth in heroic flight/escape to start a ring shout in heaven, and we see a sense of exile at the heart of Afro-New World mother-child-ness, as the Bahamian character Lias makes clear before fleeing the hurri-cane: "If I never see you no' mo' on earth, Ah'll meet you in Africa" (148).

The powerful ancestral figure of the John/Master slave tales, conflated with hoodoo's High John de Conquer root in *Their Eyes Were Watching God*, received fuller treatment in Hurston's essay "High John de Conquer" published in *The American Mercury* in 1943. Like Sunjata's epic battles in which the object was discovery of the opponent's means, John de Conquer fights "without outside showing force . . . winning his war from within" (543). He, too, traces lineage to the Orient: "He had the wisdom of the East in his head" (543). Not only is the Conqueror's manner of engagement similar to that of Mande epic, but his knack for "Hitting a straight lick with a crooked stick" recalls the purposeful indirection of pathways in Senegambian villages (Gamble 41), the intentionally random "percussive" textile patterns observed by Robert Farris Thompson as a Mande influence upon African American quilts, and the music and dance styles Hurston describes in *The Sanctified Church*: "[I]t is a rhythm of segments. Each unit has a rhythm of its own, but when the whole is assembled it is lacking in symmetry. . . . to avoid the simple straight line" (54–55). Rooted in a fragment-navigating, fragment-unifying aesthetic that might illuminate the polyphonic, collagelike forms of *The Souls of Black Folk* and *Cane*, High John de Conquer is Hurston's clearest figure for a residual African culture in America's South. She offers the conflated trickster/hoodoo root as "the source and soul of our laughter and song" ("High John" 542).

Hurston claims that "John" of the well-known tale cycle is the hero behind hoodoo's powerful High John the Conqueror root. Like Mande herbalists and the Wolof *ya-bopa* ("wide-heads") known to be conversant with tree-dwelling spirits, African American two-headed doctors and spiritualists "do John reverence by getting the root of the plant in which he has taken up his secret dwelling, and 'dressing' it with perfume, and keeping it on their person, or in their houses in a secret place" (548). Hurston adds that High John had "come from Africa . . . walking on the waves of sound" and later (with powers reminiscent of Sumamuru Kante and coastal Georgia's flying Africans) "went back to Africa, but . . . left his power here, and placed his American dwelling in the root of a certain plant" (543–44). However, the folklorist Alan Dundes argues that "accounts of the root make no mention whatsoever of a related trickster figure, and, by the same token, none of the various collections of the 'John and Marster' folktales refer to the root" (542). Since it seems uncertain that African American folk culture transmitted a connection between the tale cycle and the root, it may be more likely that Hurston, as visionary artist of the folk culture, answered the need for root figures of cultural reassembly in a mythopoetic move akin to Alex Haley's journey to *Roots*. In at least one essay, she resorted to plagiarism in order to dress up what appears to have been a disappointing interview with Cudjo Lewis, known as the last survivor of the last known ship to bring African slaves to the United States (Hemenway 96–99). But we must also remember that if there has ever been an American writer in position to connect folktale with hoodoo root, it would be Zora, who studied voodoo/obeah traditions throughout the United States and Caribbean, and—as she details in *Mules and Men*—underwent initiation ceremonies from at least six different two-headed doctors in New Orleans, after which she was fully empowered to do two-headed work (208). Whether the connection between root and tale was, like Mande *nyamakala* trade secrets, closely guarded, or whether it is a connection fully "doctored" by Hurston, it is clear her "High John" narrative operated from solid visionary authority to reassemble a hoodoo tradition.

Citing an informant's belief that "John de Conquer means power. . . . God don't leave nobody ignorant" (544), Hurston links the root's enduring power to the Conqueror's veiled signs and sounds: "[H]is singing-symbol was a drumbeat. . . . an inside thing to live by" (542). Inside black English and ancestral to it, High John came, like Du Bois's and Amelia Dawley's songs, "from Africa . . . walking on the waves of sound" (543). Even in paying lip service to English, transatlantic African sounds often signify through the motherland's semiotics: "If they, the white people, heard some scraps, they could not understand because they had nothing to hear things like that with" (543). Hurston claims that High John would travel incognito, "touristing around the plantations as the laugh-provoking Brer Rabbit" (543). Kin to Leuk-the-Hare and Bouki-the-Hyena of Wolof tales, Brer Rabbit and Brer Fox (Bouki in Louisiana tales) animated African memory in America. Their tales imparted an understanding of the *nya* or "means" so important to Sunjata and even more important to Africans enslaved in America: "He who wins from within is in the 'Be' class. *Be* here when the ruthless man comes and *be* here when he is gone" (544). This brand of briar patch mother wit, shared by John de Conquer and the means-finding Sunjata the Conqueror, offers the energy of action that Kabnis encountered in the Hole with Father John and that Ellison's narrator would seek in his basement struggles with Monopolated Light & Power. John de Conquer (as a trinity of hoodoo root/John the folk hero/Brer Rabbit) stands as Hurston's foundational "soul" ancestor.

The tales that Hurston relates concerning John de Conquer cover familiar "joy-sharing" soul territory: food and music. In her first "High John" tale, "Massa" witnesses John's theft of a pig but waits until John "had seasoned that pig *down*, and it was stinking pretty" (545). As we know from *Their Eyes Were Watching God*, High John has a reputation as a man who "could give uh flavor to *anything*." And Massa is soon less concerned with punishing John than with enjoying some seasoned soul cooking "simbled down to a low gravy" in a house he may once have played in, even nursed in as a child. To this day good barbeque is one of the few items of legal trade that regularly brings Southern whites into black communities, and Hurston here makes an expansive appeal to white readers, establishing a shared realm of American culture before signaling difference.

Mande epics often recount the struggles of heroes to win control of powerful praise-songs and their *nyama*; similarly, Hurston's High John states in another tale that "What we need is a song. . . . a particular piece of singing" (546). High John's quest for his own New World song begins from a core Senegambian trope, people "gathered up under a big hickory nut tree" (546). And since the journey, familiarly, will require enabling clothing, High John orders the group to "reach inside yourselves and get out all those fine raiments you been toting" (546). This clothing turns out to be a spiritual clothing for wandering souls that are summoned (like the Mande *ja*) outside of the body as a means of evading the slave-master's control: "Just leave your old work-tired bodies around for him to look at, and he'll never realize youse way off somewhere, going about your business" (546). The tale's "business" of transmitting an imperial memory of "something finer than this plantation . . . put away inside," begins its journey on the back of a crow that takes the group to conquer hell, where John becomes (like Sunjata visiting the Nine Queens-of-Darkness) "High Chief Devil" in "possession of power" (547–48). But since the song they are seeking is not located there, they go directly to Old Maker. What the group receives is more system than song. Like Toomer's "folk songs from soul sounds," the new song "had no words" and was "a tune that you could bend and shape in most any way you wanted to fit the words and feelings that you had" (547). Bending and shaping the hoodoo lore surrounding the High John the Conqueror root to fit the John/Massa tales, Hurston nurtured something that may have remained of the full-foliaged epic Conqueror—its root—which "could retire with his secret smile into the soil of the South and wait" (548). Tunes shaped to praise Sunjata the Conqueror's triumph over lameness had surely been shaped into "broke-legged" banjo rhythms and spirituals praising the heroic sorcery of Moses, eventually secreting an African *nyama* so thoroughly into the American birth cloth that Hurston could answer America's (and her editor's) World War II needs for national unity with her wartime offering of John de Conquer's secrets, since "We are all his kinfolks" (548). Blending fiction, folklore, and hoodoo, she used the structural flexibility of mother wit for informed doctoring of a tradition long formed by two-headed doctors. John de Conquer emerges as Hurston's root figure for a whole semiotic system that grounds the identities of the powerful black nation within the United States, and the larger (no longer Aryan) national whole.

IV

Ralph Ellison was intensely concerned with matters of identity, history, tradition, national origins: all the stuff of epic. Yet *Invisible Man* is no epic. Its hero remains nameless. And the novel moves through so much cultural and ideological shape-shifting that critics such as Thomas Whitaker have argued that nowhere in the novel is "a solid and visible identity to be found" (401). *Invisible Man* shows little interest in reaching toward a valorized Africa for a source of identity that transcends the American situation. But despite its many differences from the Sunjata and the works of epic impulse by Du Bois, Toomer, and Hurston, *Invisible Man* does have its moments of *African* American epic performance, often linked intertextually to Hurston, Toomer, and Du Bois, and sometimes—through cultural transmission—to the Sunjata. Ellison felt little need to "seek" African sources, for he recognized that he had grown up immersed in a deeply Afro-Creole navigation of New World changes. With Ellison, Africa is simply assumed as a primary source of his vernacular means. Even so, many critics have taken Ellison to task for not doing his "seeking" outside of Western history and culture. For instance, Jane Campbell has attempted to show that "the Afro-American background . . . as *Invisible Man* presents it, does not reach back into African culture but into the Western intellectual heritage," and argues that "Ellison's primary limitation lies in his assimilationist tendencies, not the least of which is his refusal to recognize the 'infinite possibilities' of Africa as well as America" (89–90). Nevertheless, I would argue that critics like Campbell misrecognize the "infinite possibilities" of Africa in America through too-rigid identities and oppositions. Ellison took up issues of power and ancestry, second sight, and soul semiotics in a manner deeply resonant with a griot-informed African American culture. Although Ellison steadfastly refused to employ "Africa" with romantic consciousness, as a sign on display, Africa is a source of long invisible cultural currents that pervade *Invisible Man*'s America.

Invisible Man's search for ancestry and identity makes the novel a quest for ritual immersion, beginning and ending in a "hole" similar to Mali Kumba Njaay's immersion at the base of the baobab Nderexeen, Sunjata's journey to the Nine Queens-of-Darkness, Georgia traditions of "seeking" in the wilderness, Du Bois's Black Belt, Toomer's basement-dwelling Father John, and Hurston's High John and Okeechobee muck. Like the griots' epic performances, Ellison's narrative of immersion is not only a quest for ancestral connection but a quest for power, understood as a kind of *nyama*. When the "Wizard-like" Bledsoe instructs the narrator that "Power is confident, self-assuring, self-starting and self-stopping, self-warming and self-justifying" (140), he is speaking with the demystified knowledge gained from his position as a black Southerner, but Bledsoe also stays true to the griots' understanding that once one accrues the *nya* or means, the battlefield scene is anticlimactic.

The genealogies of *Invisible Man* resonate with griot repertoires and with Du Bois and Toomer. Recall how Sunjata's patrilineage is traced to Mecca and the very foundation of Islam, while the ancestral mother is a buffalo from the wilderness of Du, a wild virgin who conceives Sunjata in a rape sanctioned by marriage. Du Bois suggested a similar pairing when he wrote in *Souls* "Of the Dawn of Freedom" that "two figures ever stand to typify that day. . . . the one, a gray-haired [white] gentleman. . . . the other, a form hovering dark and mother-like, her awful face black with the mists of centuries" (21). Similarly, Toomer's Kabnis claims the black earth as mother, while "God is a profligate red-nosed man about town. Bastardy; me" (82–83). *Invisible Man* opens in like manner as a woman responding to a sermon on the "Blackness of Blackness" mourns the death of her master, whom she killed but who also "gave me several sons . . . and because I loved my sons I learned to love their father though I hated him too" (10). One of the veterans at the Golden Day offers a parallel genealogy:

> "Gentlemen, this man is my grandfather!"
> "But he's *white*, his name's Norton."
> "I should know my own grandfather! He's Thomas Jefferson and
> I'm his grandson—on the 'field-nigger' side," the tall man said. (77)

It is obvious why monumental purists searching for a patronymics from Africa (in weird collusion with guardians of Eurocentric purity) would be troubled with Ellison's unembarrassed claim upon America's founders. But if we look more closely, as we did in the Buffalo of Du narrative, we might see that the seemingly disparaged maternal inheritance has much to offer.

Ellison wields the mother wit of African American ancestry in a doubly conscious manner. Dr. Bledsoe, for instance, questions the narrator over his inability to learn from either of two received sources of *nya*: "Boy, you *are* a fool. . . . Your white folk didn't teach you anything and your mother-wit has left you cold" (139). The blood ancestor who leaves the nameless narrator the most enduring legacy is a grandfather whose deathbed words are a distillation of mother wit: "Live with your head in the lion's mouth. I want you to overcome 'em with yeses, undermine 'em with grins, agree 'em to death and destruction, let 'em swoller you till they vomit or bust wide open. . . . Learn it to the younguns" (16). *Invisible Man* is probably the American novel most informed by Brer Rabbit's modes of knowledge and power, informed to such an extent that the rabbit is the one ancestor and source of identity whom the narrator claims by name. If Thomas Jefferson could be said to represent the patrilineal inheritance, then Brer Rabbit represents a mother wit born of West African traditions and New World creolization.

The lobotomy that erases all memory save for patterns of soul, song, and mother wit serves as Ellison's metaphor for the way transatlantic passage and the subsequent years of slavery and racial hostility assaulted African identities and cultures. After the operation, the patronym is gone; the attempt to identify "Who am I? . . . was like trying to identify one particular cell that coursed through the torpid veins of my body" (235). The doctors' question "WHO WAS YOUR MOTHER?" based upon their expectations of a matriarchal black family, elicits only a desire to respond through the dozens. But the next question, "WHO WAS BUCKEYE THE RABBIT?" hits upon an unerased identity connected to the dozens:

> I laughed, deep, deep inside me, giddy with the delight of self-discovery and the desire to hide it. Somehow *I* was Buckeye the Rabbit . . . or had been, when as children we danced and sang barefoot in the dusty streets:
>
>> Buckeye the Rabbit
>> Shake it, shake it
>> Buckeye the Rabbit
>> Break it, break it . . .
>
> Yes, I could not bring myself to admit it, it was too ridiculous—and somehow too dangerous. It was annoying that he had hit upon an old identity and I shook my head, seeing him purse his lips and eye me sharply.
> BOY, WHO WAS BRER RABBIT?
> He was your mother's back-door man, I thought. Anyone knew they were one and the same. . . . (236)

Emerging from the "mumble" of Africa alive in Southern rhymes, tales, speech, and song (as in the banjo player's "Guinea Gall"), Brer Rabbit merges the narrator's "I" with a corporate "we" going back to his Southern childhood and even to African ancestors (and specifically, as I will show in Chapters 4 and 5, to Senegalese ones). The first identity that the narrator steadfastly claims and answers to is Brer Rabbit, "your mother's back-door man," the truly transgressive force that disrupts hegemony.

As in the *The Souls of Black Folk*, Ellison's narrator wields enabling *nyama* through Afro-Southern folk traditions of the veil of second sight. Some of the novel's moments of greatest insight and deepest immersion in an African American semiotic are accompanied by figurations of the vision-enabling veil. Consider, for instance, the narrator's witnessing of the eviction of an old couple in Harlem. Their possessions—"nuggets of High John the Conqueror," "a small Ethiopian flag," "a faded tintype of Abraham Lincoln," "a dime pierced with a nail hole so as to be worn about the ankle on a string for luck," "a rabbit foot," and finally the "FREE PAPERS" of Primus

Provo (266–67)— elicit "a pang of vague recognition" in the narrator as these reassembled fragments of ancestral significance "all throbbed within me with more meaning than there should have been" (267). The montage of objects brings a vision of his mother and his Southern childhood, leading him to ask, "*[W]hy did I see them now, as behind a veil that threatened to lift, stirred by the cold wind in the narrow street?*" (267) He wonders if he would cling to the "junk" of history and the "bad air" of the veil in order to keep these particularly visionary soul moments. Answering the veil's vision with action, he then delivers an impromptu speech against the couple's dispossession that lands him in the Marxist "Brotherhood."

A stronger visionary moment comes when the narrator finds that he is wearing the same style of hat and shades worn by Rinehart, a numbers runner and "spiritual technologist." As the hat and veiling shades cause the "invisible" narrator to be misidentified as Rinehart, he begins to see a griot/Brer Rabbit/hip-cat-informed world of "possibility" and "fluidity" (487), a chaos-navigating style outside of the Brotherhood's notion of history: "[F]or the first time . . . I began accepting my past. . . . It was as though I'd learned to look around corners. . . . I now recognized my invisibility" (496–97). This invisibility, first envisioned in a reefer-induced immersion in the trumpeting of Louis Armstrong, offers second-sighted abilities and another sense of time: "Instead of the swift and imperceptible flowing of time, you are aware of its nodes, those points where time stands still or from which it leaps ahead" (8).

Ellison's focus is clearly not on the past but on "nodes" of time breaking out of the past and into a world of possibility. For this reason, jazz is his model for a vernacular modernism improvising upon and renewing received traditions. *Invisible Man*, therefore, celebrates "those bearers of something precious" dressed in "surreal variations of downtown styles," youths who "speak a jived-up transitional language full of country glamour, think transitional thoughts, though perhaps they dream the same old ancient dreams" (430–33).

"Jive," the etymology for which appears to be rooted in Wolof *jev*—to disparage or speak disrespectfully—is a perfect term for mediating between African disparagement of American conditions and the vernacular *play* of griot-informed banjo-cats riffing at the limits of American possibilities. Readers who dream of a "pure" imperial Africa of kings and queens will be disappointed by the hybridity of *Invisible Man*, will not recognize Leuk-the-Hare as ancestor, will not achieve the Tarawere second sight necessary for "seeing around corners," and may confuse Ellison's conscious deployment of an Afro-Southern semiotic as insignificant. But if we turn to Ellison's use of a culinary soul "erotic," we may find that the *nyama* of Afro-Creole roots of identity provides the bass rhythms to *Invisible Man*'s jived-up epic sound.

The narrator is a fresh exile in Harlem (trying to look anything but Southern or "folkish") when he meets a Southern confrere, Peter Wheatstraw, carting a load of blueprints to the shredder. Wheatstraw admonishes his homeboy not to stick blindly to the letter of any script and boasts that old-time "shit, grit and mother-wit" enable navigation of the chaos of New York (and by implication—the whole New World). Immediately after this unsolicited advice from a fellow "from the old country," the invisible narrator visits a New York diner, is offered the breakfast special of pork chops, grits, an egg, biscuits and coffee, and then—acting out of a fear of confirming whites' stereotypes—refuses to order the Southern-style special he truly desires (and that a white man subsequently orders). Much later, after a lobotomy has reduced his identifiable ancestry to Brer Rabbit, the exiled narrator reluctantly begins to act upon genuine desires. In a market scene, as he is "walking close to the windows, the snowflakes lacing swift between, simultaneously forming a curtain, a *veil* [emphasis added]," he gazes at dream books, love powders, money-drawing oil, skin whitening ointments, and amidst his instant revulsion, catches "the odor of baking yams . . . bringing a stab of swift nostalgia" (256). The old vendor's vernacular call, "Get yo' hot, baked Car'lina yam," adds to the narrator's "sudden hunger" (257). And like the okra of the Sunjata market scene, the yam becomes an erotic sign of shared identity:

> I knew that it was sweet before I broke it; bubbles of brown syrup had burst the skin.
> "Go ahead and break it," the old man said. "Break it and I'll give you some butter since you gon' eat it right here. . . .
> I broke it, seeing the sugary pulp steaming in the cold.
> "Hold it over here," he said. He took a crock from a rack on the side of the wagon.
> "Right here."
> I held it, watching him pour a spoonful of melted butter over the yam and the butter seeping in.
> "Thanks."
> "You welcome. . . .
> I took a bite, finding it as sweet and hot as any I'd ever had, and was overcome with such a surge of homesickness that I turned away to keep my control. I walked along, munching the yam, just as suddenly overcome by an intense feeling of freedom—simply because I was eating while walking along the street. (257–58)

An intensely sweet sense of rootedness overcomes the exiled narrator who—at least for this one moment—unashamedly embraces folk tradition even as he embraces the possibility of eating on the street: a violation of old-time Afro-Southern manners. What the narrator finds bizarre is that admitting to a stereotyped desire, say a love of chitlins or collards, could be considered a greater transgression than poor manners. Like the marketplace okra that links the exiled Sunjata to a reintegrated mother Mande, the yam and associated soul food provide a link to the shared joys of a maternal inheritance that the narrator had been dodging: "*Field-Niggerism*" (259), the Afro-Jeffersonian heritage that a "Golden Day" veteran had nonchalantly claimed "on the 'field nigger' side" (77). After the simple moment of recognition, "to hell with being ashamed of what you liked" (259), the narrator buys two more yams and asserts "They're my birthmark . . . I yam what I am!" (260). Deep traces of *nyama* may be read in the way this yam serves as a "birthmark." Even the word "yam" appears to be linked to the Wolof and Mandinka *nyam* and Pulaar *nyami* used as in Gullah as a general noun for "food" or as a verb meaning "to eat" (Dalgish 154). As Senegambian griots know, we *are* what we eat . . . long before we are aware of the fact.

It is no accident that the narrator's belated acceptance of a soul heritage embodied in the yam (and earlier disparaged as the "field-niggerism" evident in masterful banjo songs like "Guinea Gall") provides a linkage to Senegambian energies of action. For as Charles Joyner has explained: "Such joys as slavery allowed were centered around food . . . thus creating a desire deeper than hunger for that kind of food" ("Soul Food" 177). Joy-sharing soul ingredients, a kind of deep semiotics of mother-child-ness, bind soul foods to a whole "soul vernacular" that shapes the earliest imitative efforts and impulses of childhood. Ellison explained this inescapable semiotic element to Hollie West: "You watch a little Negro kid try to dance. . . . there is a spirit of the dance which is around him, and he observes and absorbs it before he is aware of what he is absorbing. . . . you're not going to get away from that. . . . as you become conscious as an artist, you will begin to exploit it consciously" (44). And so with cultural continuity and African origins, nurtured along preverbal, verbal, and extraverbal chains of transmission, Ellison knew he could not get away from that, nurtured as he was upon resilient soul styles.

Ralph Ellison's *Invisible Man*, like Jean Toomer's *Cane* and Zora Neale Hurston's "High John de Conquer," articulates ancestral identities, explores visionary realms of second sight and gendered double consciousness, and utilizes a deeply African American semiotics (particularly through vernacular language, song, and food ways) to signal community and provide the *badenya* grounding for successful innovation. Because these modern narratives were far removed from Africa—if not from slavery—their authors felt strong forces of discontinuity working against easy access to older forms of identity and expression. Jean Toomer's *Cane* was an elegy for old Afro-Southern sources even as it sought new forms for reassembly and transmission of what was most vital. "High John de Conquer" turned more explicitly to satisfying epic needs of African origin, heroism, and enduring modes of power/knowledge; and it did so, I believe, only through Hurston's visionary "doctoring" of the tradition by conflating root and tale cycle. Ellison, recognizing that all tradition is useful chiefly to the degree that it *is* doctored to meet ever-emergent needs, applied "shit, grit, and mother wit" to his artistry. When Ellison is accused of not properly valorizing African origins or not presenting a racial-nationalist agenda, he is in essence often being accused of not having written in a prescribed epic mode. But Africa is an invisible presence that provides much of the means and shapes much of the energy of the novel's action, and as for the assimilationist tendencies noted by critics like Jane Campbell, he is surely guilty, since according to Kimberly Benston, Ellison "has exhorted us not only to assimilate the past but also to acquire it, to *appropriate* it by interested engagement, in the context of the present" (3). Given the fractured context of its mid-twentieth-century present, *Invisible Man* came quite close to filling epic needs. The "buggy jiving" of its narrator (which I will return to in Chapter 9) is, if we consider possible Wolof etymology for vernacular use of "bug" (Wolof *begg*: to desire, love, want) and probable etymology of "jive" (Wolof *jev*: to speak disparagingly), ironically masterful.[9] For "buggy jiving" or desirous disrespect is the truest, most paradoxical and doubly conscious manner of contention with American "democracy." Tracing a strong lineage from Senegambian griots to the Tennessee banjo-cats of "Guinea Gall," the buggy jiving of "Kabnis," "High John de Conquer," and *Invisible Man* (kin to the collagelike reassemblies of a Romare Bearden or Dizzy Gillespie) works constantly to rechannel Afro-Creole energies of action. Simultaneously occulted by forces of modernism and secreted at the very core of the modern/post-modern matrix, a much hybridized, hard-to-name *nyama* emerges from the root cellars and soil of Southern landscapes and from the undergrounds of "inner cities," sounding the "rumble" of its "root-life" and leaving everywhere its unerasable, uncapturable, primordial trace.

3

Myth-making, Mother-child-ness, and Epic Renamings

Malcolm X, Kunta Kinte, and Milkman Dead

> *The fathers may soar*
> *And the children may know their names*
>
> Toni Morrison, *Song of Solomon* (1977)

I

If Du Bois, Toomer, Hurston, and Ellison, in their narratives of immersion in an incredibly "open-eyed" Afro-Creole culture, often seemed to be seeking articulation of an underground "mumble" (leading in Ellison's case to an embrace of invisible namelessness), then we can understand how the civil rights era's resurgent Pan-African spirit might call for more concrete, more explicitly nameable epics of African patrimony. Efforts to narrate continuities between Africa and America forced a confrontation with what Melville Herskovits termed *The Myth of the Negro Past* (1941): the idea that Africa was a cultural tabula rasa and that American slavery had erased any remnants of an already only nominal African heritage. Despite Herskovits's powerful intervention, scholars following in the wake of E. Franklin Frazier, who had argued that the horrific "shock" of slavery obliterated African cultural/familial heritage in America, tended to emphasize the pathology of African American folk culture and the problems posed by what Frazier had termed a dominant "matriarchate" (102–13). Many of the chapter titles of Frazier's *The Negro Family in the United States* (1939) tell the story of African American father-child-ness as a repeated narrative of flight, a story of extreme discontinuities and dislocations: "Roving Men and Homeless Women," "The Flight from Feudal America," "Fathers on Leave," "Outlawed Motherhood," "Rebellious Youth," "Divorce: Scrip from the Law." As Frazier reveals, in a nation where "reason" and tradition might rule, "as a South Carolina court held in 1809, [that] 'the young of slaves . . . stand on the same footing as other animals,'" the property interests of a master class worked to institutionalize the categorical denial of black humanity (35). Denials of black cultural "patrimony" or meaningful "matrimony" operated from a legalistic discourse and prison house of language that still serves as a barrier against articulation of a countervision.[1] When Frazier does acknowledge traces of Africa in America, as in his opening chapter entitled "Forgotten Memories," it is no accident that references to Islam and Senegambia are repeated sources of nostalgia for a lost black patrimony/patriarchy able to command respect under the very terms of the oppressor's culture. He opens *The Negro Family in the United States* with Mungo Park's accounts of Muslim-led Senegambian slave "coffles" bound for Charleston, cites Martin Delany's claim to Mandinka ancestry, and conveys Charles Ball's witnessing of Islamic worship in South Carolina as "forgotten memories" of an African scriptural patrimony. Frazier concludes that "Probably never before in history has a people been so nearly completely stripped of its social heritage as the Negroes who were brought to America. . . . of the habits and customs as well as the hopes and fears that characterized their forebears in Africa, nothing remains" (15). However, with the noted exception of the Senegambian Muslim scriptural patrimony, he views this "stripping" of the African heritage as a kind of providence since it led "preliterate African races" to evolve into "the culture of the civilized American Negro today" (359). As he presents it, outside of Islam, the African heritage offers a kind of nullity to begin with . . . even in Africa itself. We can see something of Frazier's internalization of the post-Enlightenment equation of writing with cultural patrimony, since as Henry Louis Gates Jr. has pointed out, writing had long filled a hegemonic position as the West's visible sign of reason and humanity.[2]

While white Americans scripted slavery as a kind of providential schooling for the lowest rung of humanity, Africans and their open-eyed descendants knew too well that slavery was a form of rape.[3] As we have seen, Ellison, Toomer, and Du Bois came face to face with this white rapist presence (in the white founders' Jeffersonian "strippage" of African culture and African women). Since patrimony and patronymics have been the domain of white (and male) supremacy, Afro-Creole epic-heroic narratives of resistance have operated against incredibly restricted options—particularly in the core homeland of the Deep South, the lynch land of ritual castration. Aside from flight, resistant choices in the pre–civil rights South seemed limited to suicidal confrontations (Du Bois's "Of the Coming of John," Toomer's "Blood-Burning Moon") or the kind of Brer Rabbit-like underground mother wit offered by *Invisible Man*. Given that some of the twentieth century's most steadily confrontational figures of black father-child-ness were finally pushed into patterns of flight prefigured by nineteenth-century slave narratives (Richard Wright searching freedom in Paris, and Du Bois in Accra), the ever-dislocating trope of father-flight occupies a strange, racially charged, ever-violent American space. Adding racist insult to the nation's pathological history of racist injury, the Moynihan Report (1965) labeled the black family "a pathological 'matriarchy'" that had fallen into a "deterioration" explainable by "the rampant sexual debauchery among the black population, by the instability and violence of black men, and by the pathological dominance of black women" (Hirsch 142–43). Issued at a time when heroes like Fred Shuttlesworth, John Lewis, and Martin Luther King Jr. (along with women like Selma's Marie Foster and Amelia Boynton), were taking to Southern streets and spilling their blood there, the Moynihan Report's maligning of the black family avoided America's core pathologies. As might be expected, its critical focus upon an alleged "black matriarchy" energized black nationalist efforts to restore the father to his "proper" familial location. In the quest to emplot nonwhite sources of patrimony/patronym, powerful figures such as Frederick Douglass, David Walker, or Olaudah Equiano might not offer the fullest symbolic satisfaction since the means by which they came to the written word could be said to have arrived via white men. American epics of African patrimony would locate logos/law/patronym in Africa and most often in the scriptural, Islamic cultures of Senegambia and the monumental empires of Ghana, Mali, Songhay (or, following a path popularized by the Senegalese scholar Cheikh Anta Diop, might work further back to Pharaonic Egypt and hieroglyphic writing, thereby positioning Africa as ultimate source of world patrimony).[4]

Working from paradigms strikingly similar to those of E. Franklin Frazier but drawing also upon the populist Afrocentrism of the Garvey movement, the Nation of Islam offered a corrective response to New World dislocations of black patriarchy. Emerging from the Nation of Islam and the American racial forces that shaped it, *The Autobiography of Malcolm X* (1964) reenvisioned and renamed possibilities of epic-heroic action. Nearly a decade later, the variable "X" of African ancestry became fully fleshed in the Mande/Muslim Kunta Kinte of Alex Haley's *Roots* (1976). Following Haley's groundbreaking root-work as chronicler of Malcolm X's heroism and Kunta Kinte's ancestral *nyama*, we find a Senegambian Muslim patrimony continually reinvoked, most powerfully in Toni Morrison's *Song of Solomon* (1977) but also in works as different as Ernest Gaines's *A Gathering of Old Men* (1983) and Julie Dash's film *Daughters of the Dust* (1991).[5] Clearly this scriptural Afro-Muslim heritage answered some urgent ideological needs for epic reassembly of an Africa-based community.

Like the Senegambian epics, *The Autobiography of Malcolm X* moves well beyond the representation of one heroic life and into the myths of origin of the reassembled "Nation." Malcolm describes how Elijah Muhammad (born Elijah Poole) moved from Georgia to Detroit, where he met Master

W.D. Fard, who "identified himself as 'a brother from the East'" and taught "that God's true name was Allah. . . . that the Negroes in America were directly descended from Muslims. . . . that Negroes in America were Lost Sheep, lost for four hundred years from the Nation of Islam, and that he, Mr. Fard, had come to redeem and return the Negro to his true religion" and "the black man's original language, Arabic" (206–7). Hell was on earth, and the devil was "the white race which was bred from black Original Man" (207). Although his autobiography claims spiritual patrimony in a distant, valorized homeland to the east and in a scriptural religion, the heart of Malcolm's narrative began, as the story of the Sunjata essentially does, when the chronicler Haley—after listening to the genealogies and panegyrics surrounding the Nation of Islam—asked, "I wonder if you'd tell me something about your mother?" (390). So Haley opens the book with a chapter entitled "Nightmare," recounting a scene of KKK terrorism against Malcolm's mother, pregnant with him, as the Klan seeks to intimidate his father because "'the good Christian white people' were not going to stand for my father's 'spreading trouble' among the 'good' Negroes of Omaha with the 'back to Africa' preachings of Marcus Garvey" (1). Racial violence is established as the contextual prehistory of Malcolm's life, and Garvey's Pan-African nationalism is a logical choice to a father who had seen "four of his six brothers die by violence, three of them killed by white men" (2). Turning to his mother's ancestry, Malcolm underscores the pervasive presence of violence, the sign of which is his own red hair and light skin received from his racially mixed mother: "I learned to hate every drop of that white rapist's blood that is in me" (2). Since Malcolm's Anglo-American patronym of "Little" represents the rape—both literal and cultural—of his ancestors, the new patronym of "X" works doubly to excise a white rapist patrimony and to represent the unknown variable, the "original" African patrimony reassembled in the name of a renamed God: Allah.

While the Nation of Islam valorized monumental African origins, the South continued to provide the imaginative link between Africa and the northern-based Nation. In fact, Georgia was the birthplace of both Elijah Muhammad and Malcolm's father, the Reverend Earl Little. Malcolm speaks of his father as a "very black man" (1–2), further authenticating him as "a real Georgia Negro" who "believed in eating plenty of what we in Harlem today call 'soul food'" (7). He describes his paternal aunt Ella as being "the first really proud black woman I had ever seen in my life. . . . plainly proud of her very dark skin," which was "jet black" (32–33), and offers further signs of Ella's authenticity: "[S]he was truly a Georgia Negro woman. . . . the kind of cook who would heap up your plate with such as ham hock, greens, black-eyed peas, fried fish, cabbage, sweet potatoes, grits and gravy, and cornbread" (39). Despite Malcolm's amazing mastery of vernacular styles, the Nation of Islam's redemptive mission for black patriarchy led him to distrust the Afro-Southern semiotic/erotic that is America's strongest cultural link to Africa. Speaking of Afro-Christian worship patterns, Malcolm voices a puritan disdain similar to the reactions of Toomer's Ralph Kabnis: "I had faith in the Nation: we weren't some group of Christian Negroes, jumping and shouting and full of sins" (297). His representation of women, along with his representation of "soul" styles, often carries tones of disdain heightened perhaps by the convert's rigorous austerity: the swearing off of sinful desires for women, ham hocks, and dancing. Many of his comments about women stand in opposition to the depth of character he observes in Ella. He claims that "[a]ll women, by their nature, are fragile and weak" (93) and that "I'd had too much experience that women were only tricky, deceitful, untrustworthy flesh" (226). As for dancing, Malcolm says, "You know those 'dancing jigaboo' toys that you wind up? Well, I was a live one" (57).

As Richard Turner has written, Malcolm seems to be insisting that in his preconversion days as Detroit Red he had become "the mirror image of all the racist significations that white Christian America had constructed for young African American men" (180). In much of *The Autobiography of Malcolm X*, Afro-Southern aesthetics and semiotics are treated with ambivalence due to their embeddedness in a matrix of "racist significations," while valorizations of Islam and Arabic as the black man's original ("pure") patrimony betray an uneasiness with vernacular realities. However, we must note that when Malcolm X eventually distanced himself from Elijah Muhammad, after performing the *hajj* and being renamed once more as El-hajj Malik El-Shabazz, his thinking moved toward new identity and new modes of transition.[6] Having moved himself—and many Americans—from a view of Africa as a land "of naked savages, cannibals, monkeys and tigers and steaming jungles" (7) to advocacy of "the black man's glorious history" (263), Malcolm seems to have found in Islam a wholly independent, Africa-based patrimony of literacy and flight. It allowed for a scriptural grace unbeholden to white America and a return to a belief that "everything is written" (149). Vowing to learn from the story of Icarus never to forget "that any wings I wore had been put on by the religion of Islam" (287), this militant visionary "El-hajj Malik El-Shabazz, who had been called Malcolm X; who had been called Malcolm Little; who had been called 'Big Red' and 'Satan' and 'Homeboy' and other names" (455), did much to call attention—in an ever-racialized America—to the connections and disconnections between the powers of naming and the powers of flight.

II

While El-hajj Malik El-Shabazz was murdered in the midst of transitions that would have undoubtedly led to evermore engaging forms of action, his griot (Alex Haley) survived him to join Islamic/Mandinka patrimony and Southern soul semiotics in one of the most popular (and simultaneously disparaged and dismissed) works of the twentieth century—the truly epic *Roots* (1976). Given the popular success of *Roots* (1.5 million hardcover copies of the book sold in its first eighteen months while the first televised version had over 135 million viewers), it may be the most read, most viewed work of our time, rivaled only by *Gone with the Wind*; in fact, by the final night of *Roots*' airing as TV miniseries (1977), only three of the ten most-watched television shows in American history were *not* episodes of *Roots* (Wolper 154). Through *Roots*, Haley began to introduce a global audience to the griot profession and "did more than any other individual to create an interest in griots throughout the world" (Hale, *Griots* 247). However, David Chioni Moore recently brought attention to the fact that after an initial wave of academic resistance to the authenticity and historicity of Haley's griot-received story of Kunta Kinte's capture, "*Roots* . . . has been subjected to a near-total silence on the part of the intelligentsia" ("Routes" 7). Moore convincingly argues that the adjectival cliche of "epic" often attached to *Roots* should be taken seriously if we are to understand what Haley himself called a "faction," positioned at the crossroads of history and fiction. While historians' critiques shortly after the publication of *Roots* challenged Haley's claims of tracing an enslaved eighteenth-century ancestor through a griot's narrative, Philip Nobile's article in *The Village Voice*, "Uncovering Roots" (1993), has gone further in seeking to expose Haley as a systematic scam artist who gave us "a hoax, a literary painted mouse, a Piltdown of genealogy, a pyramid of bogus research" (32). Still, in a generally scathing article, Nobile finds himself offering strange praise: "Haley's ripping yarns about his search for Kunta Kinte and his 10–year struggle to write *Roots* were part of an elegant and complex make-it-up-as-you-go-along scam" (32). Intended as an attack upon Haley's reputation, Nobile's exposé could ultimately work to bolster Haley's position as a griotlike epic artist. Like Senegambian epics, *Roots* is indeed a fiction. But it is also a "foundational" narrative of such national and diasporic popularity that for many readers it became "a sacred text" (Moore 10). Blending history, folk narrative, and a thick gumbo of cultural information, *Roots* answered the demands of epic genre and the epic needs of its audience. Informed by his chronicling of the life of Malcolm X, Haley realized that it was only by purveying *Roots* as nonfiction that he could orchestrate response to it as epic.

Although Sunjata, Kunta Kinte, and a lineage of griots emerge as epic ancestors in *Roots,* Kunta Kinte's most immediate roots run deep in American literature. Harriet Beecher Stowe gave America a myth of comparable magnitude in *Uncle Tom's Cabin* (1852), but her ancestral position to Kunta Kinte may be seen more clearly in *Dred* (1856), in which Stowe presents a rebel whose love of liberty comes from his Mandingo mother. This trope of the freedom-insistent "noble" Senegambian maroon, given variants as Senegalese Babo in Melville's "Benito Cereno" (1855), the Wolof Bras Coupé in Cable's *The Grandissimes* (1880), and the Fulbe Ben Ali in Joel Chandler Harris's *Aaron* (1896), contributed to Kunta's creation. Providing both Mandinka and Muslim patrimony, the Kinte patronym was scripted perfectly to replace the "X" long branded into American psyches and most searingly exposed in El-hajj Malik El-Shabazz's contentious readings of the dislocations of American history. While the Kinte patronym may be traced all the way back to imperial Mali's Sunjata epic, several texts in Philip Curtin's *Africa Remembered* reveal other Africans in Kunta's genealogy: Olaudah Equiano's horrific recollection of Middle Passage, Salih Bilali's recollections of Mali, and Ayuba Suleiman Diallo's (Fulbe Muslim) narrative of being captured on the Gambia River and placed on a ship bound for Annapolis. Since thousands of Muslims were enslaved in America, Haley's narrative of Kinte ancestry has strong historical grounding and was ideologically attractive to the man who had served as Malcolm X's autobiographical scribe.

The genealogical connection Haley sought to establish between Africa and America was already traceable by hundreds of Americans who needed no documents to recall specific African ancestors—often Muslims—as seen in the Georgia Writers' Project interviews. Zora Neale Hurston met with the man known as the last living African ex-slave and published "Cudjo's Own Story of the Last African Slaver." I myself have met an Alabama woman whose autobiography moves past her central role in Selma's voting rights movement to narrate her meetings in the late 1930s with Redoshi, known as Aunt Sally, one of the Africans enslaved with Cudjo (Boynton 30–34) and whom Hurston also seems to have met (Hemenway, *Zora* 117). Clearly there was no historical gap to fill that would necessitate what Philip Nobile has called a "hoax." The gap was mythic, to be filled only by a fiction.

Nobile's "exposure" of Haley may help to lay the groundwork for a better appreciation of the power of Haley's myth-making artistry. Nobile begins by examining Haley's out-of-court settlement with Harold Courlander for plagiarism and his "sampling" of passages from Mungo Park's *Travels*, Shirley Graham's *The Story of Phyllis Wheatley*, and Margaret Walker's *Jubilee*. But since, as David Chioni Moore has remarked, "plagiarism as such has never been enough to silence or discredit a text" (*Routes* 9), Nobile's real interest lies in exposing Haley's "reassembly" of chronology and motive in the representation of his genealogical search in the book's last three chapters. Nobile claims that the most damning evidence comes from Haley's own papers, recently opened in the University of Tennessee's Special Collections Library in Knoxville. The tape of Haley's 1967 encounter with Kebba Kanji Fofana (the Gambian griot who narrated Kunta Kinte's capture for

Haley) reveals a prompted response from Fofana (who apears to have been a well-informed member of a family of griot origin but not an active practitioner of the profession) and an unsurprised Haley, who had read a prepared text of Fofana's transmission four days earlier in Banjul.[7] According to Nobile, Haley's notebooks show that he met the Gambian Ebou Manga and visited the Gambia twice before meeting Professor Jan Vansina, who is represented in *Roots* as the first person to translate the African sounds of Haley's family story, the first to recognize them as Mandinka and direct Haley toward Gambia. Nobile writes that before Haley met Ebou Manga, "there were no African fragments in Haley's family story," having been cited in neither Haley's initial 1965 publication, "My Search for Roots," nor in two requests in 1966 for funding from Doubleday and *Reader's Digest* to cover expenses for a trip to Africa (35). It may be that Manga, rather than a family/griot-derived narrative, was Haley's clearest Mandinka source. The truly amazing thing in Nobile's attack on Haley is the amount of research energy devoted to proving that *Roots* indeed is a fiction. Nobile's most damaging charge against Haley's actual artistry is that Haley's *Playboy* editor "rewrote the African section—more than a fifth of the book—because Haley was trapped in a quagmire of Africana" (38), a revision for which Haley openly expressed gratitude in his acknowledgments pages. Ironically, similar editing moves have often been made in texts of the Sunjata, cutting griots' tendencies toward genealogy, praise-proverbs, and esoteric displays of cultural knowledge in favor of a cleaner narrative line, targeted for a general readership. Haley's unedited, multigeneric "quagmire of Africana" was probably even closer in spirit to the Mande epic from which he claimed descent than is the published form of *Roots*.

It may be through readings of the Mande Sunjata epic that we can best understand Kunta Kinte and Haley's epic project. Haley, who might claim Sunjata's adversary Sumamuru Kante as an ancestor, since Kante is a variant pronunciation of Kinte (Johnson x), at times seems to be transmitting a Sunjata. For instance, Djeli Mamadou Kouyate's claim that "silk cotton trees and baobabs that you see in Mali are the only traces of extinct cities" (Niane 83) is repeated in *Roots*: "Kunta's favorite sight was a lonely old oak or cedar in the middle of a field; it would send his mind back to the baobabs of Africa, and to the elders' saying that wherever one stood alone, there had been a village" (242). Just as genealogical needs in the Sunjata shift as tellings move from Mali's imperial core (where griots are concerned with tracing authority to Mecca and even to Eden) to a Gambian periphery (where griots trace origins to the prestigious imperial heartland of the Manden), Haley's epic—further removed in diaspora—focuses its genealogy on peripheral Gambia as valorized source and Kunta Kinte as "the farthest-back person." But by imagining Kunta Kinte planning a genealogical quest to the heartland of Old Mali at the very moment before he is captured and shipped into New World slavery, Haley calls attention to the unending backwards glance of a strictly genealogical foundation of identity: "Kunta . . . meant to put his eyes and feet upon that distant place called Mali, where some three or four hundred rains before, according to Omoro and his uncles, the Kinte clan had begun" (122). The tracings of genealogy ultimately lead us away from a unitary tree trunk toward fractal branchings, and we see "the dissipation rather than the enracination of identity in any kind of genetic history" (Moore, *Routes* 17). Haley's narrative return to the source (a tracing that moves more often through matrilineage than patrilineage and that must confront a white forefather, Tom Lea, who was the master/rapist of Kunta Kinte's daughter Kizzy) finally arrives at Kunta Kinte, just *one* of Haley's many great-great-great-great-great-great-grandfathers, a man who represents only ½₅₆th of Haley's bloodline (Moore 15). The reclaimed Mandinka heritage actually offers a far more distant genealogical relationship than Haley's potential claims to Irish, English, or Cherokee ancestry. From this perspective, we can see that—as David Chioni Moore argues—"the farther back one can trace a single ancestor, the *less and less* that ancestor represents you, except . . . by a process of retroactive and selective affiliation" (15). Haley's need for a rooted "point zero" indeed led him to the retroactive and selective choice of Kunta Kinte, who identified with the heroes of the Sunjata, who chose descent from the Prophet's Bilali, whose ancestor was Adam— made by God. Establishing Kunta Kinte as the fictive zero point of his own genealogical tree, Haley presented *Roots* as "faction," for only by presenting *Roots* as a genealogically rooted, "authentic" history could it be received as "a symbolic saga of all African-descent people" (Haley 580). Though *Roots* is subtitled "The Saga of an American Family," it functions more like the griots' foundational epics than like an Icelandic saga. Indeed, in his scholarly introduction to the world of *Griots and Griottes*, Thomas Hale repeatedly states his admiration for Haley's "faction" and how it "echoed the griot tradition," allowing Haley to operate as "a modern-day griot" who popularized the tradition to such an extent that "use of the term *griot* [has come] to symbolize awareness of and attachment to Africa" (254–55).

In spite of the editing of Haley's "quagmire of Africana" (his praise-proverb modes, cultural explications, and other typically epic indirections), the semiotics of West African mother-child-ness bonds permeate *Roots* and sustain its epic performance. The family narrative transmitted primarily through women repeating Mandinka sounds—*Kin-tay, Kamby bolongo, ko*— is Haley's invention of a Mandinka semiotic surviving through his family's revoicings, as with Du Bois's African lullaby and Amelia Dawley's Mende song. Kunta's first Mande sounds are extralinguistic: "[T]he first sound the child heard was the muted *bomp-a-bomp-a-bomp* of wooden pestles" (1).

The munko (saraka) cakes of pounded rice and honey prepared at his birth (2), his play around "the giant trunk of the village baobab" (7), and evening meals in Juffure all take on a significance similar to Audre Lorde's erotic "bridge" of joy-sharing identity and power. This erotic sense is one of the things most imperiled by slavery; in fact, in antebellum America the sharing of pain bridges difference more quickly than the sharing of joy, as we see when a Fulbe elder aboard the slave ship calls for solidarity around a man beaten by the crew: "Share his pain! We must be in this place as one village" (134).

At first, Kunta finds the old pleasures of a Mandinka semiotic/erotic absent in Virginia: "Missing the sound of the village women's pestles thumping the couscous for their families' morning meals, he would enter the hut of the old cooking woman and bolt down whatever she gave him—except for any filthy pork" (184). But just as market women used okra and eggplant flour as signs to reach an exiled Sunjata, Kunta's integration into American life begins with the exile's nostalgic response to things familiar: "Some days they served foods Kunta knew from his home, such as groundnuts and kanjo—which was called 'okra'—and so-so, which was called 'black-eyed peas'" (185). These foods powerfully summon remembered joys, and Kunta gradually recognizes that "he had heard all his life the very same sounds of exclamation, accompanied by the very same hand gestures and facial expressions. And the way these blacks moved their bodies was also identical. . . . these blacks laughed when they were among themselves—with their whole bodies, just like the people of Juffure" (189). In a similar manner, he begins to recognize familiar patterns in deliberately occulted forms of plantation speech: "[L]ike the Mandinkas' own secret sira kango language, these blacks shared some kind of communication known only among themselves" (191).

Kunta initially rejects identifying with others enslaved on the plantation, asking himself, "was he still an African, or had he become a 'nigger'"? (239) His model African is Sunjata, transformed into a maroon prototype for New World efforts to escape slavery: "[A]s he lay hidden beneath a bush, he found himself thinking of the Mandinkas' greatest hero, the warrior Sundiata, who had been a crippled slave so meanly treated by his master that he had escaped and gone hiding in the swamps, where he found and organized other escaped ones into a conquering army that carved out the vast Mandinka Empire" (204). But Kunta Kinte's resistance, patterned after Sunjata's triumph over lameness, results in the loss of his foot. Near death from blood loss and infection, he is saved by the familiar medicine of Bell's herbal care, "like Binta's medicines from his childhood, the herbs of Allah's earth passed down from the ancestors" (209). After regaining health, he is gradually seduced by her soul-sharing as "Bell cooked things Kunta had let her know were also grown in the Gambia, such as black-eyed peas, okra, a stew made of peanuts or yams baked with butter" (272). Haley's cultivation of a Mande semiotics reassembles *African* American identity more success-fully than does the Kinte patronym, which—since Kunta fathers no sons—serves as a matrilineal source rather than as "original" patronym. Kunta's value as a chosen ancestor lies in his resistance to plantation slavery and his authoritative claims to a scriptural African patrimony demonstrated in his ability to write in Arabic, a performance that astonishes Bell, who "seemed to take it for granted that those who had come from Africa had just climbed down from the trees" (280). But *Roots* is more than a recovery of patrimony through the naming of a single reclaimed patriarch. As Kunta begins to share joy with the griotlike Fiddler and more significantly with Bell, *Roots* moves toward the conservative group identity signified by Mande cultures as *badenya*. Mother-child-ness bonds forged by symbolic reunion in the house of Mother Africa make the novel a narrative of familial location overcoming extreme dislocation.

As Russell Adams has remarked, part of the national appeal of *Roots* was its celebration of the American dream as the genealogical narrative moved from Kunta Kinte's enslavement to the Arkansas funeral of a college profes-sor. Despite the fact that Haley enabled white Americans to begin to identify with some of the intense struggles of black Americans, the result was not a movement toward an inclusive American mother-child-ness identity but one of further fragmentation as Americans pursued separate roots in a national craze for genealogy fueled by nostalgia and age-old ideologies of ethnic "pu-rity." Nevertheless, the book and TV miniseries were germinal to America's national acceptance of African cultural identity and forced whites to look at some of the ties that yoked Europeans and Africans together as American kin: "[I]t was strangely unreal, a kind of beautiful dream the white folks were having, a lie they were telling themselves: that goodness can come from badness, that it's possible to be civilized with one another, without treating as human beings those whose blood, sweat, and mother's milk made possible the life of privilege they led" (Haley 252). *Roots* allowed a national glimpse of the national lie, but it still troubles many who argue for its im-portance. Sanford Pinsker, writing of Toni Morrison's superior prose and vision, observed that Haley's admirers might be telling themselves the lie that goodness can come from badness: "[N]o imagination, black or white, can be liberated for long, or perhaps at all, by such a hackneyed vision, by such a badly written work" (188). But those who would damn *Roots* often find themselves singing strange praises, as did Nobile, speaking of Haley's "elegant and complex make-it-up-as-you-go-along scam" (32), "the daring and grandiosity of Haley's fakery" (33), and the "savant's grace to Haley's grift" (36). This ability to make it up as you go along, to add grace to grift, has long enabled epic performance and marks the kind of bardic artistry that brought Leslie Fiedler to write that Haley "possesses, though perhaps only by fits and starts, that mythopoetic power which neither ineptness of language nor banality of ideas can impugn" (231).

To this day, Haley's "mythopoetic power" has gone unacknowledged by literary critics, even though *Roots* was one of the most significant literary/media events of the twentieth century. Despite the fact that it "has sold more copies than any other African American narrative ever written, *Roots* has been effectively 'disappeared' from contemporary literature" (Moore 8). Moore attributes the literary/academic "silencing" of *Roots* to its "middle-brow status (Haley's favorite publishing venues had been *Playboy* and *Reader's Digest*)," to the "unchallenging character of the book's politics," and to the constant "disputes about its historical veracity, its author's basic honesty, and the presence of plagiarism in all chapters of the text" (8–9). Interestingly, in Haley's case, griots themselves—like current hip-hop stars with their mainstream popularity, their up-from-the-'hood success stories, and their collagelike art of sampling—must answer to similar charges. Still the griotlike Haley has been silenced. And though *Roots* singlehandedly put griots into the American vocabulary, neither *The Norton Anthology of African American Literature* (1997) nor the more Afrocentric *Call and Response: The Riverside Anthology of the African American Tradition* (1998) includes selections from Haley's epic work, despite the fact that the latter anthology locates the roots of African American culture in griot traditions by opening with selections from the Sunjata epic (in both the text and the accompanying compact disc) and by arguing in the introduction that early black ministers and writers, "using the inherited verbal artistry and eloquence of the griots . . . crafted sermons, prayers, narratives, hymns, poems, essays, and songs to educate, uplift and stir the African American spirit toward social action" (Liggins et al 26). Haley's griot-popularizing call for diasporic reassembly has been occulted to a "mumble" even as the response to his call remains energized by the *nyama* of his root-work. More than anyone else, Haley has helped us to see that the griot connection is simultaneously an underappreciated historical reality (and source of enduring Afro-Creole *nyama*) and a Senegambia-centric, monumental fiction authored by Haley et al. In his work we see the facts of Mande Muslim origins alongside the fictions of their narration.

Haley's location of a Mandinka/Muslim patrimony in the Kinte name by way of family tales, griot narratives, and numerous archival documents, does not by itself provide the kind of psychic reassembly offered by epic performance. What was most powerful in *Roots* was the national dramatization of scenes that had previously been repressed. The televised version of *Roots* thus worked more powerfully than the book to fill its epic role. Played over several nights (as the Sunjata often is), *Roots* reached audiences gathered to watch and listen. Filmed by director David Wolper in Savannah and on the islands of coastal Georgia—"the American location that looked most like the West Africa of *Roots*" (Wolper 69)—the miniseries offered mother-child-ness reconnections in the joy sharing of Afro-Creole semiotics. Simultaneous focus on the hellishness of slavery challenged all involved, particularly in the filming of the slave ship loaded with human cargo: "[W]e put all the actors playing slaves in those narrow spaces and everyone felt it. . . . 80% of the extras refused to return" (87). The unforgettable scene of a resistant Kunta Kinte being "broken" under the lash until he finally answered to the name "Toby" became searingly emblematic of systematic attempts to dehumanize (and dispatriate) enslaved Africans—and dramatized as well the resistant power of African American naming (as the "Kin-tay" name signaled through its very survival in family narrative). *Roots* emerged as a response to problems of naming and patrimony posed in *The Autobiography of Malcolm X*. But the long slow accretion of a genealogy-based novel, the repeated panegyric to the American dream achievable through hard work, self-sufficiency, and old-fashioned pride—combined with the popular appeal of *Roots*—worked against the entry of *Roots* into emergent canons of "literature." It is true that *Roots* lacks the powers of poetic flight that we find in novels by Toni Morrison or Paule Marshall. And it is true that Haley's understanding of rooted identity is, as we say now, "unproblematized," but if Ralph Ellison has been criticized for not writing clearly enough in epic/heroic mode, Haley has been damned for doing it—and for doing it so well that his name now counts for much less than the griot traditions he celebrated.

III

While Alex Haley, Ernest Gaines, and Julie Dash have presented strong Senegambian Muslim, or simply "Singaleese" patriarchal figures, no contemporary artist has more powerfully married the Senegambian ancestor to the Afro-Creole semiotics of mother wit than did Toni Morrison in *Song of Solomon* (1977), published the year after *Roots*.[8] In *Song of Solomon* we are lured by the title to associations with conventionally erotic romance and Biblical (or canonical) texts, but as we become immersed in Morrison's novel, we find supplementations and displacements of these expectations as a West African (Fulbe/Muslim) patrimony, a doubly conscious mother wit, and a gumbo soul erotics provide means for comprehensive reassembly of the African American literary/spiritual/social landscape. Part initiation tale, part epic-heroic quest, *Song of Solomon* offers the strongest repossession/retransmission of Senegambian Muslim heritage that we have seen, in part because

Morrison responds to the call of *fadenya* flight with a grounded response that brings the whole epic project into question when the male hero begins to understand the costs of male flight (and epic-heroic acts of male transcendence). Morrison's work, unlike Haley's, is no mere panegyric to Afrocentric patrimony. Like the griots, and the strongest work of Du Bois, Toomer, and Hurston, Morrison seeks immersion in residual Afro-Creole cultural elements, which she then retransmits and critiques in an act of "'mothering' the residual into the emergent" (Wilentz xxix). As she works in griotlike fashion to "bind the culture," Morrison stays truest to the ancestors by refusing the stasis that would kill their *nyama*. Much as the ancestors themselves introduced New World information into familiar repertoires, *Song of Solomon's* shape-shifting reassembly of Afrocentric patrimony and womanist revision of its legacies of flight need not be located outside of griot-bequeathed means. The Sunjata's shape-shifting Buffalo of Du and the powers of mothers and lovers all work to mediate against the most hubristic male actions even though the women must often wield power from an "occulted" position. In her rearticulation of occulted means (*nya*), Morrison avoids mere literary folklore (or the replacement of Eurocentrism with a mirror image Afrocentrism) in order to wield a truly vital, openly emergent soul-*nyama* that "not only reflects the perspectives of Afro-American culture, but seeks to contribute in significant ways to its transformation" (Awkward 113).

Song of Solomon derives much of its transformative energy of action from the special power of African American song. We have seen how Mande griots transmit ancestral voices, reassembling ancient patrimony in performance of the Sunjata and its many praise-songs, and we have seen the importance that Du Bois attached to "the sorrow songs" and his great-great-grandmother's African lullaby. Likewise, Toomer sought occulted soul sounds in Father John and in the voices of women and singing trees, while Hurston wrote of High John de Conquer's arrival "on the waves of sound." In a manner remarkably similar to Haley's construction of Kinte ancestry from Mande sounds woven into his family narrative, Toni Morrison found voices of African remembrance in the Georgia Writers' Project's *Drums and Shadows*, from which she rerouted tales of flying Africans and Fulbe-Muslim ancestry. Amelia Dawley's Mende funeral song (kept alive by descendants who have been faithful to the sound of African memory even when they can no longer translate its Mende meanings) "bases" Morrison's *Song*. And an epic catalogue of folk facts from the *Drums and Shadows* interviews finds coherent reassembly in *Song of Solomon's* stories of flight back to Africa, tales of wings for sale, workings of conjure and birth cauls, the presence of ghostly figures and voices, communication with spirits (including a woman transformed into a bull), and retransmitted names—Coupers and Butlers (repeated as the Reverend Cooper and the Butler family), day names (informing the vigilante Seven Days), Fulbe Muslim names of Bilali's children, even the name of Solomon himself. Morrison's reshaping of the *Drums and Shadows* folk material—its saraka cake, Fulbe names, and *"Kum baba yano"* Mende song—into the title song's ring play works simultaneously to encode and unveil soul sounds shared from mothers to children in seemingly meaningless rhymes:

> Black lady fell down on the ground
> Come booba yalle, come booba tambee
> Threw her body all around
> Come konka yalle, come konka tambee
>
> Solomon and Ryna Belali Shalut
> Yaruba Medina Muhammet too
> Nestor Kalina Saraka cake
> Twenty-one children, the last one Jake! (303)

While Alex Haley based many of his claims to authority upon the presentation of researched archival "facts," Morrison's imaginative condensation of the Muslim Fulbe and the Mende folk material from the coastal Georgia narratives seeks its authority in a folk counterculture and in visionary acts of imagination.

By taking this leap of faith into the heart of an Afro-Creole counterculture, *Song of Solomon* recovers much of what had been previously left out of histories and canonical fictions as it explores relationships between song and scripture, folklore and history, even perhaps truth and fact—all observed in interface. While all New World experience is affected by this weave of voice and print, for Morrison names most often provide the point of discovery and departure: "Under the recorded names were other names, just as 'Macon Dead,' recorded for all time in some dusty file, hid from real view the real names of people, places, and things. Names that had meaning" (333). Like Alex Haley, Morrison relies upon the semiotics of mother/child bonds to trace the transmission of unique cultural and family traditions. One of the chief differences is that while *Roots* refers to history, archival fact, and academic authorities to authenticate the names in its epic narrative, *Song of Solomon* authenticates its names through dialogue with the forms and magic of Afro-Creole memory. Morrison's novel appeals to the folk living on "Not Doctor Street" for much of its authority, recognizing the power of a non–M.D./Ph.D. community that maintains self-naming agency in the face of legislating/canonical efforts to name the street "Mains Avenue." Most of the novel's names are not the names of birth certificates but are the basket names of mother wit, "names that bore witness" (330). Some of the biblical names, like "Pilate" (pilot), both certify *and* bear witness, as does the doubly conscious "*Song of Solomon.*"

As *Song of Solomon* progresses and the materialistic quest for an ancestor's gold becomes a *Roots*-like quest for identity, the novel's aptly named protagonist, Milkman Dead, comes to a mature appreciation of the *badenya* milk bonds (and basket names) of an African American semiotics. The "semiotic" has been described as the musical, presymbolic other of logos, law, patrimony. A kind of "milk bond," it is that "pattern or play of forces which we can detect inside language," which is "the 'other' of language" and "is nonetheless intimately entwined in it. . . . bound up with the child's contact with the mother's body" (Eagleton 188). When Milkman's mother Ruth finds her only antiphonal pleasure in nursing her boy well into his fourth year, a neighbor finally spies her through a window in a discovery that both weans and names her son. But even in the novel's description of Ruth's erotic pleasure in nursing, there is a premonition of how Milkman's later materialistic quest for gold might turn into a more soulful quest for mother-child-ness bonds: "She had the distinct impression that his lips were pulling from her a thread of light. It was as if she were a cauldron issuing spinning gold. Like the miller's daughter—the one who sat at night in a straw-filled room, thrilled with the secret power Rumpelstiltskin had given her: to see golden thread stream from her very own shuttle" (13). As Stephanie Demetrakopoulos has remarked, the "power and worth (gold)" that Ruth finds in nursing valorizes a systematically devalued experience (430). Here the milk (and *nyama*) of mother-child-ness bonds *is* gold. Likewise, Milkman is destined to seek revalorization of this "golden" semiotic realm (realized as presymbolic/countersymbolic "soul"). Marianne Hirsch's readings of Lacanian psychoanalysis bring her to point out that "Ruth unwittingly renames Milkman through her act of nursing, repossessing him from the symbolic, connecting him to her with a stream of milk, an alternative to the ink the fathers, white and black, use to write their children's names," and she adds that "the community engages in a similar act of repossession when they name their street 'Not Doctor Street' or their hospital 'No Mercy'" (155). Indeed, *Song of Solomon* might be best described as a text of soul repossession that will lead Milkman (and the reader) "to give up the shit that weighs you down" (179) in order to fly, not in evasion but in spirited possession of *nyama* or soul. Although Milkman's journey from his Michigan home to Pennsylvania, and finally to Shalimar, Virginia, begins as a conquistador-like, ever-dislocating quest for gold, the whole project transforms as he comes to value familial/soul connections in a Southern folk culture he once would have dismissed. In Shalimar, Virginia, where he found "Omar and Solomon shaking sacks of okra into peck baskets" (298), Milkman discovers an inventively veiled Gullah motherland transcending America with African flight and traces of Mecca. It is a place "down home" where you may know "your people."

From the two lines of its opening dedication, *Song of Solomon* seeks the powers of *fadenya* flight and the knowledge of *badenya* communication: "*The fathers may soar / And the children may know their names.*" As Morrison's "father-soaring" dedication suggests, her epic *Song* is concerned with the tensions of father-child-ness and mother-child-ness, dislocation and location, individual action and community stability. The novel celebrates the full range of play in these tensions, seen less as polar opposites than as a dialectic that when balanced is formative of healthy identity. In a narration of patrimony traceable to yet another Senegambian Muslim patriarch, Morrison encodes a deep countercritique of epic celebration of the heroic "flights" of male actors enabled by (and at the cost of) female grounding. *Song of Solomon* redirects epic notions of father-child-ness, heroism, manhood, and patrimony. Since Milkman's "Dead" patrimony (as received from his father) is a soul-killing power-crazed materialism, his heroism lies in his finding another way of being a man, another way of finding "gold." Like the Sunjata, this contemporary tale of the quest for identity demands that its hero open himself to people he had considered his inferiors: the women of his family, his lovers, and the rural folk of Shalimar, Virginia, whom he "hadn't found . . . fit enough or good enough to want to know their names" (266). After discovering that his grandfather Macon Dead "was one of those flying African children" that Solomon left behind in his transatlantic flight (325), Milkman gains access to his patrilineal means but still finds no patronym. The only clan name he arrives at comes from his grandmother's Cherokee side of the family: the Byrds. His grandmother Sing Byrd (Singing Bird) was indeed a *Bird* with transformative powers something like the Buffalo of Du, so any heritage of flight comes from both sides of the family and is a multivalent heritage of evasion ("marooning escape" from slavery and from family) and of spiritual power (transcendent spirituality and actual supernatural flight). As Susan Byrd tells Milkman after speaking about Solomon's leaving wife and family behind, "according to the story he wasn't running away. He was flying. . . . Like a bird" (322–23). Like Sumamuru Kante's final escape, like coastal Georgia slaves' transcendence, like the Cherokee Bird clan camouflaged in the mountains as Byrds, the soaring power described here goes beyond escapist flight—to reach ritual ascent enabled by immersion in *badenya* bonds so that "*the fathers may soar / and the children may know their names.*"

Gay Wilentz, who examines *Song of Solomon* in the context of women writers from Ghana and Nigeria, offers an insightful reading of Morrison's opening dedication: "[T]here is one group missing from the dedication whose presence is overpowering in the novel itself—the mothers," who teach language and bind cultures, and whose "discredited knowledge" is often "left out of recorded history" (85). While Wilentz underscores how bodies of occulted mother wit, "African values and African culture, exemplified in Pilate, are privileged in the text" (86), Wilfred D. Samuels points out (through an analogy that owes much to Alex Haley) that Pilate's "role as guide and educator—as pilot, as her name suggests—is that of griot" (15). The gifted burden of her role as spiritual pilot/griot is evident in her father's choice of her name, a choice made as that illiterate son of an African Muslim, with a respect for the calligraphy of scripture, "thumbed through the Bible, and since he could not read a word, chose a group of letters that seemed to him strong and handsome; saw in them a large figure that looked like a tree hanging in some princely but protective way over a row of smaller trees" (18). Through Pilate, Milkman will learn to acknowledge the sustaining power of mother-child-ness bonds and begin to answer the needs of those around him, maturing into the *badenya* role suggested by his name. She is the *nyamakala* pilot whose transmissions of her dead father's ghostly mumbling—"sing sing" and "You just can't fly off and leave a body" (208)—connect song, flight, and naming with the blues of abandonment, remorse, and transcendence.

Pilate, who "true to the palm oil that flowed in her veins . . . never had a visitor to whom she did not offer food before one word of conversation—business or social—began" (149), is the initiator into the novel's realm of semiotic openness. Her hospitable offerings of soft-boiled eggs, her use of herbal medicines sprinkled on Macon Dead's food to allow Milkman's conception, and her occult powers used to protect the newborn from his enraged father, all fit the patterns and motifs of powerful female "Answerers-of-Need" present in the Sunjata and repeated in African American tales and texts. True to the Sunjata, Milkman comes to understand the ancestral information veiled in Shalimar's ring-play song through an initiate's recognition of patterns of *nyama*. He first earns respect and goodwill from the men of Shalimar on a thoroughly humbling hunt. Lost and stumbling, he rests beneath a sweet gum tree and—in the manner of Jean Toomer's "Fern" and the Sunjata's Tarawere brothers hunting the Buffalo of Du—is possessed with openness to phenomena of all sorts, beginning with the sounds of hunting dogs: "[I]t was not language; it was what was there before language. Before things were written down" (278). Milkman "felt the sweet gum's surface roots cradling him like the rough but maternal hands of a grandfather," and as he listened "with his fingertips, to hear what, if anything, the earth had to say," he sensed the presence of his disturbed Michigan friend, Guitar, come to kill him (279). Milkman's initiation into self-possession resonates with Sunjata's overcoming of lameness and uprooting of the baobab; Milkman walked on the earth "like he belonged on it; like his legs were stalks, tree trunks, a part of his body that extended down down down into the rock and soil, and were comfortable there—on the earth and on the place where he walked. And he did not limp" (281). After his hunting initiation finally opens him to the community and to need-answering mutuality, the older men direct him to lodge with a woman named "Sweet" (a word that signifies the erotic through-out West Africa and the diaspora). Lorde's sense of an empathetic joy-shar-ing erotic is well conveyed in Morrison's declarative sentences extending the scene of Milkman and Sweet's lovemaking: "She sprinkled talcum on his feet. He straddled her behind and massaged her back. She put witch hazel on his swollen neck. He made up the bed. She gave him gumbo to eat. He washed the dishes. She washed his clothes and hung them out to dry. He scoured her tub. She ironed his shirt and pants. He gave her fifty dollars. She kissed his mouth. He touched her face. She said please come back. He said I'll see you tonight" (285). Milkman Dead, who had taken sexual ad-vantage of his cousin Hagar, who had stolen from his aunt Pilate, and who had received the repeated sacrifices of his mother and sisters, eventually shows himself to be capable of need-answering mutuality. That he shares this deep, mutual embodiment of spirit with Sweet, whom he would have dismissed earlier as a "whore," is striking.

In one deft simile, Morrison links the *nyama* of Milkman's newly trans-formed consciousness to residual folk means or *nya* of wielding it: "[T]he skin of shame that had rinsed away in the bathwater after having stolen from Pilate returned. . . . as thick and tight as a caul" (300). This emergent shame of infantile selfishness becomes a birth veil offering the second-sighted epiphany through which he might decipher his/Shalimar's ancestral song. Upon decoding Solomon's song, Milkman first feels its epic powers of flight, and then goes back to tell Sweet about his roots in "[t]hat flyin motherfuckin tribe" (328). Yet it can hardly come as a surprise to Sweet that an ancestral "Sugarman" would up and go. Drawing attention to the song's blues of aban-donment (and the "fucking over") of mother-child-ness bonds, she asks, "Who'd he leave behind? (328). Although he still doesn't fully "see," Milkman's response, "Everybody! . . .'O-o-o-o-o-o Solomon done fly, Solomon done gone / Solomon cut across the sky, Solomon gone home!" (328–29), calls attention to the song's multivalent renderings of "flight" and "home" and "homing." Clearly, this song of flight "back home" may be read as a hymn or blues of escape and/or as a shout of return to spiritual grounding. And home too is a fractal set of linkages running through biological, "elected" and historically/situationally forced mother-child-ness bonds connecting Milkman with "his people." Africa remains a rather distant homeland of the spirit, offering more of a source of means than any final destination.

The Afro-Creole music of *Song of Solomon*, as with Amelia Dawley's Mende funeral song and DuBois's "Mighty Myo" (*maayo*) figured as river of death, may finally call readers to dare numinous "soul" transition through the psychic abyss that would separate and further dislocate the ancestral, the living, and the unborn.[9] Though Morrison turns to yet another Senegambian (Fulbe) Muslim ancestor (via the *Drums and Shadows* information), no amount of scripturality or patronymics can navigate the New World's particularly challenging psychic no-man's land quite like the antiphonal, often polyrhythmic soul repertoire that Du Bois called "the singular spiritual heritage of the nation." *Song of Solomon's* slow accretion of "soul sounds" received from folk culture and revoiced by strong musicians like Du Bois, Toomer, Hurston, and Ellison, finally builds to a soaring grace that comes into its powers of transcendent flight through a deeply grounded knowledge. Morrison's ring-play reenvisioning of the coastal Georgia Mende song (Solomon's song) lies at the source of her Nobel Prize-winning efforts and offers a means of spiritual embodiment that runs counter to the dispiriting dislocations of plantation slavery and industrial/postindustrial consumerism. Afro-Creole music has indeed emerged as the singular means for stepping through the tragedies and transitions of a shared hemispheric/global modernity first navigated by New World Africans and their children. By reevaluating the means bequeathed by Afro-Creole legacies, *Song of Solomon* taps into the soul music that Paul Gilroy has called "a distinctive counter culture of modernity," built in large part from "the formation of a community of needs and solidarity which is magically made possible in the music itself" (36–37). So if Malcolm X credited Islam and a re-Africanized monumental patrimony for his powers of flight, Morrison turns to occulted vernacular means for an energy of action that might make a real difference.

When Milkman must in the end attempt to measure up to his Muslim ancestor's ability to fly (or to Pilate's final death-transformation from being a "Dead" back to being a "Bird"), he leaps from a cliff top to confront his murderous friend Guitar. The question of whether Milkman dies or actually flies is yet another instance of Morrison's semiotic openness, calling on the reader for response (Wilentz 98). As Milkman Dead enters more "open," more soulful modes of living, the reader too is called. Many of Morrison's readers have seen her as a magical realist, but more "open" readings might move past matters of contemporary literary "schools" or styles to step into the hermeneutic ring play of a real conjury immersed in Afro-Creole soul traditions that have navigated the convergence of forces such as Mandinka *nyama*, Yoruba *ashe*, Islamic *barakha*, and Baptist grace.[10] In a book filled with communication with the dead, a navel-less conjure woman, and veiled second sight, why should we finally pause at flight? We might question the ideological needs informing Sunjata's patrilineage from Mecca, Hurston's conflation of root and tale, and Haley's tracing of his Kinte genealogy, but if as engaged readers we ask, did Du Kamisa really wield shape-shifting Buffalo powers? can trees signify? and might Milkman—like Solomon and Sumamuru Kante before him—really soar? then given the *nyama*-laden contexts and sources of Morrison's *Song*, it seems unlikely that she would lead her readers to the cliff simply for a view of an Icarus-like fall. Rather, by building a sense of community that stretches our understanding of the limits of what is scriptable, *Song of Solomon* would have its readers know their potential for *fadenya* soaring, seeing that "If you surrendered to the air, you could ride it" (337).

Ultimately, *Song of Solomon's* panegyric to a Mande/Fulbe-informed Afro-Creole heritage works quite differently than somewhat similar projects in *Roots* and *The Autobiography of Malcolm X*. Morrison does not play by the rules of Western reason complicit with racial terror, nor does she locate ultimate authority and vision in scriptural traditions that would view writing (or monumental imperial culture) as the sign of reason. She draws authority from the Afro-Creole repertoires articulated by enslaved ancestors and rearticulated by soul visionaries like Du Bois, Toomer, Hurston, and Ellison. *Song of Solomon* fully inhabits a scriptural world, but like the griots' narration of the Sunjata, Morrison finds visionary means in a residual culture of resistance to the scriptural naming of enslaveable others. Seeking to restore soul balance through a uniquely female, uniquely individuated African American response to epic calling, *Song of Solomon* reassembles and rebalances the kind of dual agency offered by the Sunjata's epic-heroic patrimony and its occult(ed) celebration of the shape-shifting/life-giving powers of mother-child-ness and mother wit. Immersion in America's Africa-informed vernacular traditions offers a music, a value system, and an aesthetics that run counter to Enlightenment "reason" and counter to bourgeois Romantic obsessions (with self, genius, nationalism, the aesthetics of "purity" and dissociation from "nature"). Morrison reveals something of her artistic immersion in a countercultural, slavery-surviving energy of action when she has Guitar tell Milkman, "You can't get no pot of gold being reasonable. Can't nobody get no gold being reasonable. You have to be unreasonable" (183). Although Guitar eventually loses sanity by attempting to match the "logic" of white racial patriarchy, what Guitar and the Seven Days do makes perfect eye-for-eye, blood-for-blood sense, and it makes sense too that in the end he has become another gold-crazed "Western" murderer. Morrison would show us that it is a trap to play by the rules of a spirit-thieving Western "reason" and a trap to envision soul traditions as the polar opposite of Western modernity (to replace Eurocentrist rapist patrimony with a mirror image, "noble" Afrocentrism and the same old aesthetics of racial authenticity/purity/patriarchy). Instead, we might look to how the

energy of action of Afro-Creole soul traditions managed to navigate plantation slavery and dispiriting racism. Like the music the whole world already
dances to, the spiritedness of this long-resistant struggle calls for ever-emergent response to its energy of action. Africa is, without a doubt, a very real,
foundational source of African American and American cultures and consciousness. But in the end, our search for Sunjata might teach us to see—as
I believe the Sunjata epic itself may demonstrate—that any "static" search
for the distant material glories of Timbuktu or the scriptural "pure gold" of
an African Muslim patronym (as sign of reason) tends to play by the rules of
colonizing/enslaving systems and offers a less provocative/transfiguring "energy of action" than does receptivity to a much hybridized Afro-Creole *nyama*
and studied preparedness to handle it.

II

Bound Cultures/The Creolization of Dixie

N'Dioumane first saw their dust, then he saw the black bulk of
Nièye, the tawny coats of Gayndé and M'Bile, Ségue's and Bouki's
spots. He threw a palm-nut on the ground, crying, *'N'dèye yô!'*
('Mother!')

From the ground sprang up a palm tree, whose top nearly touched
the sky. He climbed it just as the beasts were upon him.

Birago Diop, *Les Contes d'Amadou Koumba* (1947),
translated, Dorothy S. Blair

4

"Two Heads Fighting"

African Roots, Geechee/Gombo Tales

The water breaking at your birth,
The cloth on which it spilled,
Behold that cloth before you!

Du Kamisa (the Buffalo-Woman),
from *The Epic of Son-Jara* as told by Fa-Digi Sisòkò

I

It took long months after my arrival as a Peace Corps fisheries volunteer in Senegal before my Wolof language skills began to coalesce enough for me to understand some of the tales told after the evening meal. But the narrators' performances had me listening even before I could follow the plots, which began to resonate with old cartoons like *Roadrunner* and *Bugs Bunny*. One night I described these cartoons, moving by association to the Macy Parade's giant cartoon balloons, and responding to questions about America's upcoming feast day, I vaguely described the family homecoming I would miss for the first time. A few days later, on Thanksgiving Day, as the group gathered to eat from the midday bowl, I sat down to a meal prepared to make me feel *chez moi*. In the bowl, on a bed of rice, were mounds of fresh Senegal River catfish stewed in okra, onion, hot peppers, and tomato sauce. If the catfish Creole served in Senegal seemed familiar, so too did the black-eyed peas served on New Year's Day for good luck, and the banjolike *halam* music frailed over the radio each night as the group told tales from a repertoire shared with Uncle Remus. I began to get a feel for the many ways Africans had shaped the culture into which I was born.

Although the word "creole" was used in the Caribbean and Latin America (including Louisiana and Florida) to signify people and things that were American born and bred, "creole," with its ever-present association with race, tends to refer to an Africa-informed New World presence. From El Inca Garcilaso de la Vega's writings on colonial Florida and Peru (1605, 1612) to George Washington Cable's *The Creoles of Louisiana* (1884), the word "creole" has been used to identify people, cultures, and languages that were born, nursed, and shaped in New World contact situations, and has been used to speak of a hybrid Americanness powerfully shaped by Africans. The New World Creole might thus be described as the true "true American," the one who is oriented not to Europe or Africa or pre-Columbian "First Nations" but to the full (often terrifying) New World mix, the one who hears America's music and speaks its language.[1]

Creole languages, created largely by enslaved Africans and their American-born children, are arguably the most American of languages, born from the enormous communicative need of New World contact situations. In North America, creole-speaking populations have resided in two important centers of African cultural dissemination: the Gullah coast of Carolina and Georgia, and Creole Louisiana. Significant to the Senegambian focus of my own telling of the American story, Gwendolyn Midlo Hall (1992) writes that Senegambians were the most important shapers of Louisiana Creole, and writers from Lorenzo Turner (1949) to Mervyn Alleyne (1980) and Charles Joyner (1984) have pointed to Senegambian impact upon the development of Gullah. In addition, the work of William Bascom (1992) points to Senegambia as an important source for many of the tales told in American vernacular and creole languages. The reasons for considerable Senegambian impact are numerous and will be considered in greater detail later in this chapter. Trade connections between Senegal and Louisiana—and to a lesser extent between Gambia and Carolina—played a large part, as did the fact that Senegal and Gambia were early sites in Africa for the development of French and English trade languages. Senegambians also came in relatively large numbers and as founding contingents to the rice-growing areas that became centers of North American creolization. They were in demand not only for knowledge of rice culture but also for service as overseers and domestic servants. Because of their numbers, their roles in early contact situations, and their often intermediary positions, Senegambians were able to shape the creolization of American culture.

As Twining and Baird have recently stated (borrowing from the work of the Caribbean poet/historian Kamau Brathwaite), linguistic models of creolization may be extended to see "creolization as a process not only in the formation of language but of society as well" (vii). I will use the examples of the Sea Islands and Creole Louisiana—locations with recognized Afro-Creole languages—as models for a cultural process occurring throughout the Deep South and throughout America. From Brathwaite's understanding of creolization as "a cultural action—material, psychological and spiritual" (296), I will turn to Senegambian narratives for sources to show that Afro-Creole narratives from Louisiana and the Sea Islands have transmitted something of Senegambian *nyama*. We may see that Senegambian energies of action have moved through Afro-Creole centers such as New Orleans and Charleston into the entire South—and finally into modern urban America—and have helped shape an American vernacular that has become a powerful agent of cultural action throughout the world.

We need not see Gullah as a remnant of a once fully creolized African American English (as Stewart 1967, 1968, and Dillard 1972, have argued) in order to use creole theory as a model from which we may approach African contributions to American vernacular language and culture. Of course, it would be a huge mistake to suppose that Creole cultures from such important port cities as New Orleans, Charleston, and Savannah were isolated from the development of vernacular language and culture in America. But going beyond diachronic patterns of descent, we might also see these Creole cultures as synchronic models or analogues for what was (and is) happening elsewhere in the South and in America, given different mixes of the same Europeans and Africans that shaped the culture(s) of Charleston and Savannah. And because the French/Spanish background of New Orleans presents an anomaly to patterns of Anglophone development in America, Louisiana tests the possibilities of synchronic analogy and also supports diachronic arguments for West African impact upon American culture since it is not the European elements that colonial Louisiana shares with South Carolina (and say Maryland); rather, it is the African (and particularly the Senegambian) elements that are shared.

Creole societies are, in the words of Michael Montgomery, "cauldrons of crisscrossing and competing cultures, nationalities, and influences" (13), so I shall not pursue a monogenetic cultural genealogy claiming unmediated Senegambian ancestry. But given that widespread cultural differences within Africa make it more feasible to focus on continuities from *some* African groups and regions rather than from Africans in general (Mufwene 1994), I will focus once again on one significant African region—the one that I know best. As I refer to Senegambian models and sources for American narratives, we must keep in mind that other African peoples, as well as Europeans and indigenous peoples, contributed to the formation of creole languages and to repertoires of creole and vernacular narrative. After all, the word "creole" was first used to mark the cultural hybridity of peoples of African and/or European descent who were born in the Americas. Creolization was understood to be a process of Americanization. Given America's cultural mix, one of the important subtexts of my argument is that the boundaries of the African cultural diaspora extend beyond racial boundaries. There is no Americanness separate from the New World's foundational African presence. To varying degrees, all Americans can turn to Wolof, Mande, and Fulbe narratives with a sense of being descendants. So it is to the narratives that I now turn.

II

One of the strengths of West African folk narrative is the way it serves as "a mode of moral inquiry" exploring relationships "between orthodox and fictional images of the world" (Jackson 1). Even when they support orthodox positions, the narratives "inspire reflection upon subjects which are usually taken for granted, and they encourage people to express preferences and to make judgements upon matters which are normally decided for them" (53). While the often subversive patterns of the trickster tales traveled exceptionally well from Africa to the Americas, more orthodox moralistic tales are common in both Senegal and the Deep South. Tales concerning the proper treatment of orphans offer a good example of the moralistic fable. Motherless children are placed in a precarious position when they must compete in *fadenya* rivalries with their half-siblings without having the benefit of *badenya* support, and typically in these tales, an orphan girl is sent by an abusive stepmother into the wilderness on a dangerous mission. Outside of the community, the spurned orphan reveals her well-bred nature in a confrontation with a bush spirit or old sorceress, who then supplies the girl with gifts that change her status back home.

A moralistic fable with regional variants, the Wolof "Kumba-with-a-Mother and Motherless-Kumba," tells how the orphaned Kumba is sent by her stepmother on a dangerous wilderness journey on which she encounters an amazingly disfigured old woman. Expressing no open-mouthed rudeness, Kumba greets the woman courteously as "Maam dey" (Grandmother) and is asked to spend the night. The woman hands her a bone that Kumba obediently places in a pot, which fills with meat. Kumba is then given a grain of millet that she pounds in a mortar that fills with couscous. Before parting the next day, Kumba receives three eggs along with instructions for breaking them in the forest. Breaking her eggs as instructed, orphan Kumba finds that gold, cattle, and attendants emerge to make her return to the village truly regal. Her envious stepmother then sends her own daughter Kumba on the journey. This second Kumba confronts the old woman rudely, asking, "Old woman, are you a person?" The girl refuses both the bone and the single grain of millet. The next morning, after the gift of three eggs, rude Kumba confuses her instructions, and the cattle that burst forth stampede and kill her (Kesteloot and Mbodj 24–31).

In Louisiana the tale of the two Kumbas was told to Alcée Fortier in Louisiana Creole French (also known as "Gombo") and was published in

1895 in a version remarkably true to the Wolof tale. The most notable departure from the Wolof tale is the "coloring" of the two Louisiana girls' names:

There was once a lady who had two daughters; they were called Rose and Blanche. Rose was bad, and Blanche was good; but the mother liked Rose better, although she was bad, because she was her very picture. She would compel Blanche to do all of her work, while Rose was seated in her rocking chair. One day she sent Blanche to the well to get some water in a bucket. When Blanche arrived at the well, she saw an old woman who said to her: "Pray, my little one, give me some water; I'm very thirsty." "Yes, aunt," said Blanche, "here is some water;" and Blanche rinsed her bucket, and gave her good fresh water to drink. "Thank you, my child, you are a good girl; God will bless you."

A few days after, the mother was so bad to Blanche that she ran away into the woods. She cried, and knew not where to go, because she was afraid to return home. She saw the same old woman, who was walking in front of her. "Ah! my child, why are you crying? What hurts you?" "Ah, aunt, mamma has beaten me, and I am afraid to return to the cabin." "Well, my child, come with me; I will give you supper and a bed; but you must promise me not to laugh at anything which you will see." She took Blanche's hand, and they began to walk in the wood. As they advanced, the bushes of thorns opened before them, and closed behind their backs. A little further on, Blanche saw two axes, which were fighting; she found that very strange, but she said nothing. They walked further, and behold! it was two arms which were fighting; a little further, two legs; at last, she saw two heads which were fighting, and which said: "Blanche, good morning, my child; God will help you." At last they arrived at the cabin of the old woman, who said to Blanche: "Make some fire, my child, to cook the supper;" and she sat down near the fireplace, and took off her head. She placed it on her knees and began to louse herself. Blanche found that very strange; she was afraid, but she said nothing. The old woman put back her head in its place and gave Blanche a large bone to put in the pot. Lo! in a moment the pot was full of meat.

She gave Blanche a grain of rice to pound with the pestle, and thereupon the mortar became full of rice. After they had taken their supper, the old woman said to Blanche: "Pray, my child, scratch my back." Blanche scratched her back, but her hand was all cut, because the old woman's back was covered with broken glass. When she saw that Blanche's hand was bleeding, she only blew on it, and the hand was cured.

When Blanche got up the next morning, the old woman said to her: "You must go home now, but as you are a good girl I want to make you a present of the talking eggs. Go to the chicken house; all the eggs which say 'Take me,' you must take them; all those which will say 'Do not take me,' you must not take. When you will be on the road, throw the eggs behind your back to break them."

As Blanche walked, she broke the eggs. Many pretty things came out of those eggs. It was now diamonds, now gold, a beautiful carriage, beautiful dresses. When she arrived at her mother's, she had so many fine things that the house was full of them. Therefore her mother was very glad to see her. The next day she said to Rose: "You must go to the woods to look for this same old woman; you must have fine dresses like Blanche."

Rose went to the woods, and she met the old woman, who told her to come to her cabin, but when she saw the axes, the arms, the legs, the heads, fighting, and the old woman taking off her head to louse herself, she began to laugh and to ridicule everything she saw. Therefore the old woman said: "Ah! my child, you are not a good girl; God will punish you." The next day she said to Rose: "I don't want to send you back with nothing; go to the chicken house, and take the eggs which say 'Take me.'"

Rose went to the chicken house. All the eggs began to say: "Take me," "Don't take me;" "Take me," "Don't take me." Rose was so bad that she said: "Ah, yes, you say 'Don't take me,' but you are precisely those I want." She took all the eggs which said, "Don't take me," and she went away with them.

As she walked, she broke the eggs, and there came a quantity of snakes, toads, frogs, which began to run after her. There were even a quantity of whips, which whipped her. Rose ran and shrieked. She arrived at her mother's so tired that she was not able to speak. When her mother saw all the beasts and the whips which were chasing her, she was so angry that she sent her away like a dog, and told her to go live in the woods. (Fortier 117–19)

Along with encouraging openness to wild forces or gifts of the spirit, the Senegambian fables must have provided useful lessons in Louisiana concerning the need for discretion. And it is likely that tales such as this served as creolizing vehicles through which the planter class learned its famous manners (Williamson, *The Crucible of Race* 39). The tale works to present good manners and open-heartedness not as a limiting social orthodoxy but as a kind of agency that enables action.

But in West Africa, as we have seen in the Sunjata epic's Buffalo of Du story, Mande hunters' narratives show how a symbiotic balance between impeccable manners and openness to "wild" agencies allows the hero to navigate a wilderness where he gains blessings and eludes curses. Often the means by which the hunter-hero is saved from an attacking animal is a gift of eggs from a witch-woman to whom he has offered food. Once thrown, the eggs become roadblocks that ensure safe flight. These same wilderness roadblocks may be traced to mark paths that we can begin to follow through a psychic wilderness that closed back around the fables and the history of their narration.

In the Buffalo of Du narrative, for example, a shape-shifting Buffalo-Woman, after being fed "yesterday's rice" and "many eggs" by two hunters advised by a jinn, gives the hunters the means by which they may kill her, including eggs that—after being tossed—burst open to become a wilderness and then finally a lake to slow her pursuit. Similar occult means of escape turn up in narratives told by descendants of the many peoples who were once vassals of the expanding Mali empire. Ali Sawse's Wolof variant has Sunjata befriend the Buffalo-Woman, cook for her, and—in apparent transgression of hunters' prohibitions against sex before the hunt—even sleep with her before she offers the items of her destruction: "[T]hrow the egg between us and it will turn into a great sea. There I will die" (Ames 78).

In his narration of the epic of Askia Mohammad, the Songhay griot Nouhou Malio recounts a similar escape that the Askia makes from the Bargantche, a people whom he cannot defeat in battle, "for he has in his stomach the milk of the Bargantche" from his mother's servant who nursed him and with whose people he now shares a "milk bond" relationship (Hale, *Scribe* 211). Having violated this milk bond relationship, the Askia receives the means to escape the Bargantche from his mother, who informs her son that he should throw an egg behind him and "[t]hat egg will become a river that will be a barrier between them" (211–13). From the broken eggshells of these epic "roadblocks," we might find moments of recognition of the gravity of American violation of milk bonds.

The Mande/Kuranko narrative "The Origin of the Yimbe Drum" provides what may be the most comprehensive model for a body of folktales that entered American folk repertoires. In the Kuranko tale the young hero's fearlessness in search of the *yimbe* drum earns the respect of a bush creature who gives him an oracular string fetish known as a *fele*. The bush spirit tells the young hero, "Whatever you want to do, first consult it. . . . say 'Sarafin Mara inse,' then it will reply 'Sedu Mara haba' and tell you what you want to know" (Jackson 160). Along with the *fele*, the spirit gives the young man "some charcoal, an egg, a bamboo cane, and a stone"(160). The hero succeeds in stealing the drum from a group of hyenas, and when they pursue him, the *fele* offers instructions: "'Sedu Mara haba, drop the egg.' It becomes an enormous lake which crossed the world from east to west. The hyenas could not cross it" (162). The shape-shifting leader of the hyenas, however, transforms into a beautiful young woman and crosses the lake to become the hero's lover. In spite of his mother's warnings against his new lover, the young hero welcomes her and is persuaded to journey into the wilderness with her, where she reverts to hyena form and is joined by her comrades. Only after climbing a series of trees (which the hyenas saw with their teeth) and offering his long-neglected *fele* a doubled sacrifice does he manage to kill his pursuers by following the oracular fetish's instructions.

The *fele* string fetish, widely used by Kuranko people, may be alive in the memory of Sapelo Island, Georgia, resident Cornelia Bailey, who has described her grandmother's "Nubie" in terms similar to the *fele*: "The Nubie is a weight at the end of a piece of string. And it's like a modern day Ouija board. The string is about 12 inches long and there's a weight on the end and it's like power of concentration. You hold it in the center of your hand and you ask it a question and it will start slowly going back and forth, going this way and that and that's the Nubie" (Bledsoe 31–32). Although the Nubie no longer directs folk to throw eggs behind them to escape pursuing forces, we can see that the escapes it directed in Africa were narrated repeatedly in antebellum America. Long occulted forces of civility and psychic wilderness emerge from Creole retellings of African hunters' tales. Indeed, these tales probably represent the strongest surviving core of an African epic-heroic tradition in America.

A wide body of hunters' tales, featuring flight from a shape-shifting bush woman, eggs tossed as impediments, escape in a tree, and assistance from the hunters' dogs or an oracular fetish entered Creole repertoires. As William Bascom has noted, the tale type that best matches this body of Senegambian tales is Type 315A, *The Cannibal Sister*, which consists of four parts: 1) A Princess Becomes a Cannibalistic Ogress; 2) The Captive Brother; 3) Magic Flight; and 4) Escape in the Tree. Working with motifs from part four of the tale—"Dogs Rescue Master in Tree Refuge"—Bascom cited fifty-eight versions from Africa, fifty-seven from the Americas, and one from Spain (158–59). Among several versions cited from Senegal and Mali, Bascom refers to Birago Diop's literary adaptation of a Wolof tale in *Les Contes d'Amadou Koumba* ("La Biche et les Chasseurs"), which features a hunter who falls for a group of shape-shifting animal seductresses intent upon killing the dogs that make him such a successful hunter. In the end it is the betrayed dogs, miraculously restored to life by the hunter's mother, who rescue him after he has been treed. It is this basic prototype, repeated in

Africa from the Sunjata epic to Birago Diop's Wolof tales, that we find retold everywhere that Africans were enslaved in the Americas.

The wild energies and carnal vision of the West African hunters' tales find their most celebrated retelling in Joel Chandler Harris's "The Little Boy and His Dogs," as Uncle Remus narrates a boy's encounter with two panther women who lure him to the outskirts of town.[2] When the frightened boy seeks refuge in a tree, the shape-shifters use their tails as axes to fell the tree; the boy then utilizes three magic eggs to gain time to shout the names of his dogs, who arrive to devour his attackers. In another Harris narrative, "The Man and the Wild Cattle," traces of the Sunjata Buffalo of Du narrative beckon from an epic past: "Dey wuz a man one time what had a bow en arrers dat done 'im some good, but dat time gone by" (524–25). He hunts "horned cattle" reminiscent of buffalo, and his two dogs Minny-Minny-Morack and Follamalinska help him to be so successful that one of the cows "[s]he 'low she gwine ter change inter a young 'oman en make 'im marry 'er" (526). When the newly married hunter eventually regains interest in hunting, his wife ties his dogs, and in the wilderness he is surrounded by the vengeful herd. Taking refuge in his third and last magic tree, the hunter calls his dogs: "'Minny-Minny-Morack! Follamalinska!'" while the cattle's axes "talk, 'Tree-down! Tree-down! Trip-trip-tree-down!'" (529). Finally breaking loose, the dogs enable the hunter to kill the cattle, including his wife, "a snow white cow."

A Louisiana Creole version of the tale makes its connections to Senegambian precedents even more clear. The Creole hunter calls his dogs "Miblé, Toumadaie, and N'Daye" (Ancelet 35), names that return us directly to Birago Diop's Wolof fable. The Creole dog "Miblé" resonates with the Wolof "M'Bile," the antelope of Diop's title; and the Creole "N'daye" comes from the Wolof "N'deye," the "mother" upon whom Diop's hunter repeatedly calls when seeking help.

Another Louisiana Creole tale, "Compair Taureau et Jean Malin," collected by Alcée Fortier, features Senegambian-style pursuit sequences and Sunjata lore. Fortier's narrator tells how the orphan Jean Malin discovers a bull in the pose of Islamic prayer:

> Ein jou, bo matin quand Jean Malin té couri cherché di bois pou limin di fé, li oua Compair Taureau dans parc qui té a genoux et pi li té apé dit:—Bouhour, madjam, fat madjam, djam, djam, djara, djara, et pi tout d'ein coup taureau tourné n'homme et li prend marché vini coté so madame. (Fortier 8)

> One day, early in the morning, when Jean Malin went to get some wood to light his fire, he saw Compair Taureau on his knees, and

saying: "Bouhour, Madjam, fat Madjam, djam, djam, djara, djara,"
and then, all at once, the bull became a man and went to see his
lady. (Fortier 9)

After exposing the man as Compair Taureau, Jean Malin must then protect
himself against an overpowering opponent set on revenge, and therefore so-
licits a *gris-gris* from Compair Lapin (Brer Rabbit). When the bull later attacks, Jean tosses his *gris-gris* of three eggs—one by one—from his refuge in
a tree, butchering Compair Taureau bit by bit with each tossed egg. Then in a
scene much like one in Fa-Digi Sisòkò's Sunjata epic, Jean utters incantations
that restore the bull's butchered pieces to life: "Alors li dit paroles yé, la téte et
pi bras sauté après corps la et n'homme la tournin taureau encore" (12). ["He
said the magic words and the head and the arms jumped to the body, and the
man became a bull again and galloped away in great haste" (13).][3]
　　African American hunters' tales guard what is probably the clearest
remnant of Senegambian epic energies of action: the extreme *fadenya*/wil-
derness orientation of the hunter-hero's world, and the core of the Sunjata
epic itself—the encounter between the second-sighted, occult-empowered
Tarawere hunters and the shape-shifting Buffalo-Woman. The above-men-
tioned Creole tale, "Compair Taureau et Jean Malin," is interesting for its
signal deviations from Senegambian pattern. The shape-shifting beast is a
man, and we have our epic hero (Jean Malin) and the animal trickster (Brer
Rabbit) occupying the same ground. As Judith Gleason points out, the hunters' tales differ from the animal fables that test ethics from a more human,
more civil space: "Hunters venture further. Sprung from experiences deeper
in the forest, involving creatures farmers haven't observed, their fables turn
fabulous, pitting a human hero against shape-shifting demonic forces" (179).
In America, the African epic hero would give way to the animal trickster
and to the scriptural figure of Moses. But Sunjata lore lingers in these hunters' tales fetched back from the daring, occult exploits of singular heroes in
the wilderness, a realm of experience limited in slavery mostly to maroons
and recast perhaps in the urban wilderness of "The Signifying Monkey" and
in "badmen" like Stagger Lee. If the Afro-Creole tales played a role in teaching manners to an often pathologically materialistic planter class, the tales
also emparted something of their open-eyed, wilderness-informed psychic
energy to an American vernacular culture hungry for kernels of psychic
truth in a pre-Freudian Victorian era.
　　In a contemporary America obsessed with airbrushed images of unreal beauty, we would do well to follow the Senegambian means of escape
offered in a series of Creole "Marriage to the Devil" tales analogous to the
Wolof fable "The Woman Who Wanted a Husband Without a Scar" (Kesteloot
and Mbodj 48–53). In a South Carolina version, a vain young woman who

vows not to marry anyone with a scratch on his back finds herself wed to a shape-shifting tiger (Christensen 10–14). The tale's American analogues often allow for the bride's escape via the familiar Senegambian pattern of miraculous eggs tossed to create wilderness roadblocks. A coastal Georgia Gullah version, "Mary Bell," as told by Charles Spalding Wylly's "Nurse Baba," has Mary Bell escape her marriage to the devil by throwing an egg behind her, "and straightway there ran a large river between them" (Wylly 153). And in a Louisiana Gombo French version, "Mariaze Djabe," the bride escapes by throwing a series of eggs: "Li cassé ein lote dezef, ein gros fleuve poussé" (Fortier 72). ["She broke another egg: a large river appeared" (73).] Thoroughly creolized in language, plot, and performance, the Creole "Marriage to the Devil" tales marry West African and West European narratives. And they work to caution us against a demonic perfectionist-idealism and its canons of unreal, pathological purity.

III

Just as the narrative content of Creole tales reveals Senegambian sources, the very structure of the languages in which the tales were told in America also draws deeply from West Africa. In Louisiana "Gombo," as is the case with many West African languages, verbs are often uninflected, are marked preverbally for aspect rather than postverbally for tense. There is relatively little distinction of gender or number. Philip Baker has identified Senegambia as a source for many of the words of African origin in Louisiana Creole (128), but Wolof and Mande influence on the structure of Louisiana Gombo French may be far more significant than the survival of Mande or Wolof lexicon. Nevertheless, at times we may find both grammatical and lexical analogies between Louisiana Creole and Senegambian languages such as Wolof; for example, in the Gombo "Marriage to the Devil" tale the plural marker "choal *ye*" (horses) is analogous to the Wolof "fas *yi*" (horses) of "The Woman Who Wanted a Husband Without a Scar." Gwendolyn Midlo Hall writes that Louisiana Creole "developed from a Portuguese-based pidgin that had been relexified with French vocabulary in Senegal" (192). Hall points to early Louisiana court records demonstrating that some slaves were arriving from Senegal already speaking the Creole that seems to have developed in France's old Senegalese trading ports of St. Louis and Goree. And in his *Louisiana Creole Dialect* (1942), James F. Broussard also claims that Gombo was developed in large part by Senegalese. Gombo subsequently became a mother tongue not only for most of South Louisiana's black population but also for many of its whites. Like many of the elite, Broussard learned Creole from his childhood nurse and spoke the language exclusively until the age of seven.

The Afro-Creole language known as Gullah or Geechee developed similarly in the South Carolina and Georgia low country, where labor-intensive rice plantations contributed to strong African cultural retention. As with Gombo French, the lexicon of Gullah is derived primarily from the colonizers' superstrate, yet Lorenzo Turner (1949) recorded so many words and narratives of Mande origin that his work has led many creolists to argue that Mende (a Sierra Leonian Mande language) probably made the most significant contribution to Gullah.[4] While the Mende/Mande connection may be the most significant, Patricia Jones-Jackson has noted continuing Gullah use of many Wolof words, as well as use of calques—direct translation of idioms—like "day clean" (Wolof *berset*), signifying "dawn." Many Wolof expressions have entered our national vocabulary, but Gullah-specific Wolof words such as "nyam" (to eat), and calques like "day clean" continue to be used in the low country. As with Louisiana Gombo, Gullah pronouns tend to make no distinction between gender, using "e" to serve for masculine, feminine, and neutral gender, and as subject, object, and indicator of possession. Verbs are uninflected. Charles Joyner writes that the Gullah verbal system's "distinction between continuing and momentary actions (aspect) rather than . . . the relative time of the action (tense)" retains grammatical patterns of West African languages like Mandinka (200). Gullah concern with aspect over tense and the language's unchanging verb stem forms appear in "De Debble an May Belle" as the devil's horse asks May Belle: "Enty you know who you marry ter? You husbun duh de Debble, an wen eh saterfy long you eh gwine bex you an kill you same luk eh done kil dem tarruh wife wuh eh bin hab befo eh bring you yuh" (Jones 95).

It is to the arguments over creole language formation that I wish to turn in order to develop a lens through which we might reread American cultural and literary performance. For if we are to understand creolization as a broad-based cultural action (most easily identifiable in linguistics, but moving—like language itself—to touch every cultural action), then we can profit from the work of linguists who have pioneered creole theory. Louisiana Gombo French and the Gullah of coastal South Carolina, Georgia, and northeast Florida belong to the family of Atlantic Creoles, languages created by enslaved Africans and their American-born children. These languages grew rapidly from the enormous communicative need of New World contact situations, becoming more elaborate as they became the primary languages of the community's communication.

Like most Atlantic Creoles, French Creole and Gullah share similarities of grammatical structure, phonology, and usage of calques, while most but not all of the lexicon is derived from the superstrate (colonial) languages. The dominance of European items in the lexicons of most Atlantic Creoles has led a few superstratists like Chaudenson (1979) to argue that

Atlantic Creoles developed from European colonials' restructuring of their own dialectical varieties into a language like the "français approximatif" that he claims served as the model for Haitian slaves. Arguing against this dialectologist position, substratists posit African roots for Atlantic Creole languages. Although West African lexical impact upon Gullah and Louisiana Creole is demonstrable (see Turner 1949, and Baker 1993), it is in the area of grammatical structure, verb aspect, phonology, conversational formulae, and signifying strategies such as counterlanguage that arguments for strong, even controlling contribution of African substrate languages have been built.

Following Sylvain's work on Haitian Creole (1936) and Turner's work in Gullah (1949), Mervyn Alleyne has been among the most persuasive proponents of the African substrate hypothesis with regard to the genesis of creoles in the New World. In *Comparative Afro-American* (1980), Alleyne makes the case that creole languages were created in a process through which the West African languages spoken by slaves were transformed in contact with European colonial languages. He sees Atlantic Creoles as West African languages lexified by European language contact and argues for a high degree of African linguistic and cultural continuity in the New World. Alleyne argues for the strong influence of speakers from the Senegambian region, site of early European-African contacts, and emphasizes the controlling role of Mande and Kwa languages in the African substrate of Atlantic Creoles (146–47). In an essay entitled "Continuity versus Creativity in Afro-American Language and Culture," Alleyne describes the creativity of creole languages and cultures as "inventiveness within a tradition" (179).

A convergent, componential hypothesis of creole genesis that takes account of the role of African substrate languages, European superstrates, and the constraining effects of Derek Bickerton's "Universal Grammar" has been proposed by Ian Hancock, who stresses the particularity of individual creoles, arguing that each creole arises from its own specific linguistic and historical gumbo in an "ongoing process" of negotiation with received "ingredients" (187). Hancock's understanding of the way "convergence" of ingredients works to encourage their retention may help us to understand and identify the persistence of Afro-Creole cultural practices that have long been masked by the presence of European analogues: "[W]here syntactic patterns happen to be shared by some, or all, of the input languages, nothing new needs to be learned, and convergence of functions will help to ensure their retention in the emerging linguistic system" (187). Too often we assume that European precedents for American cultural practices show automatic and absolute causal linkage when African, American Indian, or other traditions may have contributed something to the convergent mix of American traditions.

Salikoko Mufwene has also argued persuasively for "a mutually en-
riching coexistence" of the substrate, dialectologist, and universalist hy-
potheses (*Africanisms* 192). In his essay in *The Crucible of Carolina* (1994),
Mufwene writes that "[m]ore and more scholars assume that the structures
of AAE [African American English], Gullah, and CECs [Caribbean English
Creoles] have been determined to varying extents by both the African languages of the slaves who produced them and the colonial nonstandard English varieties of the Europeans the slaves interacted with on the plantations"
(44). And in *Africanisms in Afro-American Language Varieties* (1993) he
emphasizes componential issues such as "the proportion of speakers of different languages," "the rate of change over time of the population ratios,"
and the "founder principle . . . since the ethnolinguistic makeup of the
plantation community at the formative stage of its creole must have determined a great deal of its system" (198, 12). Stepping between intensely
ideological Eurocentric/Afrocentric poles of opposition, creolists like
Mufwene and Hancock call attention to the kinds of "componential" his-
torical/geographic variables that close readers of American literature and
culture would do well to consider.

If we are to regard Senegambian cultures as being powerful, if not
always dominant, substrate components in North American creolization,
then we must account for the sociohistorical conditions that would have
allowed transmission of language, narratives, and a base semiotics or nor-
mative matrix that Herskovits called a "grammar of culture" (81). We might
ask if Senegambians played an important role in first contacts between Europeans and black Africans. David Dalby has noted that Wolof speakers,
due to their geographic location as the closest black African people to Europe (as well as to North America), "were frequently employed as interpreters or mariners during early European voyages along the African coast"
(138). Senegal and the Gambia were important locations for the development of French and English pidgins, and Senegalese must have played a
strong role in the development of an earlier West African Portuguese pidgin; the first encounter with black Africa in Portugal's national epic *The
Lusiads* (1572) finds dark-skinned natives "who dwell by the Senegal River
with its chill, dark current" and the kingdoms of "Jalofo, where the Negroes
are split into different tribal communities; Mandinga, through whose vast
territory the Gambia winds its sinuous way to the Atlantic and where the
natives traded gold with us" (Camoens 123). Senegalese encounters with
Iberian culture predate Portuguese maritime contact, for as Gwendolyn Midlo
Hall has pointed out (29), Senegambia was a launching ground for the
Almoravide empire that ruled Spain and that is represented as having sent
"all the Negro tribes" into battle against the hero of *La chanson de Roland*:
"[A]ccursed tribesmen / As black as ink from head to foot their hides are, /

With nothing white about them but their grinders" (Sayers 125). Given the power of Senegambian drumming and the long exchange of musical instruments and styles between Senegambians and North Africans, it is likely that Senegambians from ancient Tekrur and Ghana were among those striking fear into the hearts of the companions of the hero of *El Cid* (1140): "The drums are sounding through the ranks of the Moors and many of those Christians marveled much at the sound for they had come lately to the war and never heard drums. Don Diego and Don Fernando marveled more than any; they would not have been there if the choice had been theirs" (Merwin 209). Already the Almoravides, along with their Senegambian slaves, vassals, and soldiers, had left a strong trace of black Africa upon Europe (see Bernard Lewis 69), and during the early days of European exploration and establishment of the slave trade, "Wolof speakers from Senegambia may have served as interpreters . . . lending a strong Wolof cast to the emerging pidgin" (Joyner, *Down by the Riverside* 204).

We might also ask if Senegambians arrived in North America in particularly large numbers and if they were part of a founding contingent of Africans in America. According to Michael Gomez's figures, Senegambians made up only about 14.5 percent of slaves imported into North America, with another 15.8 percent coming from Sierra Leone, from which many captive Mande speakers and Fulbe/Fula peoples disembarked (*Exchanging* 29). Recent calculations tabulated from *The Trans-Atlantic Slave Trade* database (compiled by David Eltis et al 1999) show the figures for Atlantic slave trade voyages coming from Senegambia to be 59.1 percent for Maryland, 25.2 percent for Virginia, 26.5 percent for the Carolinas, and 33.3 percent for Georgia.[5] Clearly, Senegambians constitute an absolutely crucial part of the mix in the Virginia/Chesapeake foundational heartland of North America. Philip D. Morgan writes that "slaves from two regions—Senegambia and the Bight of Biafra—constituted about three-quarters of the Africans arriving in the Chesapeake" (62) and that Senegambia "dominated the Maryland trade in the third quarter of the eighteenth century" (64). While Virginia and Maryland represent the very foundations of Anglo-American plantation slavery, nothing in their relatively slow patterns of development could match the rapid and intense Africanization of South Carolina and Georgia during the rice boom that began in South Carolina around 1710 and in Georgia with the introduction of slavery in 1750. The Charleston and Savannah markets—the focal points of Gullah culture emergent from the region's rice culture—were well known for preferring slaves from the Senegambia, a rice-producing region. Given the Charleston market's preference for Senegambians, British merchants associated South Carolina with the region of Gambia and "coupled Gambia with South Carolina more than with any other region" (Littlefield 20–21). And during the late-eighteenth-century foundational period of slavery in the Georgia colony, "large numbers were carried directly to Georgia from Gambia, Senegal, and Sierra Leone" (Smith 94). The situation in Louisiana during the early eighteenth century was similar but even more striking. Gwendolyn Midlo Hall reports that "[t]wo-thirds of the slaves brought to Louisiana by the French slave trade came from Senegambia," due in part to administrative ties and a trade monopoly that the *Compagnie des Indes* held in both Senegal and Louisiana (29). Rice was an early concern in Louisiana, too; in fact, "captains of the first two ships that brought African slaves to Louisiana in 1719 were instructed to purchase three or four barrels of rice for seeding and several blacks who knew how to cultivate rice" (Hall 122). Shaping the foundation of French Louisiana, and central to the rice boom that was foundational to the emergence of a Caribbean-style Creole culture in South Carolina and Georgia, Senegambians were significant cofounders of a creolized American culture. They came to be the preferred slaves in much of the South because of their perceived "tractability and superior intelligence" (Broussard ix), and because of their expertise with rice culture, indigo, cotton, and livestock (see Wood 28–62).

Senegambians were present in significant numbers and were in high demand in the important slave markets of Charleston, Savannah, and New Orleans; there is evidence that enslaved Senegambians were placed in positions of power or agency that would have encouraged transmission of Mande, Fulbe, Wolof, or generalized areal patterns. Southern planters seem to have preferred Senegambians over other Africans as house servants (see Holloway 12–14 and Hall 40–41). A Savannah woman chose Koomba Johnson—likely either Wolof or of Wolof ancestry—from over two hundred Georgia slaves to be her personal servant and wrote with pride and delight of Koomba's beauty and elegant sense of style (W. Johnson 93). There is evidence that Wolof women, in particular, were frequently established as concubines, even sometimes as wives of American planters (see Hall 40, and Schafer 8–31). In *Le Mulâtre*, Louisiana's Victor Séjour writes of a slave auction at which "the offering is a young Senegalese woman, so beautiful that from every mouth leaps the exclamation: 'How pretty!' Everyone there wants her for his mistress" (288). Senegambian men also tended to be placed in relatively powerful positions as drivers or overseers of plantations in low-country Carolina and Georgia, where they might be the sole managers of agricultural production during the warm-weather fever season when whites moved to summer homes. Salih Bilali, a Muslim from the Fulbe Massina region of Mali and a plantation manager on St. Simons Island in Georgia, was in a strong position as intermediary in lines of communication between his master, James Hamilton Couper, and the nearly four hundred slaves placed under his charge. Couper praised Bilali in a brief but amazingly respectful biography of his foreman that included a "Foulah" vocabulary, notes on rice-culture in Bilali's native Massina, and the assertion that "I have several times left him for months, in charge of the plantation, without an overseer; and on each occasion, he has conducted the place to my entire satisfaction" (Hodgson, *Notes* 69). Lest we doubt Salih Bilali's ability to make his "Foulah" [Fulfulde] language a powerful presence on the plantations under his control, Couper states that "[t]here are about a dozen negroes on this plantation, who speak and understand the Foulah language; but with one exception, they appear not to have been native born Foulahs; and to have acquired the language, by having been for sometime in servitude among that nation" (68). A sizeable Senegambian Muslim community lived along the Georgia coast—particularly on Sapelo Island, where Salih Bilali's Fulbe co-religionist and friend Bilali Mahomet had even stronger impact upon the over four hundred slaves under his charge on Thomas Spalding's plantation. And in Louisiana, where Mande-speakers were the dominant African enculturating force—with slave drivers being "almost universally black" (Brasseaux 57)— and where four hundred Bambara were reportedly at the core of the conspiracy of 1731 (Hall 42), sheer numbers were enough to leave considerable cultural impact. Because of their numbers, their determinative role in early contact situations, and their prestige positions as drivers and house servants, Senegambians were indeed in strong position to shape the creolization of an emergent American culture.

IV

We have seen how Senegambian tales survived transplantation from Africa to the South with plot structures often wholly intact. Motifs traveled well, along with performance aesthetics and some of the very structures of the African languages in which the tales were told. Even the functions and essential messages of the Creole tales remain true to West African ancestry. As Michael Jackson writes of Kuranko tales, the Afro-Creole tales tend to see food sharing as the most repeated sign of correct behavior, and they use images or metaphors of hunger in order to "focus a morality of cooperation and fairness by first negating such a morality" (74–75). Plantation slavery's systematic negation of morality brought the African fables to America, where their explorations of ethical ambiguities thrived, along with a tendency to utilize encoded modes of trickery and communication. "The Agreement to Sell Mothers," a common Senegambian fable that Bascom notes "originated in Africa" (201), provides an exemplary model of a food-focused tale of negated morality that turns upon occulted means of communication and was shared throughout the plantation South.

In a Mande/Kuranko version collected by Michael Jackson, Lion, Hyena, and Hare form a rice cooperative and agree to "make their mothers into sauce to be eaten with the rice" (101). After Lion and Hyena kill their mothers—who were unable to pass the test of naming the group members' code names—Hare saves his mother on the day that the cooperative members work his fields in expectation that he will provide the meal. Always a kind of griot figure because of his mastery of "sweet" language and music, Hare "decided to play some music on his little drum as the others worked" (Jackson 102). While drumming, he sings the secret names of Lion and Hyena in a masked song that reaches his own mother's ears:

> Konkofekenkie, *tintimatima, a tima tintima*
> Almantuporo, *tintimatima, a tima tintima*
> N'de l togo Tensara, *tintimatima, a tima tintima*
> (I am called Tensara . . .)
> *Ni nyina ra wo l ko i le toge konkon mangfa, tintimatima, a*
> tima tintima
> (If you don't remember that, your name will be sauce to be eaten with the rice . . .) (102)

Hare manipulates "two codes of communication at the same time . . . [so that] his songs and drum-playing are never what they seem" (Jackson 118). Using his powerful rhetorical skills of sweet talk and sweet song, Hare (the allegorized younger nephew or brother) consistently outwits his status superiors. His sweet talk and jive music are so consistently griotlike that many Wolof griots "identify hare as gewel [griot]" (Magel 191).

Alcée Fortier collected and transcribed a Louisiana Creole variant in which Compair Lapin dupes Compair Bouki, who in Louisiana (as in Francophone Missouri) retains the name of his Wolof ancestor Bouki-the-Hyena. After the animals agree to sell their mothers for grits and gumbo, Rabbit rescues his mother and tricks Bouki out of his food. Not satisfied with simply stealing Bouki's victuals, the vengeful Creole Rabbit then baits Bouki with erotic signs of power, singing in griotlike manner to advertise a "grand ball" featuring "Beautiful negresses from Senegal" (110). As the ever-gluttonous Bouki rushes to the ball, Rabbit beats his drum—"Simion, carillon painpain, Simion, carillon painpain"—and arranges for Bouki to meet his death in the clutches of Compair Tiger, disguised as the desired Senegalese woman.

Although Remus told one tale of a dupe cow named Bookay, and Bahamian tales refer to a similar dupe as B'Bouki (see Edwards), the Wolof hyena lost his name in Gullah and black English tales, becoming simply Brer Fox or Brer Wolf. Still in "Cutta cord-la," Joel Chandler Harris's Gullah tale remains true to West African form as Brer Rabbit's manipulation of two codes befuddles Brer Wolf and allows Rabbit to save his grandmother and kill his adversary. Harris's Brer Rabbit manipulates both an "open" communal Gullah and a familial African tongue that Brer Wolf has trouble replicating. The device by which Brer Rabbit saves "'e gran'mammy" and kills Brer Wolf is when Rabbit "'E hide 'e gran'mammy in top cocoanut tree . . . un 'e gi' um lily bahskit wit' cord tie on um," which she lowers and raises to receive food whenever her grandson sings "Granny!—Granny!—O Granny! Jutta cord-la!" (291). Brer Wolf, even when he spies the exchange, garbles his efforts to reproduce the message, then gets its lexicon and syntax right but proves unable to reproduce its tone closely enough to trick Granny. A trip to the blacksmith (an important power source in the Senegambian region) to have a red-hot poker thrust down his throat enables Brer Wolf to reproduce the message's tone well enough to fool Granny Rabbit, who then raises the basket containing Brer Wolf to her perch in the tree; however, Brer Rabbit arrives in time, and "'e holler 'Granny!—Granny!—O Granny! Cutta cord-la!" (292), orchestrating Brer Wolf's cartoonish fall. While most of the Senegambian and American "Agreement to Sell Mothers" tales allow for the trickster's mother to escape by cutting or breaking a cord, the most significant repeating element in the narratives is that the less scrupulous, less intelligent, less cunningly deceitful Bouki is tricked through Rabbit's skillful use of a code that Bouki proves unable to understand or reproduce.

The ability of Brer Rabbit to exclude Bouki from familial communication offered instruction on how to veil messages to achieve a degree of mastery over Ole Massa. The famed dual messages of black music provide solid examples of trickster-informed semiotics. Lawrence McIver, of coastal Georgia's McIntosh County Shouters, explains the origin of the shout "Move Daniel" in terms informed by the mother wit of Brer Rabbit:

> See, Daniel was a slave, and the slaves all were havin' a little party across the field one day. And the smoke-house was up there. . . . And they wanted to steal some of the meat, y'know, and they send Daniel in to get a piece of meat so they could put the party on sho' enough! An' ol' boss was comin' down, through there, so the slaves goin' to sing a song to let Daniel know to get out of the way. . . . So ol' boss thought that they was singin' a party song, but they was tellin' Daniel how to get out the way, so that ol' boss wouldn't put the whiplash on him. (quoted in Rosenbaum 6)

Like the subversive indirection of many of the old-time fables, McIver's explication of an old shout draws upon the manipulation of two codes as a means to trick a status superior and steal away with valued victuals.

The fact that the tales' plots and motifs often traveled from Senegambia intact does not mean that the meanings of the tales "survived" plantation slavery in some sort of fossilized essence. However, some of the most fundamental functions and meanings remain the same. Whether in West Africa or America, the trickster narratives play a flexible, didactic role, forcing individuals to "suspend orthodox solutions and reach out for resolutions that cover and highlight problems met in real life" (Jackson 262). Allegorized as Hare's corrupt status superior, Hyena is characterized by inflexibility, ineptness, and the use of rules and power for selfish personal gain (96). In contrast, the subordinate Hare wields the ethically ambiguous "wild" forces of "intelligence, mobility, flexibility, unorthodox improvisation, and play" (96). The tales are as much concerned with how to avoid the immoderate, selfishly stupid behavior of the duped status superior as they are with how to use Hare's cleverness to usurp status position and take control of the symbols of power.

Africans of different nations shipped across the Atlantic in chains and enslaved in the Americas were forced to find ways to maintain identity and build community in a wilderness more terrifying and oppressive than that of any spirit-inhabited spot along the Senegal, Gambia, or Niger Rivers. African fables that had allegorized generational conflicts and relationships between subordinate and authority positions (allowing for the "safe" incorporation of unorthodox *fadenya* forces) came to address the racialized worlds of plantation communities ruled by Bouki-like whites. The task of creating viable community had never before had such need of accessing wild *fadenya* forces from outside the domain of rules and roles—a need to suspend orthodox solutions and enter ethically ambiguous realms in order to solve real life problems (see Jackson 20–21). The trickster fables were a perfect medium through which to address these needs. And the tales *do* offer compelling allegories of race. Yet we must be careful to avoid blanket racialist readings of the allegories of African American tales.

Bernard Wolfe overstated the case for racial allegory when he reduced Brer Rabbit to "a symbol . . . of the Negro slave's festering hatred of the white man" (72). And Wolfe's blanket racialist reading was flat wrong when it led him to argue against the tales' African origins. In the Deep South, masters simply did not have the degree of cultural mastery over the slaves that Wolfe presumed. Lawrence Levine writes in *Black Culture and Black Consciousness* that there is indeed much testimony that "documents the enduring identification between black storytellers and the central figure of their tales" (113), but he adds that to read the trickster tales as "protest tales in disguise . . . ignores much of the complexity and ambiguity inherent in these tales" (114). Levine is right when he adds that "[t]he slaves' interest was not always in being like the trickster but often in avoiding being like the victims from whose fate they could learn valuable lessons" (119). Indeed, "[a]nimals were taken in by the trickster most easily when they violated many of the lessons of the moralistic tales" (120). Although no American tale can escape the terrain of "race," the Afro-Creole tales were not concerned solely with racial matters. The fabulous animal tales mocked the official plantation order, questioned Afro-Creole responses to life within the black community, and bolstered countercultural *African* American worldviews. It is the generic and functional nature of fables to provide the most flexible of locations, for as Eileen Julien writes, "Fable removes us from the space in which we are accustomed to exist and through whose atmosphere we are accustomed to look around ourselves" (139). Wielding "wild" fabulous forces that distance us from official, orthodox ideologies, the Afro-Creole tales force us to re-think all of our identities and desires.

Creolized in language and content, the Afro-Creole tales retain African elements of plot, purpose, and performance. We can understand the inventiveness of Creole cultures as what Mervyn Alleyne has called "inventiveness within a tradition." The tradition has strong Senegambian ingredients and has so thoroughly entered and shaped national menus, repertoires, and canons that these Senegambian sources have often gone unrecognized as African or even "black," and have been seen simply as American, which is a true sign of the tradition's inventive strength.

5

Creole Self-Fashioning

Joel Chandler Harris's Other Fellow

As for myself—though you could hardly call me a real, sure enough author—I never have anything but the vaguest ideas of what I am going to write; but when I take my pen in my hand, the rust clears away and the "other fellow" takes charge.

Joel Chandler Harris, letter to his daughter

I

Born of a syndicate of African and African American tellers of tales, born of particular men and women on the Turnwold plantation in Putnam County, Georgia, born of staged minstrel sketches and a white Southerner's postbellum nostalgia, Uncle Remus entered the national consciousness as the artistic, nurturing "other fellow" of Joel Chandler Harris's intensely Southern double consciousness. Careful reading of the Remus tales may move us away from "either/or" principles of cultural and racial polarity so that we might see creolization as an antiphonal continuum operating between and within black and white communities to shape a shared national culture. Harris was indeed conscious of the creolizing effects of his "other fellow" on his own dual souls, the South's, and on a national soul born from New World creolization.

Harris's characterization of Remus and his narration of the Brer Rabbit tales began by chance at the *Atlanta Constitution* in 1876 when, newly hired from the *Savannah Morning News,* he was given the job of filling a vacuum left by the departure of Sam Small and his popular Old Si sketches. Harris's first sketches were merely minstrel-like exercises in dialect. But William Owens's essay "Folk-lore of Southern Negroes" (1877) led Harris to reevaluate the trickster tales he had heard while growing up in Middle Georgia. He reviewed Owens's essay, writing that it was "remarkable for what it omits rather than for what it contains" (quoted in Brookes 15) and criticized it for being more of a primitivist listing of superstitions and speculations on Afro-paganism than a serious presentation of the folktales. Even so, the article did turn Uncle Remus in the direction of narration of the tales, which proved to be such a hit at the *Constitution* that they were reprinted nationally in 1880 as the collection *Uncle Remus: His Songs and Sayings*. However, this first book, which made Harris's reputation, remained deeply flawed due to its nature as a miscellany and its inconsistent and often ridiculous presentation of Remus. Harris's early Remus sketches included in the first book are condescending portraits of an indigent old man who serves as a humorous mouthpiece for white Atlanta's racial propaganda. It is only Harris's evolved reconception of Remus as the narrator of Brer Rabbit tales that is a creation worthy of respect.

Although *Uncle Remus: His Songs and Sayings* (1880) is more often anthologized, Harris's second book, *Nights With Uncle Remus* (1883), is his masterpiece. The first book was a miscellany collected from the newspaper pieces; *Nights* was planned much more carefully. It consists entirely of the animal fables, and instead of the little boy hearing a single tale from Remus, he hears a set of from two to five interlocking tales from an expanded cast of characters so that the reader is treated to tale-telling sessions. The extended cast allows for more development of Remus's character and allows differing voices and personalities to emerge: Gullah-speaking African Jack, Aunt Tempy the big house cook, and the young house servant Tildy. Through the expanded cast, Harris put his rapid immersion in comparative folklore to work, using his considerable skills in black American vernaculars to tell regional variants of the same tale and to account for each tale's provenance—cotton plantation, coastal rice plantation, or perhaps from the big house. Most importantly, the second book enables the reader to hear the tales in the context of their performance. Augmenting the first book's performances by Remus, *Nights* is filled with the interjections and responses of a group from which anyone (other than the boy) may be moved to tell the next tale.

It is Harris's understanding of the importance of folk narrative performance, his willingness to go to the source of performance, and his sheer delight in the language of performance that made *Nights With Uncle Remus* what may be the nineteenth century's most *African* American text. Just as the Senegalese-American poet Phillis Wheatley demonstrated her ability to immerse herself in an eighteenth-century European poetics, Joel Chandler Harris handled tales from the African continent with an ear for the matter of plot and the manner of language and semiotics. Only by valuing and submitting to African American standards of performance could Harris bridge the gaps he acknowledges in his introduction to the first volume: "I have found few negroes who will acknowledge to a stranger that they know anything of these legends; and yet to relate one of the stories is the surest way to their confidence and esteem. In this way, and in this way only, I have been enabled to collect and verify the folk-lore included in this volume" (45). Harris's increasingly developed interest in narrative performance is evident in the introduction to *Nights With Uncle Remus* in his expanded account of the way he used the tales to gain readmission into the black world of his childhood, finding in the telling, an erotic "sharing of joy [that] forms a bridge between the sharers . . . and lessens the threat of their difference" (Lorde 56). Harris writes that while he was waiting for a train to Atlanta, he heard "boisterous shouts of laughter" from groups assembled along the tracks: "The writer sat next to one of the liveliest talkers in the party; and, after listening and laughing awhile, told the 'Tar Baby' story by way of a feeler, the excuse being that some one in the crowd mentioned 'Ole Molly Har.' The story was told in a low tone, as if to avoid attracting attention; but the comments of the negro, who was a little past middle age, were loud and frequent. 'Dar now!' he would exclaim, or, 'He's a honey, mon!' or, 'Gentermens! git out de way, an' gin 'im room!'" (xv). Harris writes that the crowd was soon competing to see who could tell the best and most tales: "Some told them poorly, giving only meagre outlines, while others told them passing well; but one or two, if their language and gestures could have been taken down, would have put Uncle Remus to shame" (xvi). Tales remembered from boyhood, revivified by plot outlines sent from correspondents throughout the South and verified by Harris's participatory performance, enabled Remus to perform in his texts.

In *Nights With Uncle Remus*, when Remus, African Jack, Tildy, and Aunt Tempy get in a tale-telling session, an African performance aesthetic applies. The performances are sprinkled with the responses of the audience. In narratives 61–64, Aunt Tempy's "Dar now!" (370), "Dat's de Lord's trufe!" (371), "Man—Sir!—he's a-talkin' now!" (377), "Trufe too!" (380); African Jack's "Enty" (373), "Ah-yi-ee!" (380); Remus's "I boun' fer you, honey!" (370), "Tooby sho!" (372); and Tildy's "Eh-eh! Look out now!" (373), "Dar you is! (373), and "Watch out" (380) provide the participatory audience responses familiar to West African narrative and necessary even to effective greetings. Drawing upon his memory of tale-telling sessions, Harris recreates session after session in *Nights With Uncle Remus*. In "Mr. Hawk and Brother Rabbit," Tildy begins the story, but the more adept Uncle Remus finishes it. The bantering and increasing encouragement before and after each tale's narration mirror sessions Harris witnessed and participated in.

Harris's narrators employ at least two types of performance techniques common to West African folk narratives: ideophones and verb reduplication (Baer 193). Ideophones (verbal mimicry of sounds) are not only used frequently in the Remus tales, but they are also used in the triplet form common to West African tales. The Kuranko "Origin of the Yimbe Drum," for example, tells us that "hyena Sira seized the bamboo and cut it with her teeth—*wado-wado-wado*" (Jackson 161). And in the Wolof tale of Njaajaan N'diaye the narrator tells us that "when the porridge was cooked it went *ret ret ret*" (S. Diop 88). Likewise, in *Nights* Aunt Tempy tells of how "Brer Wolf went ter de do,' en he knock, he did—*blip, blip, blip*" (299). And Remus tells of "ole Miss Wolf whettin' 'er knife on a rock—*shirrah! shirrah! shirrah*" (152). Verb reduplication, "used to intensify, to indicate degree, magnitude, quality, or duration; and to express great excitement," is common to both the Remus tales and their African sources (Jones-Jackson 144). Kuranko narrators tell how much the hyenas enjoyed the yimbe drum: "Every evening they used to play it, play it, play it" (Jackson 159). Wolof narrators speak of how Hare waited "ba gainde nampale nampale nampale dom ya len be sur" [until Lion had nursed nursed nursed her cubs full] (Magel 354). Remus also tends to reduplicate in triplicate; Brer Fox says "I run, en I run, en I run, en de mo' w'at I run de furder de fier git" (288). And Brer Rabbit, "He diggy, diggy, diggy, but no meat dar" (113).

Nights With Uncle Remus benefits from Harris's greater attention to both his own artistry and to professional folklore. Framing and plotting are more complex in the second book, helping to make it a unified whole. The formal range of the individual narratives is also impressive in *Nights*. Along with the numerous trickster tales, *Nights* contains five origin myths and two ghost stories. *Nights With Uncle Remus* is laced with folk knowledge as is evident in the folklorist Stella Brewer Brookes's extensive list of proverbs from the Remus corpus (99–104).

One of the most significant formal features of *Nights* is the use of song interpolated into the narrative in the manner of African American and West African folk narration. Thomas Talley (1922) credited Harris as being among the first in literature to recognize the formal workings of call and response in black song. Talley writes that "[s]o well were these established parts of a Negro Rhyme recognized among Negroes that the whole turning point of one of their best stories was based upon it" (quoted in Brookes 139). Talley is referring to "Brother Fox, Brother Rabbit, and King Deer's Daughter" from *Nights With Uncle Remus*, in which Brother Rabbit, the griotlike master of music and speech, manages to trick fox into admitting to a theft that Rabbit committed. Offering the call of a reel-like tune, Rabbit seeks Fox's "confession": "Some kill sheep and some kill shote / But Brer Fox kill King Deer goat," and Brer Fox offers the formulaic, damning response: "I did, dat I did, en I'm glad dat I did" (169). Elsewhere in *Nights*, in African Jack's Gullah tale "The Cunning Snake," an "ole Affiky ooman, 'e call 'im name Coomba" (the stereotypical Senegambian woman's name), arranges a coded song of call and response so that her little girl in hiding might recognize the mother and open the door only to her. The Gullah story turns around the motif of Snake's learning to repeat the African sounds of Coomba's song: "Walla walla witto, me Noncy" (304). Matching the West African Hare's ability to manipulate dual codes of drum music and speech, the cunning Snake manipulates Gullah and an African code (while Harris shifts among at least four codes—standard English, black English, Gullah, and the African song). The sophistication of the way songs weave trickery into the plots of "The Cunning Snake" and "Cutta cord-la" (told in Gullah by the supposedly primitive African Jack) led Kathleen Light to remark that "[b]ecause of his peculiar speech and actions, Daddy Jack seems the most primitive of storytellers, but by placing in his mouth what is presumably the most sophisticated story in the volume, Harris confounds the notion of cultural evolution" with which he had flirted in his scholarly introduction to *Nights* (152).

Harris took great care with the language of the tales, which he felt to be inseparable from narrative content. Indeed, Uncle Remus was born of Harris's experiments with African American English, and it was from a growing appreciation of the vernacular that Remus found his matter. In the introduction to *Uncle Remus: His Songs and Sayings*, the author offers something of an apology for his use of dialect but announces that it is wholly "different . . . from the intolerable misrepresentations of the minstrel stage" and is "phonetically genuine" (39). He adds that his purpose is to preserve the tales in the medium through which "they have become a part of the domestic history of every Southern family" (39). As late as 1898, when the national interest had begun to turn away from local color, Harris found himself again defending his use of dialect, writing that "real dialect" differs from "lingo" in "that the first is preservative, while the latter is destructive, of language" (Collier Harris 401). Harris articulated his passion and respect for black English as a viable and expressive mode of language when the mood of the day was to see it as humorously deficient, a communicative lack. Robert Hemenway writes that "[t]he very authenticity of Harris' dialect reveals his investment in the Uncle Remus role" (17). And no less a master of the vernacular than Sterling Brown, who had serious qualms with Harris's representation of folk thought, allowed that "[t]he dialect, often meticulously rendered, rang true" (568). Harris's renditions of the vernacular are still respected enough to be used as sources for contemporary linguists studying the development of black English (see Williams 1993).

As Harris continued to conduct serious comparative thinking about vernacular performance, he came to be more and more interested in what he supposed to be a more "primitive," certainly more fully creolized vernacular—Gullah. Harris had translated a tale into Gullah in the introduction of his first book, but in *Nights With Uncle Remus* he has African Jack tell ten Gullah tales. In the introduction to *Nights,* Harris provides a Gullah glossary and adds that Gullah "is the negro dialect in its most primitive state . . . a confused and untranslatable mixture of English and African words" (xxxii–xxxiii). Although Harris's understanding of Gullah falls far short of his knowledge and passion for the Middle Georgia vernacular, his astute ear and his time spent living in Savannah provided him with enough background to make the first extensive effort at writing in Sea Island Creole. Harris seems to have solicited Charles Colcock Jones's aid in developing African Jack's Gullah tales. Jones wrote to Harris in March of 1883, referring to three tales "already gleaned," offering Harris further assistance with the Gullah language: "Familiar from childhood with the dialect. . . . I would experience no difficulty in interpreting, or in putting them in proper shape" (quoted in Baer 76). Helen Barclay, a providentially placed amateur folklorist from Darien, Georgia, was commissioned to provide Harris with outlines for much of the Gullah material for *Nights.* Writing to Harris in early 1883, Mrs. Barclay offered him "two of the real old nursery tales of alligators; and from my washerwoman, who 'use ter b'long ter Butler estet' . . . a true tale of a 'dead gose wha' I bin see wi' my own two eye'" (Collier Harris 194). The author we know as Joel Chandler Harris seems to have been quite a syndicate of black and white narrators, all walloped together.

In order to create a voice for the coastal Georgia tales and their creolized Gullah or Geechee language, Harris introduces eighty-year-old African Jack clownishly courting young Tildy: "I bin ahx da' Tildy gal fer marry me, un 'e no crack 'im bre't' fer mek answer 'cep' 'e bre'k out un lahff by me werry face. Da' gal do holler un lahff un stomp 'e fut dey-dey, un dun I shum doone gone pidjin-toe. Oona bin know da' Tildy gal?" (216). "Daddy" Jack, a trusted foreman of a rice plantation in coastal Georgia, brought from Africa when he was about twenty years old, is known as a conjurer and is the accomplished narrator of some of the book's most malicious trickster tales. In African Jack we see something of the ambivalence that Harris felt for Gullah and African cultures. Although Harris admired the African stories he had heard in Savannah and received in outline from correspondents along the Georgia coast, and was fascinated with the language, he often describes African Jack in animal terms. In one instance, "his yellow teeth shone in the firelight like those of some wild animal, while his small eyes glistened under their heavy lids with a suggestion of cunning not unmixed with ferocity" (384). Harris introduces African Jack as "a wizard, a conjurer, and a snake-charmer" (214). But, as Kathleen Light has observed, the supposedly primitive African Jack tells some of the most sophisticated stories, a point that was certainly not lost on Harris, who went to great lengths to obtain stories and outlines from the Georgia coast, an area known to be rich in both narrative and "primitive" African "survivals."

II

Harris consistently cited Africa as the source of most of the Remus tales, and he took great pride in presenting them as he had heard them himself. The degree to which he was right about West African origins and remained true to matter and manner of the tales he had heard may be gleaned from one particular Wolof tale that entered the Remus repertoire and has continued to reappear in much the same form ever since Harris's initial publication of it.

By 1893 Adolph Gerber had located a Wolof analogue for Harris's "Brother Rabbit's Love-Charm," told by African Jack in *Nights With Uncle Remus*. Gerber's Wolof source, according to Emil Magel, was Abbé Boilat's *Grammaire de la langue Woloffe* published in Paris in 1858. Boilat's language manual included four Wolof narratives presented in Wolof text and accompanied by French translations. Magel points to one of these, "Laeg aek Sagore yae," ("The Hare and the Sparrows"), as the Wolof prototype that Gerber cited for Harris's tale. Boilat's narrative recounts Hare's petitioning of Allah for more intelligence so that he might hold mastery over the other animals. Allah then gives Hare the task of filling a calabash with sparrows and bringing them back. Hare challenges the sparrows to fill his container, traps them, and brings them to Allah, who then strikes Hare on the forehead and tells him, "If I were to increase your intelligence, you would turn the world upside-down'" (quoted and translated in Magel 352). Magel himself collected a contemporary Wolof narrative in which Allah orders Hare to deliver a bag of birds, a lioness's milk, and an elephant's tusk, all of which Hare accomplishes through appeals to the animals' vanity. William Bascom notes that this widespread West African tale, "Trickster Seeks Endowments," is accompanied by one or more of the following task-motifs: "Challenging the Birds to Fill a Container," "Measuring the Snake," "Milking the Lioness," "Delivering the Elephant's Tusk," and "Delivering the Tears of the Hippopotamus." Bascom presented eighty-three variants of the tale, including thirty-one from Africa, thirty from the United States, and twenty-two from elsewhere in the New World (Guadeloupe, Cuba, Puerto Rico, Bahamas, Dominican Republic, Martinique, Saint Lucia, Grenada, Trinidad, Venezuela, Columbia, Mexico, and Guatemala), attesting to shared currents of New World creolization (40–44).

Harris offered an early version of this Afro-Creole fable in *Nights With Uncle Remus*. Uncle Remus begins the narrative, but African Jack's interruption, "Ki! . . . wut tale dis? I bin yerry de tale wun I is bin wean't fum me mammy" (262), situates the African-born Gullah speaker as a more authoritative teller. Thus Harris is able to make an unobtrusive claim for African origin of the fable and at the same time is able to signal its widespread popularity in the American South. Still, there are numerous contextual changes in African Jack's Gullah tale from what he may have heard in a Wolof mother tongue. Rather than going to Allah for more wisdom, Brer Rabbit "see one ole Affiky mans wut is bin-a hunt in da fiel' fer root en yerrub fer mek 'e met'cine truck" (262); and worried by love troubles and "a kinder idee dat may be he wa'n't ez smart ez he mought be," Brer Rabbit is told by the African root doctor that he can be fixed up with a charm bag if only he'll bring the old man an elephant tusk, a gator's tooth, and a rice bird bill. Although the African herbalist replaces Allah as Rabbit's petitioned power source in the Gullah tale, this "replacement" could reflect pre-Islamic narrative patterns predating the earliest recorded Wolof variant of the tale since the occult herbalist working in the bush is a strong power source in Senegambian traditions. After providing the items, Brer Rabbit is rewarded by the "Affiky mans" with the *gris-gris* that will allow successful courting. That African Jack, a known conjurer, is courting a girl who is listening to his tale, is—we must surmise—part of the tale's point. The tale works to reinforce extrascriptural systems of knowledge and the mother wit that nourishes both root-work and tale.

Charles Colcock Jones, whose knowledge of Gullah language and tales Harris tapped in *Nights With Uncle Remus*, wrote a volume for which Harris served as encouraging catalyst, *Negro Myths From the Georgia Coast* (1888), which includes a variant of the "Trickster Seeks Endowments" tale entitled "Buh Rabbit an de Cunjur Man." Rid of the courting frame that surrounds Harris's narrative, Colcock Jones's Rabbit apprentices himself to a conjure man, and following a period of service, "ax um fuh gen um eh full knowledge" (111). Rabbit is told to fetch a live rattlesnake and a swarm of yellow jackets. After bringing the yellow jackets trapped in a calabash, Rabbit gets his reward from the admiring Conjure Man, who tells him, "Buh Rabbit, you is suttenly de smartest ob all de animal, an you sense shill git mo an mo ebry day. Mo na dat, me gwine pit white spot on you forrud, so ebrybody kin see you had de bes sense een you head" (113).

When Rabbit goes to a conjurer for more wisdom, he is doing something socially acceptable and gets his reward for the accomplished tasks. But when Rabbit shows dissatisfaction with his natural gifts and has the audacity to petition God directly, he gets no reward for the successful completion of his tasks. In four South Carolina variants recorded by Elsie Clews Parsons on St. Helena Island (1923) and another by Albert Stoddard on Daufuskie Island (1949), Rabbit petitions the Lord for more sense, performs the assigned tasks, and is punished or sent packing for challenging the natural order.

The tale was published most recently by Patricia Jones-Jackson (1987). Recorded on Wadmalaw Island, South Carolina, "Ber Rabbit and the Lord" contains many of the tasks of Harris's tale. Rabbit must fill a bag with partridges, must catch a live rattlesnake, bring back a gator's teeth, milk a cow, and finally must even milk a bull—an impossible task common to Senegambian repertoires (see Kesteloot and Dieng 41–44). Remarkably stable over the century between *Nights With Uncle Remus* (1883) and Jones-Jackson's *When Roots Die* (1987), "Ber Rabbit and the Lord" suggests that roots are not dying, that they are still nourishing foliage.

III

Nights With Uncle Remus marks the high point of Harris's interest in the field of comparative folklore. The first Remus book's success, which resulted in a flood of correspondence with folklorists from around the world, not only strengthened Harris's sense of himself as an artist but also led him to take himself seriously as a folklorist. He subscribed to the British *Folk-Lore Journal*, became a charter member of the American Folklore Society, and collected folklore studies in his library. Harris's growing interest in the field of comparative folklore may be seen in his thirty-two-page footnoted essay written as an introduction to *Nights With Uncle Remus*. Aside from accounting for his methods of collecting tales, defending his use of dialect, offering a Gullah glossary, and presenting an analogue collected by Alfred Mercier in Gombo French, Harris makes extensive comparative reference to other published accounts to argue for the African origins of most of the tales. The folklorist Florence Baer, whose study of the Remus corpus found evidence that 122 of the 184 tales have immediate sources in Africa, writes that Harris's introduction to *Nights* "was the first truly comprehensive study of the probable origins and dissemination of Afro-American folktales documented with comparative texts from African, South American, and North American Indian sources" (190). Aside from its obvious artistic appeals to adults and children throughout the English-speaking world, *Nights With Uncle Remus*, "with its explanatory notes and inclusion of variants seems intended for serious consideration by the learned community of professional folklorists" (Baer 190).

Kathleen Light claims that Harris lost interest in professional folklore after publishing *Nights With Uncle Remus* (1883) because the sophistication of African Jack's allegedly primitive Gullah tales conflicted with the era's ethnological credo of social evolution. The theory of cultural evolution implied that narratives would become more sophisticated as a group advanced from primitive society into an industrialized literate society. But African Jack's tales, in which the trickster often utilizes two codes of communication to emerge triumphant, are clearly among the collection's most sophisticated. From the artist's point of view, the more African, more supposedly primitive tales were the strongest. Light writes that Harris had "been confused by ethnological theories, [but] there is enough evidence to conclude that he came to understand quite well how these theories degraded black folklore and thus undermined his own art" (156).

It is hard to imagine that Harris could have given up interest in folklore in 1892 over disagreement with the ethnologues' theories of cultural evolution when he could write in 1897 (in the voice of a fictional character who seems to be the author's sanctioned voice of wisdom) that although Africans "came here as savages, they were brought in close and stimulating contact with Christian civilization, and so lifted up that in two centuries they were able to bear the promotion to citizenship which awaited them . . . and to behold in their bondage here the scheme of a vast university in which they were prepared to enjoy the full benefits of all the blessings which have been conferred on them" (*Aaron in the Wildwoods* 153). Harris had an intense respect and love for black vernacular traditions; however, this respect was mitigated by a late-nineteenth-century white identity comfortable enough in condescension to leave much of the social Darwinism of the day unquestioned. Rather, his falling out with the folklorists likely came from some of their crudest examples of racial "science." For instance, David Dwight Wells attacked Harris in the *Popular Science Monthly* (1886), accusing Harris of having invented the names of the dogs in "The Little Boy and his Dogs," claiming that Uncle Remus could never have pronounced "Minny miny Morack and Follerlinsko," and taking further exception with the point in the tale where the little boy warns his mother about two panther-women by asking sharp indirect questions that caused Wells to argue that a "native African would never have asked such questions, because he was by nature lazy and indifferent" (quoted in Baer 113). Harris's belief in the tales' African origin and his respect for their genius remained strong, but his acknowledgment of African genius must have caused him consternation over cultural evolutionist theories that were almost inescapable at the time.[1] Harris's response to truths that split the comfortable edifice of white "scientific" knowledge was retreat to an Arcadian plantation aesthetic. Never again would his work have the power and sophistication of *Nights With Uncle Remus*. In 1892, announcing his retreat from late-nineteenth-century ethnology and folklore into the Arcadian realm created by his "other fellow," he offered a deeply playful preface as parting shot:

> But the folk-lore branch of the subject I gladly leave to those who think they know something about it. My own utter ignorance I confess without a pang. To know that you are ignorant is a valuable form of knowledge, and I am gradually accumulating a vast store of it. In the light of this knowledge, the enterprising

inconsequence of the Introduction to "Nights with Uncle Remus" is worth noting on account of its unconscious and harmless humor. I knew a great deal more about comparative folk-lore then than I know now; and the whole affair is carried off with remarkable gravity. Since that Introduction was written, I have gone far enough into the subject (by the aid of those who are Fellows of This and Professors of That, to say nothing of Doctors of the Other) to discover that at the end of investigation and discussion Speculation stands grinning. (*Uncle Remus and His Friends* vi–vii)

Through their fabulous plots and the laughter they provoke, the Uncle Remus stories express an intensely ambivalent double consciousness. Robert Hemenway, among others, has remarked that Harris must have had "a deep need to imagine himself as Uncle Remus," and he adds that "[i]n mimicking black speech, often calling himself Uncle Remus, signing his letters Uncle Remus, hearing himself referred to by the President of the United States as Uncle Remus, Joel Chandler Harris assumed an identity well suited to the 'other fellow' dualism of his creative life" (16–17). His artistic need for Uncle Remus, however, goes deeper than a white man's longing for his freer, less constrained "other fellow." Living in one of America's most sentimental, most nationalistic ages, Harris was clearly attracted to the more powerfully realistic worldview of the Brer Rabbit tales. Brer Rabbit's briar patch realism is a realism informed by harsh realities, but it is also a realism sharpened by the media of fable and laughter. In fact, it is only through the laughter provided by the Remus fables that Harris, a white Southerner, is able to speak "realistically" at all, for according to Bahktin, laughter "demolishes fear and piety before an object, before a world, making of it an object of familiar contact and thus clearing the ground for an absolutely free investigation of it. Laughter is a vital factor in laying down that prerequisite for fearlessness without which it would be impossible to approach the world realistically. As it draws an object to itself and makes it familiar, laughter delivers the object into the fearless hands of investigative experiment—both scientific and artistic—and into the hands of experimental fantasy" (23). As Eileen Julien notes in her reading of the "fabulous" fiction of Sony Labou Tansi, laughter "refuses to take the terms proffered by the system portrayed, it makes us step out of the ring of authority of that world" (129). It is only through the indirection of fable and the erotic realism of laughter that Harris steps out of the ring of authority of his plantation world. When Remus remarks that "ef deze yer tales wuz des fun, fun, fun, en giggle, giggle, giggle, I let you know I'd a-done drapt um long ago" (355), we can be sure that he (as Harris's "other fellow") is aware of the liberating power unleashed by fabulous laughter. Brer Rabbit allows entry into a world outside of dominant ideological systems, for he is an animal outside of human rules who exemplifies "the capacity to survive and flourish in a world in which society can be and often is predatory" (Rubin, "Uncle Remus" 166). Louis Rubin adds that "Harris knew this, but it was only when writing of Negro life in the guise of the animals that he could, as a writer, tell what he knew" (167). The fabulous realism of Uncle Remus, along with Mark Twain's Huck Finn, did much to enable the development of a truly novel American voice.

The tales' remarkable semiotic freedom keeps them ever open to interpretation. Michael Jackson describes such narratives as jokelike plays upon form, tending "to subvert the dominant structure of ideas by showing that an accepted pattern has no necessity" (52). Aware of the tales' use of racial allegory, Harris wrote in the introduction to his first collection of Remus tales that "it needs no scientific investigation to show why he selects as his hero the weakest and most harmless of all animals, and brings him out victorious in contests with the bear, the wolf, and the fox" (44). Fabulous subversion of the racial order is most clearly suggested in Brer Rabbit's trickery of Mr. Man. In "Mr. Man Has Some Meat," Rabbit and Fox work together to trick Mr. Man out of his meat. When the little white listener objects to the animals' disregard for the Eighth Commandment, Remus offers that "[i]n dem days de creeturs bleedzd ter look out fer deyse'f" (209). Harris's divided sympathies between clear-cut Victorian ethics and Remus's worldwise knowledge of survival appear again in "Brother Rabbit Outdoes Mr. Man" in which Rabbit steals Mr. Man's money. Remus explains the situation to the little boy: "Mr. Man got w'at lots er folks ain't got,—good luck, long head, quick eye, en slick fingers. . . .'twon't be long 'fo' some un'll take you off 'roun' de cornder en tell you dat 'tain't make no diffunce whar de money come fum so de man got it. Dey won't tell you dat in de meeting-house, but dey'll come mighty nigh it" (339). Born of the process of creolization, Harris and the Remus tales were creolizing double agents.

Weaving text and tale, standard English and "dialect" or Gullah, *Nights With Uncle Remus* is born of an expansive, truly multicultural American vision. In the closing Christmas pageant of *Nights*, as clearly as anywhere else in Harris's work, Remus is a nurse figure through whom Harris lays claim to the black folk tradition. Remus sings to the little master just before bed:

De big Owl holler en cry fer his mate,
    My honey, my love!
Oh, don't stay long! Oh, don't stay late!
    My honey, my love!
Hit ain't so mighty fur ter de Good-by Gate,

My honey, my love!
Whar we all got ter go w'en we sing out de night,
My honey, my love! (407)

Appropriately enough for a collection of tales for the era's white children, *Nights With Uncle Remus* concludes with this romanticized plantation lullaby in a scene staged much like the closing of an operatic minstrel show. As Uncle Remus discovered the little boy fast asleep, he "took the child in his arms and carried him to the big house, singing softly in his ear all the way; and somehow or other the song seemed to melt and mingle in the youngster's dreams" (407). Harris's enculturation into an African American erotic allowed him impressive mastery of the tales' performance, but the white man's claims to mastery over the lives and souls of black folk assured that no pursuits were too deeply shared. Whites, who had so wanted to see themselves in the parental role in their enculturation of childlike blacks, are here revealed to be enculturated children, shaped by a soul semiotics they are born into and with identities forever split and mixed. Harris is Remus—the artist, realist, and parent. And he is also the child nostalgic for the old plantation order, inventing in Remus the father's love he never knew. Harris's passion for the tales is powerfully conveyed, well informed, and only intermittently naive. His identity inhabits the divide between Remus's mastery of a profoundly unsentimental art and the little master who is born of Harris's nostalgia for an antebellum childhood. Brer Rabbit is the vehicle of their sharing, a means for admitting the little boy's studied respect for Remus. But the "erotic" power through which the tales (and so much else) entered Harris's repertoire was an erotic gone terribly awry, an erotic repressed, never fully acknowledged, an erotic popularized and used—pornographically—against the "other fellow" celebrated in the Uncle Remus texts. Indeed, the often unacknowledged impact of Joel Chandler Harris (for better and for worse) on American literature and culture calls for renewed attention.

IV

Joel Chandler Harris's respect for African American folk narratives and his genius in developing their literary vernacular performance should not be underestimated. Harris might arguably be called the greatest single authorial force behind the literary development of African American folk matter and manner. He is an important literary forefather in any attempt to trace the development of African American literature toward vernacular expression. Paul Laurence Dunbar seems to have felt quite trapped by Remus's influence. As Dunbar remarked to James Weldon Johnson, "'I've got to write dialect poetry; it's the only way I can get them to listen to me'" (35–36). And

Charles Chesnutt, who read the Remus stories to his children, wrote *The Conjure Woman* as a direct engagement with Harris.[2] Du Bois cites the Fisk Jubilee Singers as his soul source, but Harris's literary reevaluation of vernacular traditions (along with the national interest he received and the national/international interest in folklore that *Uncle Remus* helped inspire) surely shaped, even if only indirectly, Du Bois's affirmation of the vernacular. Remus, the mythic old-time negro, cast a powerful shadow upon writers of the New Negro movement. Writers as powerful as Sterling Brown and Zora Neale Hurston owe an immense debt to Uncle Remus's earlier attention to vernacular performance. To be sure, Joel Chandler Harris is often included in anthologies of African American literature—but as an amanuensis to the folk tradition and not as an Afro-Creole artist. Time and time again Harris himself stated that he was little more than an amanuensis, but to see him as such is to overvalue originality of plot and to undervalue literary performance, development of style, reevaluations of source material, and widenings of the field of literary activity. Far from being an amanuensis, Harris, in the guise of Uncle Remus and African Jack, is one of our most consciously *African* American authors. Sterling Brown's own peerless poetic efforts in blues forms taught him enough to recognize that Harris was a "true artist" and "more than a reteller" since he "altered, adapted, polished, and sharpened" the tales (*Negro* 53). Although Brown rightly condemns the first Uncle Remus of the *Atlanta Constitution* sketches as a dialect-speaking "mouthpiece for defending orthodox southern attitudes," he writes that the Remus of the trickster tales was "finely conceived . . . one of the best characters in American literature" (53).

Harris's impact upon American literature as a whole, and Southern literature in particular may be as strong as that made upon African American letters. A whole era of local colorists drew inspiration from Harris's work. His narrative bridges across an intensely biracial culture laid a foundation for popular acceptance of his contemporaries, Cable and Twain, and would help Faulkner to recognize his own "postage stamp of native soil" as worthy material. Harris presented an interracial familiarity as part of the very constitution of a distinctly Southern identity. In the opening paragraph of his introduction to *Uncle Remus: His Songs and Sayings,* he asserted that the tales and their vernacular language "have become a part of the domestic history of every Southern family" (39). But even as Uncle Remus revealed truths of a shared creolism, Harris's framing of the tales tended to hide the evils out of which creolism was forged. According to Lucinda McKeithan, the Remus tales attempt to show that "mutual affection between the races was the natural state of affairs; black men and white were part of one family devoted to maintaining a way of life which joined mansion and cabin together in common endeavors" (11–12). The Uncle Remus tales indeed appealed powerfully to nostalgia for the old order, as is evident from a letter to Harris written by Alexander Stephens, former vice president of the Confederacy: "My father had an old family servant whose name was Ben. He came from Virginia, and was quite lame from rheumatism, from my earliest remembrance. Often have I set up late at night in his house, and heard nearly every one of those stories about Brer Rabbit, Brer Fox, and Brer Terrapin, as you have reproduced them. In reading them, I have been living my young life over again" (quoted in Collier Harris 165). As long as literary creolism was expressive of the old paternalistic relationships and served as a pastoral, even feudal romance preservative of the status quo, Southerners could celebrate Creole identity as evidence of their connection to the soil and their noblesse oblige (Stafford 91–92). But if creolization became perceived as supportive of "social equality" and indicative of racial/cultural mongrelization, there could be no room for celebration of the African elements of Southern or American culture. Harris's romantic realism was built of the complexity of the white South's dual message on race and cultural identity. In the words of Bernard Wolfe, Joel Chandler Harris's other fellow, Uncle Remus, is "a monument to the South's ambivalence. . . . Harris's inner split—and the South's, and white America's" (84).

Paul Buck has written that upon publication of the Remus volumes, Harris gained "immediate recognition among white readers everywhere as the greatest authority on Negro life" (211). Ultimately, Harris's claims to a creolized biracial Southern culture were used as a means toward North–South reunion and the solidifying of a national, white racial solidarity. The Afro-Creole erotic of the Remus tales was wielded oppressively. A northern readership eager for national reunion and not at all eager to embrace African Americans en masse on northern soil or to continue the crusade for racial justice on Southern soil was happily convinced that Southern whites who had grown up on the knee of an Uncle Remus or an Aunt Tempy were bound to deal with these affable freemen in an informed and graciously paternalistic manner. Northern magazines such as *Scribner's* fueled the postbellum local color movement by publishing Southern writers like Harris, Cable, Thomas Nelson Page, and Grace King, with the announced editorial goal of seeking "to increase the sentiment of union throughout our diverse sisterhood of States" (quoted in Buck 221). As the Remus tales represented familial bonding of Southern blacks and whites under plantation paternalism, so too did plantation fiction work to bond and reunite North and South. Robert Hemenway writes that Uncle Remus, "[i]nvented as Federal troops withdrew from the South. . . . promised the North that Southerners could see the Negro's virtues and even celebrate them, which was proof that rehabilitation had occurred and that force was no longer necessary to ensure that black people would be treated with justice by their former masters" (*Uncle* 20–21). More than any other writer, Harris portrayed a land "where romance of the past still lived, a land where, in short, the nostalgic Northerner could escape the wear and tear of expanding industry and growing cities and dwell in a Dixie of the storybooks which had become the Arcady of American tradition" (Buck 235). Buck writes that "[t]he people of the North after 1877 were for the most part in substantial agreement that the Negro was not prepared for equality and that the South should be allowed to deal with the problem in its own way" (283). Due in part to writers like Harris and Arcadian presentations like Remus, "[t]he South had won its major point" (283). As Harris's contemporary, Albion Tourgée, wrote, the national literature became "not only Southern in type but distinctly Confederate in sympathy" (405).

That Joel Chandler Harris, a white Southerner, should be one of postbellum America's most intensely Africa-informed writers should surprise no one who is aware of how thoroughly creolized the Deep South had become during the antebellum period. Many of the Remus plots are West African, often Senegambian. Codes and aesthetics of performance in the Remus tales are also often strongly African. Motifs and means of trickery remain true to West African form. In short, Harris performed the tales with empathy, authenticity, and artful passion. At his best, he was a powerful realist. He enabled much that black writers would shape out of the vernacular. But his split identity wrought an Africanist art that was double-aimed. The creation of a romanticized Southern Arcady massaged northern guilt over abandoning the freedmen to disenfranchisement and lynching. The South of creolizing agency would live (in cuisine, dance, language, literature, religion, medicine, and especially music) alongside the Arcadian South of Aunt Jemima, Uncle Ben, *Gone With the Wind*, Disney's *Song of the South*, and Bill Clinton's Hope, Arkansas. Joel Chandler Harris and his "other fellow" provide us with a kind of spirit-inhabited palaver tree—or *pench*—from which we may observe points of convergence and branchings of Afro-Creole cultural forces and Arcadian myth.

6

Searching for Spiritual Soil

Milk Bonds and the "Maumer Tongue"

"[V]ernacular speech" is that which babies become accustomed to from those around them when they first begin to articulate speech; or, as it could be put more succinctly . . . that which we learn without any rules in imitating our nurse. We can also acquire another speech which is dependent on this one called by the Romans "grammar."

Dante, *De Vulgari Eloquentia*

[M]y "maumer tongue" has been so profaned by those who undertake to transcribe it, that I renounce the task.

Susan Petigru King, *Lily: A Novel* (1855)

I

It was only after the fall of the Confederacy that white writers felt much compulsion to lay claim to the deeply racialized erotics and Africa-informed vernaculars that were at the very core of their collective consciousness. Postbellum Southern writers nostalgic for the Afro-Creole world of childhood milk bonds seem to have sought "by means of a language that 'musicates through letters,'" to do what Julia Kristeva feels post-Renaissance Western writers were unable to do until the arrival of James Joyce; that is, to "resume within discourse the rhythms, intonations, and echolalias of the mother-infant symbiosis—intense, pre-Oedipal, predating the father" (*Desire* 157). The strongest fiction in this vein tapping the language and semiotics of Southern childhood (*Huckleberry Finn, Nights With Uncle Remus*, and the later possibilities springing from Faulkner's *The Sound and the Fury*) turned to various creole/vernacular modes of language in carnivalesque writing that worked to free consciousness, as Bakhtin claims polyglossia does, "from the tyranny of its own language and its own myth of language" since "it is possible to objectivize one's own particular language . . . only in the light of a language belonging to someone else, which is almost as much 'one's own' as one's native language" (61–62). Repeatedly in Southern writing, we can see black vernacular modes of expression providing the means by which artists attempt to escape the tyranny of Southern ideologies and social forms—the official grammar of church, state, and the literati. We have seen how several African American narratives of epic impulse have utilized traditions of mother wit—its soul-structures of freedom and authority—to reassemble a fragmented ancestral muse.[1] What we may now begin to see is that even after violent racial weaning and years of grammar schooling, white children nursed on a creole vernacular often imagined the muse as black or "colored" (as our national popular culture increasingly does). While the figure of this "other-wit" may be cast as Poe's Raven, as Uncle Remus, or as a jazz-cat or contemporary rapper, an incredibly powerful phenomenon of Creole agency may be glimpsed in the matrix of significations emerging from the national stereotype/archetype of the "mammy," who although she tends to be horrendously abused, often serves as a troubling source of textual authority and freedom through which white consciousness is deconstructed and the tyrannies of its language and myth of language are exposed and cut through with another, fabulous vision.

Even in antebellum Southern fiction, one finds glimmers and brooding repression of the claims that whites would later make to Afro-Creole identity. Despite her avoidance of the task of representing her Gullah "maumer tongue," the Charlestonian Susan Petigru King, in at least one scene of her novel *Lily*, revealed the degree to which her Carolina consciousness was a double one, tied, in the words of Lillian Smith, "to two umbilical cords which wrap themselves together in a terrifying tangle" (132). Anticipating the representations of many later writers, King's figure for the "other" side of her identity was her other mother: the black "maum" who taught the author her "maumer tongue."

The Creole word "maum," used in the low country in place of "aunt" or "mammy" as a titular address for older black women, may have grown from this tangle of two umbilical cords. The word can be understood to be a creolized pronunciation of "mom" or "mamma" or the French "maman." But given the low country preference for Senegalese house servants (Holloway 16), and given that Du Pratz in 1758 recommended that only Wolof servants be selected for service in Louisiana homes (Hall 41), the term "maum" or "mam" as used in South Carolina, Georgia, and Louisiana, would have been reinforced and perhaps even derived from the Wolof word "maam," signifying one's grandparent or elderly relative—as in the Wolof source tale for the Louisiana tale "Rose and Blanche" when the orphan Kumba greets a mysterious old witch-woman as "maam ndey" ("grandparent-mother" or "ancestor-mother"). "Maum," with its Wolof associations of grandparent or elder and its English associations of mother, was a term perfectly suited to expressing the black nurse's "motherhood with a difference" relationship to her white charges. It was through these women and through the "maumer tongue" that whites learned, in the words of Joel Williamson, much "in language, literature, and religion, in music and manners, and in cuisine and conjuring" to the point "that a significant amount of the African heritage that survived in the slave South survived outside the black world in the white" (*Crucible* 38). As C. Vann Woodward has written of America's umbilical tangles, "so far as their culture is concerned, all Americans are part Negro" ("Clio" 5). Among the most significant agents or "ancestors" of the Afro-creolization of America have been enculturating "maums."

Susan Petigru King's narration of two teenage girls' return to Charleston from a New York finishing school presents their homecoming as a reimmersion in a long-familiar soul semiotics. Lily is excited over the return, and she speaks passionately of the low country landscape and the feast that will be prepared for them. But her companion Alicia complains of the smell of the marsh mud and feigns ignorance of facts constitutional to low country Creole identity: Alicia asks in mid-December, "Is this the season for okra soup? I should like okra soup" (153). While Alicia is diffident in her homecoming, the author pointedly tells us that as Lily greeted the loyal family servant Plato, "[S]he shook hands with him—not daintily like one dreading contamination, but a hearty good shake" (154). Having been finished by her Afro-Creole "maumer" as well as at the New York school, Lily has the manners to inquire after the servants' "relations and their health . . . understanding their talk and their habits like one who had from childhood lived familiarly among them" (155). Some of the servants' responses suggest their Senegambian roots. King translates the greeting response "I day" as "I am here" (156), a calque from the most common Wolof response, *Mangi fi rekk* (I am here only). Lily takes special interest in greeting her "maumer, a dignified colored woman, with an immense head-kerchief, who laid her withered hands upon the light tresses of 'her child,' and patted her cheek, while tears of joy silently rolled down her face" (156).

The author's need to mark the Charleston girls' homecoming from New York with the book's only sustained interracial contact reveals something of King's own creolization. Still, the soul erotics into which the girls are reimmersed appears either to be not deeply shared or not fully valued. In fact, King's authorial manners suffer because she uses Lily's "maumer" and the young house servants not just to mark reimmersion in the familiar but as a means of repartée attacking Harriet Beecher Stowe. King's prose drips with condescension and displays a profound disrespect for her maum's basic humanity and for anyone with the temerity to criticize slavery. The narrative pointedly withdraws from the scene of greetings at just the moment when it has reentered an Afro-Creole world:

> I might make out quite an interesting chapter by detailing at length the first conversations held between the young ladies and these "slaves," who were brimfull of the adventures of the past eighteen months, and who were anxious to call for "Miss Lily and Miss 'Licia's" sympathy or good wishes; but there have been so many dreary attempts to depict the manners and customs of these "unhappy descendants of the aborigines of that delightful and interesting country—Africa" (as I once heard a distinguished senator say), my "maumer tongue" has been so profaned by those who undertake to transcribe it, that I renounce the task. (156–57)

King claims authoritative possession of her "maumer tongue" in the same breath with which she dismisses both the bondage and cultural patrimony of her "'slaves.'" Her claims to a "maumer-child-ness" repress any effort toward true self-consciousness. The novel finally renounces representation of the maumer tongue in order to sprinkle its pages with the French of elite finishing schools and descriptions of good Madeira "decanted into cut-glass of the old diamond pattern, and drunk in thin, bell-shaped glasses with straw-thick shanks" (158). But it is a decidedly gothic emplotment that brings King to have Lily be betrayed by her fiancé's passion for a free woman of color. Described as "one who was too perfect for this earth," Lily meets her death by poisoning at the hands of her competitor—the dark "Spanish beauty" hired to help with Lily's wedding dress. The novel's renunciation of the task of representing "the maumer tongue" and its easy disparagement of African humanity lead to fated emplotments of violence as a renounced Afro-Creole erotic erupts from what Lillian Smith called the segregated "Darktown of our unconscious" (90).

After the war, white Southern writers embraced Afro-Creole language to answer a variety of needs. Joel Chandler Harris's "Mom Bi: Her Friends and Enemies" tells the story of a low country "maum" as if he had gleaned it from Charleston's oral history. Harris tells us that "there was a tradition in the Waynecroft family that her name was Viola, and that it had been corrupted by the children into Bi—Mom Bi" (174). If Harris's Mom Bi is indeed scripted from low country lore, the most common Wolof article, "bi," might have replaced the article "ji" normally used with "maam" so that the children she enculturated might be speaking a form of Wolof when addressing her as "maam bi." Speculative etymology aside, Harris describes Mom Bi in terms resonant with the planters' myth of Senegambian superiority and in stereotypes of Wolof physiognomy. We read that "Mom Bi's spirit remained unbroken," and she was "superior in her methods and ideas to the common run of negroes" (173). A few years before the publication of "Mom Bi," George W. Cable had written of Louisiana Creole culture in "The Dance in Place Congo" (1886), describing "tall, well-knit Senegalese from Cape Verde, black as ebony, with intelligent, kindly eyes and long, straight, shapely noses" (37). Cast in accord with Cable's description of Wolof physical types, Harris's Mom Bi "was tall and gaunt, and her skin was black as jet. . . . Her nose was not flat, nor were her lips thick like those of the typical negro" (172). Matching descriptions of elaborate head wraps worn by Muslim women in coastal Georgia, Mom Bi's "head-handkerchief was queerly tied"; its folds "stood straight up in the air" (172).

Having served four generations of Charleston's Waynecroft family, Mom Bi is a chronicler of the family's oral history, the authorized custodian of the family's manners, and a master of the Gullah "maumer tongue." Her "frank and fearless criticism" of people inside and outside the family makes her an arbiter of how well the Waynecrofts live up to their forebears' legacy. As the Civil War rages, Mom Bi's marginality in both white and black worlds shapes her into a kind of prophetess. Blacks in the story who do not come into regular contact with whites "argued that any black who talked to white people as Mom Bi did must possess at least sufficient occult power to escape punishment" (181). And as the war begins to turn in favor of the North, she speaks publicly of the slaves' impending freedom: "Oona see dem gang er nigger down dey? Dee gwine be free, un nuttin' 't all gwine stop um. Dee'l be free, un ole Bi gwine be free. Ah Lord! when de drum start fer beat, un de trumpet start fer blow, de white folks gwine los de nigger. Ki! I mos' yeddy dem now" (182). Harris's investment in Mom Bi's story forces him to see her yearning for freedom and gives him the language to concede the righteousness of the abolitionist cause. But powerful bonds tie her (and her author) to the family she long served, working against the scripting of her full freedom.

The battlefield death of the Waynecroft's son, whom Mom Bi had nursed, afflicts her with unusual grief. Although such scenes do reinforce the pernicious myth of a Southern Arcady, to underestimate the strength of nurse bonds is to underestimate human capacity for love (even when ambivalent). It is also to underestimate the degree to which black women were able to wield some degree of power through the investment of care given to children who matured to become masters. Harris's Mom Bi explains the depth of her feelings for the slain Waynecroft boy as an embarrassed Waynecroft friend attempts to pull her away from the coffin: "Take you' han' fum off me, man! I bin cry on count dat chile mos' fo' he own mammy is. I bin nuss um, I bin worry wid um, I bin stay 'wake wid um wun ev'body wuz sleep, un I bin hol' um in my lap day un night, wun 'e sick un wun 'e well. I ain't gwine out! I ain't! I ain't!" (186–87). In this empathetic moment, Harris gives Mom Bi's Gullah a dignity and power that had been missing from the Gullah scripted in *Nights With Uncle Remus*. Mom Bi's Creole speech, less distorted than African Jack's, has a strength to match the emotional range of the bonds she feels.

When freedom comes, Mom Bi tells the Waynecrofts of her decision to go to Savannah to live with "My daughter 'Ria, w'at you bin sell to John Waynecroft" (189). She informs the Waynecrofts that she had finally, after many years, forgiven them for selling her daughter. But what she refuses to forgive is their sending their son to die in a doomed war effort. It is this scene to which Darwin Turner objects, finding that it fit too neatly the stereotype of the childless mammy who lavishes a mother's love upon her white children (120–24). I agree with Turner that Mom Bi is too type-set; however, Harris does complicate the picture in "Mom Bi" with the story's attack on slavery under even the best of conditions. And given the tangle of affection and hatred, the infinite peculiarities that obtained between individual whites and enslaved individuals on different plantations and households, Mom Bi's rage at the Waynecrofts' second transgression of her motherly bonds—bonds she had been socialized to feel were "safe"—is understandable even if it reinforces a pernicious myth. Harris's Mom Bi, trapped in the stereotypes that engendered her fictional role, still manages to find the language to challenge an Arcady that Harris himself helped build.

Following the success of Harris's Uncle Remus tales, more white Southern writers gave literary expression to their "maumer tongue," and the region began to stake conscious claim to its Afro-Creole culture, if only to show that by speaking the lingo (in essence by becoming authoritative Africanists), white Southerners might be trusted to govern African American subjects. Prior to Uncle Remus, American writers' use of African American vernaculars had met with little success. Creole languages posed particular challenges. Nevertheless, antebellum difficulty in rendering Gombo, Gullah, or African American English dialogue does not mean that Southern whites could not speak fluently in the vernacular or creole. In fact, the opposite is true. Southern speech was being thoroughly affected by black speech patterns during the duration of plantation slavery.

The English actress Fanny Kemble noted the Africanization of Southern English. During a year spent on her husband's plantations in coastal Georgia, she observed that the Gullah of the black majority had become the region's mother tongue: "[T]he utterance of many of them is more like what Prospero describes Caliban's to have been, than the speech of men and women in a Christian and civilized land: the children of their owners, brought up among them, acquire their Negro mode of talking—slavish speech surely it is—and it is distinctly perceptible in the utterances of all Southerners, particularly of the women, whose avocations, taking them less from home, are less favorable to their throwing off this ignoble trick of pronunciation than the more varied occupation and the more extended and promiscuous business relations of men" (252). Writing with a combination of a white foreigner's prejudices and clarity of vision, Kemble had a good eye and ear for American difference and for the peculiar difficulties that faced enslaved women and their mistresses. Still, Kemble looked upon slave culture with a disgust that went beyond her disgust with slavery itself. And seeing that the acculturation process cut both ways, she feared creolization as mongrelization. After less than a year spent on her husband's Sea Island plantations, she wrote that her own four year-old daughter was beginning to sound black: "Apparently the Negro jargon has commended itself as euphonious to her infantile ears, and she is now treating me to the most ludicrous and accurate imitations of it every time she opens her mouth. Of course I shall not allow this, comical as it is, to become a habit. This is the way the Southern ladies acquire the thick and inelegant pronunciation which distinguishes their utterances from the Northern snuffle, and I have no desire that S[ally] should adorn her mother tongue with either peculiarity" (280–81).

Since there was a substantial black majority along the rice coast, with as much as 75 percent of the population enslaved in the counties of coastal Georgia (Smith 33), whites may have been more inclined to learn Gullah than the slaves were to learn English. Charles Joyner writes that the creolized maumer tongue was the mother tongue of many white children who "learned their first language from a Gullah-speaking nurse, thus becoming native speakers of Gullah, and learned English as a second language" (208). Many, like Benjamin Allston Sr. of South Carolina, "apparently never really mastered English" (208). John Bennet wrote in 1909 of Charleston's linguistic situation in a manner similar to Ishmael Reed's descriptions of the New Orleans-based Jes' Grew virus: "It is true that, up to the age of four, approximately, the children of the best families, even in town, are apt to speak an almost unmodified Gullah, caught from brown playmates and country bred nurses" (339). While Gullah made its impact, particularly upon the low country aristocracy, the identification of Louisiana whites with Afro-Creole French was even more pervasive in a Creole culture that—as much as any other single source—gave its energy of action to a whole jazz age.

II

Louisiana Creole was developed in large part by Senegalese slaves (Broussard ix–x and Hall 188–200) and quickly crossed racial boundaries to become a preferred language of many upper-class whites. In 1945, Broussard wrote that Creole is "spoken bilingually with French by a large number of whites who learned it from their nurses in childhood and by others who adopted it as the language of their community" (viii). Accepted as "the language of childhood," Creole was discouraged and replaced with French as white children were weaned from its milk bonds and socialized as young white adults; however, the familiar childhood joy-sharing erotics of Gombo (or Gumbo) French would often call "older educated Louisianians to return to the language of their childhood when in reminiscent moods" since Creole was for many—as for Broussard—a native tongue, "learned from my nurse, which I used exclusively up to the age of seven" (viii-x). The Creole vernacular established itself at the bedrock of being—the language of childhood freedom and "relaxed" social modes—and served simultaneously as the language of original (perhaps true and lasting) moral authority.

Although Gumbo French became the Louisiana colony's mother tongue, it is not surprising that Louisiana's Creole writers (from the planter/poet Julien Poydras to the black Creole poets who published *Les Cenelles* in 1845) chose French rather than Creole as their language of literary expression. While the Creole language might be the medium of any true Louisiana muse, French was, alas, the French of France. Interestingly, it may have been the vernacular genius of an Anglo-American, Joel Chandler Harris—along with the influence of Cable's *The Grandissimes* (1880)—that did the most to move the standard French of a novel such as Charles Testut's *Le vieux Salomon: ou une famille d'esclaves au XIX siecle* (1872) to the Creole dialogues that add psychic depth to Alfred Mercier's *L'Habitation Saint-Ybars: ou maîtres et esclaves en Louisiane* (1881). Although Testut's novel follows a pair of enslaved lovers from their relatively happy home in Guadeloupe to their sale to an abusive Louisiana sugar planter, and contains many scenes ripe for inclusion of the Afro-Creole languages of Louisiana and Guadeloupe, all dialogue is in a standard French. However, Mercier's Remus-influenced *L'Habitation Saint-Ybars* (1881) is filled with passages written in Creole, passages that simultaneously reveal the author's nostalgia for antebellum Creole life and his criticism of that life's violent legacy. Having already published his *Étude sur la langue créole en Louisiane* (1880), Mercier was well prepared for his novel text.

L'Habitation Saint-Ybars is a portrait of life on a large Louisiana plantation and features an extensive cast of characters, but the three central characters are the French tutor Pélasge, his young white Creole charge Démon Saint-Ybars, and Démon's Bambara-Creole nurse Mamrie, who enculturates Démon into the African systems of expression that most clearly differentiate him from the French Pélasge. A Creole with Bambara grandparents still living on the plantation, Mamrie imparts something of Mande culture to the Saint-Ybars family through her role as nurse and confidante to two of the

Saint-Ybars children. In fact her very first sentence in the book, "Hé, nénaine, ga: vous piti apé tété moin" (114) (Godmother, look: your babies are taking their milk"), establishes Creole as the language of earliest milk bonds, the twins' true mother tongue. The text tells us that Mamrie "replaced" the mother, and the twins are referred to as "les enfants de Mamrie" (115).

Given the task of socializing Démon as a European, the French tutor Pélasge is astute enough to see that Démon's passion for the trickster tales told in the kitchen marks an education already begun along Afro-Creole foundations. Although Démon's father, Saint-Ybars, defends his son's love of the Gombo French tales told by people of Mande descent, he also stresses the need to wean Démon from Afro-Creole pursuits and begin his proper education:

> Il aime les contes des nègres? C'est bien naturel. Qui de nous, à son âge, ne les a pas écoutés avec plaisir? Du reste, ne nous y trompons pas, il y a dans ces récits, outre l'intérêt du drame, une malice quelquefois très fine. (109)

> He likes the blacks' tales? That's natural. Who among us at his age didn't listen to them with pleasure? But for the rest, let's not kid ourselves. There is in these tales, aside from the dramatic interest, a malice that is often quite refined.

Alluding to reasons why the fables cease to entertain white adults, Mercier shows awareness of the tales' more subversive powers.

Mercier introduces his readers to plantation life through the tour that Démon offers his French tutor. We meet the African patriarch Ima playing banjo beneath a sky described as an illuminated Qur'an, and the Orientalist context of the scene suggests that Ima could [as Reginald Hamel states (411)] signify "Imam":

> C'était une de ces belles nuits transparents et douces, où la ciel de la Louisiane rivalise de splendeur avec celui de l'Égypte ou de l'Arabie. La voûte étoilée s'ouvrait comme un immense livre écrit en lettres d'argent, de pourpre, de topaze et de saphir. (126)

> It was one of those beautiful nights, transparent and peaceful, when the Louisiana sky rivals in splendour the night sky of Egypt or Arabia. The starry vault opened like an immense book written in letters of silver, purple, topaz, and saphire.

As he listens to the African patriarch's music beneath the stars, Démon describes Ima's "banza . . . une espèce de guitar à quatre cords" ("banjo . . . a kind of guitar with four strings"), detailing its construction from a calabash resonator, snakeskin covering, cypress neck and pegs, and horsehair strings (127). Pélasge's respect for his charge's Creole knowledge is forthright: "Mon petit ami, ce que vous savez vous le savez bien, et vous l'expliquer parfaitement" (127) ("My young friend, what you know you know well, and you explain it perfectly"), and following his introduction to the banjo, the tutor's Creole education is continued with introductions to filé gumbo and the Saint-Ybars family emblem—"le sachem," a giant live oak that had once served as a sacred Choctaw landmark.

While the "Sachem" oak is the Saint-Ybars emblem, and gumbo dishes and banjo music mark Creole heritage, Mamrie remains the most powerful enculturating Afro-Creole force in the novel. Her position works, of course, to enculturate her, too. She is taught to read and write French (Voltaire, Rousseau, and Hugo), and she sings to piano accompaniment. Even though she is seen as fitting organically into the Saint-Ybars household, Mamrie is well aware of the evil of slavery. When Démon brings her some birds he has captured and caged, she replies, "[T]o oté li so la liberté é to oulé li contan. Mo sré voudré oua ça to sré di, si yé té mété toi dan ain lacage comme ça" (119) ("You took away his freedom and you expect him to be happy. I'd like to see what you would say if someone put you in such a cage"). Démon responds indignantly in Creole: "Mété moin dan ain lacage! . . . mo sré cacé tou, mo sré sorti é mo sré vengé moin sur moune laié ki té emprisonnin moin" (119) ("Put me in a cage! . . .I would break everything. I would escape and get even with everyone who had imprisoned me"). Mamrie then draws upon her moral authority and her experience of slavery to correct him:

> "Si yé té mété toi dan ain bon lacage avé bon baro en fer, to sré pa cacé arien; to sré mété toi en san, épi comme to sré oua ça pa servi ain brin, to sré courbé to latete é to sré resté tranquil comme pap là va fé dan eune ou deu jou." (119)

> "If someone put you in a cage with steel bars, you wouldn't break out; you could try till you burst, and then you'd see that it was no use, and you'd bow your head and be quiet like these parrots will be in a day or so."

She does manage to convince him to free the birds, and as he releases them, she exclaims, "[C]an michié Démon va gran, la fé ain bon maite pou nouzotte" (120) ("When Mister Demon grows up, he will make a good master for us"). Since the plantation is for Mamrie both the cage that binds her and her home, she cultivates the young master in such a way as to make her life more agreeable in old age.

Mercier makes the evils of the patriarchal system quite apparent in the whimsical, destructive power that Saint-Ybars wields. When Démon is ordered to submit to a lashing after defending his mother against his adulterous father, he refuses, and Saint-Ybars lashes his son across the face with the whip normally reserved for slaves. Mamrie hurls a hatchet toward Saint-Ybars, thereby becoming subject to execution according to the code noir. Although an assembly of forces intervenes on Mamrie's behalf to win her pardon, Mercier makes it clear that the concentration of power in the hands of a master corrupts even a "good" man and is the root cause of a manic personality split in many of the Creole men. Even the servants dearest to the family find their fates resting with their masters' shifting whims and fortunes.

Saint-Ybars's attempt to master his son Démon results in Démon's departure for study in Paris. From Paris, Démon corresponds with Mamrie in Creole. But when he returns to Louisiana as the plantation's heir following the Civil War, he greets Mamrie for the first time in French, the language of mastery. Mamrie's Creole response underscores the changes and continuity of their old bonds: "To blié parlé créol; mo oua ça; tapé parlé gran bo langage de France; epi asteur, effronté to tutéié to Mamrie" (246) ("You forgot the creole language, I can see that. You learned the nice language of France, and now, you impudent young man, you address your Mamrie as *tu*"). Démon's immersion in an Afro-Creole world, his period of study and exile in Paris, and his postwar return to Louisiana all mirror the life of Mercier. Born in 1816 to a prominent Creole family, Mercier learned Creole as a first language from his Afro-Creole nurse and spoke it exclusively until adolescence (Dickinson 71). The relationship between Mamrie and Demon is at least in part Mercier's autobiographical recapturing of a lost childhood erotic. Any true reentry into this world, however, brings with it certain highly charged recognitions.

Mercier finally takes the novel beyond nostalgia for a Creole childhood and offers a sustained moral critique of the South through a gothicism emplotted by miscegenation. Démon comes to recognize slavery as "une violation flagrante du droit humaine" (246) ("a flagrant violation of human rights"). Pélasge argues for "l'égalité publique" and asserts that post–Civil War racism is even harsher and more entrenched than was antebellum racism. And Démon's twin sister voices unorthodox ideas for which she fears "on peut me lyncher" (216) ("I could be lynched"). But it is Démon's love for Blanchette (eventually discovered to be a woman of color) that brings the text to full gothic critique.[2] Démon duels the man who reveals Blanchette to be the daughter of a slave, then stands by his intent to marry. But his greater difficulty is his fight with his family members in defense of his desire to marry a woman of color. Démon's first argument against them is simply that of a hard-headed lover: he states that he would marry Blanchette even if she were "noire comme l'ébène" (264) ("black as ebony"). His second argument is one that many Southerners found unsettling and which very few could respond to with absolute certainty: "Mais vous, Mesdames, pouvez-vous dire avec certitude quelle était la couleur de vos ancêtres?" (264) ("But you, Madames, can you say with certainty what the color of your ancestors was?"). He makes a third rather heretical argument that "nous sommes les descendants d'une race qui était au moins cousine germaine des singes" (244) ("We are descendants of a race that was at least first cousin to monkeys"). When his aunt and cousins add that race is less the issue than is Blanchette's shameful heritage of slavery, Démon counters by recalling the base ingredients that made up America's colonial pioneers: "Nous tous qui vivons sous ce ciel béni de l'Amérique, descendants de Français, d'Anglais, d'Espagnols, d'Italiens, d'Allemands, de Portugais, de Suisses, de Suédois, etc., tous nous sommes les petits fils de malheureux qui ont traversé de longs siècles, le front courbé sous le poids de la servitude" (265) ("All of us who live under America's blessed sky, descendants of French, English, Spanish, Italians, Germans, Portuguese, Swiss, Swedes, etc., all of us are the grandchildren of the wretched who crossed over, stooped from centuries under the weight of servitude"). The last argument, made by Blanchette's black great-grandmother to Démon's cousin, appeals in metropolitan French to shared texts:

> "Je vous ai vue pleurer en lisant l'histoire d'une jeune paria: vous trouvez injuste et cruel qu'il ne fût pas permis au jeune homme qui l'aimait de l'épouser, parce qu'ils n'étaient pas de la meme classe. La pitie que vous aviez pour cette paria, ne l'aurez-vous pas pour Blanchette?" (283)

> I have seen you cry while reading the story of a young outcast: you find it unjust and cruel that the young man who loves her is not permitted to marry her because they aren't of the same class. The pity that you had for that outcast, can't you feel it for Blanchette?"

L'Habitation Saint-Ybars speaks from America's literary crossroads. We have ex-slaves reading French romances and planters fully conversant with Senegambian fables. Informed by the language and contentious point of view of those fables, Mercier's text offered a deeper embrace of creolization than his white audience was ready to face.

Had Mercier written *L'Habitation Saint-Ybars* in English rather than in French, it could have capitalized on the national interest in Creole culture sparked a year earlier by Cable's *The Grandissimes* and would have raised quite a ruckus in Louisiana, the South, and the nation as a whole. But Mercier could no more divest French and Gombo from his text's interweaving of fierce social criticism and nostalgia than could Harris renounce the task of telling the Remus tales in the vernacular. The medium is indeed fabulous muse-source of the message. That Mercier's attack on racial prejudice did not provoke outrage in the South is due to the fact that *L'Habitation Saint-Ybars* has never really been read. By combining Louisiana's most substantial novelistic immersion in Gombo French with a strong critique of Creole society, *L'Habitation Saint-Ybars* was assured of a marginal reception even as it articulated forces shaping the American mainstream.

III

Julia Peterkin (1880–1961), the South's first Pulitzer Prize- winning novelist, a South Carolina plantation mistress born with a caul of second sight on a Halloween night, affirmed in *Roll, Jordan, Roll* (1933) that "[w]hite Southerners with generations of contact with Negroes behind them show markedly the influence of negro ways and ideas" (19). But her Creole vision of Southern culture was rejected by the more influential poet-critic Allen Tate, who repeatedly argued that the Southern tradition was most valuable for the degree to which it had remained profoundly European. Yet Tate did acknowledge problems with his point of view, admitting "*African* chattel slavery was the worst groundwork conceivable for the growth of a great culture of European pattern" (524). Tate wrote that "[t]he Negro slave was a barrier between the ruling class and the soil" (524), for "[t]he enormous 'difference' of the Negro doomed him from the beginning to an economic status purely. . . . the white man got nothing from the Negro, no profound image of himself in terms of the soil. . . . he was too different, too alien" (525–26). Assuming essential difference, Tate ignored the reciprocal process of enculturation in the South, but he arrived at the truth when he admitted that "[b]lack slavery could not nurture the white man in his own image," and created "deficiencies in *spiritual soil*" for a ruling class that held title to the soil but found self-imposed barriers thwarting identification with the emerging folk culture (526, emphasis added). As long as they sought truth/legitimacy in European/white "Being" rather than in the Creole realities of "Becoming," white Southern writers would find no viable muse, no spiritual soil.[3]

While Du Bois and Toomer were tilling spiritual soil in the South, serious deficiencies continued to plague white writers' attempts to cultivate "the Sahara of the Bozart," at least until Julia Peterkin realized that far too many white Southerners were what Robert Frost claimed Americans had ceased to be:

> still colonials,
> Possessing what we still were unpossessed by,
> Possessed by what we now no more possessed.
> Something we were withholding made us weak
> Until we found out that it was ourselves
> We were withholding from our land of living. (348)

Peterkin resolved to see more clearly the natural and social landscape that surrounded her and, through her active apprenticeship into Afro-Creole culture, found the means to say things "no nice South Carolina lady ever says" (Clark 222). The almost colonial loneliness she had felt as the only white woman living on her plantation "ended," she wrote, "as my interest in becoming acquainted with things began" (*Collected Stories* 71), and Julia—who had earned a master's degree in comparative religions—began to appreciate what she might learn from women such as "Maum" Lavinia Berry and Mary Weeks.

Best remembered for *Green Thursday* (1924), *Black April* (1927), and the Pulitzer Prize-winning *Scarlet Sister Mary* (1928), Peterkin had received more attention from historians and folklorists than from literary critics until the University of Georgia Press recently returned her work to print and published a compelling biography by Susan Millar Williams (1997). Despite long neglect from the literary world, Julia Peterkin was an early practitioner of Southern gothic and one of the most popular of Harlem Renaissance era writers. Du Bois wrote in *The Crisis* that *Green Thursday* was "a beautiful book"; Alain Locke wrote that "only one or two Negro writers of prose have found the depth of analysis or the penetration of spirit which . . . characterizes Mrs. Peterkin's 'Scarlet Sister Mary,'" and Sterling Brown offered her creolized fiction as a worthy model of achieving contact with spiritual soil: "From her we might get a hint of the need of going back to the soil; of digging our roots deeply therein. . . .If we do decide to try this, there could be few better mentors than Julia Peterkin" (quoted in Robeson 764).

Peterkin admitted that her first stories were exorcisms of the ugliness Southern pastoral ideology had long hidden: "I write to get rid of the things that disturb me. . . . I have to get rid of them, so I have written them out" (Overton 258–59). Her "writing out" of disturbing incidents on the plantation received first encouragement from her piano teacher, the poet Henry Bellamann, and then met with the praises of Carl Sandburg and finally H.L. Mencken, who published Peterkin's first work in 1921 but found much of it "too strong" (Clark 230). One such "too strong" story was Julia's first sustained effort from a black point of view, "A Baby's Mouth" (1922). The story tells how Maum Hannah, the plantation midwife, delivers a child born without a mouth. Maum Hannah realizes, "'Somebody got to cut a mout' fo' dat chile. . . . Dey got to. Ef dey don't, he gwine dead'" (*Collected Stories* 89), so she takes it upon herself to cut the opening that gives the child voice and sustenance. "A Baby's Mouth" may or may not have been born of such a birth on Peterkin's Lang Syne Plantation, but as Susan Millar Williams writes, the story had "special significance for Julia. . . . It dramatized the painful process of opening up, finding a voice, making noise" (49). The "gagged" voicelessness of so much of her South Carolina female experience drove Julia to try to cut a mouth through which she might (borrowing the voices of her servants and tenants) "musicate through letters" even if the music was often "too strong" in its spiraling movement between fabulous spiritual/folk vision and horrifying rage.

Another of the Mencken-rejected "strong" stories, "Missy's Twins" (1922), struck at the heart of Southern idealizations of milk-bond relationships in an unprecedented treatment of the Afro-Creole mammy. Missy, a pregnant, motherless girl cared for by the story's unnamed "Mammy," is left on the plantation without means as Mammy must accompany her little white charge to a summer residence in the mountains. Months later, riding the train back to the plantation, the little boy, "accustomed to her undivided interest," is hurt by her divided mind and questions her "with the same accent all the children she had nursed learned from her" (95). Back in the big house, she bathes him and feels the weight of a life spent "putting children to sleep" (96). When the boy's father—whom she also raised—peers into the room, she reads his troubled face, asking "Son, is you troubled 'bout somet'ing?" and finally, "How's my people?" (96). Using a standard English that stands in contrast with the Gullah his son has yet to be weaned from, the father confesses that Missy gave birth to twins—born dead—and that the babies' bodies were poorly buried in Mammy's garden:

> "The hounds—" he went on, "the hounds broke in and dug them both up—and ate them—"
> The silence was intense, like a thing in the room. The little white boy's quiet breathing seemed harsh. (98)

As Susan Millar Williams has noted, we are led to see that underneath the oft-celebrated mutual affection between "Mammy" and her "employers" there lies "an impersonal force, white supremacy. The white child sleeps in a clean white bed; black children are not safe even in their graves" (51). Peterkin's early antipastoral vision led her away from "moonlight and magnolia" nursemaids into a divided real world that engendered her need to "write out" texts of cathartic, personal healing.

Julia Peterkin's attentiveness to her world brought her more deeply

into a doubly conscious, creolized worldview. Grounded in Afro-Creole belief systems and the fabulist's faith in folk culture, her first book, *Green
Thursday*, goes beyond use of "superstition," understood by Lotman and
Uspensky as "elements of a text of an old culture whose code is lost" (412),
to emplot action through codes understood to be occulted or transformed
rather than lost. *Green Thursday*'s title story pits its hero, Killdee, against
social, natural, even supernatural boundaries. Faced with the necessity of
saving his crops, Killdee transgresses traditional law by plowing on Ascen-
sion Day—Green Thursday—when "God would send fire down from heaven
to punish men who didn't respect this day" (28). Transgressively individualistic and an admitted "sinner," the *fadenya*-oriented Killdee refuses orthodox faith: "Preachers say sinners are like goats and Christians are like sheep.
He'd a lot rather be a goat than a sheep. Goats have sense" (31). Rose, pregnant with their second child, warns him that because of his violation of the
soil on Green Thursday "Somet'ing bad'll happen to you" (38). Sure enough,
the couple's only child is burned (perhaps by lightning) and dies in the
hands of the folk healer Maum Hannah, who that very night moves from
treating the dying child to serving as midwife at the birth of their new child.
Maum Hannah, a pillar of the Afro-Christian community, consoles the couple
using a Gullah expression for the coming dawn that is a translation straight
from Wolof: "Day'll soon be clean" (48). Although Killdee pays for his transgression of orthodox folk belief in the title story, later on—in the book's
penultimate story—when he confronts the church flock and swears threats
at the deacons, he proves able to transgress the church's codes without the
retribution that followed his earlier transgression of more elemental forces.
Green Thursday, upon which Peterkin's tenant Hester worked a charm so
that "whoever read these stories, they will be seal on his heart" (Maddox
40), indeed sealed its readers in an earthy Creole soil that takes priority
over scripture. *Green Thursday*, with its representation of a young girl's spiritual "seeking" (the West African-style process of religious initiation by which
Gullah and Bahamian Christians, under the guidance of church elders, pray
in the woods, relate their dreams, and await confirmation of initiating visions or signs), is born of its author's long process of "seeking" voice and
vision in creolized "spiritual soil."[4]

Peterkin's first novel, *Black April*, stakes her most solid claim to Afro-
Creole "spiritual soil." One of the pioneering novelists (at least among whites)
in treating the Deep South's social landscape, she was also, in the words of
William Sessions, "one of the very last who can evoke with magnificent
precision the natural landscape that surrounded American life for two centuries or more" (747–48). *Black April* opens with a powerful low country
landscape and a birth. The expectant grandfather paddles a pirogue by night
across tide-flooded rice fields to Blue Brook Plantation to fetch the woman

who grounds almost all of Peterkin's fiction—Maum Hannah—whose African birthing beads are emblematic of her medicinal knowledge and power: "Maum Hanah, his own first cousin, had a string of charm beads their old grandmother had brought all the way from Africa when she came on a slave ship. They and the charm words that ruled them were left in Maum Hannah's hands. Ever since he was a boy, living on Blue Brook, he had heard people say that those beads had never failed to help a woman birth a child safely" (19). Introduction into folk knowledge begins with the birth. We learn that "a plough-share . . . ground and filed and put under the bed is the best thing in the world for birth-pains," that "[s]wift labor comes with a waning moon, not a growing one," and that "[e]bb tide is a dangerous time for sick people" (12). Like Peterkin herself, the baby boy (Breeze) is born with a caul and is assumed to be gifted with second sight.

In all of Peterkin's fiction, Maum Hannah is the communal, nurturing force of *badenya* mother-child-ness bonds. A guardian of old forms of herbal medicine, midwifery, and spirituality, she is a rooted pillar of the Afro-Christian community and an enculturating link to Africa:

> All children loved to come here and sit inside Maum Hannah's chimney on the end of a log. Big Sue used to sit there and watch Maum Hannah put ash-cake in the ashes to cook, and sweet potatoes to roast. The fire never went out in Maum Hannah's fireplace. It's bad luck for a fire to die in a house and this fire had never gone out altogether since it was first started by Maum Hannah's great-grandpa, who was brought from across the sea to be a slave. . . . The fires that burned in all the Quarter houses came from that same first fire that had burned for years and years. It was a lot older than anybody on the plantation. (112)

The fires in the quarters represent something of Creole energy of action itself—with sources in old forms of *nyama* fueled by ever-present material, a constant process of burning and becoming.

As baby Breeze grows and is initiated into the world of Blue Brook, he sees that his world is possessed of two minds. Like the dialectic of indigenous Mande practice and Islam in the Sunjata, these two minds cause Uncle Bill to declare: "I don' like charms . . . a Christian man ain' got no business foolin' wid 'em," but he admits to living between "dem two minds arguin'" (270). Breeze ponders a choice between two spiritual paths: "[H]e ought either to pray now or start learning magic" (123), and since Breeze was "born with second sight. . . . magic would be better for him than learning books" (137). Medicine is a particular field of contention. Blue Brook's inhabitants tend to avoid white doctors until all other resources have been exhausted, and they place their trust in Maum Hannah, who "knew more than any white doctor" (271).[5]

The process of Breeze's folk education allows Peterkin extensive cataloging of Afro-Creole knowledge concerning medicine, conjure, birthing, planting, animal husbandry, weather, botany, and wildlife. Interested in the ways in which shared experience creates community, she chronicles how smells and tastes of cooking (yams, greens, bacon, grits) spice activities such as a birth-night supper, where music and dance add erotic "soul" to common ingredients as Zeda calls to the group: "Yunnuh got to dance nice if you want to eat dis rice an' hash! I ain' mixin' no cool Christian stew!" (76). The birth-night supper is a scene that, like many in *Black April*, offers a semiotic kinship to Senegambian sources. One instance of this connection occurs when Breeze is taught, like Mande hunters, not to touch a woman before going hunting (139). Another such connection may be found in Peterkin's treatment of Sea Island de facto polygamy (noted by Twining 14). April, the powerful foreman of Blue Brook, follows a pattern perhaps first established by West African polygamy and then altered by the quasi-polygamous example of so many plantation masters, when he fathers children by several of the plantation women even though he has a wife. April's children by his wife Leah are his "yard children," while his children by other women are "woods colts." As with the Sunjata, much plot tension revolves around *fadenya* jealousy of "co-wives" and their children. Peterkin's relatively frank focus on such sexual matters shows a brazenness akin to that of her hero Black April and led to efforts to ostracize her from Carolina society, since according to South Carolina historian Yates Snowden, "no Southern lady should be concerned with the Negro's 'fornications'" (quoted in Durham 42).

As Breeze learns to read his landscape, the narrative focuses on the transgressive behavior of his father, April, who appears to violate the natural order by using pesticides on boll weevils and by assaulting a corrupt preacher in the church. April's dominance wanes after he exiles his son Sherry, who curses him: "I hope Gawd'll rot all two o' you feets off! I hope E will" (214–15). Astonished at April's behavior, Big Sue tells him: "[Y]ou ain' strong as dat conjure Zeda's gwine put on you" (218). Later, after April is cuckolded by Sherry, Zeda (Sherry's mother and April's ex-lover) adds a final curse reminiscent of the one Sunjata received from his mother's co-wife, making him lame and unfit to wield power: "I hope ev'y lawful yard-chile you had by Leah'll perish. I hope you' feet'll rot" (267).

April soon begins complaining about his feet. Then, in a scene in which Peterkin fictionally presents the horror she initiated with her own plantation's gangrene-stricken foreman, April soaks his feet in a medicated bath prepared by a friend, watches his toes float free, and stands shouting before crumpling to the floor. The scene of April's fall is the factual core out of which the novel—and perhaps something of Julia Peterkin's very need to write—grew. Goatlike in a world expectant of sheepish behavior, April is one persona of Julia Peterkin's own unorthodox individualism. He is also, as observed by his son Breeze, an oppressive patriarchal figure represented in language reminiscent of some of Peterkin's descriptions of her father, Dr. Mood (Robeson 775). The novel's treatment of de facto polygamy may fit too neatly into the primitivist excesses of the Harlem Renaissance era, but Peterkin's fearless hero and the brazenness of the women who desire him help to provide her with what Ralph Ellison has called the black mask of "deeply personal rebellion" (*Shadow and Act* 49). Peterkin in essence appears in black face in order to mask and find voice for unorthodox views that she (as a South Carolinian white "lady") could not otherwise express. And though *Black April* is something of a mask, it remains hauntingly tied to the lives of real people, particularly as it ends with a revoicing of her amputee foreman's last command to her, "Bury me in a man-size box—You un'erstan'?—A man-size—box—I—been—six—feet—fo'" (316). *Black April* attempts, in its guilt-haunted, embracing, catalogic way, to be the man-sized box her foreman ordered for his interment in soil to which Peterkin held title.

The novel that followed *Black April*, Pulitzer Prize-winning *Scarlet Sister Mary* (1928), turned to yet another Gullah character as an enabling mask of personal rebellion. Unified around a strong-willed woman's efforts to live outside of the confines of the patriarchal family, *Scarlet Sister Mary* appears intimately connected to Peterkin's effort to face events surrounding the birth of her son. Elizabeth Robeson writes that "[o]n a plantation filled with midwives, Dr. Mood delivered his daughter's baby and following the birth declared her unfit to bear any more children," then, as she lay unconscious, "secured the consent of her husband to sterilize her" (768–69). As Maum Lavinia Berry (the model for Maum Hannah) cared for Julia and the newborn son, Julia stepped up a questioning of male authority that culminated in what may be, as Paul Goldstein has argued, an attack against "no less a force than the patriarchal family itself" (138). Dedicated to her father, Julius Mood, *Black April* had provided Julia with the fabulist's mask through which she might voice "unspeakable" criticism—going so far as to feature a mule named Julia, a bit of "kick her father in the pants" innuendo that Susan Millar Williams claims Julius Mood "could hardly have missed," coming from his stubborn "sterile daughter, culturally half black and half white" (119). But *Scarlet Sister Mary* would be more bold in its rebellious vision and would draw less upon Maum Hannah (Lavinia Berry) as muse than upon Lavinia Berry's niece, Mary Weeks, in its celebration of self-sufficient female power (Williams 130).

We meet Mary at a time when the fifteen-year-old girl is drawn to the charmingly irresponsible July Pinesett. As Zora Neale Hurston's Janie would later feel about Tea Cake Woods, Mary "felt that she could walk on air, or fly like a bird, or blossom like a flower, when she heard his beautiful words" (22). After marriage, Mary sits alone each night as July drinks at the local juke (from Wolof *juk*, meaning "disorderly"). On Christmas Eve, the pregnant Mary sits on the back benches with the sinners at Watch Night, "hearing the story of that other Mary who was the mother of God's own son" (70), and we begin to see possibilities of a different and truer (Creole) Madonna. With the advent of spring, a plum tree outside Mary's home signals (like the pear tree in Hurston's *Their Eyes Were Watching God*) sexual vision: "The old black plum tree beside her door hid its knotty branches with soft white blossoms, which became thicker and sweeter hour by hour as the sunshine gathered strength, and when honey-bees climbed in and out of them showers of fragrant petals were scattered around the old tree's foot" (71). Since July is the bee to her flower, Mary hopes to make the marriage work. She yearns, like Hurston's Janie, to be "*any* tree in bloom."

Also like Zora's Janie, Mary has difficulty matching her vision of the tree in bloom with her knowledge of men. Taking the advice of Maum Hannah, she visits a conjurer, but July abandons her before she can "root" him with the powerful *gris-gris* she obtains. The novel then leaps fifteen years ahead to when Mary has established herself as the head of a large family, each of her children having a different father. With mother-child-ness bonds (and her erotic *gris-gris*) as her form of social security, she turns to a different mode of family values, for "she knew men at last, and she knew that not one of them is worth a drop of water that drains out of a woman's eye" (191).

Mary's psychic/sexual independence brings her into conflict with the women and deacons of Heaven's Gate Church. Like Killdee and April, she disdains congregational orthodoxies that bring people to move and think "in droves and flocks like chicken or sheep" (218). Standing in opposition to desire, the church members "laid strict rules for each other because they were too timid, too coward-hearted to come out in the open and live as they wanted to live" (218). Hurston would write similarly in *Dust Tracks*: "People need religion because the great masses fear life" (201). Condemned because none of her children were "full kin," Mary finds more power in breaking the rules than in continuing to be ruled.

Peterkin's dissatisfaction with sterilizing male control over her life seems to have driven her creation of Mary as a desired, masked double. But unlike most of the jazz-era exoticism that used black worlds as vibrant counterworlds, Peterkin's Sister Mary struggles against the same sorts of sheepishness that her author hoped to escape. *Scarlet Sister Mary* tends to treat difference through a prior acceptance of similarity, as when Mary tells

Deacon Andrew, "Men is different from womens, Cousin, but all o we has two minds enty?" (240). Later, Mary thinks movingly about difference: "Men are too much alike, with ways too much the same. None is worth keeping, none worth a tear; and still each one is a little different from the rest; just different enough to make him worth finding out. Everybody has a selfness that makes the root of his life and being" (248).

Mary is finally brought back to the flock after her first son's death, which she interprets as judgment on her life of scarlet sin. Like Killdee and April, Mary finds the limits of her will, but unlike these male heroes, she finds a place in the fold *and* is able to maintain her independent (goatish) ways. As she prepares to give an account of her vision to the deacons who debate her readmission into the church, her two minds form a plan of syncretic agency: "Should she wear the charm? Would it be sinful to wear it to-night? She looked in the glass and asked the question to herself. One of her minds said, 'Take it off.' The other mind said, 'Don't be a fool, keep it on.' The earrings shook and twinkled. The deacons were men who needed to be ruled in her favor to-night" (340).

Learning from the many black women who contributed to the artistic creation of Maum Hannah and Sister Mary, Julia Peterkin developed deeply personal, need-answering characterizations of flexibly transgressive Afro-Creole heroines. Jazz-era primitivism provided a climate for Peterkin's work, but the particular power of Peterkin's fiction is derived from her ties to the land and the people living on it. She found fresh images of self from the language and worldview of the tenant farmers who worked land to which she held title. Still, despite her respect for Afro-Creole culture, Julia Peterkin never fully faced the horrors of slavery and white supremacy, and her later works, from *Bright Skin* (1932) to *Roll, Jordan, Roll* (1933), show a steady retreat from the early desire to see things clearly, as one-time admirer Sterling Brown pointed out in a review of *Roll, Jordan, Roll*: "These people pay for their quaintness by their—at best—semi-enslavement" (quoted in David Lewis 296). Her apprenticeship to Afro-Creole culture always hovered near pastoralism, particularly since her vocation as plantation mistress interfered with honest representation of the plantation economy. She avoids having her fictional tenants confront the problems of paying rent or of giving up a share of crops they raise. Her fictional titles, nurtured by her immersion in the daily life of a South Carolina plantation, worked to reinforce her claims of entitlement to govern the people living upon her land and in her pages. Peterkin's opening of herself to Afro-Creole bodies of knowledge is encyclopedic and often soulful, but she did not open herself fully. It would be easy to argue that she treated her tenants and fictional characters much in the manner that Audre Lorde writes that men have kept women "maintained at a distant/inferior position to be psychically milked" (54). In spite of these serious limitations and her Depression-era retreat into full-blown pastoralism, something in Peterkin's Afro-Creole landscape animated her imagination in fiction, folklore, and strong-willed heroines that opened "spiritual soil" for more powerful writers who later tilled such places as the Okeechobee Muck and Yoknapatawpha County. Julia Peterkin helped open us all to our land of living, enabling others to see as she did that "[t]he breath of the earth was thick in the air, a good clean smell that went clear to the marrow. . . . it offered life to all that was fit and strong" (*Black April* 14).

IV

The contribution of Harlem-era works like Toomer's *Cane*, and the accompanying body of work by Carolina creolists like Julia Peterkin and Du Bose Heyward (*Porgy* 1925, *The Half Pint Flask* 1926, and *Mamba's Daughters* 1928) helped—in the context of international modernism's celebration of African art and the black image—to prepare Faulkner "to rediscover as an artist the black environment he had always known . . . his 'postage stamp of native soil'" (Honnighausen 206). Although most of Mississippi may not have been a location of creole language use, Faulkner was immersed in a creolized culture, shaped at its deepest foundational patterns by confluences of African and European elements, and by the remnant traces and forced absence of an old American Indian presence. In Faulkner, perhaps America's greatest literary artist, we find a man, as Edouard Glissant argues in *Faulkner, Mississippi*, whose "works operate in that troubled place where everyone in the world feels threatened by outrages from something oddly amorphous and denaturing, and we think it is the distorting shape of the Other" (31). This "threat," Glissant insists, "has a name, 'Creolization,' the unstoppable conjunction . . . (like a tumultuous and boundless Mississippi)" that brings "the damnation of those who fight it" (30). Thoroughly creolized, Faulkner's Yoknapatawpha allows him to think of neither the soil, motherhood, nor his own ancestry outside of an African(ist) America.

In *Go Down, Moses,* Faulkner's Mississippi wilderness, "the rich black land, imponderable and vast, fecund" (340), is an Africanist female figure: "He had watched it . . . retreating southward through this inverted-apex, this V-shaped section of earth between hills and River until what was left of it seemed now to be gathered and for the time arrested in one tremendous density of brooding and inscrutable impenetrability at the ultimate funneling tip (343). Ike McCaslin, initiated into the wilderness by a black Chickasaw named Sam Fathers, links the destruction of the wilderness and the evils of plantation slavery as a single crime for which "[t]he whole land, the whole South is cursed" (278). Ike decides to relinquish his plantation patrimony, "that whole edifice intricate and complex and founded upon injustice and erected by ruthless rapacity and carried on even yet with at times downright savagery not only to the human beings but the valuable animals too, yet solvent and efficient and, more than that: not only still intact but enlarged, increased" (298). Through this narrative of relinquishment, Faulkner digs deeper than Heyward or Peterkin ever did, as Ike finds his claims to the soil "as trivial and without reality as the now faded and archaic script in the chancery book in Jefferson which allocated it to them" (171). Having witnessed the whites' strippage of the land from its "First Nations" inhabitants, and being the people who most labor and observe the land, Yoknapatawpha's blacks have an emblematic and legitimate link to the land and to its flora and fauna. As Glissant observes, "When Faulkner wanted to name a particularly unusual animal, most often it would be '*the one the niggers call* this or that,' as though the name given by Blacks added clout and descriptive qualities that stemmed from some arcane knowledge" (61). Faulkner would have us see that the truest "owners" of the land are the black tenants who crop and hunt it—men like Lucas Beauchamp, who had for forty-five years worked "his own field, though he neither owned it nor wanted to nor even needed to" (35). But it is at points like this that Faulkner's mythologized spiritual soil clashes—as in Peterkin—with power politics and human needs. It is hard to imagine a man of Lucas Beauchamp's pride and resourcefulness not wanting to own and bequeath the land. And while Ike McCaslin may relinquish the material possessions of his patrimony, he proves unable in the end to relinquish the racialized possessions of psyche that his patrimony bequeathes to him: "*Maybe in a thousand or two thousand years in America,* he thought. *But not now! Not now!* . . . 'You're a nigger!'" (361). To his credit, Faulkner profoundly registers white psychic wilderness vertigo.

From its dedication "To Mammy Caroline Barr . . . born in slavery," images of motherhood, images of the autochthonous in *Go Down, Moses,* are figured in black. Much of the description of Molly Beauchamp appears drawn from Faulkner's memories of Caroline Barr. Faulkner writes that Molly Beauchamp was "the only mother he, Edmonds, ever knew, who had raised him, fed him from her own breast as she was actually doing her own child, who had surrounded him always with care for his physical body and for his spirit too, teaching him manners, behavior—to be gentle with his inferiors, honorable with his equals, generous to the weak and considerate of the aged, courteous, truthful and brave to all—who had given him, the motherless, without stint or expectation of reward that constant and abiding devotion and love which existed nowhere else in this world for him" (117). Faulkner renders the embodied power of these milk bonds in a manner similar to but stronger than Peterkin's evocations of Maum Hannah:

Even before he was out of infancy, the two houses had become interchangeable: himself and his foster-brother sleeping on the same pallet in the white man's house or in the same bed in the negro's and eating of the same food at the same table in either, actually preferring the negro house, the hearth on which even in summer a little fire always burned, centering the life in it, to his own. It did not even need to come to him as a part of his family's chronicle that his white father and his foster-brother's black one had done the same; it never even occurred to him that they in their turn and simultaneously had not had the first of remembering projected upon a single woman whose skin was likewise dark. (110)

Noting the repeating presence of such figures in Latin American and Caribbean literature, Glissant asks of Faulkner's characterizations of Caroline Barr/Molly Beauchamp/Dilsey, "How many times have we railed against her conventionality, judging her so much more unbearable, the more she corresponded perhaps to some part of the truth of the real?" (81). In *South to a Very Old Place*, Albert Murray also writes of the creolizing power of a shared Afro-Southern semiotic, but he takes Faulkner much more to task over words of gratitude and respect in eulogy of his "Mammy Caroline Barr." Murray signifies upon Faulkner's manhood and manners by asking "a hell of a lot of pretty embarrassing questions, beginning, for instance, with: 'Damn man, if the mammyness of blackness or the blackness of mammyness was so magnificent and of such crucial significance as you now claim, how come you let other white folks disrespect and segregate her like that? How come you didn't put yourself out just a little more to please her? How can fellows like you be so enthusiastic about her and yet so ambivalent and hesitant about her brothers and sisters? Man, do you really think that your reciprocation was adequate?'" (53). *Go Down, Moses*, like the best work of Peterkin, Heyward, Mercier, and Harris, is an often guilt-driven but passionate attempt at reciprocation. Albert Murray, who has tremendous respect for Faulkner's artistry, has been among the most astute readers of fiction by white Southerners. Murray notes that in Southern fiction, "the conception of *Motherhood*, for some reason almost always comes out *black*!" and he asks what happens to the "jive about the first few years of childhood being the most crucial, when the topic is the black mammy's relationship to the white child?" (54–55).

At its best, some of the creolist writing we have examined takes Murray's question to heart and recognizes an extended sense of family that cuts across racial boundaries. What Faulkner's Ike McCaslin is most deeply disgusted by is not so much slavery or even "miscegenation" but his family's denial of subsequent kinship and relations, bonds secreted in the plantation ledger, "not alone of his flesh and blood but of all his people, not only the whites but the black ones too, who were as much a part of his ancestry as his white progenitors" (268). Ike's relinquishment of his entitlement to the plantation in favor of his pursuit of spiritual soil is linked to his new, creolized reading of ancestry—his *choice* of descent from Sam Fathers, "the old man born of a Negro slave and a Chickasaw chief who had been his spirit's father if any had" (326). *Go Down, Moses* seeks its spiritual soil in the fleshpots of Egypt/Mississippi, and from its unflinching gaze into that vertigo it recognizes that the soil it inhabits is a fabulous unpossessable frontier—a frontier one can only seek to be possessed by, as the author appears to be in his immersion in Lucas Beauchamp's navigation of a local creek bottom: "Curiously enough, visibility seemed to have increased, as if the rank, sunless jungle of cypress and willow and brier, instead of increasing obscurity, had solidified it into the concrete components of trunk and branch, leaving air, space, free of it and in comparison lighter, penetrable to vision" (37).[6] What emerges from *Go Down, Moses* is a relinquishment of the old poetics of being in favor of a frontier "poetics of becoming," a Creole "poetics of the real" that has been best recognized by Martinique's great Creole writer/theorist, Edouard Glissant.[7]

The texts we've examined, all written from nineteenth-century America's core Creole centers—Charleston, Savannah, and New Orleans—and from Mississippi, a Deep South location in long commerce with them, help us to recognize what Shelley Fisher Fishkin has called our "mixed literary bloodlines," a mix so thorough that in her study of that great voice of American identity and difference, Huck Finn's, Fishkin asked *Was Huck Black?* As Albert Murray has stated, behind every American is "an Uncle Remus-derived respect for human complexity, a Brer Rabbit-derived appreciation for human ingenuity" (55). Those who would label the contemporary American scene as "the age of multiculturalism" have not been reading widely enough in our rich literary corpus, nor have they paid close attention to the cultural conditions that obtained prior to and following the nation's founding—when polylingualism and cross-cultural awareness were tools of survival rather than watchwords. The South has been a cradle for much that has so vitalized and haunted American culture, and African America has been a strong cultural agent of much that has come out of the South to shape the national identity. In a nation where shrines to Elvis abound, where Congressional Republicans slap high fives, and where Bill Clinton could swap saxophone licks with Branford Marsalis, it is high time to reevaluate the ways we read ancestry, build identity, and revere canons. Such a foundational reevaluation (not simply patterns of Saturday night slumming) could prove to be one step toward making America feel ever more Creole, more and more like home.

III

Shadows of Africans/Gothic Representations

Sincerity is telling the truth in a situation from which there is no escape except by lying.

al Junaid, quoted in al-hajj Umar Taal's
*The Spears of the Party of the Merciful Against
the Throats of the Party of the Damned* (1845)

7

The Spears of the Party of the Merciful

Senegambian Muslims, Scriptural Mercy, and Plantation Slavery

'Twas mercy brought me from my pagan land,
Taught my benighted soul to understand
That there's a God, that there's a Savior too.

Phillis Wheatley (1773)

Charno, William A. Caruthers's
The Kentuckian in New York (1834)

Evil has stunted dignity and life; Evil has stunted the mind against knowing itself.

Omar ibn Said, North Carolina (1831)

I

In chapters 1–3 we have examined some of the epic attractions posed by a monumental, scripturalist Senegambian patrimony, and have traced some of the means by which Senegambian cultures imparted something of their energy of action to emergent African American cultures. And in chapters 4–6 we took stock of how Senegambians were positioned (by their own African experiences/repertoires, and by Southern planters' needs and speculative desires) to be trusted drivers, house servants and—most significantly—the nurses or "maums" who were such strong creolizing agents upon the master class. But at a crossroads between these epic claims to Senegambian/African patrimony and white Southerners' remastered tales of an Arcadia planted in Afro-Creole spiritual soil, there is another and perhaps truer story of national horrors and violence repressed by evasive half-truths and lies. Henry Louis Gates has demonstrated that Enlightenment discourse viewed writing as "the *visible* sign of reason" (*"Race"* 8), and we have heard time and time again that enslaved Africans (like the young Senegalese Phillis Wheatley) brought with them only "oral traditions" and were awed by the Europeans' "talking books."[1] It is time to ask ourselves what happened when the epic-heroic scripturalist tradition and the Arcadian/Africanist fabulist orality became crossed? What happened when a significant number of literate enslaved Muslims gave the incontestable lie to the notion that black Africans were incapable of reason—possessing neither books nor history nor scriptural/revealed religion—were, in short, a cultural tabula rasa? The result could only be explosive, with acknowledgment on all sides of the possibility that insurrection or jihad could come from the closest, most trusted quarters. No people were better positioned to reveal the depths and dangers of the New World's foundational lies than were enslaved Muslims, and the shocks of recognition that their writing produced fueled some of America's most charged modes of writing—modes best described as gothic. While I will not argue that Senegambian Muslim scripturality is *the* source of American/ Southern gothic (the gothic, after all, was a European mode, and writers like Hawthorne reveal a powerful gothic response to the American Indian presence), what I will look to is the degree to which the presence of Muslim scripture highlights (and "charges") some of the deepest, most Manichean, most "black and white," most American modes of evasion, projection, haunting, and violence, all the stuff of American/Southern gothic. Nothing reveals so many of the occulted forces behind this fundamentally American literature of "dis-ease" than does the response of the authorial voice of slave masters to the scriptural voice of their supposed chattel. As Sylviane Diouf writes, "If these men and women could read and write, if they were not the blank slates or the primitive savages they had been portrayed to be in order to justify their enslavement, then the very foundation of the system had to be questioned" (109). This emergent questioning of the very foundation of American systems—the haunted edifice—is the special ground of the gothic.

Interestingly, even in Senegambia itself, we can find strong traces of the discourse by which scriptural mastery and possession of book religion entitles an "elect" group to "merciful" enslavement of nonscriptural "magicians." With its emphasis on the providential mercy of jihad, al-hajj Umar Taal's doctrinal work of West African Tijani Sufism (*The Spears of the Party of the Merciful Against the Throats of the Party of the Damned*) shares a discourse with Phillis Wheatley's panegyric to the "mercy" of transatlantic slavery in uprooting her benighted Senegalese soul from ways of error. Muslims have long shared an evangelistic, binary worldview with Christian co-religionists of the Book. Letters written to the French on behalf of the Tukolor/ Fulbe jihad launched by Umar Taal in 1852 near the headwaters of the Senegal and Niger show how the Umarian state offered monotheism, scriptural religion, and literacy as bonds of civilization between Muslims and Christians, linking them against "people of wickedness," "Bambara," "unbelievers," "libertines," "Magians" (Hanson and Robinson 120). Wielding a language of radical dichotomy, Umarian Islam separated peoples of the Book from mere magicians: "Know that there are only two exemplary religious communities in this age, Islam and Christianity. . . . Do not let the Magians spoil the relations between us and you" (120). Through a discourse that often paralleled the writings of European Africanists, the Umarian jihad dismissed as "Al-Magus" or Magician "those who were not People of the Book" (Hanson and Robinson 120), those who as practitioners of mumbo jumbo were liable to enslavement.

Among peoples of the Book, the scriptures themselves often become fetishized, and writing too easily becomes the visible sign of reason. Mungo Park, who repeatedly risked his life to preserve the knowledge and power inscribed in the notes for his *Travels,* wrote of how Senegambians made use of Arabic scripture in amulets and considered "the art of writing as bordering on magic" (39). Interestingly, it is after writing about the power ascribed to writing that Park introduced Western readers (who were presumed not to fetishize objects or texts) to a mask called "Mumbo Jumbo. . . . a strange bugbear, common to all the Mandingo towns, and much employed by the Pagan natives in keeping their women in subjection" (39). Introduced to Western readers as a Senegambian mask, Mumbo Jumbo soon came to represent the opposite of reason: Magian (African) difference. Increasingly, through what Abdul JanMohamed has described as "[M]anichean allegory— racial difference transformed into moral and even metaphysical difference," there grew "a field of diverse yet interchangeable oppositions between white and black, good and evil, superiority and inferiority, civilization and savagery, intelligence and emotion, rationality and sensuality, self and Other, subject and object" (80–82). Thus, we find the late-nineteenth-century author Helen Bannerman offering the following pre-scriptural genealogy: "Once upon a time there was a little black boy, and his name was Little Black Sambo. And his Mother was called Black Mumbo. And his father was called Black Jumbo" (1–3). Inescapably "Magian," born of Mumbo and Jumbo, Sambo is subjected to bookish jihad and drawn as the other side of radical racial dichotomy. African Muslims named Samba (a common name for second sons among Mande, Fulbe, Wolof, and Hausa peoples) found themselves identified as enslaveable Sambos, who might be advertised in runaway notices like the one from Savannah's *Georgia Gazette* (1775) requesting the return of "THREE NEGRO MEN: *Quamie*, about 5 feet 5 inches high and about 30 years of age; *Sambo*, about 22 years, smooth face, of the Moorish country; and *Sambo*, about 25 years and about 5 feet 5 inches high."

At question here is what happened when the growing racial ideologies behind American "Samboism" clashed with the reality of a literate Muslim slave presence in America. The presence of literate, black African Muslims as slaves in America often caused moments of doubt, challenge, and embarrassment to supporters of a racial justification of slavery. Possessing cultural values and prejudices that were at times remarkably similar to those of white Americans, and with a literate, often cosmopolitan knowledge that was clearly prior to contact with European "civilization," African Muslims could not easily be said to be benefitting from the "discipline" of slavery. Only Senegambian Muslims offered, a priori, what whites could recognize as a cultural patrimony and legitimate religion. When seriously acknowledged, the Muslim presence led American writers to gothic explosions of ideology in texts that move through the imaginary toward our real conditions—toward realities for which we have no adequate language.

II

William Alexander Caruthers (1800–1846), a Virginian who practiced medicine in Savannah and was one of the founders of the plantation novel, offered in his strongest work, *The Kentuckian in New York* (1834), a brief but powerful encounter with an enslaved Fulbe Muslim called "Charno" (from Pulaar "Cheerno"—meaning *"imam"*). Caruthers's meeting with a Fulbe Muslim named Charno appears to have been historical, but it is the imaginative impact of Charno's Arabic text that sparked Caruthers to reconsider, momentarily, his assumptions of inherent African "difference" since writing "stood as a complex 'certificate of humanity'" (Gates, *"Race"* 12). Following a meal near Savannah, Caruthers's epistolary narrator, B. Randolph, writes that "a tall, bald-headed old fellow" was summoned "who could write in his own language" (146). Randolph adds a translation to his facsimile of the text, showing it to be the Fatiha—the opening verses of the Qur'an—and offers the following response: "The old fellow's name is Charno, which it seems he has retained, after being enslaved, contrary to their general custom in that respect. I became quite affected and melancholy in talking to this venerable old man, and you may judge from that rare circumstance that he is no common character" (147). Although Charno's Arabic literacy and retention of African identity is at focus, "that rare circumstance" refers to Randolph's becoming "quite affected and melancholy in talking to this venerable old man." The "rare circumstance" is, in fact, recognition of African humanity, even perhaps recognition of the impossibility of any racial argument for sustaining plantation slavery. But Charno, like the other literate Muslims enslaved in America, must be seen as exceptional, as "no common character" in order for Randolph (and his readers) to tranquilize uncomfortable thoughts. Since Charno's ability to produce his texts comes not through slavery but in spite of it, supporters of slavery would have to regard the enslavement of this "venerable" man as an unfortunate mistake in order to avoid questioning plantation slavery's providential, civilizing mission.

To be read well, the encounter with Charno must be read in narrative context, revealed in epistolary style by B. Randolph, a young Virginian traveling through the Carolina low country. Randolph's Africanist low country scenes "transport a man into the center of Africa at once; there is the dark and sluggish stream, the dismal-looking pine barrens, and the palmetto, the oriental-looking cabbage-tree, aided by the foreign gibberish, and the unsteady light of the pine logs before the door, now and then casting a fitful gleam of light upon some of those natives of the shores of the Niger, with their tattooed visages, ivory teeth, flat noses, and yellow and blood-shot eyeballs" (118). On a journey through a cypress swamp, the famished narrator, accompanied by his trusty body servant Sam[bo], follows fenced cotton fields into "an immense negro quarter . . . many miles distant" from the master's house (145). Accepting the gracious hospitality offered by the black driver's family, the narrator receives grilled chicken and grits: "[A] sweeter meal was never made than I thus took; a fowl seasoned with salt, and a large pot of small homminy, served direct to my mouth from a large wooden spoon, without the cumbrous intervention of plates, knives, and forks" (145). As Mungo Park had learned, Randolph writes that travel and hunger may erode essentialist suppositions of difference: "Sam and I dined at the same time and from the same table, which was none other than the ground floor, covered with the head of a barrel,—hunger is a wonderful leveler of distinctions" (145). It is while seated over a barrel next to Sam, enjoying a meal in the heart of an Africanist landscape, that Randolph meets Charno, who "took the head of the barrel in his lap, and began . . . on the right side of the page" (146), producing the Arabic text inscribed in facsimile and translation in Caruthers's text.

Even as *The Kentuckian in New York* attempts to make Charno's case appear exceptional, the text shows contemplation of Charno to be connected to a quotidian yet exoticized Afro-Creole erotic: "[W]eary as I was, I could not directly get to sleep for thinking of sandy deserts, old Charno, chicken suppers, negro quarters, and Virginia Bell!" (147). The narrator's puzzlement over the meeting with Charno is dismissed as the Quixote-like narrative continues its quest for the heroine Virginia Bell. However, that quest leads through a web of associations tying hero and heroine to slave quarters where Randolph sleeplessly seeks solace in a prayer similar to this one from Charno's text: "'Guide us in the right way, the way of those with whom thou art well pleased, and not of those with whom thou art angry, nor of those who are in error. Amen!'" (147). But as we shall see, in returning to *The Kentuckian in New York* at chapter's end, efforts to dismiss disquieting realizations tend to return more ominously as gothic obsession bound for violence.

Three Muslim Fulbe whose texts gained them attention provide historical context and precedent for Caruthers's representation of Charno. The first of these men was Ayuba Suleiman Diallo, whose story was told by his amanuensis/biographer Thomas Bluett in *Some Memoirs of the Life of Job, the Son of Solomon, the High Priest of Boonda in Africa. . .* (1734). Like Alex Haley's Kunta Kinte, Ayuba Suleiman Diallo was captured on the Gambia River and brought to Annapolis, Maryland. Diallo was captured and sold while on a mission on behalf of his father, a Muslim cleric, "to sell two Negroes, and to buy Paper, and some other Necessaries" (in Austin 78–79). Through the circumstances of his capture we can see that scriptural religion not only helped to establish the dichotomies defining "Magian" others fit for enslavement but also fueled the market materially with demands for the media of scriptural communication—imported paper.

Fortunately for Diallo, racial ideologies justifying slavery as a civilizing force were not fully developed in America when he was enslaved in 1731. It was still possible to be recognized as an individual black "African gentleman" who might be freed as such, "merely from a Principle of Humanity" (77). Having initially fallen victim to his need to sell slaves for English paper, Diallo made use of his literacy to call attention to his identity as a gentleman for whom "Slavery and Confinement" were "by no means agreeable" (81). After having escaped his master, Diallo was jailed and brought before Bluett, who writes of a recognition scene prefiguring that of Caruthers's novel: "[H]e wrote a Line or two before us, and when he read it, pronounced the Words *Allah* and *Mahommed*; by which, and his refusing a Glass of Wine we offered him, we perceived he was a *Mahometan*, . . . we could perceive he was no common Slave" (80).

Throughout the biography, Bluett insists upon Diallo's attributes as a gentleman, writing of his "good nature and affability," his possession of "solid judgement, a ready memory, and a clear head," and his "strict regard to truth" (88). Regard for Diallo's status as a gentleman appears to have taken priority over preoccupations with race. James Oglethorpe, founder of the Georgia colony, purchased Diallo's freedom and enabled him to travel to England and be received by the royal family before his return to Africa. Diallo's return home by way of the Gambia is chronicled in Francis Moore's *Travels Into the Inland Parts of Africa* (1738). Moore, who had worked closely with Oglethorpe in Georgia and had published *A Voyage to Georgia Begun in the Year 1735*, was a close partner of Diallo's from August 1734 to April 1735 and writes of Diallo's reportedly Panglossian response to his enslavement: "'[H]ad I not been sold, I should neither have known any thing of the English tongue, nor have had any of the fine, useful and valuable things I now carry over, nor have known that in the world there is such a place as England, nor such noble, good and generous people as Queen Caroline, Prince William, the Duke of Montague, the Earl of Pembroke, Mr. Holden, Mr. Oglethorpe, and the Royal African Company'" (in Austin 57). While it is quite possible that these were Moore's sentiments rather than Diallo's, the belief that a scriptural God authors the creation, writing things into his book for the ultimate though not always apparent good of the Kingdom of the Faithful, may indeed have been an idea Diallo shared with his early-eighteenth-century British benefactors.

Philip Curtin suggests that Diallo, who was "probably the best known of the early African travellers to Europe" (*Africa Remembered* 17), may have helped to popularize the name "Sambo" through his claims to close contacts with a reigning king, "Sambo Gelazi" (*Africa Remembered* 17, 38). If Curtin is correct, Bluett's biography of Ayuba Suleiman Diallo provides a link between two simultaneously developing traditions: one degenerating into the Sambo myth in the Americas, and the other gathering force to become one of West Africa's most celebrated epic heroes—Samba Geladio Jegi. As slavery, American racial politics, and European colonialism gathered momentum, so too did Africanist construction of black Sambo, born of mumbo jumbo. When a literate or obviously heroic Muslim Samba came along to destroy the stereotype's validity, one then might Orientalize Samba in order to account for his textual and cultural patrimony. Even back in Senegal, when French colonial administrators encountered the epic of Samba Geladio Jegi, they explained the cultural sophistication which produced it by arguing that "the first authors of this legend, the Deniankobe, were Fulbe, that is to say, racially mixed Semites . . . and not negroes in the absolute sense of the word," and that "Semitic blood" had been "of the greatest intellectual benefit of the race" and had made possible "this half-negro 'Iliad'" and its traits of chivalry unknown among "Negroes of pure race" (Equilbecq 15, 21, 132).

Also preceding the appearance of Muslim Charno in Caruthers's *Ken-tuckian in New York* were the writings by and about another enslaved Pulaar-speaker, Omar ibn Said. Described by the chief justice of the North Carolina court, as having "the manners, principles, and feelings of a well bred gentle-man" (in Austin 455), like Ayuba Suleiman Diallo, Omar had escaped a master who he felt had misused him, attracted attention after his capture by writing upon the jail walls, and convinced a new master that he was a frail African gentleman-scholar unfit for the fields. Whites called him "Prince Moro," assuming that any literate African must be royalty, while Africans who encountered his writing in the jailhouse called him a "pray-God to the king" (452).The many Arabic texts left behind by Omar suggest that his faith weakened or perhaps became more syncretic as he aged among Chris-tians. His Presbyterian pastor reported that he long kept the fast of Ramadan and clung to Islam but that through efforts at proselytization he gradually became "by all outward signs, [a] sincere believer in Jesus Christ" (482). Although synthesis of Islamic and Christian practice was a fairly common pattern, described by Charles C. Jones in Georgia in 1842 (125), it seems best to look at the evidence Omar himself offered in an autobiographical letter written in Arabic (1831).

Omar opens his autobiographical letter by noting his birthplace in Futa Toro and his studies pursued for twenty-five years under three schol-ars, whom he acknowledges by name. He also writes briefly of his coming to America: "Wicked men took me by violence and sold me to the Chris-tians. We sailed a month and a half on the great sea to the place called Charleston in the Christian land. I fell into the hands of a small, weak and wicked man, who feared not God at all, nor did he read at all nor pray" (in Austin 467). Omar writes of his escape, of being jailed, and of his good fortune in being purchased by the Owen brothers, one of whom (John) had served as governor of North Carolina: "These men are good men. What food they eat they give me to eat. As they clothe themselves they clothe me. They permit me to read the Gospel of God, our Lord, and Savior, and King" (466). Omar seeks to clarify his conversion to Christianity by invoking Jesus as "Messiah," and "the true way," while claiming to have abandoned Islamic practice. But as Sylviane Diouf has pointed out, "Omar ibn Said may have been the only person who actually wrote—openly—an autobiography while still enslaved. The fact that it was in Arabic could act as a buffer between him and his potential readers, but he still had to be very much on his guard" (143). And Richard Brent Turner insists that although Omar "convinced the Christian community of his religious assimilation, the fact that his Arabic Bible and all of his manuscripts include references to Muhammad challenges the assumption that he was successfully converted" (38).

North Carolina whites built an increasingly pastoral legend around the life of Omar. Presenting slavery in its most benign, paternalistic form, the Omarian legend negated awareness of inherent equality by going so far as to deny Omar's blackness. In 1884, the *Raleigh Farmer and Mechanic* reported that Omar, whose "hair was straight" and whose "features and form were as perfect as those of an Apollo Belvidere. . . . was no ordinary person, and was certainly not a negro," but "had been a hereditary prince of the Foulah tribe in Arabia" (in Austin 488–89). After misrepresenting Omar's geographical origins, the Raleigh biographer offers a relatively informed review of the Fulbe presence in the antebellum South and concludes with an Uncle Remus-influenced account of how Omar "let the children climb on his knees, while he would tell them strange stories of his native Arabia" (490). And in 1968, under assault by the Civil Rights movement, the *Fayetteville News and Observer* could celebrate "Omeroh" after carefully deracinating him: "His skin was dark, but he was not Negro. His hair was straight, his features perfect, his manners those of a gentleman" (Austin 501). His legend became a strange Orientalist fixture of his master's plantation, a means of comforting white fears of the black masses: "Omeroh became part of Owen Hill, as integral a part as the magnificent Chinese export vases that stood in the hallway" (503).

Another enslaved Fulbe Muslim with whom Caruthers was almost certainly acquainted (and whose life story speaks volumes concerning antebellum America's inability to face simple truths) was a general of the armies of Futa Jallon and a son of the Muslim state's famed leader Almamy Ibrahima Sori. Captured while leading his army in battle, Ibrahima abd al Rahman was sold on the Gambia River and shipped to New Orleans, where he was resold and taken upriver to Spanish Natchez. Known as "Prince" in Natchez, he was selling potatoes one day in the market (alongside one of his countrymen named Sambo) when he noticed a white man who had once been his father's guest in Africa. After regarding Ibrahima for some time, the white man asked, "[B]oy, where did you come from?" and when this "boy" answered as Ibrahima abd al Rahman of Timbo, the possibility of return home began to grow.[2]

Ibrahima's celebrated return to Africa in 1828 occurred nearly one hundred years after that of Ayuba Suleiman Diallo in 1734. During that time span many changes had worked to heighten the racial tensions of slavery, including both the U.S. and Haitian revolutions. Since Ibrahima's inherent dignity and refusal to play the Samboesque role could not be recognized without damaging national unity, Ibrahima was accounted for as a mistakenly enslaved Moor, more Arab/Berber than "negro." Although Suleiman Diallo could be freed simply as an "African gentleman" in early-eighteenth-century colonial America, Ibrahima had to be deracinated in order to be accepted as a gentleman a century later.

It is true that enslaved Muslims may well have been eager to separate themselves from pagans fit for slave status. The fact that many enslaved Senegambian Muslims had been masters in their highly stratified Old World societies surely had an impact upon their attitude toward non-Muslims enslaved in America. Like Diallo, Ibrahima had been a slaveholder himself. His native Timbo "approximated a slave mode of production" (Robinson 55). Under his father, Ibrahima Sori, jihad against pagans was closely linked to economic interests as surplus grain produced on the area's plantations grew increasingly important to the victualing of transatlantic slave ships (Rodney 282). Attitudes of Muslim superiority, combined with prejudices of rank and a degree of ethnocentrism, affected Fulbe attitudes toward fellow slaves and toward white masters. In West Africa, according to David Robinson, as Fulbe jihads grew increasingly successful, there emerged a "sense of 'electedness' among Fulbe."[3] It is not surprising that Ibrahima abd al Rahman and his captured soldier, Samba, may have felt little racial solidarity with enslaved African Americans. After all, Ibrahima was a member of an elite within a Fulbe elite. If whites, seeking to keep their racial categories free of problems posed by a fully literate and noble slave such as Ibrahima, offered to recognize him as something other than "nigger," he would have had ample reason to navigate the options. His first biographer, the editor of the *Natchez Southern Galaxy*, Cyrus Moore, wrote that Ibrahima's "appearance indicates the Foolah rather than the Moor"; however, "Prince states explicitly, and with an air of pride, that not a drop of negro blood runs in his veins" (in Austin 135). According to Griffin, who aided in securing Rahman's liberty, "He places the negro in a scale of being infinitely below the Moor" (135). Griffin adds that "[h]is prejudices, however, have been so far overcome as to allow him to marry, and he now has a numerous offspring" (135). While Ibrahima is quoted as refusing Negro identity, he also, according to Griffin, underscored the self-serving hypocrisy of American Christian practice:

> "the Testament very good law; you no follow it; you no pray often enough; you greedy after money. . . . you want more land, more neegurs; you make neegur work hard, make more cotton. Where you find dat in your law?"
>
> On being asked if such were the case in his own country, "No, no" he replied with much earnestness, "I tell you, man own slaves—he join the religion—he very good—he make he slaves work till noon—go to church—then till the sun go down they work for themselves—they raise cotton, sheep, cattle, plenty, plenty." (142–43)

Having married a black American woman with whom he fathered enslaved children, and having been addressed for forty years as "boy" in Mississippi,

Ibrahima abd al Rahman developed an empathetic understanding of the ways that Samba might be rendered as Sambo.

After winning his own freedom and that of his wife, Ibrahima used his white patrons and contacts in order to try to secure the freedom of his children for passage to Liberia. Working from contacts established by the competing Natchez newspaper editors Cyrus Griffin and Andrew Marschalk, and posing as a Christian convert, Ibrahima received aid from President John Quincy Adams, Henry Clay, Francis Scott Key, and the wealthy Charles Tappan. The many Arabic texts of "the Lord's Prayer" that he wrote as gifts for his admirers are transcriptions of *Al-Fatiha,* the same opening surah of the Qur'an inscribed by Charno in *The Kentuckian in New York.*[4] Although Ibrahima may have claimed to be a Christianized Arab/Berber "Moor" to the mutual convenience of white patrons and himself, when he was in Boston in 1828 seeking funds to help free his children, he was toasted as a black African at a public dinner sponsored by prominent black Bostonians. The toasts, which were printed in the *Boston Centinel* and *American Traveler,* varied from patronizing hopes of Ibrahima's ability to Christianize benighted Africa to revolutionary statements in praise of Haitian independence. The most sensitive of the toasts was offered by David Walker: "Our worthy Guest, who was by the African's natural enemies torn from his country, religion, and friends, and in the very midst of Christians, doomed to perpetual though unlawful bondage, may God enable him to obtain so much of the reward of his labor, as may purchase the freedom of his offspring" (in Austin 164). One year later, Walker would publish his *Appeal,* making him the most hated black man in America. Three years later, Nat Turner would become the man who most haunted the white South; however, following Southern republication of the Boston toasts, the ex-slave whom Southerners had conveniently agreed to dismiss as a "Moor" suddenly became menacingly black and Jacobin.

Andrew Marschalk, one of the Natchez editors who had been a patron of Ibrahima, reacted to the toasts in outrage (touched with a bit of self-serving political cynicism). Using the toasts as propaganda in Andrew Jackson's presidential campaign of 1828, Marschalk printed and distributed an election year anti-Adams pamphlet in which Domingo Williams's toast, "carrying with it the real Domingo feeling," was highlighted: "May the slaveholders of the world be like the whales in the ocean, with the thrasher at their Back and the Swordfish at their belly until they rightly understand the difference between Freedom and slavery" (in Austin 199). Announcing an intention to wake his readers "ere the horrors of St. Domingo, of Rio de Janeiro are reacted here," Marschalk called Southerners to unify behind Jackson, reminding his audience of its precarious position: "Look at the last census of the white and black population of Mississippi and Louisiana, and ask yourselves what must be the consequences if our blacks are inoculated with the doctrines contained in the toasts which Mr. Adams' official journal announces, as being 'received with hearty cheering'" (200–01). Marschalk, who had once praised Ibrahima as having "a character for honesty and integrity which is almost beyond parallel" (151), and who had asserted that Ibrahima was "a dignified captive, a man born to command, unjustly deprived of his liberty, and who has become the victim of a cruel and savage practice (the curse of our land) and deprived of what is held so dear to us" (134), resorted to Africanist manipulation of election-year hysteria, linking a suddenly "savage" Ibrahima to northern political interests, proclaiming, "Long enough have we been the submissive slaves of the senseless representatives of the equally senseless natives of Africa" (202).

As Ibrahima suddenly became dangerous in Boston, all the old Mississippi pretensions to his identity as a white Moor were dropped; and we see clear fears of a resistant epic-hero who would restore black freedom, African patrimony. One Jacksonian editorial of 1828 stated that "If Mr. Adams had sought the world over he could not have found a better instrument than this negro to work upon the prejudices of the people of Pennsylvania, New Jersey, New York, and New England," a negro known "to have an education superior to most white people . . . ambitious, proud, daring, altogether unfit to go at large in the United States" (Austin 216, 214). What was perhaps most threatening was that as an African Muslim, Ibrahima was in literate command of a language Americans could not read. The New Orleans *Louisiana Advertiser* (1828) accused this "tool" of John Quincy Adams of "preparing the way for the horrid scenes of Hayti to be reached here. . . . this self same negro who is traveling through the Northern states in a splendid carriage, at the expense of Government, is almost daily employed in inundating the Southern states with private letters" (215). The hysteric power accorded to Ibrahima was such that a handbill distributed just four days before the election reminded Louisianans "that ANDREW JACKSON IS A MAN OF THE SOUTH, A SLAVE HOLDER, A COTTON PLANTER" and that Adams and Clay had employed "an emancipated NEGRO TO ELECTIONEER FOR THEM" since "they thought they could not be withstood when they had AFRICA AT THEIR BACK!" (Austin 226). The handbill called for fervent Southern populist resistance against the most intriguing Fulbe/Yankee elitist alliance: "THE HOUSE OF TIMBOO . . . AND QUINCY! What a coalition of Royalty to bamboozle the NORTH and destroy the SOUTH! Firm, united let us be—Rallying round the Hickory Tree" (226).

Following Jackson's victory in the 1828 election, his partisan forecasters of slave revolt must have seen themselves as prophets when Nat Turner led America's bloodiest revolt in 1831. Senegambian Muslims had long driven the fear of God into shamelessly avaricious white colonists, with the first known African slave revolt being led by Wolof slaves in 1522 on the Hispaniola plantation of Christopher Columbus's son, and one of the New World's best organized revolts being the Muslim revolt of 1835 in Bahia (Diouf 145–46, 153–63). Furthermore, as Sylviane Diouf points out, the early leaders of the New World's most successful revolt (Haiti) were likely Muslim. Macandal is recorded as being a highly literate Muslim (probably a Mande marabout), while Boukman (who came to Haiti from Jamaica) may well have received his English name, Bookman, from being "a 'man of the book,' as the Muslims were referred to even in Africa" (151–52). It is possible that Islam may have provided part of the inspiration for Nat Turner himself, though the sources matter less than the violent reality of the kind of revolt that whites had long feared. Turner, who read the gaps between jihads of African warrior marabouts, the prophetic modes of Old Testament/ Qur'anic patriarchs, and a Christian world awaiting a violent revelation, stated that he was in communion with "the Spirit that spoke to the prophets in former days" (Gray 135). His spiritual search and charismatic authority, like al-hajj Umar Taal's combination of mystic Sufi practice and jihad, led him to discover "on the leaves in the woods hieroglyphic characters, and numbers, with the forms of men in different attitudes, portrayed in blood, and representing the figures I had seen in the heavens" (137). Nat Turner was not simply a reader of "natural" signs but a reader of scriptural signs as well, a "bookman" who wielded the Book as a weapon, for "the time was fast approaching when the first should be last and the last should be first" (138).

Turner describes his book learning in the magical manner of epic childhood feats: "I have no recollection whatever of learning the alphabet—but to the astonishment of the family, one day, when a book was shewn to me to keep me from crying, I began spelling the names of different objects" (134). Somehow young Nat acquired a sense of the power of the scripted word, an understanding that may have come from his mother Nancy. Stephen B. Oates writes in *The Fires of Jubilee* that "According to black and white tradition, Nancy was a large, spirited, olive-skinned young African," whose "home was supposed to have been in the North's Nile River country" (10–11). Beginning with the most reliable information—that Nat Turner's mother was an African purchased in 1799—and adding oral tradition of her being olive-skinned, from the North's Nile River country, and marched hundreds of miles to the coast, it is not unreasonable to suggest that she was from a Muslim people (or a people well exposed to Islam), perhaps even Fulbe from the Massina. The Niger and Nile had long been confused, and capture along the headwaters or bend of the Niger would have been followed by a long march to the coast. If she were Muslim, she would have been familiar with the power of the written word, and may have instilled her son with a desire to read scripture within the context of tales of messianic jihad.[5] Although a possible Muslim background for Nat Turner remains mere speculation, we know that his revolt, if not nurtured by a parent's tales of Arabic scripture and an heroic Samba, did demonstrate the utter falsity of the Sambo myth to white Southerners whose greatest (and hard to acknowledge) fear was of literate black men like Ibrahima abd al Rahman, David Walker, or Nat Turner. It was this very fear that drove whites away from seeing the truth. As John Blassingame argues, "With Nat perennially in the wings, the creation of Sambo was almost mandatory for the Southerner's emotional security. Like a man whistling in the dark to bolster his courage, the white man *had* to portray the slave as Sambo" (230). As Blassingame adds, "The more fear whites had of Nat, the more firmly they tried to believe in Sambo" (233). White paranoia of black holy warriors fueled the plantation fiction of Sambo (as presented in works such as Caruthers's *Kentuckian in New York*), but African Muslims, with claims to a non-European scriptural religion, offered the most obvious, most unavoidably unsettling refutation of Samboism.

III

No single enslaved African left such a forceful impression upon the American imagination as did Bilali Muhammad, a Fulbe Muslim from the Futa Jallon mountains who was enslaved, purchased by Thomas Spalding in the Bahamas, and later made manager of Spalding's Sapelo Island, Georgia, plantation. Singled out in print as early as 1829 by Zephaniah Kingsley, Bilali served as a model for two of Joel Chandler Harris's children's books— *The Story of Aaron (So Named) the Son of Ben Ali* (1896) and *Aaron in the Wildwoods* (1897). Bilali was a much recalled patriarch in the Georgia Writers' Project's interviews *Drums and Shadows* (1940), offered Muslim patrimony to Toni Morrison's *Song of Solomon* (1977) and Julie Dash's film *Daughters of the Dust* (1991), and anchored the historical imagination of William McFeely in *Sapelo's People* (1994), as well as the sense of heritage in descendant Cornelia Bailey's *God, Dr. Buzzard, and the Bolito Man* (2000). Bilali is particularly well remembered because he left behind a large family, authored an Arabic text (popularly known as the "Bilali Diary"), and served as headman on a cotton/sugar/corn producing plantation where he was answerable to his owner for nearly five hundred African American slaves. What was most striking about Bilali Muhammad was this enslaved African's authority and self-possession, his leadership of a Muslim community, and his insistence that he would be—as his Arabic text states—a servant who recognized his only true master as Allah.

Zephaniah Kingsley appears to have been the first writer to take note of Bilali. Kingsley offered Bilali's armed defense of Sapelo Island against the British during the War of 1812 as evidence that Africans need not be wholly feared and might be persuaded to share common interest with whites. Given that Bilali was remembered as a loyal but fiercely independent-minded head-man who stated to his master that should the British attack the island, "I will answer for every Negro of the true faith, but not for the *Christian dogs* you own" (Lovell 104), and given that Bilali is reported to have defended Sapelo with a band of eighty slaves armed with muskets, it appears that the Muslim population on Sapelo Island may indeed have been large and that its leader was willing to tell his Christian "owner" face to face and "in no uncertain terms what he thought of his master's religion" (Diouf 92). The tales circulating in Georgia about Bilali provided Joel Chandler Harris with a strong subject for romantic fiction, but Harris first felt compelled to recast Bilali's unsettling nobility as Arab rather than "negro" in keeping with the political and psychological correctness of the day.

In *The Story of Aaron (So Named) the Son of Ben Ali*, the child heroes—Buster John, Sweetest Susan, and their black playmate Drusilla—visit Aaron, who "was foreman of the field hands" and knew "the language of animals" (4). We are informed that "Aaron was the most remarkable slave in all the country round, not because he was tall and finely formed, nor because he carried himself as proudly as a military officer, but because he had a well-shaped head, a sharp black eye, thin lips, and a nose prominent, but not flat. Another remarkable feature was his hair, which, instead of being coarse and kinky, was fine, thick, wavy, glossy, and as black as jet" (5). Aaron's true identity is revealed when the children come to recognize him for what he is not:

> "You think I'm a nigger, don't you?" He turned to Buster John.
>
> "Of course," said the youngster without hesitation. "What else are you?"
>
> "I'll show you." From his pocket Aaron drew a little pack-age—something wrapped in soft leather and securely tied. It was a memorandum book. Opening this small book, Aaron held it toward Buster John, saying "What's here?"
>
> "It looks like pothooks," replied the boy, frankly.
>
> "Ain't a word in it I can't read," said Aaron. (11–12)

Aaron's ability to produce and read a text in "the talk of Ben Ali" is his certificate of humanity, proving that "he was no nigger."

The historical Bilali gave his manuscript to an author of children's stories, the Reverend B.L. Goulding, who seems to have brought it to Harris's attention (Austin 275, 288). Harris then put his imagination to work concerning both Bilali and the manuscript's untranslated contents:

[T]he book was a diary of events that had happened to Ben Ali after he landed in this country, being written in one of the desert dialects; but the first few pages told how the Arab chief happened to be a slave.

Ben Ali was the leader of a band that made constant war on some of the African tribes in the Senegambian region. With their captives, this band of Arabs frequently pushed on to the Guinea coast and there sold them to the slave traders. These excursions continued until, on one occasion, the Arabs chanced to clash with a war-loving tribe, which was also engaged in plundering and raiding its neighbors. The meeting was unexpected to the Arabs, but not to the Africans. The Arabs who were left alive were led captive to the coast and there sold with other prisoners to slave traders. Among them was Ben Ali, who was then not more than thirty years old. With the rest, he was brought to America, where he was sold to a Virginian planter, fetching a very high price. Along with him, in the same ship, was an Arab girl, and she was also bought by the planter. Nothing was said in the diary in regard to the history of this girl, except that she became Ben Ali's wife, and bore him a son and a daughter. The son was Aaron, so named. The daughter died while yet a child. (13–14)

Working from the remarkable but not altogether unusual life of a man who was definitely African and Senegambian (Fulbe from the Futa Jallon mountains), Harris worked carefully to avoid recognizing "a nigger" as a man much like himself.

Created during the peak era of radical racism, Harris's *The Story of Aaron* moved the children of his fiction away from the influence of Remus and into the company of an Arab who could talk with the animals. Bilali's Arab identity allowed escape from racial irregularities in the Southern— and increasingly national—defense of slavery as a civilizing force. In *Aaron in the Wildwoods* (1897), for example, a once ardent abolitionist comes to postbellum awareness that slavery had indeed been a providential force:

that though they came here as savages, they were brought in close and stimulating contact with Christian civilization, and so lifted up that in two centuries they were able to bear the promotion to citizenship which awaited them; and that, although this end was reached in confusion and doubt, tumult and bloodshed, it was given to human intelligence to perceive in slavery, as well

as in the freedom of the slaves, the hand of an All-wise Providence, and to behold in their bondage here the scheme of a vast
university in which they were prepared to enjoy the full benefits
of all the blessings which have been conferred on them, and
which, though they seem to have been long delayed, have come
to them earlier than to any other branch of the human race. (153)

Much as Harris repressed Ben Ali's (Bilali's) blackness in order to account
for his literacy, Harris had to repress his own considerable Brer Rabbit-derived knowledge in order to write (during a decade in which an American
was lynched every other day—with two-thirds of the victims being black)
that "two hundred and odd years of slavery, as it existed in the American
republic, is a small price to pay for participation in the inestimable blessings
and benefits of American freedom and American citizenship" (153–54).[6]

Joel Chandler Harris presented the Arabic diary of Ben Ali as a certificate of humanity, and since African Americans allegedly owed their education into "the full benefits" of humanity to "the vast university" of slavery,
no black African could be acknowledged to have produced a text unbeholden
to the white man's schooling. The actual historical document written by
Bilali Muhammad, through its iconic scriptural presence, damns the arro-
gance and avarice of white Christian relations to the Creation. As William
McFeely writes, Bilali's text is more than a text; it "is an icon, in the true
sense—a holy object connecting Africa to America in the hand of a deeply
religious man" (*Sapelo's People* 36). Although much of Bilali's thirteen-page
text remains unreadable due to ink smudging and seepage, Bradford Martin
writes that it appears to be a composite of Arabic texts recalled from his
studies in Timbo in the Futa Jallon, with portions of the document bearing
a resemblance to Ibn Abi Zayd Al Qayrawani's well-circulated legal treatise,
the *Risala*. In one legible section of the text, Bilali takes up the theme of
ritual washing before prayer: "And his right hand wipes off the right foot up
to the ankle / And his left hand wipes off / The left foot up to the ankle / And
he puts both hands / In the water container / And with them wipes his head"
(Martin 598). Following the section on ritual washing, Bilali moved into
repetition of praise-phrases, writing as many as seven times, "O God, I bear
witness that there is no god but God," usually adding "And Muhammad is
the Messenger of God" (598). Bilali's iconic text bears insistent witness in a
land of institutionalized, utterly hypocritical blasphemy.

If Michael Gomez is right in arguing that antebellum Islam's "most
salient impact was its role in the process of social stratification within the
larger African American society" (60), he does well in devoting some fifteen
pages of discussion to Bilali Muhammad and another Fulbe Muslim enslaved in coastal Georgia, Salih Bilali. Salih Bilali's situation on St. Simons

Island was remarkably similar to that of his Fulbe friend and co-religionist on Sapelo Island. Both Muslim Fulbe men were purchased in the Bahamas and became head drivers on plantations run by men known for agricultural ingenuity and a relatively "benign" plantation paternalism. Like Sapelo's Bilali, Salih Bilali was instrumental in keeping a number of Couper's slaves from deserting to the British in 1815. After John Couper's son, James Hamilton Couper, became Salih Bilali's master and took him to his rice plantation on the mainland, young Couper found himself depending heavily on Bilali's expertise. We know that on at least one occasion, James Hamilton Couper, at the request of a fellow plantation owner in Savannah—the ex-consul to Tunisia, William Brown Hodgson—listened intently to his head driver's African experiences; Couper offered a biographical letter on the life of Bilali in response to Hodgson's request for material for his *Notes on Northern Africa, the Sahara, and the Soudan* (1844). Couper's letter to Hodgson speaks of a formidable Pulaar-speaking community working under his headman at Hopeton: "a dozen negroes . . . [who] acquired the language by having been for some time in servitude among that nation" (68). Bilali appears to have adapted rapidly to his opportunities:

> Tom, whose African name was Sali-bul-Ali, was purchased about the year 1800, by my father, from the Bahama islands, to which he had been brought from Anamaboo. His industry, intelligence, and honesty, soon brought him into notice, and he was successfully advanced, until he was made head driver of this plantation, in 1816. He has continued in that station ever since, having under him a gang of about four hundred and fifty negroes, which number, he has shown himself fully competent to manage with advantage. I have several times left him for months, in charge of the plantation, without an overseer; and on each occasion, he has conducted the place to my entire satisfaction. He has quickness of apprehension, strong powers of combination and calculation, a sound judgement, a singularly tenacious memory, and what is more rare in a slave, the faculty of forethought. He possesses great veracity and honesty. He is a strict Mohometan; abstains from spiritous liquors, and keeps the various fasts, particularly that of the Rhamadan. He is singularly exempt from all feeling of superstition; and holds in great contempt, the African belief in fetishes and evil spirits. He reads Arabic, and has a Koran (which however, I have not seen) in that language, but does not write it. (68–69)

Couper's fairly knowledgeable discussions with his bondsman reveal an incredibly indebted respect. The letter also establishes the strong managing role that Bilali held on the plantation and makes one wonder how Couper might have justified his right to hold such a man in chattel slavery. Couper seems to have tried to press Salih Bilali to claim racial difference from other Africans of the region under discussion (ranging from the Bamana capital of Segou to Djenne and Timbuktu downriver on the Niger), but Bilali stated—and Couper dutifully recorded—that he "knows of but one race of negroes, occupying the country" and that they "vary somewhat in color" (323). Bilali, whom Couper describes as having "brownish black" skin and "woolly" hair, would account for no "difference in origin" or no substantive "difference in physical appearance" distinguishing himself from other Africans of the Old Mali region (323). The only difference that seems to have mattered to Bilali was a scriptural one, a prejudice against pagans shared quite fully with his master, for Couper writes that after being captured and transported out of his Muslim homeland, Bilali "met with a nation of cannibals," and "to use his own expression, the people had no religion, until he came to this country" (324).

James Hamilton Couper's interview with Salih Bilali is a testament to the range of African knowledge that planters had and the relatively open-eyed receptivity with which they could receive useful information. Along with detailed information on the architecture, dress, dyes, education, wild-life, and uses of domestic animals of the Niger Bend region, Couper pre-sents his headman's lengthy description of Fulbe rice culture and then offers a list of other Fulbe crops that Bilali supervised on Hopeton plantation—known primaily for its rice production but also for its agricultural experi-mentation. Couper concludes his letter with a list of Pulaar numerals and vocabulary, items that, given the relatively large Pulaar-speaking commu-nity on Hopeton, found their way into the area's Afro-Creole linguistic rep-ertoires.[7] Although Couper's letter is remarkably accepting of Bilali's humanity *and* his Africanity, it finally remains evasive in that it avoids reflective curi-osity about the psyche or inner workings of this remarkable man.

Couper's Salih Bilali interview appeared in a work obsessed with illu-minating "the dark continent," William B. Hodgson's *Notes on Northern Af-rica, the Sahara and Soudan* (1844), which was an addition to the first serious ethnological study of Africa written by an American, Hodgson's *The Foulahs of Central Africa and the African Slave Trade* (1843). A Savannah planter and Orientalist who had served as American consul in northern Africa and Tur-key, Hodgson opens *The Foulahs of Central Africa* by complaining that "*mys-terious darkness*, has ever, from the earliest ages, opposed the curiosity of man, to investigate the condition of the continent" (2), but he finds a glim-mer of light in the scriptural religion practiced by Fulbe (Foulah) peoples and goes to great lengths to racialize this difference: "The Foulahs are *not* negroes. They differ essentially from the negro race. . . . They may be said to occupy the intermediate space between the Arab and the Negro. All travelers concur in representing them as a distinct race, in moral as well as in physical traits" (4). Attracted by "the moral superiority of the Foulahs," Hodgson found them "destined to be the great instrument in the Future civilization of Africa" since "[w]herever the Foulah has wandered, the pagan idolatry of the negro has been overthrown; the barbarous *Fetish* and greegree have been abandoned; anthropophagy and cannibalism have been suppressed; and the horrible sacrifice of human beings to propitiate monstrous gods of the negro barbarian, has been supplanted, by the worship of the true God" (6–7).[8] Although Hodgson fully credits "the humanizing influence of the Koran," he describes the struggle to civilize the dark continent in the scriptural language of crusade, a war that—given the moral nullity of Africa—would be decided finally in a struggle between Western and Oriental canons: "In Africa—in the land of the degraded negro—the gospel now stands face to face with the Koran. . . .From the Senegambia to the Equator, along this vast extent of coast, Christianity has her stations; and she opposes by *her Book*, the further advance of the Moslem's Book" (14).

In his repeated arguments for the Christian mission in Africa, Hodgson stressed the parallel discourse of Islamic practice and pointed to Islam as the most effective and perhaps the safest means of gradually lifting a benighted continent from the darkest mumbo jumbo described in *The Foulahs of Central Africa and the African Slave Trade*: "AFRICA,—torrid, pestilential, savage, mysterious—reserved and guarded by the most terrible and resistless influences of nature, as the unconquered, uninvaded home of a peculiar and degraded race—the 'white man's grave,' the fatal road on which European enterprise in conquest, colonization, exploration, art, science, philanthropy and religion, has for five hundred years cast away thousands of noble wrecks" (1). What must have been the horror of the Savannah planter to see that his colonial forebears had surrounded their descendants with such a "savage," "resistless," "degraded" race that could produce a Nat Turner or a Denmark Vesey? What must have been the horror of recognition to see that the South had become almost an Africa? Wielding a Manichean discourse, and troubled by a supposedly essential difference between literate, scriptural Fulbe and other peculiarly degraded Africans, Hodgson—like Harris and so many of the admirers of Ibrahima abd al Rahman and Omar ibn Said—was forced to admit Muslim Fulbe as nominal whites or Arab/negro mulattos in order to keep the metonymic apparatus of "absolute" racial difference intact. Enslaved Muslims were to be encouraged in their intermediary plantation positions and in their scriptural "alliance" with Christians against black fetishry. But race itself was America's great fetish, and whites knew it even if they could not acknowledge or voice such deeply intuited American experience. Ibrahima abd al Rahman, Omar ibn Said, Bilali Muhammad, and Salih Bilali were—like Caruthers's Charno—

clearly black Africans unbeholden to whites and clearly the equals or superiors of their masters under the very terms of the masters' cultural judgments. In a "free" nation whose patriots had announced the ideal of liberty or death, the presence of enslaved black Muslims producing Arabic texts cut through the Africanist ideological "house of mirrors" to strike fear of God, fear of life itself, into the psyches of whites who stopped for even a moment to reflect.

Just to the south of Hodgson's Savannah, Zephaniah Kingsley (a slave trader and planter long settled in Spanish Florida) considered the perilous position of Southern planters, the numerous New World slave revolts, and wrote a unique defense of slavery entitled *A Treatise on the Patriarchal or Co-operative System of Society* (1829). Although Kingsley agreed with Hodgson about many matters, not the least of which was the desirability of continuing with a slave economy, Kingsley was far less interested in saving Africans' souls (or his own) than he was in saving America's prospects for a viable future. In fact, Kingsley was about as far as a Southern planter could be from Hodgson's language and ideas, writing not of "the degraded negro," "moral superiority," or "mysterious darkness," but of the goal of creating a deeply creolized, interracial American populace by "exposing and removing a prejudice that not only continues to entail ill health and degeneracy on the people, but completely neutralises the physical strength of the country, by placing one portion of the inhabitants in hostile array against the other" (10). Kingsley saw the mixing of the races as a way of improving the strength and health of the general populace and as the surest means to resolving divisive problems of racial difference. In advocating *métissage*, Kingsley wrote that

> The intermediate grades of color are not only healthy, but when conditions are favorable, they are improved in shape, strength, and beauty, and susceptible of every amelioration. Daily experience shows that there is no natural antipathy between the casts on account of color; and it only requires to repeal laws as impolitic as they are unjust and unnatural; which confound beauty, merit and condition in one state of infamy and degradation on account of complexion, and to leave nature to find out a safe and wholesome remedy for evils which, of all others, are now the most deplorable, because they are morally irreconcilable to the fundamental principles of happiness, and self preservation. (10)

Zephaniah Kingsley, whose experiences in West Africa, the Caribbean, and Spanish Florida taught him enough to begin to see through color prejudice, offered full creolism and racial hybridity as the hope of the young nation.

Taking no stock in Sambo caricatures, Kingsley knew that the possibility of sustained revolt was real and offered *métissage* as a strong bridge across a color line that he crossed irrevocably with his attentiveness to his Wolof wife and their children, his eventual despair over racial prejudice in the United States, and his relocation of his family to Haiti.

In Havana around 1806, Kingsley purchased a Wolof teenager (likely at least nominally Muslim) named Anta Majigeen N'diaye. She soon became pregnant by Kingsley. Back in Florida he would later speak of their marriage "in a foreign land" (Cuba or Spanish Florida?) where the ceremony was "celebrated and solemnized by her native African custom, altho' never celebrated according to the Christian usage" (Schafer 13). Although Kingsley practiced a Creole/Old Testament patriarchal style of virtual polygamy and had children by several slave mistresses, it was Anna Majigeen Jai Kingsley and her children, all freed, whom he fully acknowledged in his will: "She has always been respected as my wife and as such I acknowledge her, nor do I think that her truth, honor, integrity, moral conduct or good sense will lose in comparison to anyone" (14). Anna became a large landowner and slaveholder, as she benefited from deeds given by her husband and from a Spanish grant for service during the patriot war of 1813. But after Spain's cession of Florida and the introduction of U.S. law, the security that Anna and the Kingsley children had enjoyed was threatened. Kingsley added a codicil to his will warning of "the illiberal and inequitable laws of this territory" and advising his loved ones to keep a legal will on hand until they could emigrate "to some land of liberty and equal rights, where the conditions of society are governed by some law less absurd than that of color" (31). While Southerners feared the example of Haiti, Kingsley, worried over the fate of his children, negotiated with Haiti's President Boyer, bought land, and emigrated with family and slaves.

It was at a point when he was agitating against Anglo-Florida's increasingly repressive racial policies, but before he came to despair and sought refuge for his family in Haiti, that Kingsley published his *Treatise* (1829), advocating full citizenship for free people of color with long-term solutions coming through complete *métissage*. Citing his knowledge of Spanish Florida, New Orleans, Brazil, and the British, Spanish, French, and Dutch colonies in the Americas, Kingsley pragmatically argued that "a smaller degree of prejudice against color" should replace "fear and force in governing these people," adding that North Americans should profit from the wisdom of more openly creolized South America, where "free colored people, many of whom, being rich and liberally educated, enjoy great respectability, and having the same interest with the whites, and great influence with the slaves, form a barrier to insurrection" (9). Among several examples cited as evidence that blacks might be relied upon to help uphold a racially open but socially stratified society, Kingsley offered the first known mention in print of the two Bilalis: "I know two instances, to the southward, where gangs of negroes were prevented from deserting to the enemy by drivers, or influential negroes, whose integrity to their masters, and influence over the slaves prevented it; and what is still more remarkable, in both instances the influential negroes were Africans, and professors of the Mahomedan religion" (13–14). Kingsley's pragmatic philosophy of self-interest was, for the most part, remarkably free of Africanist mumbo jumbo. His respect for Africans, particularly for Senegambian Muslims like Bilali, Salih Bilali, and his own wife Anna Jai Kingsley, was such that he knew representations of Sambo to be self-deluding lies hatched by masters rightly fearful of revolt. But his vision of an interracial, deeply and openly creolized society (informed in large part by his marriage to a Wolof woman) would be viewed over the next 150 years as the ultimate heresy against Western civilization: mongrelization, amalgamation. Only the most tortuous, haunted and violent gothic modes of narrative could face/evade/defer/face and navigate America's foundational lies and foundational polyculturalism. And nothing sparked such gothic musings quite like the presence of "noble" Senegambians and the Arabic texts they produced as witness to an irrefutable humanity.

IV

Although the planter/slaver Zephaniah Kingsley's racial preconceptions appear to have been formidably altered by his openness to the realities he witnessed in Africa, the Caribbean, and Florida, founders of the plantation novel like John Pendleton Kennedy in *Swallow Barn* (1832) and William Alexander Caruthers in *The Kentuckian in New York* (1834) tended to let their ideological preconceptions limit their abilities to witness. However, to return to Caruthers's informative work, we see that *The Kentuckian in New York* cannot succeed at excluding unsettling elements of plantation life. Beneath Caruthers's representations of loyal body servants lies a clear dread of insurrection. Caruthers's Virginian B. Randolph admits that on the rice and cotton plantations "slavery is intolerable; a single individual owning a hundred or more, and often not knowing them when he sees them. . . . The slaves are plantation livestock" (115). The owner's inability to recognize his numerous slaves signals a dangerous loss of control, as seen by the reliance upon black drivers, "an odious animal, almost peculiar to the far south" (116), elevated "to an authority which . . . I doubt whether any ignorant negro can exercise without injury to himself and his fellows" (II. 72). Maligning the considerable hospitality proffered earlier to him by the family of a driver, Randolph also seems to be repressing the admiration he so clearly felt for the Muslim Charno in questioning "whether any ignorant negro" could be capable of exercising viable "authority." Deeply embedded fears certainly fuel Randolph's (and the author's) repression of full knowledge and recognition of black (and white) humanity.

The Kentuckian in New York admits the grave worries of planters inhabiting—indeed, almost colonizing—an Afro-Creole landscape:

> "[Y]ou know that I have not, when in health, habitually looked at the dark side of things; but I must confess to you that the recent circumstances have conjured up exceedingly unpleasant anticipations. What can we do to prevent the realization of these apprehensions? We cannot set slaves free among us. Such a course would dissolve the social compact. It would set at defiance all laws for the protection of life, liberty, and property, either among them or the whites. It would present the strange anomaly of a majority under the control of the minority, and a majority possessing personal without political freedom; which state of things could not last, because anarchy and confusion would usurp the place of law and government. To emancipate them where they are, would be, then, to surrender life, liberty, and property,—and for what? to render justice to these poor creatures? Would it be rendering justice to them or ourselves? Would it be any reparation of an hereditary wrong, to plunge the subjects of that wrong, with ourselves, into irretrievable ruin, to attain nominal justice? (II. 71–72)

Led by fear of revolt to look at "the dark side of things," Caruthers's text offers, amidst much ideological hedging, a tacit admission of "an hereditary wrong" and a fairly straightforward recognition of the reversal of property and power that could result from emancipation of the African American majority in the Deep South. The South is revealed to be a dark continent, perilously beyond white control. A look at the dark side of things of course brings a mirroring focus on the self and the social/historical origins of self. What the conscious mind then recognizes as foundational moral wrong and shortsighted blunder is covered up by a Manichean ideology, governed in Africanist thought (even more completely than in the Orientalist discourse that Edward Said here describes) "by a battery of desires, repressions, investments, and projections" (8). Nearly lost between Caruthers's depictions of Sambo—"deeply imbued with that strong feudal attachment to the family"—and the masters' dread of "the lawless outrages and uncontrollable fury of the savage mob" (II. 72), is the novel's earlier scene of discourse with Charno, whose Arabic literacy so troubled Randolph as to cause him to become "quite affected and melancholy . . . and you may judge from that rare circumstance that he is no common character" (147).

Babo and Bras Coupé

Malign Machinations, Gothic Plots

And my soul from out that shadow that lies floating on the floor
Shall be lifted, "Nevermore."

Edgar Allan Poe, "The Raven" (1845)

Flights of troubled gray fowl, kith and kin with flights of troubled gray vapors among which they were mixed, skimmed low and fitfully over the waters, as swallows over meadows before storms. Shadows present, foreshadowing deeper shadows to come.

Herman Melville, "Benito Cereno" (1855)

When I try sometimes to stand outside and look at it, I am ama-aze at the length, the blackness of that shadow! . . .It brheeds a thousan' cusses that nevva leave home but jus' flutter-h up an' rhoost, my-de'-seh, on ow heads.

Honoré Grandissime,
George W. Cable's *The Grandissimes* (1880)

I

As startling to American readers as the Raven's one word, "Nevermore," Arabic texts produced by enslaved Senegambians offered unrelenting, hard-to-avoid assertions of African dignity/spirit/reason, backed by an Afro-Muslim classical past and backed as well by shades of Haiti's own violent assertion of "Nevermore" to slavery. Still there has been a reluctance to face the full power of these forces in America, just as there has been a reluctance to read the most quotidian hauntings of Poe's native Virginia into his "classic" poem of haunting. In a *PMLA* article entitled "The Raven and the Bust of Pallas: Classical Artifacts and the Gothic Tale," Patricia Merivale remarked that "[s]tatues and stories come together most strikingly . . . in some of the fantasies that have been woven around the things that the Greeks and Romans made and left behind, where the past is dug up to strangely edify the present" (960). However, Merivale's intriguing article stops short of a reading that would "strangely edify" Poe's poem in its uniquely American gothic context. In Poe's "The Raven," a poem of such enduring power that it now has a National Football League team named after it, all access to the classical past, the marble bust of Pallas and "the radiant maiden" of high European culture, is an access blocked by "this ebony bird," "thing of evil," a Caliban-like "fiend" that Poe's speaker would send "back into the tempest." The raven's one repeated word appears at first to be slavish parrotry, "Caught from some unhappy master whom unmerciful disaster / Followed fast and followed faster till his songs one burden bore" (944). But for Poe, inhabiting a South haunted by the shadow of Haiti, Nat Turner, and sectional conflict, the raven perched on the bust of Pallas responds in the willful manner of Caliban only to curse: "'On this home by horror haunted—tell me truly, I implore— / Is there—*is* there balm in Gilead?—tell me—tell me, I implore!' / Quoth the Raven, 'Nevermore'" (945). The bird's black plumes cover the classical statuary; the Raven's shadow, in fact, covers the speaker with a presence that is irrevocably haunting:

> And the Raven, never flitting, still is sitting, *still* is sitting
> On the pallid bust of Pallas just above my chamber door;
> And his eyes have all the seeming of a demon's that is dreaming,
> And the lamplight o'er him streaming throws his shadow on the floor;
> And my soul from out that shadow that lies floating on the floor
> > Shall be lifted—nevermore! (946)

While Poe's speaker alternately addresses the Raven as "Prophet" and "thing of evil," the poem itself is a prophecy of much of the form and content of the gothic American narratives that would follow. Whatever else the Raven is, it is sign and symbol of a slavery-haunted, race-haunted New World, forever creolized and distanced from the purities of any Old World classical past. Poe's use of the hauntingly repetitive tale and the poem's triadic representation of black Raven, pallid Pallas, and shadow-struck figure set the stage for later writers such as Melville, Cable, and Faulkner, to excavate a past that is never quite past strangely edifying and channeling the present.

II

In Melville's "Benito Cereno," things half-spoken from the past cast their haunting energies of action upon the present, casting shadows even darker than those of Poe's Raven. When Melville's readers first view the foundering ship that the Yankee Captain Delano intends to save, we see above its canvas-covered figurehead the sentence "SEGUID VUESTRO JEFE ('follow your leader')" chalked alongside the more stately inscription of the ship's name, "SAN DOMINICK" (40). Toward the end of the tale, the canvas breaks loose in a moment of recognition, revealing "death for the figurehead, in a human skeleton, chalky comment on the chalked words below, FOLLOW YOUR LEADER" (88). We discover that a supposedly Samboesque Senegalese body servant, Babo, has authored the sentence and has used his master's fresh bones to illustrate a succinct text of rebellion, as the ship's Spanish captain Benito Cereno attests in his deposition: "that the Negro Babo showed him a skeleton, which had been substituted for the ship's proper figurehead—the image of Christopher Colon, the discoverer of the New World; that the Negro Babo asked him whose skeleton it was, and whether, from its whiteness, he should not think it a white's, that . . . the Negro Babo, coming close, said words to this effect: 'Keep faith with the blacks from here to Senegal, or you shall in spirit, as now in body, follow your leader,' pointing to the prow" (95). Along with its mocking erasure of racial difference and its reversal of racialized roles, Babo's message conveys meanings that are historically situated and are indeed intended to edify the reader's present. As Eric Sundquist writes in *To Wake the Nations* (1993), "When the skeleton is exposed in the place of Cristobal Colon's image, it is the Columbian myth itself—the entire story of New World history told from the European American point of view—that is stripped down to the rudiments of its own carnage: the master becomes the sacrificial emblem of his own vicious system of power" (170). Like Poe's raven-mounted bust of the goddess of wisdom, Melville's skeletal displacement of Columbus questions the Old World heritage from a New World crossroads of disillusioned horror. The *San Dominick*, christened in honor of the founder of the Dominican order (early advocates of the African slave trade), becomes a ship of rebellion, conjuring associations with the revolution on San Domingo (Haiti).[1]

Like Poe's "The Raven," Melville's text utilizes a triad of figures, replacing the Raven, pallid Pallas, and the shadow-struck speaker with Senegalese Babo, the Yankee Captain Delano, and the shadowy Spanish captain Benito Cereno. Jean Yellin writes that "[t]he story projects a shifting triad of figures, envisioned in the distant past as American, Spaniard, and African but more familiarly recognized by *Putnam's* readers as Yankee, Slaveholder, and Negro" (217). Using this flexible triad, Melville emplots a rereading of American history bound for shocking confrontation with his contemporary world.

Captain Amaso Delano, through whom much of the reader's perception of the narrative is filtered, is a liberal New England Yankee whose condescending smugness is characteristic of "the expansionist, anti-Catholic, Anglo-Saxonist mentality of America in the 1850's" (Zagarell 246). According to Eric Sundquist, Delano also "represents both the founding fathers, who sanctioned slavery even as they recognized its contradiction of the Rights of Man, and the contemporary northern accommodationists" who sought compromise with chattel slavery (*To Wake* 154). Delano's "innocent" ideology, shared by much of Melville's readership, keeps him and unsuspecting readers from learning from experience.[2]

Delano repeatedly remarks upon the Spanish captain's difference. As Delano misreads him, Benito Cereno appears alternately as languid, noble, and plotting. Cereno, "shadowed by his devoted slave Babo, is typical of numberless portraits done in the plantation tradition" and "as an American type suggests the Cavalier, our closest approximation to European aristocracy" (Yellin 218, 221). Benito Cereno's intimacy with Babo focuses our attention on Don Benito as both a Southern and hemispheric *criollo*, a carrier of "'traces and taints' that Americans feared as challenges to their own redemptive mission in the New World" (Ladd, "Direction" 530). In fact, Delano's (and Western Europe's) condescension for Cereno (and Iberian peoples) rests in part upon recognition that Spanish language, culture, and genes were strongly influenced by the Moorish presence. But it is in Senegalese Babo that Cereno meets a man who draws the Old World spectre of the Moor and the New World spectre of San Domingo together.

The role of the rebel leader Babo has provided the primary source of contention among readers of Melville's novella. The text of "Benito Cereno" informs us that Babo is "a small Negro of Senegal, but some years among the Spaniards," who leads the revolt aboard the *San Dominick* (93). Literate in Spanish, Babo uses his intimate knowledge of master/slave roles to dictate his fiction of black submission aboard the African-controlled ship. He is indeed a trickster in the tradition of Brer Rabbit (Leslie and Stuckey 296). True to historic pattern, Babo has been read as the source or representation of evil in the novella. According to Rosalie Feltenstein (and the "traditional" or canonical reading) "Babo is not simply a representation of evil, he 'is blackness'" [*el negro*]; "Babo is evil" (252–53). However, it is my contention that Babo, the dictator of the fiction within Melville's tale, is the text's authorial figure. Babo's insurrectionary pleasure authorizes the tale and mirrors the bitter pleasures of the novella's plotting artist. Both Babo and Melville rely upon predictable ideological responses to trap the witless reader, and both finally refuse commentary, choosing, through recognition of the inadequacies of language, silence.

Melville's hijacking of his historical source, Captain Amaso Delano's *Voyages*, reveals much about artistic command in "Benito Cereno." The few liberties that Melville took with Delano's original account and the Peruvian depositions that Delano included as evidence are significant. Melville changed the names of the ships *Tryal* and *Perseverence* to the *San Dominick* and the *Bachelor's Delight*. Melville's change of the date of the maritime revolt from 1804 to 1799 worked to underscore "the spectral presence of San Domingo" (Sundquist, *To Wake the Nations* 141). The macabre figurehead of Aranda's skeleton overlaid on the image of Columbus was an authorial invention along with Babo's chalked inscription. But Melville did not invent the terror-inspiring execution of Aranda, nor did he invent Babo's literacy or his effort to lead the ship back to Senegal. What Melville did in rereading and rewriting his source was to consistently intensify the terrorism of Babo's leadership of the revolt while, according to Rosalie Feltenstein, elevating the character of Cereno (247). This "blackening" of the Senegalese rebels and "whitening" of the Christian captain underscores a possible Manichean allegory that allows readers like Feltenstein to follow the lead of the white captains "to emphasize Babo as the origin of evil" (248). Melville's plot leads too many readers to declare in the Delanoesque language of the critic Richard Fogle that "[t]he black is evil; the white is good, since we take the side of the whites and accept the verdict of a white court of law" (Fogle 121). Such a reading is not only a result of America's historically racialized, polarizing identities (working to control who "we" are), but is also a result of Melville's manipulation of racist ideologies in a rebellious replotting of the Senegalese rebel plot.

The original Peruvian depositions included in Amasa Delano's *A Narrative of Voyages and Travel, etc* (1817) make it clear that the criminal case was "conducted against the Senegal Negroes" who led the revolt: "twelve full grown negroes, aged from twenty-five to fifty years, all raw and born on the coast of Senegal" (23–24). We are informed that the historical Babo was the group's "ring leader," that his son Muri and his henchman Atufal were also at the core of the revolt, and that the group "held daily conferences, in which they discussed what was necessary for their design of returning to Senegal" (25–26). Many of the insurgents mentioned by name do show evidence of being from Senegal. Babo (rendered from the common Fulbe name Baaba) was probably Fulbe, as were Muri (Mory) and Atufal (Artu Faal). Both Faal and Babo appear to have attended Qur'anic schools in Senegal since Cereno testified that they could write "in their language" (27), probably in Arabic, though perhaps in Pulaar. Cereno testified that in an effort to preserve his remaining crew, he "agreed to draw up a paper, signed by the deponent, and the sailors who could write, as also by the negroes, Babo and Atufal, who could do it in their language, though they were new, in which he obliged himself to carry them to Senegal, and they not to kill any more" (27). The contract was respected until the arrival of Delano's ship. At that point, Babo's son Muri, "a man of capacity and talents, performing the office of an officious servant, with all the appearance of submission of the humble slave, did not leave the deponent one moment, in order to observe his actions and words; for he understands well the Spanish, and besides there were thereabout some others who were constantly on the watch and understood it also" (28). Although Babo is described as the leader of the historical revolt, Muri played a strong role and served during the fighting "as captain and commander of them" (29). Leadership of the revolt appears to have been dispersed among the Senegalese insurgents and drew upon the assistance of Creole slaves. Cereno describes the women too as being participants, and it may be that many of them were also Senegalese since they communicated in an intimate manner with the Senegalese men who were at the plot's center. Captain Cereno testified that "the negresses of age, were knowing to the revolt, and influenced the death of their master . . . they began to sing, and were singing a very melancholy song during the action, to excite the courage of the negroes" (29).[3]

In sum, the historical documents of Cereno's deposition reveal a well-planned revolt led by a core of Senegalese insurgents who were literate (probably in Arabic) and who utilized terror to achieve their goals. Babo and Atufal appear to have been the leaders, but Babo's son was the one who posed as Cereno's body servant and who commanded the rebels in battle, perhaps due to the younger man's stronger Spanish skills and greater degree of acculturation—allowing him to communicate more effectively with Cereno, the Spanish crew, and the Creole insurgents.

Melville made so few changes in Delano's narrative and in the deposition that Newton Arvin called his novella "an artistic miscarriage. . . . lifted bodily" from Delano because Melville was "too tired to rewrite at all" (238–39). However, the changes Melville made are crucial to his plot and intent, crucial to the text's ability to lead critics such as Richard Fogle to state that the text's message is "that reality is a mystery and hard to read, and . . . that evil is real and must be recognized" (118), which is true enough, save for Fogle's comfortable conclusion that Babo is the text's source of evil. Melville's rewriting of Delano invites—even plots—just such a Manichean reading. First, Melville collapsed the leadership of the revolt into one figure, Babo, in a move that allows the insurgents to be seen as a demonic mass following one demonic will. Melville accentuates Babo's mental prowess by insisting on his small stature, and he hides his Senegalese identity until Cereno's final deposition. In fact, Melville does away with the Senegalese identity of all of Babo's cohorts. Since there was a romanticized and voluminous literature on the supposed moral and intellectual superiority of Senegalese, Melville may have feared that Senegalese—ironically Sambo's main source—were the one group for whom sentimentally racist readers may have found a Sambo performance least "natural." He replaces the Senegalese with Ashanti, "famous for their ferocity" (Emery 320). Melville's Delano reacts emotively to this recast Babo: "[I]t was not without humane satisfaction that Captain Delano witnessed the steady good conduct of Babo" (43), whose behavior toward his master was like that of "a shepherd's dog" (41). Delano's romanticized pastoralism works to pull the wool over the careless reader's (and his own) eyes until the conclusion reveals Babo as author of the plot. The move from pastoral to gothic horror, along with the recognition of Sambo as a man capable of elaborate orchestrations of terror, easily brought readers to locate the story's evil in Babo. Although Melville plotted for first-time readers to misread, and may even have plotted the misread rereadings of critics who saw Babo as the text's figure of evil, it is possible that Melville may have indeed sided consciously or unconsciously with many elements of his critics' racial assumptions. Since authorial intent is elusive and can never provide "the last word," we must reread what the text itself authorizes, what it does and makes possible in its tortuous emplotment.

Melville's text is less concerned with the evil that is out there in the "real" world than with the manner in which evil breeds and thrives in our imagining of the real, in the mutual, shared misrecognition through which individuals are rendered as subjects. If "Benito Cereno" is about any one thing, it is about ideology, "the imaginary relationship of individuals to their real conditions of existence" (Althusser 241). Melville's text indeed "lays bare the elaborate ideology" of an "expansionist, anti-Catholic, Anglo-Saxonist" America, disclosing "what Americans did not know, why they did not know it, and the potential consequences of that ignorance" (Zagarell 245–46). As J.H. Kavanagh has written, "At stake in this text is not the 'problem of evil' . . . but the problem of ideology as figured in Delano" (362). Rather than finding the locus of evil in Senegalese Babo, we would do well to look to the imaginative deficiencies of those like Captain Delano, who are "unwilling to appear uncivil even to incivility itself" (Melville 57). And we must understand that incivility, in its most topical form in Melville's America, had to be understood in terms of one's stance in regard to slavery and its Southern apologists.

First, the text of "Benito Cereno" makes it clear that Delano is a fool whose naivete is wholly in step with the national ideologies of Manifest Destiny and the racial stagecraft of minstrelsy. After foreshadowing revolt with gray seas and "[f]lights of troubled gray fowl" (37), Melville invites his reader to suspect Delano's perceptions. Delano is described as "a person of a singularly undistrustful good nature, not liable except on extraordinary and repeated incentives, and hardly then, to indulge in personal alarms any way involving the imputation of malign evil in man. Whether in view of what humanity is capable, such a trait implies, along with a benevolent heart, more than ordinary quickness and accuracy of intellectual perception, may be left to the wise to determine" (38). The good captain's thoughts are "tranquilizing" as he decides that "there was a difference between the idea of Don Benito's darkly preordaining Captain Delano's fate and Captain Delano's lightly arranging Don Benito's" (60). Time and time again, Delano's self-serving, paternalistic misrecognitions are born of the false differences he marks, differences which are not at all generous but rather support the hierarchy through which Delano wields power.

Delano eagerly confuses the imaginary relationships of minstrelsy with the real relationships that minstrelsy was meant to hide. The "affectionate zeal" of Babo's devoted role as body servant builds on a false, Samboesque erotic that masks the ugliest realities. Furthermore, the text's dialogues are laden with a double-talk mastered by Babo to torture Cereno, trick the witless Delano, and give pleasure to fellow insurgents and conspiring readers. In one such scene, Cereno is forced to praise Babo, telling Delano it is Babo to whom

> "chiefly, the merit is due of pacifying his more ignorant brethren, when at intervals tempted to murmurings."
>
> "Ah master," sighed the black, bowing his face, "don't speak of me; Babo is nothing; what Babo has done was but duty."
>
> As master and man stood before him, the black upholding the white, Captain Delano could not but bethink him of the beauty of that relationship which could present such a spectacle of fidelity on the one hand and confidence on the other. The scene was heightened by the contrast in dress, denoting their relative positions. (47–48)

The text makes it clear that we can not locate the source of the problem in Babo, for "what Babo has done was but duty," the same duty our revolutionary forebears found at Bunker Hill and San Domingo. The spectacle of "fidelity" and "confidence" surrounding plantation slavery shows itself to be a ritualized imaginary relation enacted to hide real relations. Althusser has remarked of ideology, "this imaginary relation is itself endowed with a material existence" (243), as Melville's text also notes in the "contrast in dress, denoting their relative positions" (48).

The scene in which Cereno relates the death of Aranda is another clear play upon Delano's dullness. Delano confidently remarks, "Were your friend's remains now on board this ship, Don Benito, not thus strangely would the mention of his name affect you" (51). Since Aranda's bones have replaced the *San Dominick*'s figurehead of Columbus to serve as warning that all on board may indeed follow their leader (as we know from the rereading forced upon us in Cereno's deposition), the Spanish captain understandably cringes in the face of Yankee ignorance. Delano's remark upon the Spaniard's reaction is typical: "How unlike are we made!" (51).

At another moment, Delano takes comfort in the "pleasant sort of sunny sight" of "a slumbering Negress. . . . like a doe in the shade of a woodland rock. Sprawling at her lapped breasts was her wide-awake fawn" (63). Racial ideology repeatedly serves as a tranquilizing screen to obfuscate Delano's perception of reality: "There's naked nature, now, pure tenderness and love, thought Captain Delano, well pleased" (63). Informed by Mungo Park's descriptions of the aid offered by women when Park was in extreme duress in the Senegambia, Melville had Delano draw sentimental reactions from Park's descriptions of Senegambian women: "Ah! thought Captain Delano, these, perhaps, are some of the very women whom Ledyard [originally in *Putnam's* written "Mungo Park"] saw in Africa, and gave such noble account of" (63).[4] Delano, whose ideology accounts for natural racial difference, can not see that the real difference here is between the humane treatment that Senegambian women accorded to Mungo Park and the brutal treatment these women receive in the hands of white slaveholders and through the complicity of "good" men like Delano. When the text informs us that "[t]hese natural sights somehow insensibly deepened his confidence and ease," alert readers become ill at ease with both Delano and the insensibility in which we may be too easily trapped. But readers eager to accept the false erotic depicted in the "affectionate zeal" of Babo's role as body servant and the "natural sights" of a black "dam" nursing her "fawn" are led unwittingly into a labyrinth of violence.

As Delano grows increasingly uncomfortable aboard the *San Dominick* and begins to suspect a plot, his racism leads him not to suspect the Africans but the Spaniard(s): "The whites, too, by nature, were the shrewder race. A man with some evil design, would he not be likely to speak well of that stupidity which was blind to his depravity, and malign the intelligence from which it might not be hidden? Not unlikely perhaps. But if the whites had dark secrets concerning Don Benito, could then Don Benito be any way in complicity with the blacks? But they were too stupid. Besides, who ever heard of a white so far a renegade as to apostatize from his very species almost, by leaguing in against it with Negroes?" (65). Since everything Delano says is suspect—but often useful for being a negative image of the truth— we have reason to suspect that Melville's text is finding ways to speak well of the captain's stupidity, that Babo is maligned in such a purposeful way as to make the author himself a "renegade" leaguing with blacks. Too many Delanoesque readers have stuck with the man of their own "species," even when Melville follows this passage with the Spanish sailor's clue of the Gordian knot "[f]or someone else to undo" (66), and we find Delano confounded, "knot in hand, knot in head" (66). The knot-headed Yankee captain, like the compromise-driven power structure of Melville's day, hopes "by ignoring the symptoms, to get rid of the malady" (66).

Melville is ceaseless in his ridicule of Delano, who "took to Negroes, not philanthropically, but genially, just as other men to Newfoundland dogs" (73). One such textual moment occurs when Delano comforts himself with the timely appearance of his men's boat: like "a Newfoundland dog; the sight of that household boat evoked a thousand trustful associations" (67). In response to this passage, Kavanagh remarks that "Ideology is precisely that network of 'a thousand trustful associations,'" used to "secure his position as 'master'" (368–69). Delano's tranquilizing ideology reasserts itself again to veil dangers: "What I, Amasa Delano—Jack of the Beach, as they called me when a lad . . . I to be murdered by a horrible Spaniard? Too nonsensical to think of? Who would murder Amasa Delano? His conscience is clean" (67). Invited to ponder the degree to which Delano's conscience (and America's own) is clean, we are also allowed to glimpse the nonsensical nature of the privilege that Americans regularly attach to the national history. And when Delano states "fie, fie, Jack of the Beach! you are a child indeed; a child of the second childhood, old boy; you are beginning to dote and drool, I'm afraid" (67), close readers can only say "indeed."

Readers who regard "Benito Cereno" as an allegory of good and evil, with the evil manifest in Babo (see Feltenstein, Fogle, and Kaplan), are, as we have already noted, often unable to explain Melville's slight rewriting of Cereno's depositions. Newton Arvin felt "Melville was too tired to rewrite at all," so "except for a few trifling details, he leaves it all as he found it, in the drearily prosaic prose of a judicial deposition" that shows an "absence of strong conviction" (238–40). However, recent critics suggest that Melville's use of the depositions is both lock and key to understanding the conviction with which the novella was written.

Despite the apparent closure of the deposition, the story of the Senegalese revolt and its repression is obsessively retold: "Again and again it was repeated how hard it had been to enact the part forced on the Spaniard by Babo" (102). The repetition of the difficulty of Cereno's brief role points to how difficult Sambo roles must be on a ground, every inch of which is "mined into honeycombs under you" (102). Following the revolt, the unenlightened Delano continues to sing his own smug praises, speaking of the "pleasant" temper of mind that enabled him, despite "the sight of so much suffering, more apparent than real," to interweave "good-nature, compassion, and charity" in such a way as to survive through ignorance and remain ignorant in survival (102). Delano's ability to see the crew's suffering as "more apparent than real" is built wholly on imaginary relationships to real conditions. It is the same ideology that allowed canonical readings like Rosalie Feltenstein's to assert that "Babo is evil. . . . is blackness" and that "slavery is not the issue here; the focus is upon evil in action in a certain situation" (254). We must ask, what might that certain situation be if not the situation of slavery built on ideologies of racial difference and white privilege, all mined into honeycombs beneath our shining city on a hill?

Since so much of what Delano, Don Benito, and Babo say in the novella is intended for several different readings at once, and since only Babo—and then only momentarily—is in control of the multivalent possibilities of his speech and actions, we must be careful with Cereno's final interpretive conversation with Delano: "[Y]our last act was to clutch for a monster, not only an innocent man, but the most pitiable of all men. To such degree may malign machinations and deceptions impose. So far may even the best man err in judging the conduct of one with the recesses of whose condition he is not acquainted. But you were forced to it, and you were in time undeceived. Would that, in both respects, it was so ever, and with all men" (102–3). Although Cereno appears to be referring to Delano's suspicion of his being a pirate, the "last act" was actually Delano's clutching an African "monster," an "innocent" man pushed to murderous violence in pursuit of freedom. Only through redeployment of the "malign machinery" of racist ideology is it possible to read Don Benito's statement at face value. The text probes recesses deeper than that. And though it is indeed possible that "we are using Melville's text to effect a more irreversible break from an ideology than he could" (Kavanagh 359), given Melville's elaborately veiled plotting against his readers—even against the world and language in which he drew breath and thought—it is hard to imagine that he was unaware of the messages of revolt veiled in Don Benito's final communicative effort. The text itself—its reenactment and reversals of the spectacle of slavery—functions as a gothic, insurrectionist medium that gives voice to horrific New World energies of action

After trading places with Babo, Cereno possesses a fuller, doubly conscious awareness of the malign machinations of the master/slave roles. But Delano has no capacity for learning from experience; he tells Cereno that "the past is passed; why moralize upon it? Forget it. See, yon bright sun has forgotten it all, and the blue sea, and the blue sky; these have turned over new leaves" (103). When Delano asks, "What has cast such a shadow upon you?" Cereno utters his last words: "The Negro" (103). Like the knowledge of Southern planters following the violence of Haiti and Nat Turner, Cereno's knowledge could be primarily a resolve for sterner oppression. Even more likely, Cereno's shadow-haunted knowledge is a knowledge of plantation slavery's doomed design or perhaps a feeling of what Barbara Ladd has called "black surrogacy . . . the moral 'contamination' of the slaveholder" by slavery ("The Direction" 532). This "shadow of the negro" could be felt consciously only when whites began to recognize the real conditions of shared humanity in moments that tore through the ideological fog of imaginary relationships. Following recognition, often in the aftermath of violence, one might retreat to tranquilizing ideology, one might choose additional violence, or as with Melville's text, "There was silence. . . . There was no more conversation that day" (103).

The text's authorial voice yields in the end. Babo "whose brain, not body, had schemed and led the revolt—his slight frame, inadequate to that which it held, had at once yielded to the superior muscular strength of his captor" (103). Just as Babo is defeated—not through right or superior vision but through sheer force—Melville's narrative plot yields to forces beyond its control. Even after Melville's long silence of neglect, when he was taken up in the early twentieth century as canonical, the traditional reading of this text "with its 'reality is a mystery' and 'evil is real,' marks the passage of 'Benito Cereno' into the court of a 'literary' ideological apparatus—its self-anticipated fate, for which it prepared its own ambiguous silences" (Kavanagh 377). Should we truly follow our plotting leader, we might in the end come to see a new bust replacing Poe's "pallid Pallas." When we see how that "hive of subtlety, fixed on a pole in the plaza, met, unabashed, the gaze of the whites" (104), we might see not just the head of a Senegalese rebel in a Lima plaza, but the author's double and our own.

III

After the Civil War, "the shadow of the negro" continued to be a powerful cultural/literary presence as American racial disingenuousness, rather than healing with abolition, festered into "an enduring cultural and social disaster" (Wyatt 212). An ex-Confederate, George Washington Cable, was among those writers most dedicated to resisting the post-Reconstruction South's reconstitution of much of the old racial order. Michael Kreyling has noted similarities between Cable's *The Grandissimes* (1880) and Melville's "Benito Cereno," adding that "[t]he wraithlike f.m.c. [free man of color] is as haunting a symbol of 'the shadow of the African' as the one that hovers above Amasa Delano's narrative" (xv). Both Melville and Cable confronted the triad of Senegalese insurgent, Yankee, and Creole-Southerner in obsessive retellings of historical slave insurrections, locating a peculiarly American "blackness of darkness" (Cable's phrase) at the very heart of New World societies. Both writers veiled their attacks on contemporary times by casting their tales in analogous historical settings: Melville using San Domingo to speak of American pre–Civil War tensions and expansionism; and Cable using Louisiana's transition from French to U.S. rule to speak of post-Reconstruction transitions in the South. And both texts confront ravenesque shadows through disorienting gothic narratives of Senegalese revolt. It is once again the exceptional Senegalese slave who haunts the consciousness and ideologies of slaveholders and general readers. Like Melville's novella and Poe's poem, Cable's novel repeatedly recasts statuesque foundational shadows—with a decidedly Haiti-inflected energy of action—to hauntingly edify the present.

In Cable's novel, the Wolof maroon Bras Coupé is "a statue of indignation in black marble" (174). By the end of *The Grandissimes*, the memory of Bras Coupé is sculpted into a voodoo weapon—packed in a coffin-shaped box and slipped into the home of a respected Creole patriarch: "He removed the lid and saw within, resting on the cushioned bottom, the image, in myrtle-wax, moulded and painted with some rude skill, of a negro's bloody arm cut off near the shoulder—a *bras coupé*—with a dirk grasped in its hand" (314). This voodoo object of rememory is emblematic of a violent energy of action rippling into the present from the past. It precipitates one of Southern fiction's first racial lynch scenes when the black woman who is caught with the wax voodoo figure meets a perverse end at the hands of some of the very men she had wet-nursed.

Cable sought to carry his message of protest to the same kinds of genteel readers against whom Melville had plotted his veiled revolt. To make the unpopular theme of racial protest palatable to an audience desirous of patching up sectional differences, Cable found an attractive means of drawing his readers into the narrative. Louisiana was both exotic and culturally distinct enough to offer the novelist maneuvering room. The choice of an historical setting—the time of the French cession (1804)—allowed for a critique of the Southern Reconstruction and readmission into the Union. Barbara Ladd writes that *The Grandissimes* was so successful in its implied critique that there developed "a tendency to represent the defeated South as 'creole,' to attempt to read the reconstruction of the postbellum white Southerner in terms of the nationalization of white creoles during the cession years" ("The Direction" 532). But Cable's first effort with the core of the novel, a story about an uncommon African's resistance to slavery ("Bibi") was rejected at least twice by *Scribners* and also at the *Atlantic* "on account of the unmitigatedly distressful effect of the story" (Bikle 48). Cable seems to have taken the advice his Creole character, Honoré Grandissimme, gave to a naive Yankee apothecary: "Mr. Frowenfeld, you never make pills with eight corners eh? . . . No, you make them round; cannot you make your doctrines the same way?" (152–53). The exquisite descriptions of the Louisiana spring, the masked Creole ball, the "Gumbo" language, and a Montague-Capulet romance all serve to round the corners of the "unmitigatingly distressful" core of the Bras Coupé story so that the narrative might find a readership and challenge racist orthodoxies.

If we are to compare Cable's romance of redemption from the evils of Southern history with Melville's masked exposure of evils both hemispheric and human, we would do well to return to the triads of Poe's "Raven": the statuesque figure of whiteness, the haunting bird of blackness, and the shadow-struck Creole. Anchoring the narrative voice of Cable's novel is Joseph Frowenfeld, a Yankee apothecary of German descent who represents both "the coming of Anglo-American ways to Creole Louisiana" and the coming of Yankee ways to the South (Rubin, *Cable* 83). He arrives "armed with the truth" (39). Even though he changes as he gains the experience and skill to make his ideological pills more palatable, he is never wrong, only innocent, always managing to illuminate the trace of darkness detected in the Creoles: "Frowenfeld, large, white, and immovable, stood close. . . . the largest thing in the room was the big, upraised white fist of Frowenfeld" (240–41). The "grave pale face of Frowenfeld" serves as the conscience of the best Creoles (245). His Germanic energy and his medicinal avocation resist the moral contamination of Louisiana's Afro-Creole presence: "[H]e was brain-weary. Even in the bright recollections of the lady and her talk he became involved among shadows, and going from bad to worse, seemed at length almost to gasp in an atmosphere of hints, allusions, faint unspoken admissions, ill-concealed antipathies, unfinished speeches, mistaken identities and whisperings of hidden strife. The cathedral clock struck twelve and was answered again from the convent tower; and as the notes died away he suddenly became aware that the weird, drowsy throb of African song and dance had been swinging drowsily in his brain for an unknown lapse of time" (96). Frowenfeld fights to clear his head of the Africanist atmosphere. But his self-possession is more fully challenged when facing the "untamable beauty" of the quadroon Palmyre Philosophe. After baring her "superb shoulder" so that Frowenfeld could tend her gunshot wound, the Delanoesque apothecary finds that "[i]t was many an hour . . . before he could replace with more tranquilizing images the vision of the philosophe reclining among her pillows" (135–36). As he grows increasingly aware of Palmyre's sexual appeal, he feels her touch to be "poisonous," her presence a "disrelish." Throughout everything Frowenfeld's whiteness remains untainted. As Anna Elfenbein writes, Frowenfeld's "moral rectitude pointedly differentiates him from almost all the Creole males, and it is depicted as an aspect of his Northern European, which is to say, his German (in effect his Anglo-American) Protestant nature" (92).

Cable's characterization of the white Creoles is doubly aimed, focusing first on the particularities of Louisiana Creole culture, and more generally on the creolized South as a whole. Representative of the Creole and

Southern elite, Agricola Fusilier's very name joins Southern idealization of the agricultural and martial. Fusilier continually corrects young Frowenfeld's political views, speaking for Louisiana's (and the South's) "undivided public sentiment": "H-my young friend, when we say, 'we people,' we *always* mean we white people. The non-mention of color always implies pure white; and whatever is not pure white is to all intents and purposes pure black. When I say the 'whole community,' I mean the whole white portion; when I speak of the 'undivided public sentiment,' I mean the sentiment of the white population" (59). While he corrects Frowenfeld, Fusilier does express a willingness to "stand by you, *right or wrong*" (227) provided that "you" don't upset the cornerstone of order, for "[i]f the different grades of race and society did not have corresponding moral and civil liberties, varying in degree as they vary-h-why! *this* community at least, would go to pieces!" (227)

Cable goes to great pains to show the degree to which the Creoles (and Southerners as a whole) have been marked by a West African semiotic. The Creoles tend to speak Gombo French among themselves, and many of them, Agricola for instance, speak African languages such as Wolof (173). Aurore Nancanou, the charming heroine of the novel, grew up with her quadroon playmate Palmyre and regularly consults Palmyre for voodoo divinations and *gris-gris*. A voodoo erotic (a red ribbon worn for the loa Miché Agoussou) and the Gombo French of their shared childhood bind Aurora to Palmyre and indeed "charm" Aurore as an erotically darkened yet still "pure" white heroine. Since Aurora is "touched" with tastes and beliefs of an Afro-Creole world from which white adults are supposed to have been weaned, she offers traces of an old, repressed Afro-Creole erotic acceptable only in childhood or in the quaint charms of a white Creole woman. As Louis Rubin has remarked, what are regarded as negative traits among Creole men in the novel—sensuality, backwardness, moral laxness—become attractive features in the eroticized Creole women. Among the Creole men, only Honoré Grandissime and his cousin Raoul are depicted in a favorable light, and both of them are morally improved by contact with Frowenfeld. Raoul is a dilettante who paints "pigshoes" (pictures), but his true artistry appears in performance of Creole song, through which he adds local color that thickens the text's gumbo.

Honoré Grandissime is the novel's central Creole, the one whom Frowenfeld most leads toward genuine moral growth. When we first meet Honoré, he is an unidentified Creole, urging Frowenfeld to adopt the local views and "get acclimated" to Louisiana since "the water must expect to take the shape of the bucket" (37). But even as he meets Frowenfeld for the first time—by the grave of Bras Coupé—Honoré admits the possibility of other ideological shapes, allowing how "that negro's death changed the whole channel of my convictions" (38). Honoré—the administrator of the

Grandissime family holdings, a "Creole of the Creoles"—immediately makes it clear that he does not wish to be mistaken "for one of your new-fashioned Philadelphia 'negrophiles'" (38). But early on, Frowenfeld does indeed mistake Honoré's identity as it turns out that there are two Honoré Grandissimes, and the one we meet first by name (Frowenfeld's landlord) is an older, slightly darker half-brother whom we eventually discover to be a free man of color (f.m.c.). Educated together in Paris, Honoré Grandissime and Honoré Grandissime f.m.c. represent Louisiana's and the South's racially doubled, fraternal nature.

It is the voodoo practitioner Palmyre Philosophe who sustains and wields much of the *nyama* of old haunting actions. One of the text's most intriguing characterizations, Palmyre is a Gombo-speaking woman "of the quadroon caste, of superb stature and poise, severely handsome features, clear, tawny skin and large, passionate black eyes" (57). Like the *signares* of St. Louis du Senegal, whom French colonialists described similarly, Palmyre is "a barbaric and magnetic beauty" admired also for her "mental acuteness, conversational adroitness, concealed cunning and noiseless but visible strength of will" derived from the most impressive available genealogy: "Such a type could have sprung only from high Latin ancestry on the one side and—we might venture—Jaloff African on the other" (59–60). Palmyre has her own servant, a "dwarf Congo woman, as black as soot" (71), described elsewhere as "snarling and gnashing like an ape" (201). Although Palmyre's high Latin/Wolof blood stands in exceptional contrast to that of her apelike dwarf Congo servant, even Palmyre is a "barbaric beauty," possessing "a femininity without humanity,—something that made her with all her superbness, a creature that one would want to find chained" (71). A strange combination of female power and powerlessness, Palmyre is the "poisonous blossom of crime growing out of crime" (134), and her dreams of free agency turn toward revenge. Palmyre, the remarkable Latin-Wolof woman, wins her freedom "more for fear than from conscience' sake" after her introduction to Bras Coupé makes her finally "untamable" (147).

After building an "atmosphere of hints and allusions" surrounding the mention of Bras Coupé, *The Grandissimes* scripts three different narrations of "The Story of Bras Coupé" midway through the novel. Set in March of 1804, the tale begins with the Wolof prince's arrival on the schooner *Égalité* in 1795, the year of Louisiana's Pointe Coupée slave conspiracy. The historical conspiracy, informed by "revolutionary developments in France and Haiti," included Africans (several of whom were from the Senegambian region), black Creole slaves, free men of color, white Jacobins, and an indentured servant (Hall 344–74), and ended when "twenty-three slaves were hung, their heads cut off and nailed on posts at several places along the Mississippi River from New Orleans to Pointe Coupée" (Hall 344). The Pointe

Coupée conspiracy may provide the historical background for Cable's Bras Coupé narrative, as Alfred Bendixen has briefly suggested (30).

Cable drew not only from the enduring fears and hysteria surrounding the Point Coupée conspiracy but also from legends surrounding the historical figure known as Bras Coupé, a maroon outlaw remembered as one of the best Bamboula dancers of Congo Square. Cable wrote his daughter Lucy that when he first began to write, he "took great pains to talk with old French-speaking negroes" from whom he heard the story of Bras Coupé (Bikle 179–80). We might assume Bras Coupé to have been perceived differently by black and white Creoles. Following his death, the *New Orleans Daily Picayune* described him as "a semi-devil and a fiend in human shape" who lived a life "of crime and depravity," while Afro-Creole tradition remembers him as a rebel with strong voodoo powers (Asbury 245–46). When Bras Coupé was finally killed, his body was, like the bodies of Babo and the Pointe Coupée conspirators, publicly exposed to intimidate slaves who dreamed of freedom (247).

Like the narrative of Babo's insurrectionist plot, the tale of Bras Coupé is obsessively retold, narrated in the novel three times on the same day: by Honoré f.m.c. to Frowenfeld, by Raoul to the whole Grandissime clan, and finally by the white Honoré to Frowenfeld. We hear how after arriving on the *Égalité* the royal African captive gave a name in Jaloff (Wolof), which when translated into French as Bras Coupé, "made himself a type of all Slavery, turning into flesh and blood the truth that all Slavery is maiming" (171). Purchased by Agricola Fusilier and resold to a Spanish planter, Bras Coupé kills the driver who attempts to make him work. When the overseer summons the Spanish master to see this royal, "dauntless captive," the master takes one look and recognizes the African for the man he is, by seeing what he is not:

> "This man is not a Congo," he said.
> "He is a Jaloff," replied the encouraged overseer. "See his fine, straight nose; moreover, he is a *candio*—a prince. If I whip him he will die." (172)

Just as Palmyre's Wolof-Latin ancestry sets her apart from her apelike Congo servant, Bras Coupé's exceptional Wolof identity is marked by difference from supposed Congo physiognomy and behavior. In *The Creoles of Louisiana*, Cable wrote similarly of the selection of prized body servants: the preferred African house servants were "not the dull, ill-featured Congo or fierce Bambara, imported for the plantations, but the comely Yaloff and Mandingo" (45–46). And in his "The Dance in the Place Congo," Cable also distinguished Senegambians from other Africans, speaking of "tall, well-knit

Senegalese from Cape Verde, black as ebony, with intelligent, kindly eyes and long, straight, shapely noses . . . and in contrast to these, with small ears, thick eyebrows, bright eyes, flat, upturned noses, shining skin, wide mouths and white teeth, the negroes of Guinea, true and unmixed"(37).

When a translator is needed, someone who might "render a Jaloff's meaning into Creole French or Spanish" (173), Agricola Fusilier is recommended, but he refuses to use his Wolof skills to interpret for a slave. Finally, Fusilier suggests the Latin-Wolof quadroon Palmyre: "[S]he has picked up as many negro dialects as I know European languages" (173). Palmyre "attired herself in a resplendence of scarlet and beads and feathers that could not fail the double purpose of connecting her with the children of Ethiopia and commanding the captive's instant admiration. . . . and when she spoke to him in the dear accents of his native tongue, the matter of strife vanished from his mind" (174). As Bras Coupé becomes enamored of her, she tries to convince him to become a plantation driver since "[a]n African of this stripe had been found to answer admirably as a 'driver' to make others work" (174). He agrees to the position of driver on the condition that he be wedded to Palmyre (who loves the white Honoré). She attempts to reject this condition but is commanded by the Spanish master to silence, "[a]nd she was silent; and so, sometimes, is fire in the wall" (175).

While Bras Coupé learns to speak the Gombo that is so rooted in his Wolof mother tongue, Palmyre reconsiders the options presented her through the Wolof prince, whom she does not "love," but rather identifies as her double: "She rejoiced in his stature; she reveled in the contemplation of his untamable spirit; he seemed to her the gigantic embodiment of her own dark, fierce will, the expanded realization of her lifetime longing for terrible strength" (175). After long assessment, she decides to "let the silly priest have his say," for she hopes to show Bras Coupé's "mighty arm how and when to strike" (178). But the wedding party ends in disaster when Bras Coupé, drunk for the first time, strikes his master, curses the men of the party, and flees into the cypress swamp. The blow delivered to his master, "punishable in a white offender, by a small fine or a few days' imprisonment . . . assured Bras Coupé the death of a felon; such was the old *Code Noir*" (180–81). With Bras Coupé in the swamp, Palmyre is unable to teach him "the lesson she had hoped to teach him": "She had heard of San Domingo, and for months the fierce heart within her silent bosom had been leaping and shouting and seeing visions of fire and blood. . . . The lesson she would have taught the giant was Insurrection" (184).

After dispensing a Wolof curse and disappearing into the night's cypress swamp—or as Cable terms it, "the blackness of darkness" (181)—the maroon returns months later to deliver another curse upon both master and land in the mutually shared Gombo: "Mo cé voudrai que la maison ci là et tout ça qui pas femme ici s'raient encore maudits! (May this house and all in it who are not women be accursed)" (187). He adds an additional curse similar to the one threatened by Sunjata upon the King of Mema: "May weeds cover the ground until the air is full of their odor and the wild beasts of the forest come and lie down under their cover" (187).[5] In the scene of Bras Coupé's cursing of the land, it is difficult to accept the worshipful attitude with which he approaches Palmyre's white mistress, who makes no effort to use her influence over him, for "she thought Bras-Coupé had half a right to do it. . . . and like her brother Honoré—looks at both sides of a question" (188). But his sympathy for the ladies provides one way of getting genteel readers to look at the other side of questions of liberty in a post-Reconstruction South moving rapidly to limit newly established rights of black freemen.

When Bras Coupé is finally caught while dancing the Calinda in Congo Square, his Spanish master decides to overlook the capital offense of assault and has him "suffer only the penalties of the crime he had committed against society by attempting to be a free man" (191). According to the terms of the Code Noir, the Wolof prince is shorn of his ears, branded on both shoulders, hamstrung, and whipped. The cursed master dies shortly after Bras Coupé's maiming. And finally, in a highly sentimental scene that Melville or Faulkner would never have dreamed of scripting, Bras Coupé, hamstrung and near death, cradles the mistress's baby boy in his arms in a redemptive moment: "[I]t smiled, its mother's smile, and put its hand upon the runaway's face, and the first tears of Bras Coupé's life, the dying testimony of his humanity, gushed from his eyes. . . .The curse was lifted" (193). When questioned by a priest, "Do you know where you are going?" the dying Wolof prince "with an ecstatic, upward smile, whispered, 'To—Africa'—and was gone" (193).

Although Bras Coupé apparently lifted the curse upon the Southern soil, much of what follows in the novel—a lynching, a homicide, and a suicide—suggests that if the curse lifts, it lifts like a boomerang. The sentimentalized tale of Bras Coupé has a range of effects upon its various tellers and audiences. The Grandissime beauties respond to Raul's telling by affirming that "it was a great pity to have hamstrung Bras Coupé, a man who even in his cursing had made an exception in favor of the ladies," but since "they could suggest no alternative," they "dispersed, retired and went to sleep confirmed in this sentiment" (194). For them, Bras Coupé's story is a pathetic gothic romance of unrequited love and lifted curses rather than an encounter with evil detectable in even the most superficial readings of Babo's insurrection. For Frowenfeld, however, "the story stirred deeper feelings" (194). After having heard Bras Coupé's name repeated in an "atmosphere of hints and allusions" throughout the novel, Frowenfeld first hears the story from Honoré f.m.c., and then urges the free man of color to give his energy and wealth to "the cause of the down-trodden race with which this community's scorn unjustly compels you to rank yourself" (195). Later in the day, when the white Honoré overhears Frowenfeld getting down to the bedrock problems—"the double damage of all oppression. . . . the shadow of the Ethiopian . . . [and] the glare of the white man" (196–97)—the white Creole tells Frowenfeld the by-now-familiar story, pouring it out as a confession and remarking in the end that "[y]ou may ponder the philosophy of Bras-Coupé in your study, but I have got to get rid of his results" (198).

After the tale of Bras Coupé, *The Grandissimes* moves toward romance and the violence associated with modern Southern gothic. Palmyre increasingly becomes the medium of the resistance earlier embodied by Bras Coupé. Honoré f.m.c., moved by Frowenfeld and by the white Honoré's increasing willingness to recognize their fraternity, asserts himself against the community's racial code. What follows is a remarkably public recognition of interracial fraternity as the two brothers announce their joint business— "Grandissime Brothers"—a venture that outrages the family and leads to Agricola Fusilier's death following his provocation of his darker kinsman.

Through recognition of the creolized fraternal bonds in *The Grandissimes*, Cable sought to forge a new identity, not simply in "the little, hybrid city of Nouvelle Orleans," but for the fully hybrid South (11). Yet he knew that a work of art that attempted to cut through Southern ideologies to get to real familial relationships would meet with rejection. Seeking to propagandize, he made his "pills" round rather than eight-cornered, "softening" the tale of Bras Coupé (and the violence it engenders) with exquisite local color and pairings of romance that end happily for the white Creole couples and impossibly for the black Creoles. Unfortunately, it was the pastoral mask that readers like William Dean Howells seized upon rather than the condemnation and frightening disorientations—to which fellow Southerners like Grace King, Adrian Rouquette, and Charles Gayarré took quick offense.

In his biography of Cable, Louis D. Rubin has written that "if the modern Southern novel has been characterized by its unconscious attempt to deal honestly with the complexity of Southern racial experience, then *The Grandissimes* was the first important work of fiction written by a Southerner in which that attention is manifested" (78). *The Grandissimes* stands as an important ancestor of Southern modernism. But for all of its power and well-intentioned (quite conscious) vision, the novel falls short of its goals. The reflexivity evident in Melville's characterization of Delano is what is most notably absent in Cable's presentation of Frowenfeld and *The Grandissimes*. Frowenfeld's judgments are always just; his immovable surety always provides the answer to political questions. While in Melville's tale,

Delano's Africanist language is emplotted as a mask through which we might come to see the gaps between ideology and real relations, Cable's Africanist prose (evident, for example, in his differentiation of Wolof and Congo characteristics and also in his smug anti-Latin bias) often betrays his substantial effort. Frowenfeld (along with the narrator, who is closely tied to Frowenfeld's point of view) regards Creoles with a racialized condescension similar to that found in Delano's attitude toward the Spanish captain. Cable later wrote in *The Creoles of Louisiana* of Creoles as being "slack-handed and dilatory. . . . wanting in habits of mature thought and self-control. . . . valorious but unreflecting" (70–71). In Melville, even the most naive reader finally learns not to trust Delano's perceptions, but Frowenfeld's perceptions, while not always informed of the nuanced genealogies and relationships of the novel, are the book's unquestioned moral bedrock. All essential difference must assimilate to Frowenfeld and be affected by his uplifting presence. *He*, the unquestioned center, will never be hybridized by cultural interchange or climate. Melville achieves his success largely through a decentering ideological distancing from Delano, while it is Cable's inability to distance himself from Frowenfeld that most damages the gothic power of *The Grandissimes*.

The Grandissimes is a flawed but quite important late-nineteenth-century American novel. Cable achieves his greatest success through his many-shaded characterizations of the Latin Creoles (allegorical Southerners) who most directly feel "the shadow of the Ethiopian." While in Melville's text we can never be sure what Benito Cereno has learned when speaking of "the shadow of the negro," Cable's Honoré Grandissime more clearly confronts the shadow of the Ethiopian (and its crippling energies of action) by recognizing that it is the glare of the white man that creates Africanist shadows. Still, the shadows seem most heavily cast from the black characters—from Bras Coupé and Palmyre to Honoré f.m.c., the "dwarf Congo," and the deftly depicted Clémence (the Virginia-born market woman who functions as the novel's choral "signifier" and who is finally lynched).

Melville's narrative identifies with Babo's plotting to such a degree that Melville becomes a co-plotter with the Senegalese insurgent. Melville makes use of existing stereotypes concerning Africans in order to plot the reader's response. Cable's Bras Coupé is also born of stereotypes—the royal captive, the superior Wolof/Senegambian, the uncommon slave—to play upon the sympathies of a genteel readership. However, Cable acquiesces to sentiment and racial ideology instead of confronting and wholly subverting the Africanist characterizations of Creole society. Nowhere does Cable deeply identify with his exceptional Senegalese subjects as Melville did with Babo. Cable would engage Africanist shadows in a manner considered revolutionary in the South, yet his artistic imagination falls short of the kind of fraternal identities across the color line that his book advocates and that Melville achieved.

Nonetheless, we must note that Cable, who was hounded out of the South, was brave enough in his convictions to assault Southern ideologies that were rapidly solidifying behind post-Reconstruction "redemption" and its accompanying radical racism. American literature became, as Albion Tourgée claimed, "Confederate in sympathy" (405), at just the time that Cable was taking a strong stand as an ex-Confederate condemning segregation, disenfranchisement, and lynching. Northern readers and artists were doing what Frowenfeld actively resisted, becoming acclimated to Southern-style racism in a climate of national hysteria that gave rise to literary works such as those by Thomas Dixon and films such as *The Birth of a Nation* (1914). The decades of 1890–1910 saw the rebirth of a radically racist white nation.[6]

Poe's antebellum fear of the raven and its shadow, Melville's exhumation of San Domingo and the still-active evils of America's founding, and Cable's romance-coated plunge into "the double damage of all oppression," point to the degree to which Africanist shadows variously permeate the national consciousness. As Owen Wister's narrator finds to his utter disorientation in *Lady Baltimore* (1905), parts of Charleston, like New Orleans, or any of America's "inner" cities, may take one "abruptly, as with one magic step, out of the white man's world into the blackest Congo," into places that "teem and swarm with negroes" (175). Such an African(ist) presence—with its accompanying historical/discursive causes—seems to cast a ravenesque shadow upon American whiteness, disrupting "white" dreams of an untroubled purity and hegemony. But the "glaring" gaze of the white consciousness, "teeming and swarming" with Africanist thoughts and activities, is the true source of haunting, creating a white consciousness that can never coincide with white constructions of self. Wister notes of Charleston, "As cracks will run through fine porcelain, so do these black rifts of Africa lurk almost invisible among the gardens and the houses" (175). It was in such a labyrinthine gothic milieu that Faulkner would place Quentin Compson, probing the almost invisible rifts, the shade-filled houses, the heap of broken images that America's Africanist discourse so easily attributes to its African American presence.

"Never Once but Like Ripples"

On Boomeranging Trumps, Rememory, and the Novel as Medium

"Confound it, Carothers . . . what the hell kind of Senegambian
Montague and Capulet is this anyhow?"

Faulkner's *Go Down, Moses* (1942)

—*You are my brother.*
—*No I'm not. I'm the nigger that's going to sleep with your sister.*

Faulkner's *Absalom, Absalom!* (1936)

I

William Faulkner was the most powerful American writer of a generation
whose grandparents once fought in the bloody battles of the Civil War. African slavery was not yet *was* to Faulkner's generation of Southerners. His
grandparents had owned slaves.[1] Narratives of slavery and even of Africa
were handed down by family members and acquaintances, by both
slaveholders and ex-slaves. Tied like Quentin Compson to "garrulous outraged baffled ghosts . . . telling him about old ghost times" (*Absalom* 9),
Faulkner's generation was also the generation of Southerners that came of
age during World War I, expatriated to Europe or New York, breathed the
air of international modernism and contributed powerfully to it. Members
of this generation drew knowledge of Africa from family stories told in Mississippi or Georgia, and then reencountered Africans—particularly
Senegalese soldiers—in wartime Europe. In Faulkner's short story "Crevasse,"
the same author who writes of traces of Senegambia in Jefferson, Mississippi, brings us into a WWI chalk cavern in France: "[T]he sergeant moves

the torch. It streaks laterally into the darkness, along a wall, a tunnel, into yawning blackness, the walls faceted with pale glints of chalk. About the tunnel, sitting or leaning upright against the walls, are skeletons in dark tunics and bagging Zouave trousers, their moldering arms beside them; the captain recognizes them as Senegalese troops of the May fighting of 1915, surprised and killed by gas" (472). As with Melville, we follow our narrative's "leader" on a labyrinthine Africanist passage "into yawning blackness" to find the skeletal remains of gassed Senegalese soldiers, all signs of difference erased save for the uniforms. Their bones stand witness to the latest Western atrocities and serve—like Sutpen's Haiti—to mark old crossroads forever linking Africa, Yoknapatawpha's county seat of Jefferson (as well as the nation's own Jeffersonian foundations), and Europe. The twentieth century suddenly forced Southerners (and all Americans) to face the broader world that had so shaped our colonial and antebellum beginnings. Recognizing forces of violent genesis that America has unceasingly attempted to distance as "other," Faulkner stared unflinchingly at our most haunting energies of action. His open-eyed texts have served as a medium of historical/contemporary confluences that we are only beginning to acknowledge. To paraphrase Edouard Glissant, these "unstoppable conjunctions" have a name, "Creolization," the confluent source of our deepest hauntings and of our national and hemispheric genius.[2]

Southerners of Faulkner's generation were peculiarly conscious of history, of the old ghost times of plantation slavery alongside the new ones of gas warfare and jazz/blues recordings. Allen Tate, in his essay "The Profession of Letters in the South," noted "the peculiarly historical consciousness of the Southern writer," a consciousness informing "the curious burst of intelligence that we get at a crossing of the ways" (533). Tate argued elsewhere (in "The New Provincialism") that "[w]ith the war of 1914–1918, the South reentered the world—but gave a backward glance as it stepped over the border: that backward glance gave us the Southern renascence, a literature conscious of the past in the present" (545). Emphasizing the role that Southern defeat, poverty, and agrarianism played in Southern consciousness of the past in the present, Tate managed to repress the reciprocal "crossing of the ways" presented by slavery and its legacies of racial difference marked in black and white: a consciousness of the past in the present if ever one existed.

Modernist fiction is not known for historical consciousness but rather for underscoring "the essential contemporaneity of all significant human experience" (Hayden White 31). As C. Vann Woodward noted in *The Burden of Southern History* (1960), "A Hemingway hero with a grandfather is inconceivable, and he is apparently quite as bereft of uncles, aunts, cousins, and in-laws, not to mention neighbors and poor relations" (31). If then, the postmodern text distinguishes itself by its "attempt to think the present historically in an age that has forgotten how to think historically in the first place" (Jameson ix), Southern modernists—black and white—seem uniquely positioned for postmodern readings of the frontiers of American consciousness. The South produced two historically conscious modernist "renaissances" rooted in crossroads needs to reassess the past. Writers of the Harlem renaissance looked Southward in order to take stock of Afro-Creole folk culture and its African roots. Toomer's *Cane*, Arna Bontemps's *Black Thunder*, and much of the work of Zora Neale Hurston and Rudolph Fisher reached through layers of history and vernacular folk soundings, moving southward and to Africa. Meanwhile, writers of the Southern renaissance turned obsessively to historically grounded questions of race, identity, and legitimacy. The works of Robert Penn Warren, Allen Tate, Andrew Lytle, Eudora Welty, and Faulkner are grounded in an awareness of the manner in which the past shapes contemporary thoughts and actions. Although we must acknowledge the contributions of many Southern modernists (noting, for example, Toomer's development of montage techniques and Hurston's innovations in vernacular narrative), Faulkner did the most to develop a language and style for divining our origins and sounding/deferring/resounding the damned attempt to silence creolization's unstoppable conjunctions.

As Ralph Ellison and Albert Murray have insisted, Faulkner was not that far removed from the African presence in America. My own undergraduate writing teacher, the Vanderbilt Agrarian Andrew Lytle, introduced me to a remnant of antebellum Africanist knowledge, when after I spoke with him about my experiences as a Peace Corps volunteer in Senegal he responded enthusiastically, voicing his respect for Senegalese culture, saying in effect that Senegalese were valued as the most intelligent, the most attractive, and the most dependable slaves. It was he who made me aware of the existence of Arabic documents written by enslaved Senegambians, and it was he who pointed me toward typologies of Senegambians in American fiction as I turned to his story of the fall of the old order, "Jericho, Jericho, Jericho," in which Uncle Ike, "head man in slavery days. . . .[a] tall Senegalese. . . .[whose] forehead shone like the point, the core of night," defends his mistress and the plantation gold from Civil War bushwhackers (14). Although we could extend discussion of the varied uses of Senegambian characters in twentieth-century American literature, what I shall investigate in this closing chapter is the haunting effect of Africanist speculation itself as it is channeled by a gothic medium shaped by the earlier channeling presence of Senegambian insurrectionists and slave-authored Arabic texts. As we have seen, the shadows most haunting Caruthers's, Melville's, and Cable's texts were cast by the glare of whiteness in confrontation with literate or noble Senegambians who proved difficult to fully or categorically "other." Gothic twistings and turnings of the nation's historical romance gone awry provided a medium of registering sudden shocks of recognition of the illegitimacy of whiteness and provided a way of adopting and exploring what Ellison, in *Shadow and Act*, called "the black mask of humanity."[3] Riffing off of Ellison's observations, Toni Morrison—in chapter 2 of *Playing in the Dark* ("Romancing the Shadow")—again calls our attention to the "shadow that is companion to this whiteness—a dark and abiding presence that moves the hearts and texts of American literature with fear and longing" (33). Having examined some of the ways in which Senegambians imparted a strong trace of their energies of action to this shadow of fear and longing, let us now turn to look more closely at the shadow itself, an historically active mask imbued with its double-voiced *nyama*.

Accepting in outraged recapitulation the location of modern racial slavery (and its host of illegitimacies) at the very foundation of the New World design, Faulkner makes it clear that "what is founded on slavery and oppression cannot last," but Faulkner's truest manner of cutting "a new path through the maze of the world" rises from his narrative enactments of the powers that would resist creolization and African American agency (Glissant 95). As Glissant insists, it "is through sounding this damnation, this denial, that the work draws, not a lesson, but a new vision. . . . [that] measures what reversals must occur in sensibilities before new alliances . . . can become deliberate" (95). The Creole disclosures of Faulkner's texts can help us to read and renavigate the ways in which America's unique claims to freedom are highlighted by the Africanist presence of an enslaved population. His soundings of the damnation of white repression of creolization (and free African American agency), when read against Ellison's and Morrison's strong contrapuntal voicings of a much freer agency, may bring us to some of our most charged crossroads, where we may begin to divine energies of action linking our Creole pasts, presents, and futures.

Absalom, Absalom! is Faulkner's most haunted and tortuous narrative. It is a text that functions as medium between antebellum ghosts, two ragtime-era Harvard roommates (Quentin Compson and Shreve McCannon), and our own postmodern reading present. Quentin feels the full burden of Southern/national history in a passage that resonates with recognition of how foundational moments and their enduring energies of action may shape our present:

> *Maybe nothing ever happens once and is finished. Maybe happen is never once but like ripples maybe on water after the pebble sinks, the ripples moving on, spreading, the pool attached by a narrow umbilical water-cord to the next pool which the first pool feeds, has fed, did feed, let this second pool contain a different temperature of*

water, a different molecularity of having seen, felt, remembered, re-
flect in a different tone the infinite unchanging sky, it doesn't matter:
that pebble's watery echo whose fall it did not even see moves across
its surface too and the original ripple-space, to the old ineradicable
rhythm. . . . (261)

Quentin could have served as the prototype for Allen Tate's formulation of Southern "consciousness of the past in the present." Had Tate probed more honestly and more deeply into this historical consciousness, he would have discovered that in Faulkner's Mississippi there can be no understanding of origins of action or energy of action outside of an understanding of foundations based on racial difference. The introduction of African chattel slavery into the New World Eden has long been seen as the "original sin" that destroyed American innocence, but it has been primarily Southern (and Caribbean/Latin American) writers—and none more powerfully than Faulkner—whose works remind us that we have no pastoral escape from ever-rippling collective and personal memory.

The tale of Thomas Sutpen's design to bequeathe an inheritable patrimony begins "as though by outraged recapitulation evoked" through the voice of a speaker—Rosa Coldfield—possessed to become the tale's medium, "as if it were the voice which he haunted where a more fortunate one would have had a house" (8). From Rosa's haunted voice (by which we know language to be haunted edifice enough) Sutpen's shade comes to life in Quentin's (and the reader's) psyche. As if confronted by a promotional movie poster, we see Sutpen accompanied by "his band of wild niggers" and "the captive French architect" he brought from Haiti to build the ostentatious Mississippi domain of "Sutpen's Hundred" (8). Quentin "seemed to watch them overrun suddenly the hundred square miles of tranquil and astonished earth and drag house and formal gardens violently out of the soundless Nothing and *clap them down like cards on a table* beneath the uppalm immobile and pontific, creating the Sutpen's Hundred, the *Be Sutpen's Hundred* like the oldentime *Be Light*" (8–9). We see Sutpen's house and gardens placed on the table like cards and find ourselves playing an already dealt game.

Although Thomas Sutpen's (and the South's) doomed design serves as the ostensible topic of *Absalom, Absalom!*, it is Quentin Compson—who ends the book with Shreve and begins it here with Miss Rosa—who is the novel's truest subject:

Then hearing would reconcile and he would seem to listen to
two separate Quentins now—the Quentin Compson preparing
for Harvard in the South, the Deep South dead since 1865 and

peopled with garrulous outraged baffled ghosts, listening, having to listen, to one of the ghosts which had refused to lie still
even longer than most had, telling him about old ghost times;
and the Quentin Compson who was still too young to deserve
yet to be a ghost, but nevertheless having to be one for all that,
since he was born and bred in the Deep South the same as she
was—the two separate Quentins now talking to one another in
the long silence of notpeople, in notlanguage, like this: *It seems
that this demon—his name was Sutpen—(Colonel Sutpen)—Colonel Sutpen.* (9)

Caught between Mississippi's "old ghost times" and the modernizing outside world signified by Harvard and Quentin's college roommate Shreve,
Quentin "was not a being, an entity, he was a commonwealth" (12). He
immediately displaces Rosa as medium of the shade-glutted narrative as he
begins rehearsing the tale to himself even as she tells it. Silences, like the
one in which Quentin begins his internal narration, permeate the book,
augmenting the ominous silences of "Benito Cereno" and *The Grandissimes*.
Quentin's style, like those of all the speakers, is formed by a garrulous
"notlanguage" adapted to plumbing the depths of mind and consciousness,
a sentence style piled with subordination and negation that serves not simply to represent an action but to become the medium of actions from old
ghost times rippling into the present of singular reading subjects who are
always more "commonwealth" than romantic individual.

Faulkner's sentences work, as Peter Brooks has remarked, as "an evo-
cation through outraged recapitulation, where there is evidently a need not
only to remember but also—in Freud's terms—to repeat and to 'work through'
an as yet unmastered past, from motives that are highly charged emotionally but not specified or yet specifiable" (252). Although the novel's motives
may not be specifiable, the source of many of the shadows evoked, Africanist
"blackness of darkness," lies at the base of Sutpen's design and provides the
very sign of difference: the "monkey nigger" that barred young Thomas
Sutpen's passage at the door of a Tidewater planter.[4] Brooks argues that in
"this moment of barred passage, Sutpen discovers the existence of difference: difference as an abstract and formal property which takes precedence
over all else—since, for instance, it is more important than the content of
the message he was supposed to deliver" (258). Sutpen's pride leads him to
plot to overcome the limitations of his poor white ancestry and cross over
the bar of difference to pass as planter aristocrat, his image of which is
rooted in "the colonialist slave cultures of the Deep South and the Caribbean" (Ladd, "The Direction" 525). Through New Orleans and Haiti, highly
Africanized colonialist locations, Faulkner investigates the manner in which

racial difference was inscribed at the very base of the American design to make "a country all divided and fixed and neat with a people living on it all divided and fixed and neat because of what color their skins happened to be and what they happened to own" (221).

Charles Bon of New Orleans enters the novel as a mysterious and attractive Creole, who befriended Thomas Sutpen's son Henry at the University of Mississippi, courted Henry's sister, served in the Confederate army with Henry, and was finally murdered by Henry at the gates of Sutpen's Hundred. Bon is Henry's mentor, the older Creole friend "whose clothing and walk and speech he had tried to ape, along with his attitude toward women and his ideas of honor and pride too" (110). At times almost an allegorical figure of the old colonialist coastal South, Charles Bon is also a corrupting "threat" to Henry's innocence. Like Henry's father Thomas Sutpen, and like Faulkner the author, Bon is an elaborate plotter—at least in the psyches of those who narrate his story. We read how in New Orleans Bon seeks to have his intended brother-in-law Henry accept the inconsequentiality of Bon's marriage to a New Orleans octoroon: "[H]e took the innocent and negative plate of Henry's provincial soul and intellect and exposed it by slow degrees to this esoteric milieu, building gradually toward the picture which he decided to retain, accept" (110). Bon operates almost as Delano imagined the Spaniard Benito Cereno to act and certainly as Babo *did* act: "the exposures brief, so brief as to be cryptic, almost staccato, the plate unaware of what the complete picture would show, scarce-seen yet ineradicable—a trap" (111). Bon's exposure of Henry (and the reader) to Creole New Orleans is accomplished in a manner similar to Henry James's seduction of Strether in the Paris of *The Ambassadors.* Yet New Orleans is doubly dangerous, for it has all of the Catholic Old World decadence of Paris along with the Africanist horrors of Conrad's *Heart of Darkness.* The scenes of cryptic stacatto seduction in Creole New Orleans seed the whole style of *Absalom, Absalom!*

What Bon is trying to get Henry to accept is acknowledgment of the constructedness (rather than God-ordained engendering) of the colonialists' racial design, a design that had been imitated by Mississippi's antebellum planter-pioneers but that could not be unapologetically embraced in the language of Christian democracy. Slowly, as Bon leads Henry through the Vieux Carré's streets, past courtyards and shuttered facades,

> it was as though to Henry the blank and scaling barrier in dissolving produced and revealed not comprehension to the mind, the intellect which weighs and discards, but striking instead straight and true to some primary blind and mindless foundation of all young male living dream and hope—a row of faces

like a bazaar of flowers, the supreme apotheosis of chattelry, of human flesh bred of the two races for that sale—a corridor of doomed and tragic flower faces walled between the grim duenna row of old women and the elegant shapes of young men trim predatory and (at the moment) goatlike: this seen by Henry quickly, exposed quickly and then removed, the mentor's voice still bland, pleasant, cryptic, postulating still the fact of one man of the world talking to another about something they both understand, depending upon, counting upon still, the puritan's provincial horror of revealing surprise or ignorance. (112)

All that Bon and Henry might share is based upon this understanding of racial difference as foundational design. Bon [at least in Mr. Compson's telling] makes it clear that this design entails certain patriarchal responsibilities since it was created by man rather than by God: "We—the thousand, the white men—made them, created and produced them; we even made the laws which declare that one eighth of a specified kind of blood shall outweigh seven eighths of another kind" (115).

Having exposed Henry to the attractions and responsibilities of the colonialist American design, Bon, "the gambler not quite reduced to his final trump" (117), plays Henry's reactions, knowing that it will be the marriage to the octoroon (potential bigamy) that will cause Henry to object to Bon's intent to wed Henry's sister. Bon skillfully plays a withheld card: "the trump now, the voice gentle now: 'Have you forgot that this woman, this child, are niggers? You, Henry Sutpen of Sutpen's Hundred in Mississippi? You, talking of marriage, a wedding, here?" (118). By playing the race card and having it acknowledged as trump, Bon implicates Henry in the country's foundational laws and assumptions. Indeed, the "race card" is trump only because it is recognized and played as such.

Faulkner's core Creole site for the dramatization of the moral "blackness" of the foundational design is, appropriately, Haiti. As we have seen in the demonizing of Ibrahima abd al Rahman, Zephaniah Kingsley's pamphleteering for assimilationist racial policies, Melville's *San Dominick*, and Palmyre's desire to teach Bras Coupé the lesson of San Domingo, Haiti lurked as a spectral presence in the white American imagination. Young Thomas Sutpen chooses the heart of the hemispheric plantation design and a position as overseer there as the means to proceed with his own designs in Mississippi. Once in Haiti, his success depends in large part upon how successfully he opens himself to creolization: "the patois he had to learn in order to oversee the plantation" (248). Faulkner as author internalizes the Creole knowledge that Sutpen learned when he "realized that he would not only need courage and skill, he would have to learn a new language, else that design to which he had dedicated himself would die still-born" (248). Yet creolization is the very denaturing floodgate of confluences that Sutpen (like Yoknapatawpha and Faulkner himself) fears and ultimately attempts to resist. Later in Yoknapatawpha, the Creole language that Sutpen spoke with his slaves appears as "some dark and fatal tongue of their own" (36). Creolization seems to offer an unsettling and—for Faulkner's Jefferson, Mississippi—denaturing fatality. But Faulkner himself proceeds to divine a new, confluent language. Two Faulknerian sentences are enough to evoke, in outraged recapitulation, the stream of historical consciousness by which we enter a voodoo-inhabited clearing:

> a spot of earth which might have been created and set aside by Heaven itself, Grandfather said, as a theatre for violence and injustice and bloodshed and all the satanic lusts of human greed and cruelty, for the last despairing fury of all the pariah-interdict and all the doomed—a little island set in a smiling and fury-lurked and incredible indigo sea, which was the halfway point between what we call the jungle and what we call civilization, halfway between the dark inscrutable continent from which the black blood, the black bones and flesh and thinking and remembering and hopes and desires, was ravished by violence, and the cold known land to which it was doomed, the civilized land and people which had expelled some of its own blood and thinking and desires that had become too crass to be faced and borne longer, and set it homeless and desperate on the lonely ocean—a little lost island in a latitude which would require ten thousand years of equatorial heritage to bear its climate, a soil manured with black blood from two hundred years of oppression and exploitation until it sprang with an incredible paradox of peaceful greenery and crimson flowers and sugar cane sapling size and three times the height of a man and a little bulkier of course but valuable pound for pound almost with silver ore, as if nature held a balance and kept a book and offered a recompense for the torn limbs and outraged hearts even if man did not, the planting of nature and man too watered not only by the wasted blood but breathed over by the winds in which the doomed ships had fled in vain, out of which the last tatter of sail had sunk into the blue sea, along which the last vain despairing cry of woman or child had blown away—the planting of men too; the yet intact bones and brains in which the old unsleeping blood that had vanished into the earth they trod still cried out for vengeance. And he overseeing it, riding peacefully about on his horse while he

learned the language (that meagre and fragile thread, Grandfather said, by which the little surface corners and edges of men's secret and solitary lives may be joined for an instant now and then before sinking back into the darkness where the spirit cried for the first time and was not heard and will cry for the last time and will not be heard then either), not knowing that what he rode upon was a volcano, hearing the air tremble and throb at night with the drums and the chanting and not knowing that it was the heart of the earth itself he heard, who believed (Grandfather said) that earth was kind and gentle and that darkness was merely something you saw, or could not see in; overseeing what he oversaw and not knowing that he was overseeing it. (250–52)

While Sutpen rides and "oversees," he is also to some degree "ridden" by the vodou/voodoo *loas* (divine mysteries) and utterly changed. He becomes their "horse."[5] This possessing change, like the ever-rippling conjunctions of creolization, rides the tale's retelling. As we hear Sutpen tell General Compson the tale of the founding of his wealth, we are transported (through Quentin's evocative transmission of his Grandfather's narrative) from a chilly winter room in Boston back to Jefferson, and then—from that Mississippi effluvium of the Jeffersonian dream—to shadows of Haiti itself.[6]

While Haiti appears to be close to the source of the first New World rippling, Mr. Compson and Quentin also describe the ripple effect of history as a perpetual game of cards with unchanging trumps. Mr. Compson says that Sutpen "told Grandfather, dropped this into the telling as you might flick the joker out of a pack of fresh cards without being able to remember later whether you had removed the joker or not, that the old man's wife had been a Spaniard" (252). Since every trump card in the deck of *Absalom, Absalom!* is a race card, Faulkner's most astute readers know the reason for Sutpen's abandonment of the Haitian wife and will be expectant of the eventual reappearance of the joker in the deck: the race card that will also explain Henry's murder of an Africanized Charles Bon. In works by Anglo-American writers, the dark Spaniard or Latin Creole is almost always a figure tainted by Africa, thus the "ravenesque" ambiguity of Benito Cereno, the two Honoré Grandissimes, and Charles Bon. As Melville teased his readers through Delano, Quentin teases the reader to see the insurrectionist patterns caused by the very rules of the game. What lies behind Quentin's eventual suicide is this: his half-conscious recognition that the only way to avoid the game's tainted deck is to refuse to play.

Beginning with his willful subdual of Haitian insurrectionists, Sutpen, whom both Rosa and Shreve refer to as "the demon," becomes a Satanic figure. It is Sutpen who entered the "throbbing darkness. . . . walked out into the darkness and subdued them" (254). And after proving himself to be darker, more horrifyingly devilish in pursuit of his willful design than the supposedly devilish voodoo practitioners, Sutpen becomes engaged to the planter's daughter, Eulalia Bon. We are here reminded of the Creole and Senegambian "Marriage to the Devil" tales as a Bon marries the most materialistic dispiriting demon, establishing a legacy of bonds and bondage. And it is this recognition of being wed to the Devil that hits Sutpen's Mississippi wife Ellen Coldfield when she enters a boxing match in the barn, "seeing not the two black beasts she had expected to see but instead a white one and a black one, both naked to the waist and gouging at one another's eyes as if their skins should not only have been the same color but should have been covered with fur too," and she sees what Sutpen (and, figuratively, the whole white South) has been driven to do and become "perhaps as a matter of sheer deadly forethought toward the retention of supremacy" (20–21), while forcing the heirs of this Creole wilderness into silent witnessing.

Having conceived his racialized design of entry into the planter class afer having been barred by a "monkey nigger" from delivering a message to a Tidewater Virginia planter's front door, Sutpen—like so many self-made Americans—is a gambler who has been playing with a marked deck but insists upon winning "fair." When fate or the *nyama* of his acts forces Sutpen to decide whether to allow his daughter to marry his unacknowledged, "passing" (or "passed"/past) son, he clings to the strange, always already damned design of New World whiteness: "[E]ither I destroy my design with my own hand, which will happen if I am forced to play my last trump card, or do nothing, let matters take the course which I know they will take and see my design complete itself quite normally and naturally and successfully to the public eye, yet to my own in such fashion as to be a mockery and a betrayal of that little boy who approached that door fifty years ago" (274). Should he play the race card and push Henry to murder his "black" half-brother, Sutpen is assured that for the moment he can bar threatening interracial passages. If he does not play the card, all doors will be open to an amalgamation that has in fact already occurred and that threatens the legitimacy of the patrimony he intends to bequeath. The narrative itself drifts away from its original moorings in the actions of Thomas Sutpen. As Shreve comes to understand the Africanist element of Quentin's narrative, he asks Quentin: "[Y]ou wouldn't have known what anybody was talking about if you hadn't been out there and seen Clytie. Is that right?" (274). Clytie, whose name invokes the curse of the house of Atreus, is the enduring witness of old atrocities and the ravenesque guardian of the door. The very presence of Sutpen's black daughter, Clytie, alters the direction of Quentin's narrative. We are returned to the repeating trope of the card game, already dealt, trumps already called, as Quentin and Shreve accept the old, unchanging rules.

Quentin plays his cards so masterfully and exposes Shreve to the subtleties of racial semiotics to such a degree that Shreve challenges Quentin's hard-won authority over the telling. Shreve interrupts, "'He played that trump after all'" (277). And Quentin responds to the challenge: "'Wait, I tell you! . . . I am telling'" (277). But just at this point, when Quentin reveals new information about a tale repeated over three generations of his family, Shreve usurps the tale, causing Quentin to question the incarnation of the narrative voice: "Am I going to have to hear it all again he thought I am going to have to hear it all over again I am already hearing it all over again I am listening to it all over again I shall never listen to anything else but this again forever" (277). Shreve's voice assumes greater authority as he and Quentin illuminate the contingencies of history and of all writing: "the two of them creating between them, out of the rag-tag and bob-ends of old tales and talking, people who perhaps had never existed at all anywhere, who, shadows, were shadows not of flesh and blood . . . but shadows in turn of what were . . . shades too" (303). By entering the tale as narrator, participating "in the creating of this shade whom they discussed (rather, existed in)" (316), Quentin's Canadian roommate enables the old shades' reincarnation and forces Quentin into deeper recognition of issues that were repressed elements of his narrative. In this tale, as Edouard Glissant has observed, "Thought rides from one person to another, the way the loas (divinities of the voodoo religion) ride those they have chosen to possess" (176). With Quentin and Shreve—as with the narration of the entire text—a "'continuous stream of consciousness' . . . [l]ike a tumultuous Mississippi," runs through tellers and readers through "an astounding blur of pronouns, almost all of them . . . indefinite," like a Creole/voodoo *loa* moving through chosen "horses" (Glissant 176).

Finally, when Shreve rather casually suggests a reason for Bon's attraction to Judith Sutpen: "[M]aybe the possibility of incest. . . . maybe if there were sin too maybe you would not be permitted to escape, uncouple, return.—Aint that right?" (323) Quentin is rendered speechless. The opposite force of creolization's confluences, incest—the retreat to original purities—makes perfect psychic sense as a motivating source of desires and fears. Repeatedly responding "I don't know," Quentin represses acknowledgment of incestuous desires that Shreve so glibly presents in the narrative (and that Quentin, in *The Sound and the Fury*, acknowledges feeling for his sister Caddy). But repression of incestuous desires, as with repression of knowledge of the depravity of America's foundational design, leads to tortuous reenactment. Identities (and historicity) collapse beneath the riding of thought, moving through the "four of them and then just two—Charles-Shreve and Quentin-Henry" (334). They repeat and imagine the pair's journey to Creole New Orleans, Quentin playing the role of Henry, "who knew but still did not believe . . . that which . . . would be like death for him to learn" (335). Shreve sets the stage—a New Orleans drawing room that the narrator tells us "was probably true enough" (335)—and they mutually conjure Bon's dark Haitian-born mother "whom Shreve and Quentin had likewise invented and which was likewise probably true enough" (335). Through their reincarnation of old shades, Shreve/Charles and Quentin/ Henry quickly see that Mr. Compson's idea of Henry's repugnance to Bon's marriage to an octoroon could not have been what led Henry to kill Bon, for "the octoroon and the child would have been to Henry only something else about Bon to be, not envied but aped" (336). Given the narrative evidence supplied by Quentin, Shreve arrives again at incest, stabbing at Quentin's heart as he speaks of Henry: "Jesus, think of the load he had to carry . . . faced with incest, incest of all things that might have been reserved for him, that all his heredity and training had to rebel against on principle, and in a situation where he knew that neither incest nor training was going to help him solve it" (340). Quentin increasingly identifies not just with Henry but also with Bon, a young man who wants recognition from his father but who is dismissed from his father's house just as Sutpen was originally dismissed by a Tidewater planter's "monkey nigger" in a moment that birthed a design hell-bent upon repetition. Ironically, Sutpen's design works to cast his ac-knowledged "white" son Henry (who has already been "aping" his invisibly "black" brother) into the role of "monkey nigger." Bon tells Henry, "He just told you, sent me a message like you send a command by a nigger servant to a beggar or a tramp to clear out" (341). This is the Manichean boomerang of Southern and American history: the invention of "niggers" ultimately works to cast the "white" male characters of the Sutpen story into "black" roles— demon Sutpen, the aping messenger-boy Henry, and the Africanized Creole Bon/Quentin (Sutpen never regards women as anything but chattel).

The old Shreve-Bon/Quentin-Henry pairing immediately collapses "since now both of them were Henry Sutpen and both of them were Bon, compounded each of both yet either neither" (351). And they arrive at old Sutpen's playing of his final trump in a Confederate camp: "He must not marry her, Henry. His mother's father told me that her mother had been a Spanish woman. I believed him; it was not until after he was born that I found out that his mother was part negro" (354–55). Afterwards, Bon con-fronts Henry: "So it's the miscegenation, not the incest, which you can't bear" (356). Bon then, in a repetition of a scene in *The Sound and the Fury*— when Dalton Ames challenged Quentin to shoot him—hands Henry a pis-tol.[7] Like Quentin, Henry cannot shoot: *"You are my brother"* (356). But Bon is both contemptuous and suicidal in provocation: *"No I'm not. I'm the nigger that's going to sleep with your sister. Unless you stop me, Henry"* (358). Quentin, whom we know from the start to be "two separate Quentins," is again split between Henry's honor-upholding role as protecting white brother and Bon's role as "the nigger who's going to sleep with your sister."

Quentin's attempts to repress erotic desire, which Audre Lorde tells us is "firmly rooted in the power of our unexpressed or unrecognized feeling. . . . that power which rises from our deepest and nonrational knowledge" (53), lead him to link sexuality with moral/racial blackness, a dark continent of impurities. Over the course of a narrative told from many points of view but held together primarily by Quentin, Bon is the black joker in the deck, almost invisible, represented as whatever the narrators need him to be. Barbara Ladd writes that "[a]s African, as 'black beast,' as 'the nigger that's going to sleep with your sister,' and yet as brother nonetheless, Charles Bon represents all that the post-1890 white Southerner most feared: the gradual usurpation of political, familial, and economic purity" ("The Direction" 545). In *The Crucible of Race* (1984), Joel Williamson points out that in the hysterical heyday of radical racism (1889–1915), the generation of blacks who had not been raised under the supposedly "civilizing" bonds of slavery were perceived by whites to be reverting to an innately African savagery. Lynchings occurred with unparalleled spectacle and frequency—including one in Oxford that ten-year-old William Faulkner likely witnessed (Williamson, *William Faulkner* 158–63). So sharply were ideology and morality racialized in a Manichean manner that, as Williamson argues, "[b]y about 1900 it was possible in the South for one who was biologically pure white to become black by behavior. A white person could cross over to blackness" and become "a white nigger" (*The Crucible* 467). Since "there were unseen 'niggers,' men with black hearts under white skins," a kind of always already schizophrenic consciousness intensified in the South, leaving a strong imprint upon men of Quentin Compson's and Faulkner's generations. If as the antebellum Mississippian Henry Hughes remarked, "Amalgamation is incest" (quoted in Sundquist, *Faulkner: The House Divided* 97), then incest (invoked here as a sign for the unspeakably tabooed) would be the kind of black behavior white Mississippians so feared and desired. In the Deep South, incest is the logical end of the apartheid state's retreat from Creole confluences, a retreat from the "other" into the familiar terrain of racial/cultural purities.

Incest becomes a provisional name for an unspeakable act: the foundational sin cursing the Atreus-like house of Sutpen, the South, and America. While the illegitimacy of chattel slavery (and the categorical "othering" of humanity) is the foundational sin, the words "miscegenation" and "amalgamation" mark the inevitable consequences of the system. The very idea of "miscegenation" speaks not of the erotic sharing of joy but of the pornographic: of the ways planter patriarchs used sex to capitalize their plantations, of the systematic denial of kinship bonds, and of the systematic repression of the deepest human feelings. The pornographic, as Audre Lorde writes, "is a direct denial of the power of the erotic" (54). In much of Faulkner's work "miscegenation" and its binary twin, incest, become names for the pornographic, names and impulses born of repression of the erotic. This always racially colored repression of the erotic may well have reached its most horrific intensity during Faulkner's and Quentin Compson's child-hoods—the peak period of radical racism and lynchings. Quentin's black "other fellow," the trumping "joker" in his stacked deck, mirrors/shades all that he represses and projects, and binds him for suicidal violence. Quentin is thus reduced to being a kind of "horse" for Africanist ideologies that "ride" and possess him. When Shreve finally narrates and openly voices Quentin's intuited recognition of race as the withheld (and damning) trump in Sutpen's hand, Shreve's language shows itself to be a kind of crude amal-gamation: "Aint that right? Aint it? By God, aint it?" to which Quentin adds one exasperated word of assent: "Yes" (359).

Although Clytie (Thomas Sutpen's black daughter) is identified as "the one who owns the horror" (369–70), we know that it is finally Quentin, the South, the thought-ridden nation that all own it. Quentin's much antici-pated dialogue with Henry Sutpen, whom Clytie has tended in the haunted Sutpen house for four years, reveals no new information and in fact tells us more about Quentin than about the Sutpens. We are finally brought back to Poe's shadow-haunted speaker in "The Raven" as Quentin mutters "'Never-more of peace. Nevermore of peace. Nevermore Nevermore Nevermore'" (373). After the fire that destroys the decaying Sutpen mansion and kills both Henry and Clytie, the remnant sign of the raven's shadow resides in the idiot howl-ing of the last living Sutpen: Charles Bon's black grandson Jim Bond, whose name speaks of the whole American romance gone awry—in a fall from grace—from French "bon" (good) to bondage. Jim Bond's howling among the Sutpen ruins sounds the furies with which *Absalom* ends, while the Ca-nadian Shreve is led by the Sutpen tale to foresee the inevitability of North America's unending path of creolization, stating glibly that "in a few thou-sand years, I who regard you will also have sprung from the loins of African kings" (378). The key word here is "also," as Yoknapatawpha's Quentin meets his double in Charles Bon and the howling of Jim Bond. Quentin knows that for him it is already so. But African genetic descent is less the issue for Quentin than is his descent from Africanist discursive traditions that—by employing Africans as signs "for the repressed or irrational other of rationality" (Gilroy 45)—forge a glaring whiteness, a wholly unattainable, wholly pathological model of being. Rather, it is an antierotic or pornographic model of terror. By accepting the existence of the "nigger" as bar of difference and by reading it as the trump card, Quentin has inherited a repressed identity bound to resurface and which must, according to his code of logic and honor, lead to the murder of his own "inner-nigger" who harbors sexual fantasies for a sister

who must be kept pure.[8] Quentin and Shreve's narration amounts to a se-
ance in which the reader is left to decide whether a partly African shade is
conjured and/or whether Bon becomes one more manifestation of "the shadow
of the African," the shadow self that is "simply the return of the repressed—
simply an unconscious projection of Quentin's own psychic history" (Irwin
16). What Faulkner makes clear is the utter futility, the suicide of attempting
to silence the shadow by killing an African.

As Eric Sundquist has attested, the theme of *Absalom, Absalom!* is "the
haunted mind of the South—and of the nation—its house still divided by
racial nightmares" (*Faulkner, Race* 26). But the novel's deepest message of
haunting comes only through the tale's functioning as Creole voodoo/spiri-
tualist medium. More than a ghost tale, *Absalom's* riding of thought works
like a possessed medium or oracular mask, sounding damning channels of
Africanist resistance to creolization's "unstoppable conjunctions." As
Edouard Glissant remarks, "It is through sounding this damnation, this
denial, that the work draws, not a lesson, but a new vision . . . by changing
our poetics," moving us from a "poetics of Being" (primordial purities or
origins) to a frontier "poetics of becoming" (95–96, 226).

More fully than any American writer since Melville, Faulkner sought
dialogue with the ghosts of the land that produced him. Rather than agreeing
with Joyce's Stephen Dedalus that history is the "nightmare" from which we
must awaken if we are to be saved, Faulkner seems to invite demons into
nightmarish texts with a conviction that it is only through facing and ac-
knowledging those demons designed in us that we may aim for something
more than endurance or material acquisition and consumption. By following
the shadow to its source, we arrive finally not at an African but at the Africanist
design as it controls the gothic turnings of the American romance. Obsessions with incest and racial murder direct Quentin's Sutpen tale and Quentin's
own prescribed fate, since as Hayden White writes of the patient in psychoanalysis, he "has overemplotted these events, has charged them with a meaning so intense that, whether real or merely imagined, they continue to shape
both his perceptions and his responses to the world long after they should
have become 'past history'" (87). If we accept the Freudian notion that the
repressed is bound to return as compulsive repetition, then we might most
profitably turn to the medium of the gothic/spiritualist novel and to its most
obsessive reincarnations of old tales, to find that which history has repressed,
the past we claim to no longer possess and that most fully possesses us.

II

More powerfully than most narrative modes, gothic/neo-hoodoo "riding of
thought" opens the living to the ancestral dead and manages to divine that

which the nation's history has repressed and which we fear may leave us "nevermore at peace." Ralph Ellison's *Invisible Man* makes no bones about its groundedness in a nineteenth-century gothic tradition. From the moment Ellison draws upon "Benito Cereno" for an epigraph: "'You are saved,' cried Captain Delano, more and more astonished and pained; 'you are saved: what has cast such a shadow upon you?'" we can expect to reencounter shadows of Africans. But this time the encounter comes with a signal difference. For rather than the silences and secondhand narration of Babo, Bras Coupé, and Charles Bon, it is the shade himself who narrates. After announcing "I am an invisible man," Ellison's narrator establishes his difference from the spectral lineage running from "The Raven" to Quentin Compson: "I am not a spook like those who haunted Edgar Allan Poe. . . . I am a man of substance" (3). As with Charles Bon, others "see only my surroundings, themselves, or figments of their imagination—indeed, everything and anything except me" (3). Invisibility is clearly "[a] matter of the construction of their *inner* eyes" (3). But the white gaze takes on a very material, forceful presence, shaping economies and some of the limits of American possibility. Ellison's shade makes these discoveries as he charts "how the world moves: Not like an arrow, but a boomerang. (Beware of those who speak of the *spiral* of history; they are preparing a boomerang. Keep a steel helmet handy.) I know; I have been boomeranged across my head so much that I now can see the darkness of lightness. And I love light" (6).

Rejecting the progressive vision of history instilled in him by schoolteachers and the Marxist "Brotherhood," Ellison's narrator comes to see that the more powerful forces that shape our lives can not be contained or even imagined in any written history. Instead, *Invisible Man* navigates a "merging fluidity" that is our "only true history of the times, a mood blared by trumpets, trombones, saxophones, and drums, a song with turgid, inadequate words" (480, 433). Facing three young hipsters who "speak a jived-up transitional language" and who might easily be the grandfathers of today's rappers, the narrator ponders the possibility that they might be reserved high cards in the hand: "What if history was a gambler, instead of a force in a laboratory experiment, and the boys his ace in the hole? What if history was not a reasonable citizen but a madman full of paranoid guile and these boys his agents, his big surprise! His own revenge? For they were outside, in the dark with Sambo, the dancing paper doll" (431). We begin to see history, as with Faulkner, not simply as a canon of texts but also as all the unrecorded acts that have left impressions in minds and speech. Ellison is concerned here with old energies of action retraced everywhere in the present, in the gin mills, barber shops, beauty shops, juke joints, and churches; in such places "[a] whole unrecorded history is spoken" (460) in a music and medium working like the Faulknerian sentence to give "a slightly different sense of time . . . those points where time stands still or from which it leaps ahead" (8).

While Ellison relied upon blues, jazz, and folk motifs to represent the "merging fluidity" of unrecorded energies of action from the past rippling through present transitions, Faulkner's "riding of thought" depended more upon "stream of consciousness" and the long sentence. As he remarked in a talk given at the University of Virginia, Faulkner saw the long sentence as a useful medium for dialogue with mysteries and ancestries that form consciousness from sources deeper than Western romantic individualism:

> [N]o man is himself, he is the sum of his past. There is no such thing really as was because the past is. It is a part of every man, every woman, and every moment. All of his and her ancestry, background, is all a part of himself and herself at any moment. And so a man, a character in a story at any moment of action is not just himself as he is then, he is all that made him, and the long sentence is an attempt to get his past and possibly his future into the instant in which he does something. (Gwynn and Blotner 84)

This is the project of *Invisible Man*. Sandwiched between the narrative present of prologue and epilogue, we find the structural equivalent of one long (twenty-five-chapter) episodic sentence that attempts to get the past (and maybe something of the future) into the moment of the narrator's contemplation of emergence from his neo-gothic basement. Through an understanding of his past (and the training of his readers' inner eyes) he narrates the possibility of his visibility.

Invisible Man makes the strongest claims since Du Bois's *The Souls of Black Folk* to the full crossroads of America's "classical" history and the nation's unrecorded vernacular histories. Ellison's novel calls all identities into question, particularly "white" ones constructed upon compulsive, pornographic violence and repressed knowledge of a familiar, shared erotic—as he makes clear in one long Faulkner-signifying sentence:

> I remember too, how we confronted those others, those who had set me here in this Eden, whom we knew though we didn't know, who were unfamiliar in their familiarity, who trailed their words to us through blood and violence and ridicule and condescension with drawling smiles, and who exhorted and threatened, intimidated with innocent words as they described to us the limitations of our lives and the vast boldness of our aspirations, the staggering folly of our impatience to rise even higher; who, as they talked, aroused furtive visions within me of blood-froth spar-

kling their chins like their familiar tobacco juice, and upon their
lips the curdled milk of a million black mammies' withered dugs,
a treacherous and fluid knowledge of our being, imbibed at our
source and now regurgitated foul upon us. (109–10)

Although this relationship of "familiar difference" is historically strongest
in the South, no American could be wholly unfamiliar with his or her
African(ist) sources, a fact that throws all identities built upon a rigid color
line into the truly real chaos of denied fluidities: our dammed blood-ties,
milk-bonds, and riverine creolizations. This is one of the Invisible Man's
crucial recognitions, for though he recognizes his own peculiarly American
invisibility, he comes to see that the visibility of all Americans is false: "knowing now who I was and where I was and knowing too that I had no longer to
run for or from the Jacks and Emersons and the Bledsoes and the Nortons,
but only from their confusion, impatience, and refusal to recognize the beautiful absurdity of their American identity and mine" (546). The American
identity/destiny embraced in *Invisible Man* is fully Creole, "not prophecy but
description," since "one of the greatest jokes in the world is the spectacle of
the whites busy escaping blackness and becoming blacker every day, and the
blacks striving toward whiteness, becoming quite dull and gray" (564).

Like *Absalom, Absalom!*, Ellison's *Invisible Man* speaks along usually
unregistered frequencies, revealing the difference that race has made in the
American design. Maritza Stanchich argues that *Absalom* "serves largely as
an exercise to exorcise not only the demon of Sutpen but the evil premise of
America," an exercise that ends in "frustrated futility" and never grants any
of its "Caribbean, mulatto and African characters . . . status as narrator"
(614, 616). But Faulkner's registering of the damnation of Jefferson's design
(both Yoknapatawpha's seat of Jefferson, Mississippi, and the larger
Jeffersonian national design) and the damnation of all white resistance to
forces of creolization opens a space that could be more fully articulated only
through the narrative voicings and fully inspirited embodiment of African
American writing.[9] *Invisible Man* sounds, embodies, and calls conscious attention to the Africanist myopia at the heart of the Jeffersonian design. Making music of invisibility, Ellison signifies upon foundational gaps, such as
those glaringly present in Jefferson's *Notes on the State of Virginia* (1786), in
which Jefferson writes that "never yet could I find that a black had uttered a
thought above the level of plain narration" (188–89). What the contrapuntal narrative of *Invisible Man* sounds most clearly—through Faulkneresque/
Louis Armstrong-inspired riffs and the music of "old Bad Air's horn" (568),
is an all-inclusive, expansive affirmation of the foundational "principle" of
freedom so central to the Jeffersonian dream: "Was it that we of all, we,
most of all, had to affirm the principle, the plan in whose name we had been

brutalized and sacrificed—not because we would always be weak nor because we were afraid or opportunistic, but because we were older than they, in the sense of what it took to live in the world with others, and because they had exhausted in us some—not much, but some—of the human greed and smallness, yes, and the fear and superstition that had kept them running" (561). It is no accident that an African American contrapuntal perspective has provided the most consistent and reliable narration of our multicultural American dream/nightmare. As Toni Morrison has shown us most recently in *Playing in the Dark*, an unfree Africanist presence gave first definition to the American dream of freedom. The truest dreamers of the New World dream—bringing to the dream something foundational and intensely Afro-Creole—have been people like David Walker, Frederick Douglass, Zora Neale Hurston, Ralph Ellison, and Martin Luther King.

In *Invisible Man*'s final recognition scene, Ellison gives voice to voices that had been excluded from the founders' dream. *Invisible Man* gives voice to the nightmare-shadow of the African that so haunted Benito Cereno, Honoré Grandissime, and Quentin Compson. Encountering Mr. Norton, whose incestuous desires for his daughter were brought to mixed thrills and horror in Trueblood's vernacular narrative of incest, the unrecognized invisible man reaches out with words Norton once wielded over the black college student he could never really "see"; our invisible narrator tells this wealthy white trustee of a Tuskeegee-like school (and a kind of double for the nation's founders): "I'm your destiny, I made you. Why shouldn't I know you?" (565). It is as if Charles Bon (or the shadow cast by the suicidal bright side of Quentin Compson's divided consciousness) were able to step into the Boston winter and confront Quentin in the flesh. This invisible man, whose repertoire operates along spectral frequencies, shows himself to be the perfect contrapuntal medium for Omni-American expression. Through his basement sounding of some of the depths of the American romance gone awry, Ellison makes the idea of a truly Creole, truly American romance possible, asking, "Who knows but that, on the lower frequencies, I speak for you? (568)

III

If shadows of Africans and the hauntings of American history fed the higher frequencies of Faulkner's and Ellison's gothic texts, we find haints in their most concrete, literal forms in Toni Morrison's *Beloved* (1987). Differing from the shades of *Absalom, Absalom!* and from the trope of invisibility articulated by Ellison, the ghost that haunts 124 Bluestone Road is an incarnate spirit from the dead. More than Africanist shadow (but historically "compounded" with such shades), *Beloved* emerges from the horrific infanticide of her mother Sethe's reaction to the racial design in American history, and she emerges too from Afro-Creole belief systems that prepare people to hear her speak from "the other side." Sethe, whose body and toil supplied the ink with which recorded histories and Africanist texts were written, and whose back is lashed and scarred with a chokecherry tree that is a simultaneous trace of both African tradition and American slavery, knows that "it is always now," that "nothing ever dies." More powerfully than Quentin's suicidal dialogue with Mississippi shades or Ellison's holed-up narrator's recognition of his designed invisibility, *Beloved* forces its central character, Sethe, to repeat a haunting past with enough difference and intensity to become dispossessed of some of its most treacherous ghosts. The process of confrontation with unspeakable "rememory" *or nyama* enables Morrison's novel to move from gothic horrors to romance. This resultant romance, unlike Ellison's parting (and quite lonely) affirmation of the American principle, affirms an older principle: the embodied soul erotics of family and love.

But we must recognize one thing: the ghosts in *Beloved* are real and not easily placated. As Morrison responded to Ted Koppel at the Olympic gathering of Nobel laureates in Atlanta in 1995, "[Y]ou may think the dead are inarticulate. I cannot *tell* you how much they have to say, and how often. The job is usually just to tell them to *please* shut up" (850). Morrison's novel appears to be the result of long dialogue with the ghosts of Margaret Garner and the daughter whom she killed after being surrounded by slave catchers following an attempted escape from slavery in Kentucky (See Gilroy 64–67). Unlike Quentin Compson, Morrison's Sethe sees no escape from the ripple effect of time and history, for "she knew that death was anything but forgetfulness" (4). Sethe informs her daughter's spectral incarnation that her plan "was to take us all to the other side where my own ma'am is" (250) and defends her killing of her daughter as an emancipation from the sure spiritual death of Schoolteacher's harsh mastery: "[I]f I hadn't killed her she would have died and that is something I could not bear to happen to her" (246). The resultant ghost, and something of the *nyama* or energy of Sethe's violent action lodges in the house on 124 Bluestone Road. Nothing that the baby's ghost does can truly surprise Sethe, her child Denver, and her mother-in-law Baby Suggs since "they understood the source of the outrage as well as they knew the source of light" (4). The source of *Beloved's* Faulkneresque "outraged recapitulation" and the garrulousness of its ghosts may be traced to specific actions—Sethe's killing of her child—but the deeper source lies in the larger American design. One Twenty-Four Bluestone Road becomes a symbolic lodgement for the hauntings of our national edifice: "Not a house in the country aint packed to its rafters with some dead Negro's grief" (6).

Since as Morrison says, masters "had to dehumanize not just the slaves but themselves" in order to sustain plantation slavery (in Gilroy 221), *Be-*

loved leads us to encounter terrors more disturbing than the haunting presence of African American ghosts. In fact, Morrison reveals whites as the most spectral presence of *Beloved*, for they render themselves more "otherly" than the ghosts they create. Stamp Paid asks "What *are* these people? You tell me, Jesus. What *are* they?" (222). The reincarnate ghost, Beloved, recognizes them (in a manner signifying upon *Invisible Man*) as "the men without skin" (265). This blurring of ghostliness renders the "real" ghosts of the dead less terrifying than the possibility of becoming, like Rosa Coldfield, Quentin Compson, and Sethe's husband Halle, a living, flesh and blood ghost. Again, it is men without skin, like Quentin, who are clearly the owners of the terror: "[A]nybody white could take your whole self for anything that came to mind. Not just work, kill, or maim you, but dirty you. Dirty you so bad you couldn't like yourself anymore" (308).

True to its gothic historicist genre, *Beloved* presents history as a haunting and time as a labyrinth in which "it is always now" (259). Memories and transmissions of Africa meld with the tortuous products of the enslavers' Africanist ideology. Even more than the horrifying stories of Babo's revolt and Bras Coupé's *marronage*, the tale of *Beloved* (like the tales of slavery itself) "was not a story to pass on" (336). Therefore, the story remains ever ready to erupt. Sethe "worked hard to remember as close to nothing as was safe. Unfortunately her brain was devious" (7). What joy Sethe does remember from slavery days is so mixed with loss as to have little to offer in the symbolic mode of language, although an enduring semiotic seems to fortify her: "Of that place where she was born (Carolina maybe? or was it Louisiana?) she remembered only song and dance. . . . that world of cooing women each of whom was called Ma'am" (38). Sethe's Afro-Creole Gullah or Gumbo roots, the women who all serve her as "Ma'am" (Wolof—"grandparent/ancestor"), initiate her into a world quite different from the world of enslavers, an otherness that—far from being nullity—is rich with what Audre Lorde recognizes as the erotic: "a resource within each of us that lies in a deeply female and spiritual plane" (53). Sethe's memories of an Afro-Creole childhood erotic are tied most clearly to the way the Afro-Creole slave community "danced the antelope" (the Mande *chi-wara?*) through which they maintained linkage to the other side (both Africa *and* a spiritual realm): "They shifted shapes and became something other. Some unchained, demanding other whose feet knew her pulse better than she did" (38). No longer remembering the African or Creole language used in her old home in Carolina or Louisiana, Sethe struggles to pick "meaning out of a code she no longer understood" (77). Although she fears "rememory" and its boomeranging *nyama* emplotting present actions, she feels strangely relieved when the baby ghost of her house—after a period of disappearance—returns reincarnate as a young woman to whom Sethe says "Thank God I don't have to rememory or say a thing because you know it" (235). For Sethe all things are "wrapped in a timeless present" (226). Talking about time, she says "It's so hard for me to believe in it. Some things go. Pass on. Some things just stay. I used to think it was my rememory" (44). "Rememory" in *Beloved* has a strong double agency. It works as a semiotic medium for sustaining spiritual elements derived from West Africa and from the transcendence of expressive arts thriving in the face of slavery, but it is also a house of horrors, as R. Baxter Miller remarks of the nation's remembrance of "race" and how we "hide but never displace the historical trace of slavery and the subsequent sign of racial segregation in America" (2). More than any single ingredient of America's common history, plantation slavery and its enduring signs lurk beneath the surface of our national discourse to remind us how little is truly past. As life in Mississippi had taught Quentin that *"Maybe nothing ever happens once and is finished,"* Sethe tells her daughter Denver about "the bloody side of the Ohio," saying that "if you go there—you who never was there—if you go there and stand in the place where it was, it will happen again. . . . even though it's all over—over and done with—it's going to always be there waiting for you" (45).

There is a past waiting for us all, a "nightmare" of history in which we find ourselves reenacting the old narrative scripts, consigned by ideologies and language itself to follow old designs. Despite a drive to forget much of the past, black Americans have kept a strong historical sense alive, more fully and accurately alive than perhaps any other group of Americans. And despite (no, most likely *because of*) deep strains of conservatism evident in extended family structures, religious affiliation, and racial-nationalist ideologies, African Americans have more interest than any other American group in changing some of the more pathological elements of the American design. Alice Walker has noted that black writers tend to be involved in a moral/physical struggle that is too pressing for the thick "gloom of defeat" she finds in many white writers and most noticeably in Faulkner: "Perhaps this is because our literary tradition is based on slave narratives, where escape for the body and freedom for the soul went together, or perhaps this is because black people have never felt themselves guilty of global, cosmic sins" (5). Morrison's project certainly differs from Faulkner's, Cable's, and Melville's works. Rather than romancing the shadow that serves as highlighting or haunting backdrop for white America's dreams of freedom, Morrison brings black figures "to the historical and narrative foreground" (O'Donnell 227). And unlike Ellison's *Invisible Man*, *Beloved* speaks primarily to the historical and psychic concerns of an African American community of readers.

Beloved is both a slave narrative of the most tortuous ascent and a novel of gothic-Creole immersion.[10] When Sethe informs us "I got a tree on

my back and a haint in my house" (18), we see a uniquely American coales-
cence of African and Africanist cultural forces. The pornographic scarrage
of slavery finds most explicit figuration in Sethe's narrative of the incident
in which she reported that several white boys had assaulted her and sucked
her milk dry, an assault for which she—the victim—was punished with a
brutal whipping that ripped her back to a bloody mess: "when it closed it
made a tree. It grows there still" (20). Only through dialogic, antiphonal
immersion in the pains and scarrage of a re-membered history is real ascent
(or avoidance of *Invisible Man's* "boomerang") possible. Sethe's lover Paul D
attempts such immersion with his healing, loving caress: "He rubbed his
cheek on her back and learned that way her sorrow, the roots of it; its wide
trunk and intricate branches" (21). But the pain that Paul D feels as he
learns the depths of Sethe's scarrage is too intense for him; the tree that had
long been a source of divinity and panegyric vision becomes simply the scar
tissue of slavery: "a revolting clump of scars. Not a tree, as she said. Maybe
shaped like one, but nothing like any tree he knew because trees were invit-
ing; things you could trust and be near, talk to you if you wanted to as he
frequently did since way back when he took the mid-day meal in the fields
of Sweet Home" (26). While the tree on Sethe's back serves as a text of the
horrors of the "peculiar institution," its figuration as tree remains emblematic of a scarred but thriving Afro-Creole spirituality—the tree-talking to
which Paul D alludes. More than a figure of the perniciousness of the American racial design, the chokecherry tree (both a choking and a sweetness)
inscribed in the highly literate, vernacular-informed prose of a spiritual descendant, charts a contrapuntal way of navigating history's boomerang. It is
a figure of both African and Africanist "rememory."

This branching tree is simply one in a whole Creole forest, double-
voiced and double-visioned. Just as there were two Quentin Compsons—
the ghost ridden Mississippi Quentin and the one of modern Harvard
possibilities—so too are there two tropical forests in *Beloved*. When Paul D
looks at himself through his old master's eyes, "he sees one thing," and
when he looks through "Sixo's another" (328). Quentin's black peers inhabit a world simultaneously more split and more whole than anything the
Compsons could imagine:

> Even the educated colored: the long-school people, the doctors,
> the teachers, the paper-writers and businessmen had a hard row
> to hoe. In addition to having to use their heads to get ahead, they
> had the whole weight of the race sitting there. You needed two
> heads for that. Whitepeople believed that whatever the manners,
> under every dark skin was a jungle. . . . In a way, he thought,
> they were right. The more coloredpeople spent their strength

trying to convince them how gentle they were, how clever and loving, how human, the more they used themselves up to persuade whites of something Negroes believed could not be questioned, the deeper and more tangled the jungle grew inside. But it wasn't the jungle blacks brought with them to this place from the other (livable) place. It was the jungle whitefolks planted in them. And it grew. It spread. In, through and after life, it spread, until it invaded the whites who had made it. Touched them every one. Changed and altered them. Made them bloody, silly, worse than even they wanted to be, so scared were they of the jungle they had made. (244)

In *Beloved*, as in America, there is a tropics of West African ways; there is a tropics of white Africanist modes, and there is every sort of imaginable hybrid filling gaps between. In spirited reliance upon an Afro-Creole tropics, Morrison seeks to hack a way through the pernicious "plantation" of "whitefolks'" jungles into the heads of Africans (and into the heads of "whitefolks" themselves). Bearing traces of Africa, Africanist slavery, and the uniquely African American contrapuntal textual quest for freedom, *Beloved* integrates many traditions, much of our history, and in the process offers an "imaginative appropriation of history" enabling American ability to recognize and acknowledge our past, since as Morrison notes: "The struggle to forget which was important in order to survive is fruitless and I wanted to make it fruitless" (Gilroy 222).

Much of what *Beloved* summons into "rememory" creates a sacred New World "Clearing" for a West African erotic, a non-millennial worldview celebratory of the fluidity of time and of the connected pleasures of the spirit and the body. Baby Suggs preached "that the only grace they could have was the grace they could imagine. That if they could not see it, they would not have it" (107). Moments of possession of grace and dispossession of haunting spirits come through attentiveness to the initiating mysteries, the motherpower of a presymbolic semiotic.[11] For example, it is Beloved's humming of a song that Sethe invented for her children that brings Sethe to recognize the spirit of her dead daughter. And we encounter an assembly of thirty women whose presymbolic "sound" prepares the final scene of Sethe's dispossession by immersing her in an old semiotic: "[T]hey stopped praying and took a step back to the beginning. In the beginning there were no words. In the beginning was the sound, and they all knew what that sound sounded like" (318). As "the voices of women searched for the right combination, the key, the code, the sound that broke the back of words" (321), their "sound" guides Sethe to attack Schoolteacher (refigured in the house's white landlord—the ex-abolitionist Bowdin) in a therapeutic reenactment that rescripts her earlier killing of Beloved. By avoiding the boomerang through reenacted repetition of foundational events, Sethe achieves the possibility of being something other than a live shade and can become for the equally emergent Paul D, as he acknowledges, "a friend of my mind" (335). Going deeper, further back (to presymbolic birthing sounds), and into more spiritually embodied spaces than either Faulkner or Ellison, *Beloved* struggles toward romance and moves through collective and personal horror to fetch a future that might offer freer possibilities of action.

Working from Afro-Creole understandings of energies of action akin to *nyama*, and from Ellison's "boomerang" and Quentin Compson's observation that *"Maybe nothing ever happens once and is finished"* (261), Toni Morrison's *Beloved* serves as medium of "rememory" that holds all of the remembered, repressed, and consciously pondered past in the moment where "it is always now" (259). Though Morrison moves Sethe toward fuller possibilities of romance with Paul D, self, and community, unacknowledged and repressed energies of racist Africanist action remain to haunt all Americans and threaten to leave us "nevermore at peace." But the source from which Morrison offers healing energies of action that Faulkner and even Ellison could not fully proffer is her submission to the soulful power of the erotic. This power, to which we all have access, has long been under assault by evangelical scripturalist religions that have the unusually effective ability to make "others" of human beings (not to mention animals, plants, rivers, and whole landscapes). Morrison immerses her work and vision in a feel for the sounds before language, the semiotic realm of milk bonds and mother-child-ness, and—in the process—turns to Africa and to Afro-Creole traditions that, relatively speaking, value "soul" and souls.

If America is to grow into a nation built upon solid, shared, creolized "spiritual soil," Americans must open themselves to the African elements of the national culture, elements that have long been repressed in official histories. With such an opening, the nation might be able to draw in full upon Afro-Creole "gifts of the spirit" to accompany gifts of sweat, milk, blood, and knowledge that have long been accepted or appropriated without reservation. Such acknowledgment, such opening, must be accompanied by its double: meaningful acknowledgment of the haunting, warped, recurrently violent modes of being to which we all were bound in the founding of America. America's accelerated growth of violence, of alienation, of suicidal antierotic modes of living can be slowed only by different modes of identifying ourselves and others. These different modes, which might be described—following Du Bois and James Brown—as soul-modes, are not restricted to African cultural repertoires but are modes and attitudes that West African and Afro-Creole expressive traditions have tended to recognize, respect, and transmit. The music and dance of African American soul transmissions/transitions seem to be what is most quintessentially American—at the base of our every movement and sound, part of the means of our energy of action. As we work to read Africa and Africanist ideologies into their long-standing core position in American identity, culture, and literature, we are taking a step toward finding historical truth and needful balm for festering, long-ignored wounds. And as we come to respect some of the energies of action channeled through the pharmacopoeia of the Senegalese *mocho'o* (medicine worker), we may return to the vital work of treating the foundational "mojo" of transatlantic chattel slavery, a "mojo" that is (in its ever-rippling causes and effects) a source of the nation's most enduring curses and simultaneously a source of our peculiarly American genius.

Notes

Introduction

1. An example of the critical/editorial "mainstreaming" of these notions may be found in the introduction to *The Norton Anthology of World Masterpieces* (1995), in which the editors equate the unhyphenated "American" with "Western"/"European"/"white-Anglo," and ignore the Omni-American cultural and ethnic diversity at the core of our foundational mix: "Though as a nation of immigrants we are continually in the process of redefining our collective life, that life for three centuries was defined primarily through ideas and experiences brought with them by immigrants from Britain and the countries of western and eastern Europe. This tradition constitutes the American half of such terms as African American, Asian American, German American, Hispanic American, Irish American, Italian American, Polish American, and the rest. So far as our collective life in this country has roots, these are to be found in the Western tradition" (Mack et al xxiv).

2. Henry Randall reported that Jefferson "used to mention as his first recollection his being handed up and carried on a pillow by a mounted slave, as the train set off down the river towards Tuckahoe" (I, 11). Fawn M. Brodie's biography, *Thomas Jefferson: An Intimate History*, brought this bit of Jefferson lore to my attention, as she uses it for a bit of foregrounding for later discussion of his sexual relationship with Sally Hemings (47).

3. David Dalby's recognition of Wolof contribution to the language of America's musical counterculture (1969, 136–40) predates my own discoveries of Wolof-Southern heritage, as I was living in Senegal from 1983–1985. Mary Louis Pratt's *Imperial Eyes: Travel Writing and Transculturation* (1992) provides interesting parallels to my own study, as she also relies upon questions of travel and the linguistic notion of "contact zones" to develop a revisionist focus on literary vision and gaze.

4. I am indebted to Michael Jackson's *Allegories of the Wilderness* for my understanding and phrasing of "ethical ambiguity."

5. Henry Louis Gates surveys Enlightenment-era privileging of writing as *the* generic sign of reason in his introduction to *"Race," Writing, and Difference.*

6. John Miller Chernoff coined the phrase "polyrhythmic sensibility" in *African Rhythm and African Sensibility*. My efforts to "think . . . contrapuntally" (Said 336) have benefitted from Chernoff's discussion of polyrhythmic musical/philosophical sensibilities, from Christopher Miller's Mande/Sunjata-centered readings of Francophone novels in *Theories of Africans* (1990), and from Said's contrapuntal methods in *Culture and Imperialism* (1997).

7. Crafts-caste groups in the region include Mande *nyamakala*, Wolof *neeno*, and Fulbe *neenbe*.

8. Chernoff's formulation of West African "polyrhythmic sensibility" may provide a provocative basis for understanding New World Creole religions and what

Charles Joyner in *Down by the Riverside* calls "Afro-Christianity." Look also to Jon Butler's *Awash in the Sea of Faith* and the work of Albert Raboteau (from *Slave Religion* to *A Fire in the Bones*).

9. See Dena Epstein's groundbreaking *Sinful Tunes and Spirituals* (1977) as well as the Geechee-specific focus of Art Rosenbaum's *Shout Because You're Free* (1998).

10. In "el apellido," the Cuban poet Nicolás Guillén searches "My roots and the roots / of my roots" (262), demanding, "look at my coat of arms: it has a baobab," and asking, among many possible lost patronyms, if his real name might not be "Wolof? / Nicolas Wolof, perhaps?" (264). And Aimé Césaire of Martinique coined the word "negritude" via arboreal tropes expressive of erotic soul: "My negritude is neither tower nor cathedral / it takes root in the red flesh of the earth / it takes root in the ardent flesh of the sky" (67–69).

11. As usual, Thomas Jefferson is particularly enlightening. His letter to Francis Gray (March 4, 1811), "What Constitutes a Mulatto?" (Padover 1022–23), reveals his continuing obsession with miscegenation (and his guilt/concerns over his children with Sally Hemings) and offers an amazingly drawn out mathematical equation noting the degrees of "crossing" necessary for the "clearing" of black blood. In Jefferson we see the severe limitations of foundational whiteness as metonym of enlightened reason.

12. Ralph Ellison, with his honed eye for significant detail, has noted in *Going to the Territory* that Eliot (St. Louis-born and England-bound) once spoke of himself as having been "a small boy with a nigger drawl" (161).

1. Imperial Mother Wit, Gumbo Erotics

1. A recent manifestation of Pan-African *badenya* in the United States may be found in the Organization of Badenya in the Americas, a New York-based organization promoting Pan-African cultural exchange and celebration among African immigrants. The organization recently cosponsored a concert featuring Miriam Makeba, Mande *jaliya* (griot) music, and Yoruba "spiritual songs." *New York Times,* Sunday, May 14, 2000, AR 11.

2. For an overview of African epics and epic traditions, see Belcher's *Epic Traditions of Africa,* and for an introductory anthology of African epics, see Johnson, Hale, and Belcher's *Oral Epics from Africa.*

3. See Michael Jackson's *Allegories of the Wilderness: Ethics and Ambiguity in Kuranko Narratives.*

4. See Hall, 163–65, and Fontenot, 114–26, for Bamana/Mande sources of amulets in Louisiana.

5. Numerous tales of flying Africans may be found in the Georgia Writers' Project's *Drums and Shadows.* For taboos against chicken in coastal Georgia, see *Drums and Shadows,* 118, 187.

6. See Coolen, and also Conway on banjo prototypes.

7. These "saraka" rice cakes, a West African culinary pleasure, are named from the Arabic-derived "sarax," meaning to sacrifice or give to charity, and used as a noun for any charity gift. See Sylviane Diouf, *Servants of Allah,* 191; and also Cornelia Bailey, *God, Dr. Buzzard, and the Bolito Man,* 135.

8. Sterling Stuckey's *Slave Culture* argues that the ring shout played a major role in the Africanization of Christianity in the plantation South. While Parrish and Turner point to an Arabic source for the word "shout," the ring dance itself is indigenous to West and Central Africa. We can see the griots doing a kind of ring shout around the newly installed Maali Kumba Njaay in the Wolof narrative, "The Baobabs Nderexeen and Werugeen" discussed in this study's introduction. Charles Joyner coined the phrase "creolization of culture"in *Down by the Riverside* (xxi).

9. Margaret Washington Creel has written on the Sierra Leonian sources of the Gullah religious initiatory tradition of "seeking," *"A Peculiar People"* 286–97. In *Changing Our Country Marks*, Gomez elaborates on the connection between "seeking" and the Sande/Poro bush retreats practiced by Sierra-Leonian Mande-speakers. The Bamana/Mande Komo society presents another informative link to Gullah "seeking," (see Dieterlen's and Cissé's *Les fondements de la societé d'initiation du Komo*). Finally the *hajj*, which Sunjata makes with the help of a jinn, might be considered a kind of advanced initiation-retreat into Islam.

10. See Sengova, 175–200.

11. *Florida Times-Union*, Monday, February 24, 1997, A-1 and A-17.

12. David Levering Lewis notes that "Emerson had used the term 'double consciousness' in 'The Transcendentalist'" (281–82). While Rampersad and others have written of Du Bois's debts to Goethe, Emerson, St. Paul, and Hegel (see Williamson on Du Bois as Hegelian, 399–413), my intent is to focus upon the under-recognized African and black vernacular sources without negating the European ones.

13. When I served in the Peace Corps in northern Senegal, my close friend and coworker, Sekou Dabo (from a Mandinka village in the southern Casamance region), revealed to me the spiritual necessity of his return home for burial if he should die. James Collier, a drum maker from coastal Georgia, shared this concern: "Fuh the spirit tuh rest in the grave folks have tuh be buried at home. They nevuh feel right if they buried from home" (Georgia Writers' Project 62–63). For other West African sources for the need for home burial, see the Georgia Writers' Project appendix (195–96).

14. These questions, addressed by Gomez in *Exchanging Our Country Marks* (277), are discussed in detail throughout his book, but especially in chapters on Bamana and Fon/Yoruba influence (38–58), Sierra Leonian and Akan influence (88–113), and Igbo influence (114–53)of African American culture and their confluence in an Africanized Christianity (244–90).

15. See Williamson, *The Crucible of Race*, for a reading of radical racism 1889–1915 and its relationship to *The Souls of Black Folk* (111–413).

16. My focus on the "issues of travel, movement, displacement, and relocation that emerge from Du Bois's work" (117) owes much to Paul Gilroy's study of "the tension between roots and routes" (133) in *The Black Atlantic*.

2. Of Root Figures and Buggy Jiving

1. When Thomas Talley, son of ex-slaves, published the first substantial collection of Afro-American secular folk poetry in 1922, he was drawing upon a body

of "black hillbilly music," song after song of which could be heard four years later over the airwaves of Nashville's WSM Saturday night "barn dance" program, which soon became the Grand Ole Opry (Charles Wolfe *Negro Folk Rhymes* xxv). Wolfe points to Senegal as the occulted source remembered in "Guinea Gall."

2. Gay Wilentz's *Binding Cultures*, with its comparative focus on Nigerian and African American women's writing—and its argument that women have often worked as mothering "culture-binders,"—offers precedent and useful counterpoint to my own work.

3. Ellison's friend Albert Murray sees black Americans as *The Omni-Americans*, the Americans who were first oriented to America's multiethnic New World experience.

4. See Julia Kristeva, *Polylogue* and *Desire in Language*.

5. Kristeva's presymbolic semiotic might work in a manner analogous to creole substrate languages. See Mufwene, *Africanisms* 23.

6. My language here (and elsewhere in this project) is indebted to Chris Bonghe, who writing of "an anxiety about cultural origins and traditions that are in the process of becoming ever more occulted under conditions of modernity," adds in passing that "first-level works of modernism like Jean Toomer's *Cane* (1923) or Carpentier's *Ecuè-Yambo-Ó* (1933) are attempts at bringing this secret to light, at making the Black Southern or Afro-Cuban tradition speak its originary truth, without excessively foregrounding the conditions of narration that make this speech possible" (167).

7. I am using "erotic" here in the conventional sense of the word, but we should keep Lorde's amplification of "erotic" possibilities and power in mind.

8. Eileen Julien has written on modern African novels' relationships to epic, initiation, and fable. Her insightful discussion of the importance of indigenous African genres to the narration of "Francophone" African novels offered informing precedent to my study.

9. See David Dalby on etymologies for "bug" and "jive" (138–40).

3. Myth-making, Mother-child-ness, and Epic Renamings

1. It must be pointed out that the lack of parallelism between the English words "patrimony" and "matrimony" has worked to underscore the erasure of woman's agency in favor of white male property rights and cultural heritage. The relatively balanced view of gender presented in the Sunjata (and in most West African languages themselves) offers a counteragency that few readers would have been prepared to utilize until recently. Women from Afro-Creole cultures, however, were prepared by Africa-based traditions and by slavery itself to assume relatively strong positions of womanhood. See bell hooks's *Ain't I a Woman*.

2. See Gates, *"Race," Writing, and Difference* 8.

3. Outcries against the rape of black women (and simultaneous castration of black manhood) are a repeated feature of early African American literature. Olaudah Equiano writes, "[I]t was almost a constant practice with our clerks, and other whites, to commit violent depredations on the chastity of the female slaves; and to these atrocities I was, though with reluctance, obliged to submit at all times. . . . I have

known them to gratify their brutal passion with females not ten years old" (Gates, *The Classic Slave Narratives* 74). Frederick Douglass adds, "[T]he fact remains, in all its glaring odiousness, that slaveholders have ordained, and by law established, that the children of slave women shall in all cases follow the condition of their mothers, and this is done too obviously to administer to their own lusts, and make a gratification of their wicked desires profitable as well as pleasurable" (256–57). Henry Highland Garnet, of Mandinka ancestry, was even more forthright in his indictment of white rapists and his rhetorically powerful questioning of black manhood:

> Think of your wretched sisters, loving virtue and purity, as they are driven into concubinage and are exposed to the unbridled lusts of in-carnate devils. Think of the undying glory that hangs around the an-cient name of Africa—and forget not that you are native-born American citizens, and as such you are justly entitled to all the rights that are granted to the freest. . . . You act as though you were made for the special use of these devils. You act as though your daughters were born to pamper the lusts of your masters and overseers. And worse than all, you tamely submit while your lords tear your wives from your em-braces and defile them before your eyes. In the name of God, we ask, are you men? Where is the blood of your fathers? (Gates et al. *The Norton Anthology of African American Literature* 285)

4. See Diop's *The African Origin of Civilization*. Well before Diop's work, the West Indian writer Edward Wilmot Blyden articulated a vision laying claim to an-cient Egyptian patrimony: "I felt that I had a peculiar 'heritage in the Great Pyra-mid'—built before the tribes of man had been so generally scattered, and therefore before they had acquired their different geographical characteristics but built by that branch of the descendants of Noah, the enterprising sons of Ham, from whom I descended. The blood seemed to flow through my veins. I seemed to hear the echo these illustrious Africans. I seemed to feel the impulse of these stirring characters who sent civilisation to Greece—the teachers of the fathers of poetry, history, and mathematics—Homer, Herodotus and Euclid" (in Gilroy 209). Blyden's apprecia-tion of Islam (over indigenous modes of "paganism") as an identifiable and valid source of African patrimony/civilization receives attention in chapter 4 of V.Y Mudimbe's *The Invention of Africa* (1988).

5. Gaines's *A Gathering of Old Men* dramatizes the coalescing *badenya* solidar-ity of a group of old men who for the first time enter into *fadenya* transgression of racial codes by standing with the octogenarian "Singaleese" Mathu and refusing to give him up on murder charges to the sheriff. Although Mathu is "the only one we knowed had ever stood up" (31), his valorization of blackness or Africanity does not work in an entirely positive manner upon a diversely "black" community: "Mathu was one of them blue-black Singaleese niggers. Always bragged about not having no white man's blood in his veins. He looked down on all the rest of us who had some, and the more you had, the more he looked down on you" (51). Coalescing behind Mathu, the old men of the Louisiana parish come into a true sense of shared manhood.

Julie Dash's film *Daughters of the Dust*, turns yet again to Senegambian Muslim sources of patrimony. Though her film celebrates African and Gullah women, the film's patriarch, Bilal (patterned after Sapelo Island's Pulaar-speaking Bilali Muhammad) offers stunning scenes of a scriptural/Islamic black patrimony that differs from both European sources and from the "neo-pagan" inheritance of Gullah mother wit/root-work.

6. It is worth considering that the Nation of Islam may have arisen, at least in part, from southern memories of African Islamic practice. Elijah Muhammad, born Elijah Poole in southern Georgia, may have been prepared to accept Islam by contact with surviving Islamic traditions in a region of Georgia well known for its antebellum Muslim presence. Elijah's father was a Baptist minister named Wali Poole, and *wali,* which means "holy man" or "saint" in Arabic, might well indicate the same Senegambian Muslim identity that the name "Walley" identified in various runaway notices from the *Charleston (South-Carolina) Gazette* and the Savannah *Gazette of the State of Georgia* (Gomez, "Muslims in Early America." 710). Gomez asks "Did Elijah Muhammad, when he converted to Islam in 1931, do so because the words enjoining him to Islam were in some way familiar, reminiscent of concepts and ideas he had been exposed to as a child?" (710). Given that the *Drums and Shadows* interviews in coastal Georgia reveal a lively memory of African Muslims as late as 1940, Islam may trace a continual presence in the Americas, a presence that through its existence in Spanish Florida (St. Augustine) would predate Protestantism in North America.

7. See Hale, *Griots and Griottes* 251.

8. Again, I refer to Gaines's Mathu in *A Gathering of Old Men* (1983) and Dash's Bilal in *Daughters of the Dust* (1992). We find a rare instance of a Senegalese ancestress in Gaines's *The Autobiography of Miss Jane Pitman* (1971) in which Miss Jane remembers a "tall, straight, tough, and blue-black" woman, her hard work, her love of fish and rice (*cheb-u-jen*), and "them Singalee songs" she sang. Gwendolyn Midlo Hall identifies Senegambians as the formative African cultural group in Louisiana, and Hall notes a particularly strong Senegambian presence in Gaines's native Pointe Coupée Parish.

9. Wole Soyinka, *Myth, Literature and the African World* 148–49.

10. From readings of Morrison, Paule Marshall, Gloria Naylor, Julie Dash, Tina Ansa, Ishmael Reed (in the U.S.), and Simone Schwarz-Bart, Alejo Carpentier, Erna Brodber, Wilson Harris, and others in the Caribbean, we might well propose a voodoo hermeneutics.

4. "Two Heads Fighting"

1. See William Carlos Williams, *In the American Grain*; Vera Kutzinski, *Against the American Grain*; Albert Murray, *The Omni-Americans*; and the work of Edouard Glissant, Wilson Harris, and the nineteenth-century Cuban poet Jose Marti. My understanding of "Americanness" is as a colonial/post-colonial phenomenon since pre-Columbian peoples inhabited a land that was not named after Amerigo Vespucci and was altogether different from the post-Columbian "Americas." In this sense, the native *American* is the Creole.

2. See Judith Gleason on carnal vision, 151–227.

3. In *The Epic of Son-Jara* we find the Nine Queens-of-Darkness piecing together a slaughtered bull in a similar manner, 152–53.

4. See Joko Sengova's "Recollections of African Language Patterns in an American Speech Variety: An Assessment of Mende Influences in Lorenzo Dow Turner's Gullah Data" (175–200).

5. Cross-tabulations were calculated for <sc>MAJSELRG*MAJBUYRG<\> (Majority Selling Region, Majority Buying Region). Total counts of Atlantic slave trade voyages coming from Senegambia were 13 for Maryland, 63 for Virginia, 149 for the Carolinas, and 20 for Georgia. For voyages from Sierra Leone, we find 0 for Maryland, 8 (3.2 percent) for Virginia, 95 (17 percent) for the Carolinas, and 19 (31.7 percent) for Georgia.

5. Creole Self-Fashioning

1. We should recall that Du Bois, too, in his remarks upon African religion, could write of an evolutionary process moving (via slavery and Americanization) from "the heathenism of the Gold Coast to the institutional Negro church of Chicago" (*The Souls of Black Folk* 135).

2. See Baker, *Modernism and the Harlem Renaissance* 41–43.

6. Searching for Spiritual Soil

1. Wilson Harris argues in an essay entitled "The Place of the Poet in Modern Society" (1966) that "the crucial problem for the modern poet [is] . . . to visualize a structure which is, at one and the same time, a structure of freedom and a structure of authority" (quoted in Kutzinski 49).

2. We might contrast Mercier's treatment of Blanchette with Kate Chopin's "Desiree's Baby" and Armand's moral blackness, which seems to emerge in Chopin's handling of the story as a "natural" but invisible emblem of Armand's "true race."

3. See Edouard Glissant, *Faulkner, Mississippi*: "Certainly, when established traditions—races—come into clashing contact, there is a great temptation to get beyond nettlesome crossbreeding by retreating to primordial unity. We seek truth in Being, trying to insure ourselves against the risks in Becoming. That is, we try to return to a source that would legitimize everything" (78).

4. Margaret Washington Creel discusses Sea Island "seeking" in detail.

5. Wonda Fontenot's *Secret Doctors: Ethnomedicine of African Americans* (1994), and J.E. McTeer's *Fifty Years as a Low Country Witch Doctor* (1976, 1995) attest to black patients' preference for Afro-Creole ministers of healing over white doctors and hospitals.

6. In "Faulkner and Women," Toni Morrison has this to say: "And there was something else about Faulkner which I can only call 'gaze.' He had a gaze that was different. It appeared, at that time, to be similar to a look, even a sort of staring, a refusal-to-look-away approach to writing that I found admirable" (297). I would like to thank my Roanoke College student Emily Davis for directing me to look closely at this unflinching "creek bottom" passage of Faulkner's.

7. Glissant, *Faulkner, Mississippi* 226, 56.

7. The Spears of the Party of the Merciful

1. See Henry Louis Gates, *The Signifying Monkey.*

2. See Austin, *African Muslims in Antebellum America* (209) and Alford, *Prince Among Slaves.*

3. Robinson writes, "They had developed systems for writing their language in the Arabic alphabet and a pedagogy for teaching those who were illiterate. They believed that their language had been blessed by the Prophet and was second in value only to Arabic. They may well have crystallized at this time the contrast be- tween the intelligence, honour and honesty which characterized them as ruling classes, and the 'uncivilized' behavior of their slaves, whose numbers expanded dra- matically in the course of the *jihads*" (81–82).

4. When Ibrahima returned to Africa, he also returned to open practice of Islam but died in Liberia before he could go home to Timbo. See Alford 165–83.

5. McFeely's biography of Frederick Douglass speculates that Douglass too might have had Muslim ancestry (3–5), which given the importance of Senegambia to Maryland trade, would not be surprising. We know that Henry Highland Garnet and Martin Delany proudly claimed Mandinka grandparents. It may be that Islamic reverence for the written word, passed down through the family, had an impact upon the drive and passion for literacy of early African American writers.

6. At the time of publication of *Aaron,* (during the decade from 1888–1898) the "university" of racialized Americanism was lynching more African Americans each year than during any other period of American history. For extended discus- sion of this era of "radical racism," look to Joel Williamson's *The Crucible of Race.*

7. Note Lorenzo Dow Turner's recording of Fulfulde numerals in Georgia (255).

8. Hodgson recommended use of the Arabic alphabet in Christian missionary efforts in Africa. His *The Gospels, Written in the Negro Patois of English, with Arabic Characters, By a Mandingo Slave in Georgia* offers a Gullah text written in the Arabic alphabet (10). Hodgson also presents a survey "of several educated Mohammedan negroes imported into the United States," outlining the lives of Suleiman Diallo, Ibrahima abd al Rahman, Omar ibn Said, and Salih Bilali (5–8). Hodgson's is the first comprehensive account of Arabic literacy among slaves in the United States, and he seems to have been the foremost collector of Arabic texts written by Africans enslaved in America, possessing along with the Arabic transcription of Gullah a letter by Ibrahima abd al Rahman and several letters from Omar ibn Said, with whom Hodgson corresponded in Arabic on several occasions. Quite a collector, Hodgson in fact wrote that he owned "an excellent and worthy Foolah, now at an advanced age" and "some Mandingoes, Eboes, Goulahs and Guinea people" (8–9).

8. Babo and Bras Coupé

1. Sandra Zagarell ("Reenvisioning America") and Eric Sundquist (*To Wake the Nations*) have been among the critics who have most usefully invoked the pres- ence of Santo Domingo in readings of Melville's novella.

2. It is, for example, the Delanoesque reader who most accounts for the popular-

ity of the plantation novel. For a brief survey of the development of nineteenth-century plantation literature, look to J.V. Ridgely's *Nineteenth-Century Southern Literature*.

3. Baron Roger records two successful group returns to Senegal by Senegalese freedmen (and women) from Cuba in 1819 and 1822. See Diouf, 58.

4. Seymour Gross has identified Mungo Park as Melville's original source (122–23).

5. We find a similar curse in the Sunjata epic, "Niane" (47).

6. See Joel Williamson, *The Crucible of Race*, on radical racism and Thomas Dixon.

9. "Never Once but Like Ripples"

1. See Joel Williamson, *William Faulkner and Southern History*.

2. Glissant, *Faulkner, Mississippi* 30.

3. While Toni Morrison's *Playing in the Dark* stands as a landmark recharting of the American literary/cultural/psychic territory, too little notice has been given to the degree to which it is a contemporary reenvisioning and advancement of material presented earlier by Ralph Ellison in *Shadow and Act*, and *Going to the Territory*.

4. The phrase "blackness of darkness" is Cable's from *The Grandissimes* 274.

5. "Vodou" is the most accepted spelling for Haiti's incredibly rich popular religion. I use the word "voodoo" to refer to Afro-Creole religions in general (or to speak specifically of the Louisiana-based spiritual practices historically known as "voodoo") and to signify always operative Africanist modes of discourse, as we see in diabolical Hollywood "voodoo" or in terms like "voodoo economics." "Voodoo" thus speaks of dual agencies: the enduring powers of the Afro-Creole mysteries and of Africanist othering. See Deren, Métraux, and Cosentino for useful overviews of Haitian vodou.

6. Maritza Stanchich's "The Hidden Caribbean 'Other' in William Faulkner's *Absalom, Absalom!*: An Ideological Ancestry of U.S. Imperialism" offers an archeology of representations of Haiti that works contrapuntally (from the influence of Edward Said's *Culture and Imperialism*) to help us engage Faulkner more fully.

7. John Irwin (1975), Estella Schoenberg (1977), Eric Sundquist (1983), Peter Brooks (1984), Barbara Ladd (1994), Edouard Glissant (1999), and the various writings of Joel Williamson, Toni Morrison, and Ralph Ellison have had a strong influence upon my readings of Faulkner, particularly concerning the racial dimensions of Quentin's suicide and his reenactments of confrontations with Dalton Ames and Caddy from *The Sound and the Fury* (as first articulated by Irwin).

8. See Sundquist (1983) on racial dimensions of Quentin's suicide 106–11.

9. Glissant, *Faulkner, Mississippi* (55).

10. I am, of course, once again referring to Robert Stepto's evocative conceptualizations of narratives of ascent and immersion.

11. I borrow the term "motherpower" from an unpublished essay by Amanda Gross titled "Motherpower and the Creative Life."

Works Cited

Adams, Russell L. "An Analysis of the 'Roots' Phenomenon in the Context of American Racial Conservatism." *Presence Africaine* 116 (1980): 125–40.

Alford, Terry. *Prince Among Slaves*. New York: Oxford Univ. Press, 1977.

Alleyne, Mervyn C. *Comparative Afro-American: An Historical-Comparative Study of English-Based Afro-American Dialects of the New World*. Ann Arbor, Mich.: Karoma, 1980.

———. "Continuity versus Creativity in Afro-American Language and Culture." *Africanisms in Afro-American Language Varieties*. Ed. Salikoko S. Mufwene. Athens: Univ. of Georgia Press, 1993. 167–81.

Althusser, Louis. "Ideology and Ideological State Apparatuses (Notes Towards an Investigation)." *Critical Theory Since 1965*. Ed. Hazard Adams and Leroy Searle. Tallahassee: Florida State Univ. Press. 239–50.

Ames, David. "The Lion of the Manding." *A Treasury of African Folklore*. Ed. Harold Courlander, New York: Crown, 1975. 71–78.

Ancelet, Barry Jean. *Cajun and Creole Folktales: The French Oral Tradition of South Louisiana*. New York: Garland and the World Folktale Library, 1994.

Appiah, Kwame Anthony. *In My Father's House: Africa in the Philosophy of Culture*. New York: Oxford Univ. Press, 1992.

Arvin, Newton. Introduction. *The Grandissimes*. By George W. Cable. New York: Hill and Wang—American Century Series, 1968.

———. *Herman Melville*. 1950. New York: Viking, 1966.

Asbury, Herbert. *The French Quarter: An Informal History of the New Orleans Underworld*. New York: Knopf, 1936.

Austin, Allan. *African Muslims in Antebellum America: A Sourcebook*. New York: Garland, 1984.

Awkward, Michael. "'Unruly and Let Loose': Myth, Ideology, and Gender in *Song of Solomon*." (1990) *Modern Critical Interpretations: Song of Solomon*. Ed. Harold Bloom. Philadelphia: Chelsea House, 1999.

Baer, Florence. *Sources and Analogues of the Uncle Remus Tales*. Helsinki: Folklore Fellows Communications, 1981.

Bailey, Cornelia, with Christena Bledsoe. *God, Dr. Buzzard, and the Bolito Man: A Saltwater Geechee Talks About Life on Sapelo Island*. New York: Doubleday, 2000.

Baker, Houston. *Modernism and the Harlem Renaissance*. Chicago: Univ. of Chicago Press, 1987.

Baker, Phillip. "Assessing the African Contribution to French-Based Creoles." *Africanisms in Afro-American Language Varieties*. Ed. Salikoko S. Mufwene. Athens: Univ. of Georgia Press, 1993.

Bakhtin, Mikhail M. *The Dialogic Imagination*. Trans. Caryl Emerson and Michael Holquist. Austin: Univ. of Texas Press, 1981.

Ball Charles. *Slavery in the United States: A Narrative of the Life and Adventures of Charles Ball, A Black Man.* 3rd ed. Pittsburgh: John T. Shyrock, 1854.

Bannerman, Helen. *The Story of Little Black Sambo.* 1899. New York: Frederick A. Stokes, [1900?].

Barry, Boubacar. *Le Royaume du Waalo.* Paris: Editions Karthala, 1985.

———. *Senegambia and the Atlantic Slave Trade.* Trans. Ayi Kwei Armah. Cambridge, UK: Cambridge Univ. Press, 1998.

Barton, William E. "Old Plantation Hymns." *The Social Implications of Early Negro Music in the United States.* Ed. Bernard Katz. New York: Arno/*The New York Times,* 1969. 75–89.

Bascom, William. *African Folktales in the New World.* Bloomington: Indiana Univ. Press, 1992.

Bass, Ruth. "Mojo." *Mother Wit from the Laughing Barrel: Readings in the Interpretation of Afro-American Folklore.* 1973. Ed. Alan Dundes. Jackson: Univ. Press of Mississippi, 1990. 380–87.

Belcher, Stephen. "Constructing a Hero: Samba Gueladio Djegui." *Research in African Literatures* 25.1 (1994): 75–92.

———. *Epic Traditions of Africa.* Bloomington: Indiana Univ. Press, 1999.

———. "Of Birds and Millet: Problems in West African Mythology." *Yearbook of Comparative and General Literature* 43 (1995): 52–66.

Bell, Caryn Cossé. *Revolution, Romanticism, and the Afro-Creole Protest Tradition in Louisiana 1718–1868.* Baton Rouge: Louisiana State Univ. Press, 1997.

Bendixen, Alfred. "Cable's *The Grandissimes*: A Literary Pioneer Confronts the Southern Tradition." *Southern Quarterly* 18.4 (1980): 23–33.

Bennett, John. "Gullah: A Negro Patois." *South Atlantic Quarterly* 7 (1908): 332–47.

Benston, Kimberly, ed. *Speaking for You: The Vision of Ralph Ellison.* Washington: Howard Univ. Press, 1987.

Bickerton, Derek. *The Roots of Language.* Ann Arbor, Mich.: Karoma, 1981.

Bickley, R. Bruce, Jr., ed. *Critical Essays on Joel Chandler Harris.* Boston: G.K. Hall, 1981.

Bikle, Lucy Leffingwell Cable. *George W. Cable His Life and Letters.* New York: Scribner's, 1928.

Bird, Charles S. "Heroic Songs of the Mande Hunters." *African Folklore.* Ed. Richard Dorson. Bloomington: Indiana Univ. Press, 1972. 275–93.

———. Introduction. *The Songs of Seydou Camara.* Seydou Camara and Charles S. Bird. Bloomington: African Studies Center, Indiana University, 1974.

Bird, Charles S., and Martha B. Kendall. "The Mande Hero." *Explorations in African Systems of Thought.* Ed. Ivan Karp and Charles S. Bird. Bloomington: Indiana Univ. Press, 1980.

Blassingame, John W. *The Slave Community.* New York: Oxford Univ. Press, 1979.

Bledsoe, Christena. "Touring Sapelo's Hog Hammock." *Georgia Poverty Journal* 1994: 31–47.

Bongie, Chris. *Islands and Exiles: The Creole Identities of Post/Colonial Literature.* Stanford, Calif.: Stanford Univ. Press, 1998.

Bowen, Barbara. "Untroubled Voice: Call-and-Response in *Cane.*" *Black American Literature Forum* 16.1 (1982): 12–18.

Boynton, Amelia Platts. *Bridge Across Jordan: The Story of the Struggle for Civil Rights in Selma, Alabama*. New York: Garland, 1984.

Braithwaite, William Stanley. "The Negro in American Literature." *The New Negro*. 1925. Ed. Alain Locke. New York: Atheneum, 1969. 29–46.

Brasseaux, Carl A. "French Louisiana's Senegambian Legacy." *Senegal: Peintures Narratives*. Maurice Dedieu collector. Lafayette: University Art Museum/ Univ. of Southwestern Louisiana, 1986. 52–60.

Brathwaite, Edward. *The Development of Creole Society in Jamaica*. Oxford: Oxford Univ. Press, 1971.

Brodie, Fawn M. *Thomas Jefferson: An Intimate History*. New York: Norton, 1974.

Brookes, Stella Brewer. *Joel Chandler Harris—Folklorist*. Athens: Univ. of Georgia Press, 1950.

Brooks, Cleanth. *William Faulkner: The Yoknapatawpha Country*. New Haven, Conn.: Yale Univ. Press, 1963.

Brooks, Peter. *Reading for the Plot: Design and Intention in Narrative*. New York: Knopf, 1984.

Broussard, James F. *Louisiana Creole Dialect*. Baton Rouge: Louisiana State Univ. Press, 1942.

Brown, Sterling. "Arcadia, South Carolina." *Opportunity: A Journal of Negro Life* 12 (Feb. 1934): 59–60.

———. *The Negro in American Fiction*. 1937 New York: Arno/*The New York Times*, 1969.

Buck, Paul H. *The Road to Reunion, 1865–1900*. Boston: Little, Brown and Company, 1937.

Bulman, Stephen. "The Buffalo-Woman Tale: Political Imperatives and Narrative Constraints in the Sunjata Epic." *Discourse and its Disguises: The Interpretation of African Oral Texts*. Ed. Karin Barber and P.F. Moraes Farias. Birmingham, UK: Birmingham University African Studies, 1989. 171–88.

Butler, Jon. *Awash in a Sea of Faith: Christianizing the American People*. Cambridge, Mass.: Harvard Univ. Press, 1990.

Cable, George Washington. *The Creoles of Louisiana*. New York: Scribner's, 1884.

———. "The Dance in the Place Congo." *The Social Implications of Early Negro Music in the United States*. Ed. Bernard Katz. New York: Arno/*The New York Times*, 1969. 32–47.

———. *The Grandissimes*. 1880. New York: Hill and Wang—American Century Series, 1968.

Camara, Seydou. *The Songs of Seydou Camara: Vol. I: Kambili*. Ed. and trans. Charles Bird with Mamadou Koita and Bourama Soumaoro. Bloomington: African Studies Center, Indiana University, 1974.

Camoens, Luis Vaz de. *The Lusiads*. Trans. William C. Atkinson. 1952. Baltimore: Penguin, 1973.

Campbell, Jane. *Mythic Black Fiction: The Transformation of History*. Knoxville: Univ. of Tennessee Press, 1986.

Carriere, Joseph Medard. *Tales from the French Folklore of Missouri*. Evanston, Ill.: Northwestern Univ. Press, 1937.

Caruthers, William Alexander. *The Kentuckian in New York*. 1834. Ridgewood, N.J.: Gregg Press, 1968.

Césaire, Aimé. *Cahier d'un retour au pays natal*. 1947. Paris: Presence Africaine, 1983.

Chaudenson, Robert. *Les creoles francais*. Paris: Fernand Nathan, 1979.

Chernoff, John Miller. *African Rhythm and African Sensibility: Aesthetics and Social Action in African Musical Idioms*. Chicago: Univ. of Chicago Press, 1979.

Christensen, A.M.H. *Afro-American Folklore Told Round Cabin Fires on the Sea Islands of South Carolina*. 1892. New York: Negro Univ. Press, 1969.

Clark, Emily. *Innocence Abroad*. New York: Knopf, 1931.

Cliff, Michelle. "If I Could Write This in Fire, I Would Write This in Fire." *If I Could Write This in Fire*. Ed. Pamela Maria Smorkaloff. New York: New Press, 1994. 355–70.

Conway, Cecilia. *African Banjo Echoes in Appalachia*. Knoxville: Univ. of Tennessee Press, 1995.

Coolen, Michael Theodore. "Senegambian Archetypes for the American Folk Banjo." *Western Folklore* 43.2 (1984): 117–32.

Cosentino, Donald J. ed. *Sacred Arts of Haitian Vodou*. Berkeley: UCLA Fowler Museum of Cultural History, 1995.

Courlander, Harold, ed. *A Treasury of African Folklore*. New York: Crown, 1975.

Creel, Margaret Washington. *"A Peculiar People": Slave Religion and Community-Culture Among the Gullahs*. New York: New York Univ. Press, 1988.

Curtin, Philip D. *Africa Remembered*. Madison: Univ. of Wisconsin Press, 1967.

———. *The Atlantic Slave Trade: A Census*. Madison: Univ. of Wisconsin Press, 1969.

Dalby, David. "Americanisms That May Once Have Been Africanisms." *Mother Wit from the Laughing Barrel: Readings in the Interpretation of Afro-American Folklore*. Ed. Alan Dundes. Jackson: Univ. Press of Mississippi, 1973. 136–40.

Dalgish, Gerard M. *A Dictionary of Africanisms: Contributions of Sub-Saharan Africa to the English Language*. Westport, Conn.: Greenwood, 1982.

Dash, Julie. *Daughters of the Dust: The Making of an African American Woman's Film*. New York: New Press, 1992.

Delano, Amasa. "Particulars of the Capture of the Spanish Ship Tryal, at the Island of St. Maria; With the Documents Relating to the Affair." 1817. *Benito Cereno*. Barre, Mass.: The Imprint Society, 1972. 13–39.

DeJean, Joan. "Critical Creolization: Grace King and Writing on French in the American South." *Southern Literature and Literary Theory*. Ed. Jefferson Humphries. Athens: Univ. of Georgia Press, 1990. 109–26.

Demetrakopoulos, Stephanie. "The Nursing Mother and Feminine Metaphysics: An Essay on Embodiment." *Soundings: An Interdisciplinary Journal* 65.4 (1982):430–43.

Deren, Maya. *Divine Horsemen: The Living Gods of Haiti*. (1953) Kingston, N.Y.: Documentext, McPherson, 1970.

Diawara, Manthia. "Canonizing Soundiata in Mande Literature: Toward a Sociology of Literature." *Social Text* 10: 2–3 (1992): 154–68.

Dickinson, S.D. "Creole Patois in the Novels of Dr. Alfred Mercier." *Louisiana Literature* 8.1 (1991): 69–80.

Diedhiou, Djib. "La sorcellerie aujourd'hui." *Famille et Developpement* 38 (1984): 33–59.

Dieterlen, Germaine. *Essai sur la religion Bambara*. Paris: Presses universitaires de France, 1950.

Dieterlen, Germaine, and Youssouf Cissé. *Les fondements de la societé d'initiation du Komo*. Paris: Mouton, 1972.

Dillard, J.L. *Black English: Its History and Usage in the United States*. New York: Random House, 1972.

Dilley, Roy. "Spirits, Islam and Ideology: A Study of a Tukolor Weavers' Song (Dillere)." *Journal of Religion in Africa* 17.3 (1987): 245–79.

Diop, Birago. *Les Contes d'Amadou Koumba*. 3rd ed. Paris: Presence Africaine, 1961.

———. *Leurres et lueurs*. Paris: Presence Africaine, 1960.

Diop, Cheikh Anta. *The African Origin of Civilization*. Ed. and trans. Mercer Cook. Westport, Conn.: Lawrence Hill, 1974.

Diop, Samba. *The Oral History of the Wolof People of Waalo, Northern Senegal*. Lewiston, N.Y.: Edwin Mellen, 1995.

Diouf, Sylviane A. *Servants of Allah: African Muslims Enslaved in the Americas*. New York: New York Univ. Press, 1998.

Du Bois, W.E.B. *The Souls of Black Folk*. 1903. New York: Bantam, 1989.

Dunbar, Paul Laurence. *The Complete Poems of Paul Laurence Dunbar*. 1913. New York: Dodd, Mead, 1962.

Dundes, Alan, ed. *Mother Wit from the Laughing Barrel: Readings in the Interpretation of Afro-American Folklore*. 1973. Jackson: Univ. Press of Mississippi, 1990.

Durham, Frank. Introduction. *The Collected Short Stories of Julia Peterkin*. Ed. Frank Durham. Columbia: Univ. of South Carolina Press, 1970.

Eagleton, Terry. *Literary Theory: An Introduction*. Minneapolis: Univ. of Minnesota Press, 1983.

Elfenbein, Anna Shannon. *Women on the Color Line: Evolving Stereotypes and the Writings of George Washington Cable, Grace King, Kate Chopin*. Charlottesville: Univ. Press of Virginia, 1994.

Eliot, T.S. *The Waste Land and Other Poems*. New York: Harcourt, 1934.

Ellison, Ralph. *Going to the Territory*. New York: Random House, 1986.

———. *Invisible Man*. 1952. New York: Vintage, 1972.

———. *Shadow and Act*. 1964. New York: Signet, 1966.

Eltis, David, Stephen D. Behrendt, David Richardson, and Herbert S. Klein. *The Trans-Atlantic Slave Trade: A Database on CD-ROM*. Cambridge, UK: Cambridge Univ. Press, 1999.

Epstein, Dena. *Sinful Tunes and Spirituals*. Chicago: Univ. of Chicago Press, 1977.

Equiano, Olaudah. *The Interesting Narrative of the Life of Olaudah Equiano or Gustavus Vassa, the African, Written by Himself*. 1789. *The Classic Slave Narratives*. Ed. Henry Louis Gates Jr. New York: Mentor, 1987. 1–182.

Equilbecq, Francois-Victor. *La legende de Samba Gueladio Diegui*. Dakar: Les Nouvelles Editions Africaines, 1974.

Faulkner, William. *Absalom, Absalom!* New York: Random House, 1936.

———. "Crevasse." *Collected Short Stories of William Faulkner*. New York: Random House, 1950.

————. "Funeral Service for Mammy Caroline Barr, 1940." *Essays, Speeches, and Public Letters by William Faulkner.* Ed. James Meriwether. New York: Random House, 1965.

————. *Go Down, Moses.* 1942. New York: Vintage, 1973.

————. *The Sound and the Fury.* 1929. New York: Random House, 1956.

Feltenstein, Rosalie. "Melville's 'Benito Cereno.'" *American Literature* 19 (1947): 61–76.

Fiedler, Leslie A. *What Was Literature?* New York: Simon and Schuster, 1982.

Fishkin, Shelly Fisher. *Was Huck Black?: Mark Twain and African American Voices.* New York: Oxford, 1993.

Fogle, Richard Harter. "Benito Cereno." *Melville: A Collection of Essays.* Ed. Richard Chase. Englewood Cliffs, N.J.: Prentice-Hall, 1964. 116–25.

Fontenot, Wonda L. *Secret Doctors: Ethnomedicine of African Americans.* Westport, Conn.: Bergin and Garvey/Greenwood, 1994.

Fortier, Alcée. *Louisiana Folk-Tales in French Dialect and English Translation.* New York: American Folklore Society, 1895.

Frazier, E. Franklin. *The Negro Family in the United States.* 1939. Chicago: Univ. of Chicago Press, 1969.

Frost, Robert. *The Poetry of Robert Frost.* Ed. Edward Connery Lathem. New York: Holt, Rinehart and Winston, 1969.

Gaines, Ernest J. *The Autobiography of Miss Jane Pitman.* 1971. New York: Bantam, 1972.

————. *A Gathering of Old Men.* New York: Random House, 1983.

Gamble, David P. *The Wolof of Senegambia.* London: International African Institute, 1957.

Garnet, Henry Highland. *An Address to the Slaves of the United States of America.* 1843. *The Norton Anthology of African American Literature.* Eds. Henry Louis Gates Jr. and Nellie Y. McKay et al. New York: Norton, 1997. 280–85.

Gates, Henry Louis, Jr. "Introduction: Writing 'Race' and the Difference It Makes." *"Race," Writing, and Difference.* Ed. Henry Louis Gates. Chicago: Univ. of Chicago Press, 1986. 1–20.

————. *The Signifying Monkey: A Theory of African American Literary Criticism.* New York: Oxford Univ. Press, 1988.

Gerber, Adolph. "Uncle Remus Traced to the Old World." *The Journal of American Folk-Lore.* 6.23 (1893): 245–57.

Georgia Gazette [Savannah]. May 24, 1775.

Georgia Writers' Project. *Drums and Shadows: Survival Studies Among the Georgia Coastal Negroes.* 1940. Athens: Univ. of Georgia Press, 1986.

Gilroy, Paul. *The Black Atlantic: Modernity and Double Consciousness.* Cambridge, Mass.: Harvard Univ. Press, 1993.

Gleason, Judith. *Oya: In Praise of an African Goddess.* San Francisco: Harper, 1992.

Glissant, Edouard. *Faulkner, Mississippi.* Trans. Barbara Lewis and Thomas C. Spear. New York: Farrar, Straus and Giroux, 1999. Trans. of *Faulkner, Mississippi.* 1996.

Goldstein, Paul. "Julia Peterkin's *Scarlet Sister Mary*: A Forgotten Novel of Female Primitivism." *Southern Studies* 22.2 (1983): 138–45.

Gomez, Michael. *Exchanging Our Country Marks: The Transformation of African Iden-*

tities in the Colonial and Antebellum South. Chapel Hill: Univ. of North Carolina Press, 1998.

———. "Muslims in Early America." *The Journal of Southern History* 60.4. (1994): 671–710.

Goody, Jack. *The Interface between the Written and the Oral.* Cambridge, UK: Cambridge Univ. Press, 1987.

Gray, Thomas R. *The Confessions of Nat Turner.* 1831. *Black Writers in America.* Ed. Richard Barksdale and Keneth Kinnamon. New York: Macmillan, 1972. 163–72.

Grayson, William John. *The Hireling and the Slave, Chicora, and Other Poems.* Charleston: McCarter, 1856.

Grimke, Angelina Weld. "Tenebris." 1927. *The Norton Anthology of African American Literature.* Ed. Gates et al. New York: Norton, 1977. 945.

Gross, Seymour L. "Mungo Park and Ledyard in Melville's Benito Cereno." *English Literature Notes.* Dec. 1965. 122–23.

Guillén, Nicolas. *Obra poetica.* Vol. 1. Havana: Editorial Letras Cubanas, 1980. 2 vols.

Gwynn, Frederick L., and Joseph L. Blotner, ed. *Faulkner in the University* 1959. Charlottesville: Univ. Press of Virginia, 1995.

Hajek, Friederike. "The Challenge of Literary Authority in the Harlem Renaissance: Jean Toomer's *Cane.*" *The Black Columbiad: Defining Moments in African American Literature and Culture.* Ed. Werner Sollors and Maria Diedrich. Cambridge, Mass.: Harvard Univ. Press, 1994.

Hale, Thomas A. *Griots and Griottes: Masters of Words and Music.* Bloomington: Indiana Univ. Press, 1998.

———. *Griot, Scribe, Novelist: Narrative Interpreters of the Songhay Empire.* Gainesville: Univ. of Florida Press, 1990.

Haley, Alex. *Roots.* New York: Dell, 1976.

Haley, Alex, and Malcolm X. *The Autobiography of Malcolm X.* 1965. New York: Grove, 1966.

Hall, Gwendolyn Midlo. *Africans in Colonial Louisiana: The Development of Afro-Creole Culture in the Eighteenth Century.* Baton Rouge: Louisiana State Univ. Press, 1992.

Hamel, Reginald, ed. *L'Habitation Saint-Ybars.* By Alfred Mercier. Montreal: Guerin litterature, 1989.

Hancock, Ian. "Creole Language Provenance and the African Component." *Africanisms in Afro-American Language Varieties.* Ed. Salikoko S. Mufwene. Athens: Univ. of Georgia Press, 1993. 182–91.

Hanson, John, and David Robinson. *After the Jihad.* East Lansing: Michigan State Univ. Press, 1991.

Harris, Joel Chandler. *Aaron in the Wildwoods.* New York: Houghton Mifflin, 1897.

———. *The Complete Tales of Uncle Remus.* 1955. Boston: Houghton Mifflin, 1983.

———. "Mom Bi." *Balaam's Master.* 1891. Freeport, N.Y.: Books for Libraries, 1969.

———. *Nights With Uncle Remus: Myths and Legends of the Old Plantation.* Boston: Osgood, 1883.

———. *The Story of Aaron (So Named) The Son of Ben Ali Told by His Friends and Acquaintances.* Boston: Houghton Mifflin, 1896.

————. *Uncle Remus and His Friends: Old Plantation Stories, Songs, and Ballads with Sketches of Negro Character*. Boston: Houghton Mifflin, 1892.

————. *Uncle Remus: His Songs and Sayings*. 1880. Ed. Robert Hemenway. New York: Penguin, 1982.

Harris, Julia Collier. *The Life and Letters of Joel Chandler Harris*. Boston: Houghton Mifflin, 1918.

Harris, Trudier. "Adventures in a 'Foreign Country': African American Humor and the South." *Southern Cultures* 1 (1995): 457–65.

Hartsock, Nancy. "Foucault on Power: A Theory for Women?" *Feminism/ Postmodernism*. Ed. L. Nicholson. New York: Routledge, 1990.

Hemenway, Robert. Introduction. *Uncle Remus: His Songs and Sayings*. By Joel Chandler Harris. New York: Penguin, 1982. 7–31.

————. *Zora Neale Hurston: A Literary Biography*. Urbana: Univ. of Illinois Press, 1977.

Herskovits, Melville J. *The Myth of the Negro Past*. 1941. Boston: Beacon, 1958.

Hill, Patricia Liggins et al, eds. *Call and Response: The Riverside Anthology of the African American Literary Tradition*. New York: Houghton Mifflin, 1998.

Hirsch, Marianne. "Knowing Their Names: Toni Morrison's *Song of Solomon*." *Modern Critical Interpretations: Song of Solomon*. Ed. Harold Bloom. Philadelphia: Chelsea House, 1999.

Holloway, Joseph. "The Origins of African-American Culture." *Africanisms in American Culture*. Ed. Joseph Holloway. Bloomington: Indiana Univ. Press, 1990. 1–18.

Hodgson, William B. *The Foulahs of Central Africa and the African Slave Trade*. Savannah, 1843.

————. "The Gospels Written in the Negro Patois of English, with Arabic Characters, by a Mandingo Slave in Georgia." New York: Ethnological Society of New York, 1857.

————. *Notes on Northern Africa, the Sahara and Soudan, in Relation to the Ethnography, Languages, History, Political, and Social Conditions of the Nations of Those Countries*. New York: Wiley and Putnam, 1844.

hooks, bell. *Ain't I a Woman: Black Women and Feminism*. Boston: South End Press, 1981.

Hughes, Langston. "Jazzonia." *The New Negro*. 1925. Ed. Alain Locke. New York: Atheneum, 1969. 226.

Hurston, Zora Neale. "Cudjo's Own Story of the Last African Slaver." *Journal of Negro History* 12.4 (1927): 648–63.

————. *Dust Tracks on a Road*. 1942. New York: Harper, 1991.

————. "High John de Conquer." *Mother Wit from the Laughing Barrel*. Ed. Alan Dundes. Jackson: Univ. of Mississippi Press, 1990. 541–48.

————. *Mules and Men*. 1935. New York: Harper and Row, 1990.

————. *The Sanctified Church*. Berkeley, Calif.: Turtle Island, 1983.

————. *Their Eyes Were Watching God*. 1937. New York: Harper, 1990.

Innes, Gordon. *Sunjata: Three Mandinka Versions*. London: School of Oriental and African Studies, University of London, 1974.

Irele, Abiola. "Africa: The Mali Empire of Son-Jara." *The Norton Anthology of World Literature*. Expanded ed. Vol. 1. Mack et al. New York: Norton, 1995.

Irvine, Judith. "Registering Affect: Heteroglossia in the Linguistic Expression of Emotion." *Language and the Politics of Emotion: Studies in Emotion and Social Interaction.* Eds. Catherine A. Lutz and Lita Abu Lughoa. Cambridge, UK: Cambridge Univ. Press, 1990. 126–61.

Irwin, John T. "Doubling and Incest/Repetition and Revenge." *William Faulkner's Absalom, Absalom!* Ed. Harold Bloom. New York: Chelsea House, 1987.

Jackson, Michael. *Allegories of the Wilderness: Ethics and Ambiguity in Kuranko Narratives.* Bloomington: Indiana Univ. Press, 1982.

Jameson, Fredric. *Postmodernism, or The Cultural Logic of Late Capitalism.* (1991) Durham: Duke Univ. Press, 1994.

JanMohamed, Abdul R. "The Economy of Manichean Allegory: The Function of Racial Difference in Colonialist Literature." *"Race," Writing, and Difference.* Ed. Henry Louis Gates. Chicago: Univ. of Chicago Press, 1986. 78–106.

Jefferson, Thomas. *Notes on the State of Virginia, Written in the Year 1781, Somewhat Corrected and Enlarged in the Winter of 1782, for the Use of a Foreigner of Distinction, in Answer to Certain Queries Proposed by Him.* 1782. *The Portable Thomas Jefferson.* Ed. Merril D. Peterson. New York: Penguin, 1975.

Johnson, James Weldon. "Preface." *The Book of American Negro Poetry.* 1922. Ed. James Weldon Johnson. New York: Harcourt Brace Jovanovich, 1969. 3–48.

Johnson, John William. *The Epic of Son-Jara: A West African Tradition.* Bloomington: Indiana Univ. Press, 1986.

Johnson, John William, Thomas Hale, and Stephen Belcher, eds. *Oral Epics from Africa: Vibrant Voices from a Vast Continent.* Bloomington: Indiana Univ. Press, 1997.

Johnson, Whittington B. *Black Savannah, 1788–1864.* Fayetteville: Univ. of Arkansas Press,1996.

Jones, Charles Colcock. *Negro Myths From the Georgia Coast.* Boston: Houghton Mifflin, 1888.

Jones-Jackson, Patricia. *When Roots Die: Endangered Traditions on the Sea Islands.* Athens: Univ. of Georgia Press, 1987.

Joyner, Charles. *Down by the Riverside: A South Carolina Slave Community.* Urbana: Univ. of Illinois Press, 1984.

———. "Soul Food and the Sambo Stereotype: Foodlore from the Slave Narrative Collection." *Keystone Folklore Quarterly* (winter 1971): 171–77.

Julien, Eileen. *African Novels and the Question of Orality.* Bloomington: Indiana Univ. Press, 1992.

Kane, Moustapha and David Robinson. *The Islamic Regime of Fouta Tooro.* East Lansing: African Studies Center, Michigan State University, 1984.

Kaplan, Sidney. "Herman Melville and the American National Sin." *Images of the Negro in American Literature.* Eds. Seymour Gross and John Edward Hardy. Chicago: Univ. of Chicago Press, 1966.

Kavanagh, J.H. "That Hive of Subtlety: 'Benito Cereno' and the Liberal Hero." *Ideology and Classic American Literature.* Ed. Sacvan Bercovitch and Myra Jehlen. Cambridge, UK: Cambridge Univ. Press, 1986. 352–83.

Keita, Cheick Mahamadou Cherif. "Fadenya and Artistic Creation in Mali: Kele Monson and Massa Makan Diabate." *Research in African Literatures* 21.3 (1990): 103–14.

Kemble, Frances Ann. *Journal of a Residence on a Georgian Plantation in 1838–1839*. Athens: Brown Thrasher/Univ. of Georgia Press, 1984.

Kesteloot, Lilyan, and Bassirou Dieng. *Du tieddo au talibe*. Dakar: Presence Africaine, 1989.

Kesteloot, Lilyan, and Cherif Mbodj. *Contes et mythes Wolof*. Dakar: Les Nouvelles Editions Africaines, 1983.

King, Susan Petigru. *Gerald Gray's Wife and Lily: A Novel*. Durham: Duke Univ. Press, 1993.

Kingsley, Zephaniah. *A Treatise on the Patriarchal or Cooperative System of Society as it Exists in Some Governments, and Colonies in America, and in the United States, Under the Name of Slavery, with its Necessity and Advantages*. 1829.

Klein, Martin A. "Social and Economic Factors in the Muslim Revolution in Senegambia." *Journal of African History* 13.3 (1972): 419–41.

Kolmerten, Carol A., Stephen M. Ross, and Judith Bryant Wittenberg, eds. *Unflinching Gaze: Morrison and Faulkner Re-envisioned*. Jackson: Univ. Press of Mississippi, 1997.

Koppel, Ted. Moderator. "The Nobel Laureates of Literature: An Olympic Gathering."Panel Discussion I, April 24, 1995. *The Georgia Review* 49.4 (1995): 832–56.

Kreyling, Michael. Introduction. *The Grandissimes*. George W. Cable. New York: Penguin, 1988. vii-xxii.

Kristeva, Julia. *Desire in Language: A Semiotic Approach to Literature and Art*. Ed. Leon S. Roudiez. New York: Columbia Univ. Press, 1980.

———. *Polylogue*. Paris: Editions du Seuil, 1977.

Kutzinski, Vera. *Against the American Grain*. Baltimore: Johns Hopkins Univ. Press, 1987.

Ladd, Barbara. "'An Atmosphere of Hints and Allusions': Bras Coupé and the Context of Black Insurrection in *The Grandissimes*." *Southern Quarterly* 19.3 (1991): 63–76.

———. "The Direction of the Howling: Nationalism and the Color Line in Absalom, Absalom!" *American Literature* 66.3 (1994): 525–51.

Lauter, Paul. *Canons and Contexts*. New York: Oxford Univ. Press, 1991.

Laye, Camara. *The Guardian of the Word*. Trans. James Kirkup. New York: Vintage, 1984.

Leslie, Joshua, and Sterling Stuckey. "The Death of Benito Cereno: A Reading of Herman Melville on Slavery." *Journal of Negro History* 67 (1982): 287–301.

Levine, Lawrence. *Black Culture and Black Consciousness: Afro-American Folk Thought from Slavery to Freedom*. New York: Oxford Univ. Press, 1977.

Lewis, Bernard. *Race and Slavery in the Middle East*. New York: Oxford Univ. Press, 1990.

Lewis, David Levering. *W.E.B. Du Bois: Biography of a Race 1868–1919*. New York: Henry Holt, 1993.

———. *When Harlem Was in Vogue*. New York: Knopf, 1981.

Light, Kathleen. "Uncle Remus and the Folklorists." *Southern Literary Journal* 7.2 (1975): 88–104.

Littlefield, Daniel C. *Rice and Slaves: Ethnicity and the Slave Trade in Colonial South Carolina*. Baton Rouge: Louisiana State Univ. Press, 1981.

Locke, Alain, ed. *The New Negro.* 1925. New York: Atheneum, 1969.

Lorde, Audre. "Uses of the Erotic: The Erotic as Power." *Sister Outsider.* Trumansburg, N.Y.: Crossing Press, 1984.

Lotman, Yurij, and B.A. Uspensky. "On the Semiotic Mechanism of Culture." *Critical Theory Since 1965.* Ed. Hazard Adams and Leroy Searle. Tallahassee: Florida State Univ. Press, 1986. 410–22.

Lovell, Caroline Couper. *The Golden Isles of Georgia.* Boston: Little, Brown, 1933.

Lytle, Andrew. *A Novel, A Novella, and Four Stories.* New York: McDowell, Obolensky, 1958.

Mack, Maynard, et al, eds. Preface. *The Norton Anthology of World Literature.* Expanded ed. Vol. 1. New York: Norton, 1995. xxi-xxvii. 2 vols.

MacKethan, Lucinda. *The Dream of Arcady: Place and Time in Southern Literature.* Baton Rouge: Louisiana State Univ. Press, 1980.

Maddox, Marilyn Price. "The Life and Works of Julia Mood Peterkin." M.A. thesis, University of Georgia, 1956.

Magel, Emil. "The Source of Bascom's Analogue 'Trickster Seeks Endowments.'"*Research in African Literatures* 10.3 (1979): 350–58.

Martin, B.G. "Sapelo Island's Arabic Document: The 'Bilali Diary' in Context." *Georgia Historical Quarterly* 77.3 (1994): 598–601.

McCluskey, John Jr. Introduction. *The City of Refuge: The Collected Stories of Rudolph Fisher.* Ed. John McCluskey Jr. Columbia: Univ. of Missouri Press, 1987. xi-xxxix.

McFeely, William S. *Frederick Douglass.* New York: 1991.

———. *Sapelo's People: A Long Walk to Freedom.* New York: Norton, 1994.

McKay, Nellie. *Jean Toomer, Artist: A Study of his Literary Life and Work.* Chapel Hill: Univ. of North Carolina Press, 1984.

McNaughton, Patrick. *The Mande Blacksmiths: Knowledge, Power, and Art in West Africa.* Bloomington: Indiana Univ. Press, 1988.

McTeer, J.E. *Fifty Years as a Low Country Witch Doctor.* 1976. Columbia, S.C.: R.L. Bryan, 1995.

Melville, Herman. *Bartleby and Benito Cereno.* Mineola, N.Y.: Dover, 1990.

Mercier, Alfred. "Etude sur la langue creole en Louisiana." *Les Comptes-rendus Athenee Louisianais.* July 1, 1880: 378–83.

———. *L'habitation Saint-Ybars ou maitres et esclaves en Louisiane.* 1881. Montreal: Guerin litterature, 1989.

Merivale, Patricia. "The Raven and the Bust of Pallas: Classical Artifacts and the Gothic Tale." *PMLA: Publications of the Modern Language Association.* 89 (1974): 960–66.

Merwin, W.S. Trans. *Poem of the Cid.* New York: Mentor, 1962.

Métraux, Alfred. *Voodoo in Haiti.* (1959) Trans. Hugo Charteris. New York: Schocken, 1972.

Miller, Christopher. *Blank Darkness: Africanist Discourse in French.* Chicago: Univ. of Chicago Press, 1985.

———. *Theories of Africans.* Chicago: Univ. of Chicago Press, 1990.

Miller, R. Baxter. "The Southern Trace of Black Critical Theory." *Xavier Review* 11.1–2 (1991): 1–53.

Mitchell, Carolyn A. "Henry Dumas and Jean Toomer: One Voice." *Black American Literature Forum* 22.2 (1988): 297–309.

Montgomery, Michael, ed. *The Crucible of Carolina: Essays on the Development of Gullah Language and Culture*. Athens: Univ. of Georgia Press, 1994.

Moore, David Chioni. "Revisiting a Silenced Giant: Alex Haley's *Roots*—A Bibliographic Essay, and a Research Report on the Haley Archives at the University of Tennessee, Knoxville." *Resources for American Literary Study* 22. 2 (1996): 195–249.

———. "Routes: Alex Haley's *Roots* and the Rhetoric of Genealogy." *Transition* 64 (1994): 4–21.

Morgan, Philip D. *Slave Counterpoint: Black Culture in the Eighteenth-Century Chesapeake and Lowcountry*. Chapel Hill: Omohundro Institute of Early American History and Culture, Williamsburg, Virginia, and Univ. of North Carolina Press, 1998.

Morrison, Toni. *Beloved*. New York: Knopf, 1987.

———. "Faulkner and Women." *Faulkner and Women: Faulkner and Yoknapatawpha*, Eds. Doreen Fowler and Ann J. Abadie. Jackson: Univ. Press of Mississippi, 1986. 292–302.

———. *Playing in the Dark: Whiteness and the Literary Imagination*. New York: Random House, 1992.

———. *Song of Solomon*. New York: Signet, 1977.

Mufwene, Salikoko, ed. *Africanisms in Afro-American Language Varieties*. Athens: Univ. of Georgia Press, 1993.

———. "Misinterpreting *Linguistic Continuity* Charitably." *The Crucible of Carolina*. Ed. Michael Montgomery. Athens: Univ. of Georgia Press, 1994. 38–59.

Murray, Albert. *The Omni-Americans: New Perspectives on Black Experience and American Culture*. New York: Outerbridge and Dienstfrey, 1970.

———. *South to a Very Old Place*. New York: McGraw-Hill, 1971.

Murray, Joseph. *Santería: An African Religion in America*. Boston: Beacon, 1988.

Niane, D.T. *Sundiata: An Epic of Old Mali*. Trans. G.D. Pickett. London: Longman, 1965.

Nobile, Philip. "Uncovering Roots." *The Village Voice* 38.8 (1993): 31–38.

Novak, Phillip. "Signifying Silences: Morrison's Soundings in the Faulknerian Void." *Unflinching Gaze: Morrison and Faulkner Re-envisioned*. Eds. Carol A. Kolmerten, Stephen M. Ross, and Judith Bryant Wittenberg. Jackson: Univ. Press of Mississippi, 1997. 199–216.

Oates, Stephen B. *The Fires of Jubilee*. New York: Harper and Row, 1975.

O'Donnell, Patrick. "Faulkner in Light of Morrison." *Unflinching Gaze: Morrison and Faulkner Re-envisioned*. Eds. Carol A. Kolmerten, Stephen M. Ross, and Judith Bryant Wittenberg. Jackson: Univ. Press of Mississippi, 1997. 219–227.

Overton, Grant M. *The Women Who Make Our Novels*. New York: Dodd, Mead, 1928.

Padover, Saul K. ed. *The Complete Jefferson*. New York: Duell, Sloan and Pearce, 1943.

Palmer, H.R. *Sudanese Memories*. 1928. London: Frank Cass, 1967.

Park, Mungo. *Mungo Park's Travels*. 1795. London: Henry Frowde and Hodder and Stoughton, n.d.

Parrish, Lydia. *Slave Songs of the Georgia Sea Islands*. 1942. Athens: Univ. of Georgia Press, 1992.

Parsons, Elsie Clews. *Folk-lore of the Sea Islands, South Carolina*. New York: American Folklore Society, 1923.

Peterkin, Julia. *Black April*. Indianapolis: Bobbs-Merrill, 1927.

———. *The Collected Short Stories of Julia Peterkin*. Ed. Frank Durham. Columbia: Univ. of South Carolina Press, 1970.

———. *Green Thursday*. 1924. New York: Knopf, 1927.

———. *Roll, Jordan, Roll*. New York: Robert O. Ballou, 1933.

———. *Scarlet Sister Mary*. Indianapolis: Bobbs-Merrill, 1928.

———. "Vinner's Sayings." *Poetry: A Magazine of Verse* 25.5 (1925): 240–43.

Pinsker, Sanford. "Magical Realism, Historical Truth, and the Quest for a Liberating Identity: Reflections on Alex Haley's *Roots* and Toni Morrison's *Song of Solomon*." *Studies in Black American Literature Volume I: Black American Prose Theory*. Edited by Joe Weixlmann and Chester J. Fontenot. Greenwood, Fla.: Penkvill, 1984. 183–97.

Poe, Edgar Allan. *The Complete Tales and Poems of Edgar Allan Poe*. New York: Random House—The Modern Library, 1965.

Poydras, Julien. *La prise du Morne du Baton Rouge par Monseignor de Galvez*. New Orleans: Antoine Boudousquie, Imprimeur du Roi et du Cabildo, 1779.

Pratt, Mary Louis. *Imperial Eyes: Travel Writing and Transculturation*. New York: Routledge, 1992.

Pringle, Elizabeth Allston. *A Woman Rice Planter*. 1913. Columbia: Univ. of South Carolina Press, 1992.

Progoff, Ira. *Jung's Psychology and its Social Meaning*. New York: Grove, 1953.

Raboteau, Albert J. *A Fire in the Bones: Reflections on African-American Religious History*. Boston: Beacon, 1996.

———. *Slave Religion: The "Invisible Institution" in the Antebellum South*. New York: Oxford Univ. Press, 1978.

Rampersad, Arnold. *The Art and Imagination of W.E.B. Du Bois*. Cambridge, Mass.: Harvard Univ. Press, 1976.

Ransom, John Crowe. "Reconstructed but Unregenerate." *I'll Take My Stand*. Twelve Southerners. 1930. Baton Rouge: Louisiana State Univ. Press, 1977. 1–27.

———. *Selected Poems*. New York: Ecco, 1977.

Ravenel, Beatrice. *The Yemassee Lands: Poems of Beatrice Ravenel*. Ed. Louis Rubin Jr. Chapel Hill: Univ. of North Carolina Press, 1969.

Reinecke, George. "Alfred Mercier, French Novelist of New Orleans." *Southern Quarterly* 20 (1982): 145–76.

Ridgely, J.V. *Nineteenth-Century Southern Literature*. Lexington: Univ. of Kentucky Press, 1980.

Ringe, Donald A. "The Double Center: Character and Meaning in Cable's Early Novels." *Studies in the Novel* 5 (1973): 52–62.

———. "Narrative Voice in Cable's *The Grandissimes*." *Southern Quarterly* 18 (1980): 13–22.

Robeson, Elizabeth. "The Ambiguity of Julia Peterkin." *Journal of Southern History* 61. 4 (1995): 761–86.

Robinson, David. *The Holy War of Umar Tal*. Oxford: Clarendon, 1985.

Rodney, Walter. "Jihad and Social Revolution in Futa Djalon in the Eighteenth Century." *Journal of the Historical Society of Nigeria*. 4.2 (1968).

Romero, Fernando. *Quimba, Fa, Malambo, Neque: Afronegrismos en el Peru*. Lima: Instituto de Estudios Peruanos, 1988.

Rosenbaum, Art. Jacket notes. *The McIntosh County Shouters*. 1984. Smithsonian Institution, Folkways Cassette Series, 04344, 1993. 6.

——. *Shout Because You're Free: The African American Ring Shout Tradition in Coastal Georgia*. Athens: Univ. of Georgia Press, 1998.

Rosenberg, Madelyn. "A big player in Virginia Music." *Roanoke Times Extra*. Friday, Aug. 4, 2000. 12.

Rouquette, Dominique. "La jeune fille des Bois." *Library of Southern Literature*. Vol. X. Ed. Edwin Anderson Alderman and Joel Chandler Harris. Atlanta: Martin and Hoyt, 1909. 4598–99. 16 volumes.

Rubin, Louis D., Jr. *George W. Cable: The Life and Times of a Southern Heretic*. New York: Pegasus, 1969.

——. "Uncle Remus and the Ubiquitous Rabbit." *Critical Essays on Joel Chandler Harris*. 171–84.

Said, Edward. *Culture and Imperialism*. New York: Alfred A. Knopf, 1993.

——. *Orientalism*. 1978. New York: Vintage, 1994.

Samuels, Wilfred D. Liminality and the Search for Self in *Song of Solomon*." *Modern Critical Interpretations: Song of Solomon*. Ed. Harold Bloom. Philadelphia: Chelsea House, 1997. 5–28.

Sayers, Dorothy. Trans. *The Song of Roland*. Baltimore: Penguin, 1957.

Schafer, Daniel L. *Anna Kingsley*. St. Augustine, Fla.: St. Augustine Historical Society, 1994.

Schoenberg, Estella. *Old Tales and Talking*. Jackson: Univ. Press of Mississippi, 1977.

Scudder, Harold H. "Melville's 'Benito Cereno' and Captain Delano's Voyages." PMLA 42 (1928): 502–32.

Séjour, Victor. "The Mulatto." Translation Philip Barnard. *The Norton Anthology of African American Literature*. Gen. Eds. Henry Louis Gates and Nellie Y. McKay. New York: Norton, 1997, 286–99.

Sengova, Joko. "Recollections of African Language Patterns in an American Speech Variety: An Assessment of Mende Influences in Lorenzo Dow Turner's Gullah Data." *The Crucible of Carolina*. Ed. Michael Montgomery. Athens: Univ. of Georgia Press, 1994. 175–200.

Sessions, William A. "The Land Called Chicora." *Southern Review* 19.4 (1983):736–48.

Simms, William Gilmore. "The Edge of the Swamp." *Southern Writing 1585–1920*. Eds. Richard Beale Davis et al. New York: Odyssey, 1970. 489–91.

Smith, Lillian. *Killers of the Dream*. 1949. New York: Norton, 1994.

Smith, Julia Floyd. *Slavery and Rice Culture in Low Country Georgia, 1750–1860*. Knoxville: Univ. of Tennessee Press, 1985.

Soyinka, Wole. *Myth, Literature and the African World*. 1976. New York: Cambridge Univ. Press, 1995.

Stafford, John. "Patterns of Meaning in *Nights with Uncle Remus*." *American Literature* 18 (1946): 89–108.

Stanchich, Maritza. "The Hidden Caribbean 'Other' in William Faulkner's *Absalom, Absalom!*: An Ideological Ancestry of U.S. Imperialism." *The Mississippi Quarterly* XLIX 3 (1996): 603–17.

Stepto, Robert B. *From Behind the Veil: A Study of Afro-American Narrative.* Urbana: Univ. of Illinois Press, 1979.

Stoddard, Albert H. *Gullah Animal Tales from Daufuskie Island, South Carolina.* Ed. Will Kilhour. Hilton Head Island, S.C.: Push Button, 1995.

Stuckey, Sterling. *Slave Culture: Nationalist Theory and the Foundations of Black America.* New York: Oxford Univ. Press, 1987.

Sundquist, Eric. *Faulkner: The House Divided.* Baltimore: Johns Hopkins Univ. Press, 1983.

———. "Faulkner, Race, and the Forms of American Fiction." *Faulkner and Race: Faulkner and Yoknapatawpha 1986.* Ed. Doreen Fowler and Ann J. Abadie. Jackson: Univ. Press of Mississippi, 1987.

———. "Introduction: W.E.B. Du Bois and the Autobiography of Race." *The Oxford W.E.B. Du Bois Reader.* Ed. Eric Sundquist. New York: Oxford Univ. Press, 1996.

———. *To Wake the Nations: Race in the Making of American Literature.* Cambridge, Mass.: Harvard Univ. Press, 1993.

Talley, Thomas W. *Negro Folk Rhymes (Wise and Otherwise).* 1922. Knoxville: Univ. of Tennessee Press, 1991.

Tate, Allen. *Collected Poems 1919–1976.* New York: Farrar, Straus and Giroux, 1977.

———. *Essays of Four Decades.* Chicago: Swallow, 1968.

———. "Remarks on Southern Religion." *I'll Take My Stand.* Twelve Southerners. 1930. Baton Rouge: Louisiana State Univ. Press, 1977. 155–75.

Testut, Charles. *Le vieux Salomon ou une famille d'esclaves au XIXe siecle.* New Orleans: No 200 Rue Chartres, 1872.

Thompson, Robert Farris. *Flash of the Spirit.* New York: Vintage, 1983.

Toomer, Jean. *Cane.* 1923. New York: Liveright, 1975.

Tourgee, Albion. "The South as a Field for Fiction." *Forum* VI, Feb. 1888, 405.

Turner, Darwin. "Daddy Joel Harris and His Old-Time Darkies." *Critical Essays on Joel Chandler Harris.* Ed. R. Bruce Bickley Jr. Boston: G.K. Hall, 1981. 113–29.

Turner, Lorenzo Dow. *Africanisms in the Gullah Dialect.* 1949. Ann Arbor: Univ. of Michigan Press, 1973.

Turner, Richard Brent. *Islam in the African American Experience.* Bloomington: Indiana Univ. Press, 1997.

Twining, Mary Arnold. "An Examination of African Retention in the Folk Culture of the South Carolina and Georgia Sea Islands." Ph.D. dissertation, Indiana University, 1977.

Twining, Mary Arnold, and Keith E. Baird, eds. *Sea Island Roots: African Presence in the Carolinas and Georgia.* Trenton, N.J.: Africa World Press, 1991.

Vega, El Inca Garcilaso de la. *The Florida of the Inca.* Ed. and trans. John Grier Varner and Jeanette Johnson Varner. Austin: Univ. of Texas Press, 1962.

———. *Royal Commentaries of the Incas and General History of Peru.* Trans. Harold V. Livermore. Vol. 2. Austin: Univ. of Texas Press, 1986.

Walker, Alice. *In Search of Our Mothers' Gardens.* New York: Harcourt, 1983.

Warren, Robert Penn. *Brother to Dragons: A Tale in Verse and Voices.* New York: Random House, 1979.

Waterman, Richard Alan. "African Influence on the Music of the Americas." *Mother Wit from the Laughing Barrel: Readings in the Interpretation of Afro-American Folklore.* 1973. Ed. Alan Dundes. Jackson: Univ. Press of Mississippi, 1980. 81–94.

Werner, Craig. "Black Dreams of Faulkner's Dreams of Blacks." *Faulkner and Race: Faulkner and Yoknapatawpha, 1986.* Ed. Doreen Fowler and Ann J. Abadie. Jackson: Univ. Press of Mississippi, 1987. 35–57.

West, Hollie. "Travels with Ralph Ellison Through Time and Thought." *Speaking for You: The Vision of Ralph Ellison.* Ed. Kimberly Benston. Washington: Howard Univ. Press, 1990. 37–44.

Whitaker, Thomas R. "Spokesman for Invisibility." *Speaking for You: The Vision of Ralph Ellison.* Ed. Kimberly Benston. Washington: Howard Univ. Press, 1987. 386–403.

White, Hayden, *Tropics of Discourse: Essays in Cultural Criticism.* Baltimore: Johns Hopkins Univ. Press, 1978.

White, Newman I. *American Negro Folk Songs.* Cambridge, Mass.: Harvard Univ. Press, 1928.

Wilentz, Gay. *Binding Cultures: Black Women Writers in Africa and the Diaspora.* Bloomington: Indiana Univ. Press, 1992.

Williams, Selase W. "Substantive Africanisms at the End of the African Linguistic Diaspora." *Africanisms in Afro-American Language Varieties.* Ed. Salikoko Mufwene. Athens: Univ. of Georgia Press, 1993. 406–22.

Williams, Susan Millar. *A Devil and a Good Woman, Too: The Lives of Julia Peterkin.* Athens: Univ. of Georgia Press, 1997.

Williamson, Joel. *The Crucible of Race: Black-White Relations in the American South Since Emancipation.* New York: Oxford Univ. Press, 1984.

———. *William Faulkner and Southern History.* New York: Oxford Univ. Press, 1993.

Wister, Owen. *Lady Baltimore.* 1905. Nashville: J.S. Sanders, 1992.

Wolfe, Bernard. "Uncle Remus and the Malevolent Rabbit: 'Takes a Limber-Toe Gemmun fer ter Jump Jim Crow.'" *Critical Essays on Joel Chandler Harris.* Ed. Bruce Bickley. Boston: G.K. Hall, 1981. 70–84.

Wolfe, Charles. Jacket Notes. *Altamont: Black Stringband Music from the Library of Congress.* Rounder Records, 0238, 1989.

———. Introduction. *Negro Folk Rhymes (Wise and Otherwise).* By Thomas Talley. 1922. Knoxville: Univ. of Tennessee Press, 1991.

Wolper, David L. *The Inside Story of TV's "Roots."* New York: Warner, 1978.

Wood, Peter H. *Black Majority: Negroes in Colonial South Carolina from 1670 through the Stono Rebellion 1741.* 1974. New York: Norton, 1975.

Woodward, C. Vann. *The Burden of Southern History.* New York: Vintage, 1960.

———. "Clio with Soul." *Journal of American History* 1, no. 56 (June 1969): 5–20.

Wright, Jay. *The Double Invention of Komo.* Austin: Univ. of Texas Press, 1980.

Wyatt, David. "Faulkner's Hundred." *The Southern Review* 33.1 (1997): 197-212.

Wylly, Charles Spalding. *The Seed That Was Sown in the Colony of Georgia 1740–1870.* New York: Neall, 1910.

Yellin, Jean. *The Intricate Knot: Black Figures in American Literature, 1776–1863.* New York: New York Univ. Press, 1972.

Zagarell, Sandra A. "Reenvisioning America: Melville's 'Benito Cereno.'" *ESQ* 30.4 (1984): 245–59.

Index